THE DEVELOPMENT
OF INTELLIGENCE

The Development of Intelligence

edited by
Mike Anderson
The University of Western Australia, Perth

Psychology Press
a member of the Taylor & Francis group

Psychology Press Ltd., Publishers
27 Church Road
Hove
East Sussex
BN3 2FA
UK

British Library Cataloguing-in-Publication Data
A catalogue record for this book is available from the British Library.

   ISBN 0-86377-844-5 (hbk)
   ISSN: 1368-2563

Typeset by Mendip Communications Ltd., Frome, Somerset
Printed and bound in the UK by Biddles Ltd., Guildford and King's Lynn

In memory of Neil O'Connor

Contents

List of contributors

Mike Anderson, Department of Psychology, The University of Western Australia, Nedlands, Perth WA 6019, Australia.

John Colombo, University of Kansas, Infant Study Centre, Department of Human Development, University of Kansas, Lawrence, KS 66045, USA.

Alice J. Corkill, Cognitive Interference Laboratory, University of Nevada, Las Vegas, NV 89154-3003, USA.

Robin Corley, Institute for Behavioral Genetics, University of Colorado, Boulder, CO 80309, USA.

Helen Davis, School of Psychology, South Street, Murdoch University, Perth, WA 6150, Australia.

Frank N. Dempster, Cognitive Interference Laboratory, University of Nevada, Las Vegas, NV 89154-3003, USA.

Janet E. Frick, Department of Psychology, University of Georgia, Athens, GA 30602-3013, USA.

Howard Gardner, Harvard University Project Zero, 323 Longfellow Hall, Appian Way, Cambridge, MA 01238, USA.

Graeme Halford, School of Psychology, University of Queensland, Queensland 4072, Australia.

David A. Hay, School of Psychology, Curtin University of Technology, Perth, WA 6845, Australia.

Robert M. Hodapp, Moore Hall, Graduate School of Education, UCLA, Box 95152, Los Angeles CA 90095 1521, USA.

Ted Nettelbeck, Department of Psychology, University of Adelaide, Adelaide SA 5005, Australia.

J. Steven Reznick, Department of Psychology, CB # 3270, University of North Carolina, Chapel Hill, NC 27599-3270, USA.

Herman H. Spitz, 389 Terhune Road, Princeton, NJ 08540, USA.

Irene Styles, School of Education, South Street, Murdoch University, Perth, WA 6150, Australia.

Bruce Torff, Hofstra University, 100 Fulton Avenue, Hempstead, Long Island, NY 11550, USA.

Edward, F. Zigler, Sterling Professor of Psychology, Department of Psychology, Yale University, New Haven, CT 06520, USA.

Preface

Psychology has too few luminaries but at least two of them are central to the topic of this book.

Alfred Binet may well have become the first serious applied psychologist when he was commissioned by the French authorities to develop tests to identify children in need of special education, but his legacy to psychology is much greater even than the legacy of the intelligence tests he invented. His legacy is three-fold. First, his notion that intelligence is a property of the higher faculties of the mind has influenced theories of intelligence, particularly in the United States and Europe, and has proved to be the major counterpoint against the British tradition championed by Charles Spearman. Second, Binet's genius was his formulation (and subsequent measurement) of the concept of mental age that has been so influential for the study of the development of intelligence. Third, he gave a job to Jean Piaget—our second luminary.

Piaget's early career involved developing Binet's tests. Piaget's genius was to realise that errors on intelligence test items might be even more informative than the total test score used in Binet's calculations of mental age (and subsequently Stern's calculation of IQ). Piaget thought of himself as a genetic epistemologist—Where does our knowledge of the world come from? What are the origins of intelligence in the child? What are the causes of intellectual development? These are some of the deepest questions in psychology and in some measure I hope that this book will bring students up to date on the scientific attacks on these questions.

I believe that the need for a book such as this is pressing. We live in dangerous times for the scientific study of intelligence. First we had *The bell curve* (Herrnstein & Murray, 1994) a book focused on IQ and with an explicit political agenda that went to number one in the US bestseller list (if not to number one in the psychologists' charts). While this may have whetted the appetite of many a publisher for views on intelligence, a mere 18 months later another book running pretty much the same argument is withdrawn from publication by its publisher, after a volley of adverse publicity (Brand, 1996). It seems, then, that the considerable progress, both theoretical and empirical, in understanding intelligence that has been made in the last 15 years might be threatened by ideological issues that, in truth, stand apart from scientific investigations. The central goal of this book is to provide young researchers with growing interests in the field with an authoritative statement of what has been done, where the field is headed, and suggestions about how best one might get there. I fervently hope that this book will draw in individuals more interested in the science of intelligence than in its politics.

This book will present the student of intelligence and development, not with one particular theoretical line, but with many. The contributions present both the necessary background and the leading research for students new to the field. The book will provide the necessary information on current methodology, data, and theory and will allow the reader to come to their own considered judgement about the nature and causes of the development of intelligence. Collectively the contributions should provide a future research student with the necessary methodological and theoretical armoury to consider making their own exploration on the field.

In the first chapter I present an overview of what I see as the pressing questions in the development of intelligence and why I chose the particular contributors for this book. Each of the following chapters is an excellent review of a specific area and can be read as such in their own right. Nevertheless, the field is very diverse and my aim is to provide a more general framework within which the other chapters can be oriented.

The first part focuses on the assessment of intelligence from two different perspectives. The first chapter by Irene Styles looks at traditional psychometric measures during childhood and contrasts the approach taken by those who followed factor analysis as the royal road to the intellect and those psychologists most interested in the measurement properties of the tests themselves. The second chapter by John Colombo and Janet Frick summarises the very recent research methods in testing intelligence in infancy and reviews the provocative data that suggests that new measures of information processing can predict later IQ. Such an enterprise was deemed well-nigh futile as little as 20 years ago.

The second part contains two chapters central to the book—to what extent is the development of intelligence controlled by genetic processes? In Chapter Four David Hay provides a guide to modern behaviour genetic analysis, focusing on cognitive development during childhood. Hay points out that modern behaviour genetics has moved beyond estimating heritabilities and now provides methods for locating the source of environmental influences on cognitive development. The picture presented is a more dynamic view of the influences of nature and nurture on the development of intelligence. In Chapter Five Steven Reznick and Robin Corley show how the techniques of behaviour genetics can even be applied to the development of intelligence during infancy. It turns out that behaviour genetics can be used to analyse intelligence at a finer grain than that of the heritability of IQ, namely, the extent to which genetically controlled development in infancy can be characterised as changes in general or specific abilities. In an analysis of the Bayley test of infant intelligence, they show that there is a particularly high genetic contribution to non-verbal intelligence measures and one that shows some independence from the genetic contribution to verbal abilities.

The third part of the book is, perhaps, the most diverse and deals with a broad cross-section of psychological approaches to understanding changing intellectual performance during development. In Chapter Six Bruce Torff and Howard Gardner present the case for regarding intelligence as a collection of independent abilities that develop across the lifespan. In Chapter Seven Helen Davis and I argue that the most central question is whether developmental changes and individual differences lie along the same dimension. We argue that there is a case for regarding individual differences and developmental change to be the province of quite different processes that contribute differentially to intelligence at different ages through development. In Chapter Eight, Graeme Halford argues that intelligence is best characterised in terms of the processing of relations. The development of intelligence involves the increasing differentiation of representations which allow higher order relations to be represented. In Chapter Nine Frank Dempster and Alice Corkill argue that the three dominant theoretical perspectives of recent developmental theory, knowledge-base, resources and strategies, may well have had their day. They put the case that "neo-interference theory" comprising notions of both interference from competing representations and inhibition of irrelevant information, can explain a variety of across-the-board changes and individual differences in infant search, selective attention, memory, comprehension, and reasoning—in short, intelligence.

The fourth part deals with atypical intellectual development and what challenges such examples may offer for general theories of the development of intelligence. In Chapter Ten Ted Nettelbeck reviews current theories on the nature of savants (individuals of low IQ who are, nevertheless, capable of some astonishing cognitive feats such as calendrical calculation) and draws some general implications for theories of the development of intelligence. Herman Spitz in Chapter Eleven returns to the issue of nature and nurture in development and critically reviews a number of studies of educational interventions that have claimed to have raised intelligence. In Chapter Twelve Bob Hodapp and Edward Zigler ask what the development of individuals with mental retardation can tell us about the normal development of intelligence.

The final part contains a single chapter by me that attempts to produce a synthesis of what I think I have learned from the contributions in this book (a great deal, believe me) and where I think the future research directions may be. This is done in the hope that you, the reader, may well be in the vanguard of the next generation's research effort.

REFERENCES

Brand, C.R. (1996). *The g factor*. New York: John Wiley & Sons.
Herrnstein, R.J. & Murray, C. (1994). *The bell curve: The reshaping of American life by differences in intelligence.* New York: Free Press.

Mike Anderson

Acknowledgements

Any edited volume depends, at base, on the quality of the chapters and I wish to thank the authors of the chapters in this book for their excellent contributions. For my own part I would like to thank Corinne Reid who has contributed so much in so many different ways—the book really would not have been possible without her. Thanks are also due to the "Big Lab" research group at UWA—Simon Davies, Helen Davis, Suzanne Dziurawiec, Linda Jeffery, Justin McLernon, Jeff Nelson (special thanks to Jeff for producing Fig. 1.1), Corinne Reid, and Mary Smyth. Once Linda Jarrett and Kathryn Russel of Psychology Press took charge of the manuscript things moved with alacrity and I would like to thank them for nursing the book home. Finally, this book is dedicated to Neil O'Connor who died in October 1997. Neil's work, in collaboration with Beate Hermelin, is a model of how to do interesting, significant, and clever research in cognitive development and intelligence. But the legacy of a great man is more than the published word. I, like many others, miss an inspirational teacher and a good friend.

Studies in Developmental Psychology
Published Titles

Series Editor
Charles Hulme, University of York, UK

The Development of Intelligence
  Mike Anderson (Ed.)
The Development of Language
  Martyn Barrett (Ed.)
The Social Child
  Anne Campbell & Steven Muncer (Eds)
The Development of Memory in Childhood
  Nelson Cowan (Ed.)
The Development of Mathematical Skills
  Chris Donlan (Ed.)
The Development of Social Cognition
  Suzanne Hala (Ed.)
Perceptual Development: Visual, Auditory, and Speech Perception in Infancy
  Alan Slater (Ed.)

INTRODUCTION

CHAPTER ONE

Project development—the shape of things to come

Mike Anderson

The University of Western Australia, Perth

Dah doo di dah doo (akin to the tune from the film *Close Encounters of the Third Kind*). The story told in this book has an eerie, yet familiar, quality. You know the kind of thing. Late one night somewhere in the Arizona desert Bart Thompson, a rocket scientist working for the Earth Federation Alpha Centauri Project, is driving home. Alone. Suddenly he notices in his rear-view mirror a couple of headlights approaching at high speed. He only has a second to panic because the next thing he knows he awakes in a four-by-four cell with nothing but a jug of water, a crust of bread, and a slop-out bucket. Slowly picking himself up he paces the room. There is nothing to see. Suddenly a voice comes from the walls, the ceiling, the floor. "Bart, tell me all you know about Project Development".

Bart is genuinely mystified. "I am a rocket scientist. Why am I here? What do you mean Project Development?"

"Bart, tell me about your work."

Bart, being fascinated by his work and reassured by the end of the Cold War, spills the beans. As he finishes his story with some gusto, the walls floor and ceiling approach at high speed . . . Bart bursts awake with a start, lashed with sweat. His panic-stricken breathing wakens his wife from her gentle slumber.

"Darling, whatever is the matter? You are trembling so. By the way a man from something called Project Development called. Did he find you today?

"Bart? Bart?"

Dah doo di dah doo.

Each of the contributors in this book was approached by the man from Project Development (you guessed it, me) and was asked to tell you, the student, about his or her work. None of the contributors knew the content of the others' chapters, though they knew who the contributors were going to be. I suspect that many of the contributors in this book will be unfamiliar with each other's work. This is a little unusual because edited books usually bring together a collection of researchers who publish in the same journals, attend the same conferences, and so on. But in this case the contributors come from quite different research areas with different approaches. So what are the common themes in this book? What is Project Development about?

The development of intelligence is an attempt on my part to influence the next generation who will research the central question of this book—what is the nature of intelligence and how does it develop? I hope to do this in a number of ways. First, I want to provide you with a synopsis, or map, of all the relevant areas of research activities. What better way to do this than have each story told by those who know it best, namely, the contributors in this book? Second, scientific expeditions into new territory require a methodological armoury. This book will provide you with a review of the major research methodologies in the area. Third, your route (that is the methodology you choose, or even better, the methodology you develop) will depend on what part of the territory you wish to explore. This book represents a tour of the major theoretical issues and perspectives that are out there. An army of academics can be an anarchic bunch. And no doubt the authors here would, individually, offer quite different advice on where your explorations might best bear fruit. But, rejoicing in the spoils of editorship, here is mine.

MAPPING THE TERRAIN

An intellectual terrain can look very different when approached from different directions. On the frontiers of knowledge, there are no maps—there are only the journal notes from individual expeditions. Each of these builds on a number of increasingly well-known trails, but the fact that many of these trails criss-cross the same territory is largely unrecognised. Figure 1.1 represents my own perspective on the intellectual terrain, where I have organised topics relevant to intelligence along three major dimensions.

The first dimension represents the various *structural* accounts of intelligence. The classical psychometric debate pits Spearman's (1904) concept of *g*, or general intelligence against Thurstone's (1938) conception of a number of specific Primary Mental Abilities. However, the classical debate has largely centred around alternative methods of analysing

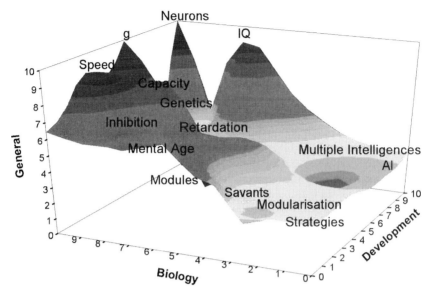

FIG. 1.1   Topics and constructs defining the research terrain of the development of intelligence. The terrain has three dimensions: *Biology*, ranging from the experiential (0) to the biological (10); *Developmental*, ranging from changing (0) to steady-state (10); and *General*, ranging from specific (0) to general (10).

intelligence test batteries, something that most contributors to this book would see as an overly narrow approach and somewhat tangential to the major current debates in the field. Nevertheless, the central issue of whether there is a need to posit a general factor of intelligence or whether intelligence is better characterised as a collection of independent abilities appears as a theme in many of the chapters.

The second dimension is the central *ontogenetic* one—what is the nature of the processes underlying developmental change in intelligence? This dimension ranges from the view that changes in intelligence through the developmental years amounts to nothing more than the simple accrual of knowledge acquired through a general learning mechanism, to those that argue for qualitative changes in the structure of cognition as intelligence develops. Obviously, this dimension embeds a common concern with the first dimension. If there is a mechanism of developmental change in intelligence is this better described in terms of a change in some global single factor underlying cognition or are there independent developmental paths for different cognitive abilities? For example, do changes in cognitive capacity or speed of processing underlie the increasing problem solving ability of children, or is this better explained by qualitative changes in cognition brought about by processes of modularisation or by the cultural development of specific abilities?

The third dimension is the *genesis* question—classically referred to as the nature/nurture debate. Is the development of intelligence caused by biological or by experiential factors? For many the answer to this question will determine much of our social and educational policies. Given this it is little wonder that much heat has been generated by attempts to determine the relative influence of genes and environment on intelligence. Aside from the consequences of the sociopolitical fall-out, the nature/nurture issue has had an impact on theories of intelligence because of the scientific issues surrounding the *appropriate level of description and explanation*. Is intelligence better understood in biological or cultural terms? The appropriate level of description is a general concern for psychological research but there is an added *frisson* in the case of intelligence caused by the only too obvious difficulties inherent in separating the scientific issues from the political.

The scientific issues surrounding the nature/nurture question are most directly tackled in the chapters on behaviour genetics and on abnormal development. However, while the fact that this question is the source of much scientific obscurantism and political angst is largely implicit in this book, it hangs like storm clouds over our intellectual terrain. So even by way of warning rather than guidance it is incumbent of me to draw your attention to the major impact that this question has had on research.

The politics of IQ

There is little doubt that the history of research in intelligence has been steeped in political controversy. Most obviously, the idea that there might be a single, biological, genetically determined basis to differences in measured IQ has lent itself to predominantly right-wing political interpretations. The caricature that intelligence is fixed and largely uninfluenced by environmental differences (something, by the way, no active researcher believes) has led to a number of odious social policies. For example, the policy of Eugenics advocates that high-IQ individuals should be encouraged to reproduce and low-IQ individuals discouraged to reproduce so that society as a whole can be improved. Intelligence tests were also central to the control of immigration to the United States in the early part of this century, leading to the restriction of entry to certain nationalities on the (plainly ludicrous) grounds that the average IQs of their population were supposedly in the feeble-minded range. These and many other political consequences of the misinterpretation of the data on the genetic basis of IQ differences have been well documented by Gould (1981, 1996). Lest you believe that this is all old hat, we have seen in the last few years a re-run of the old debate. The publication of *The bell curve* (Herrnstein & Murray, 1994) assembled the political argument in its most sophisticated form to date. Essentially, the argument in *The bell curve* boils down to a historical association (not a logical deduction) of a series of propositions:

- Intelligence, as measured by IQ, is a good predictor of social outcomes (poverty, unemployment, single parenthood, criminality, and so forth).

- Differences in intelligence cause these social outcomes rather than the other way around.

- Differences in intelligence are largely biologically based; consequently, so are social outcomes.

- Race differences in social outcome are explained by race differences in intelligence.

- The conjunction of the previous points mean that race differences in social outcome are caused by biological differences and consequently unchangeable.

These propositions are an explosive mix of fact and fantasy. I have tackled this tangled web in another place and it would lead us too far from our central goal to explore the issue in the required depth here. Suffice to say that this chain of reasoning is logically inadequate and has no empirical justification. Although the case for there being a substantial genetic contribution to individual differences in IQ is as close to a hard fact as there is in psychology, there is no evidence that race differences in IQ are genetically based or that social outcome is an inevitable consequence of biological differences. Be aware that any research in intelligence can be dragooned in the service of political agendas. Indeed, a research interest in intelligence requires a sensitivity to political debate. This sensitivity is a requirement of the researcher not just because of the potential for offence but because in the current climate of political sensibilities the possibility of disseminating the results of your research may depend on it. For example, Christopher Brand, a lecturer of 20 years' standing at Edinburgh University, had a book on general intelligence (Brand, 1996) pulped by the publisher after some controversial press coverage of the author's political views. Forewarned is forearmed.

Levels of description and explanation

Science would be simpler if there was a clear dichotomy between the "data out there" and the scientific theories that are constructed to "explain" the data. However, there is no clear dichotomy between data and theory because before very long the bulk of the data have been generated through attempts to test the scientific theories themselves. This leads to a problem of the *incommensurability* of different scientific frameworks. Theories can take such a different perspective on the terrain that they do not know what to make of the data generated by a theory outside their own framework. Constructs, methods, and ultimately the data to be explained can be quite different even though the topic area, "intelligence", is ostensibly the same. There are a number of different perspectives on what might seem to be merely different perspectives on the same "thing", namely, intelligence. Most obviously, research on individual differences in IQ, cognitive development, and mental retardation might seem to be attempts to approach intelligence from different directions. And yet these research areas (and there are many other areas relevant to the broader construct "intelligence") generate their own questions, their own methodologies, and their own theories and, before long, their central constructs cannot be translated in any simple fashion into the constructs of alternative perspectives. In science, synthesis is preferable to a proliferation of approaches. But synthesis is only possible where there is a genuine commonality, a "natural kind" as it were, in the material studied from the many perspectives. I believe that there is a commonality in the case of the development of intelligence and, consequently, I believe that all the many different approaches represented in this volume have something to say to each other. Exchanging information is the starting point of synthesis.

These considerations are present for any scientific endeavour. However, for psychology the fact that there are also different *levels* of description and explanation complicates the matter further. When we meet any phenomena in psychology we have a number of levels of description and explanation available to us. The three major levels in the study of intelligence are: the behavioural (including cultural); the cognitive/computational; and the biological/neurophysiological (including genetic). These different levels can be considered to range from high to low and map onto Eysenck's recipe (adapted from Hebb) on how to study intelligence scientifically. Eysenck divides constructs of intelligence into three distinct levels: intelligence A, which is its biological substrate; intelligence B, which is the conversion of intelligence A by cultural forces into what we know; and intelligence C which is behaviour manifested in intelligence test performance. Many would recognise these distinctions but Eysenck, for one, goes further in adopting a *reductionist* stance. He believes that a comprehensive theory of intelligence must first wait for a comprehensive theory of intelligence A (Eysenck, 1988). What this ordering implies is that the important aspects of intelligence will be best captured by a theory of its neurophysiological basis and, indeed, such theories are on offer (Hendrickson & Hendrickson, 1980; Jensen, 1982).

Yet, as I have argued elsewhere (Anderson, 1992), it is not at all obvious that discovering the precise neuronal basis of intelligence (even supposing this is possible independently of adequate descriptions at the other levels) is a prerequisite for studying intelligence B or intelligence as a cognitive construct. Indeed, I believe the opposite—there are no constraints that I can see on the cognitive theory of intelligence imposed by alternative physiological theories. However, I do agree with Eysenck that the other end of this explanatory dimension (intelligence C, or to quote Boring's famous dictum "Intelligence is what the tests test") has run out of theoretical steam. The promised structure of intelligence that was to be revealed by the use of factor analysis, as if by magic, has not materialised (Gould, 1981, 1996).

It is clear that others also take an opposite view to Eysenck. For example, Gardner (1983), although accepting as nearly everyone does that there are biological correlates, and perhaps determinants, of "intelligence" has argued that intelligence can only be considered in the social and cultural context in which it has evolved and functions. In other words, focusing on the biological loses sight of the very phenomenon of interest.

These alternative levels of description exacerbate the incommensurability of theoretical frameworks. It is important, then, to decide on the appropriate level of description in a search for commonality across the approaches represented in this book. So what does set the level of description? In my view it is the questions that we want to answer. So what are these questions? In many ways this book represents my attempt at laying out the terrain that, when explored, will yield these central questions. Before we consider why this book has been structured in the way it has been, I will demonstrate the way I have used this process before in formulating my own theory of intelligence and development. As you may well have deduced by now, scientific explorations are founded on an iterative process of question setting and answer finding.

SETTING A RESEARCH AGENDA

My own theory of intelligence and development (Fig. 1.2), the theory of the Minimal Cognitive Architecture underlying individual differences and cognitive development (Anderson, 1992; and see Chapter Seven), evolved through an attempt to answer what I saw as the central questions surrounding intelligence and development. I assembled those questions as

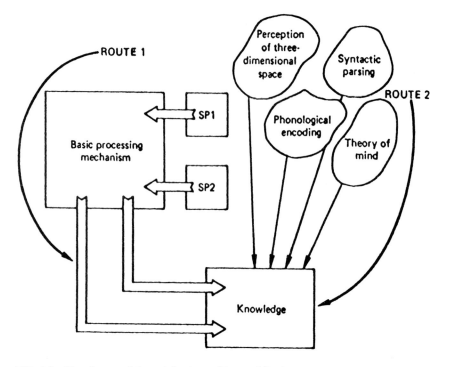

FIG. 1.2   The theory of the minimal cognitive architecture.

a series of agenda items that an adequate theory would minimally have to address. The agenda items came in two clusters, one concerned with regularities in the data and the other with the exceptions to those regularities.

The regularities are:

1. Cognitive abilities increase with development.
2. Individual differences in intelligence are remarkably stable with development.
3. Cognitive abilities covary.

I argued that a biologically based theory was well equipped to explain such regularities by, for example, associating general intelligence (regularity 3) with variation in neural functioning, a parameter that in turn improved with age (regularity 1). The stability of individual differences (regularity 2) is less well accommodated without additional assumptions but, all in all, a biologically based, lower-level theory accommodates the regularities well. However, things change when we consider the exceptions to these regularities.

The major exceptions are:

4. Some individuals of normal or above-average general intelligence have specific problems or deficits in particular aspects of cognitive functioning, for example, in reading or spelling.
5. The corollary of item 4 is that there are individuals of very low IQ who are capable of remarkable cognitive feats (savants).
6. While some relatively simple problems are the very stuff of intelligence tests and beyond the reach of many individuals considered mentally retarded those same individuals are capable of what are "everyday" cognitive activities such as acquiring language or seeing in three dimensions which are vastly more "computationally" complex.

I argued that a lower-level biologically based theory did not have the theoretical constructs to embrace both the regularities and the exceptions to those regularities. Rather, a higher level of description and explanation (a cognitive level) was necessary to embrace both clusters of agenda items. In this way, then, the explanatory agenda for a theory can be used to set the appropriate level of description and explanation and crucially alters the kind of research questions that can be asked and the methodologies that can be employed to answer them.

Clearly, my own theoretical position and previous research agenda outlined earlier has guided my choice of contributors to this book. Note that many of them have been chosen precisely because their views differ fundamentally from my own. The theory is covered in detail in Anderson (1992) and a more contextual (for this book) version is provided in Chapter Seven. A brief summary of the central propositions is presented in the next section. You may find it useful to bear my theory in mind when considering the contributions from the others, as inevitably I viewed the potential importance of these contributions through this particular theoretical lens. On the other hand, if you feel you want to read the chapters *de novo,* as it were, then skip the next section.

THE THEORY OF THE MINIMAL COGNITIVE ARCHITECTURE

The theory of the Minimal Cognitive Architecture argues that intelligence tests measure intelligence through assessing knowledge but that knowledge itself is acquired through two different routes and these two routes are differentially related to IQ differences and developmental change.

The first route to knowledge acquisition is through thinking. In the Minimal Cognitive Architecture thought is constrained by the speed of a basic processing mechanism (BPM) and it is this speed that is the fount of general intelligence, or IQ. Speed of processing is hypothesised to be unchanging with development and constitutes, therefore, the innate component of individual differences. However, there is more to differences in thinking than speed of processing or its psychometric consequence— general intelligence.

The architecture argues for a particular relationship between general and specific abilities. Individual differences in thinking are the consequence of the constraint on specific modes of thought (specific abilities) by the speed of the BPM. It is this constraint that gives rise to general intelligence. Problem-solving algorithms generated by two *specific processors*, one specialised for verbal representations and the other for spatial, are implemented by the BPM. The higher the speed of the BPM the more complex the algorithms that can be implemented. Each specific processor has a *latent* power, which can be regarded as its potential ability. The latent power of the specific processors is normally distributed in the population and uncorrelated with each other (an individual can be high on one and low on another) and uncorrelated with the speed of the basic processing mechanism. However, the observed performance of a specific processor, or its *manifest* ability, is consequently a function of two factors: the latent power of the processor and the speed of the basic processing mechanism—at slow speeds only the simplest algorithms can be implemented irrespective of the specific processors' latent power. The basic processing mechanism represents a knowledge-free, biological constraint on thought. Variation in the speed of the basic processing mechanism is the primary cause of *individual differences* in general intelligence. Individual differences in the latent powers of the specific processors are the basis of more specific cognitive abilities, *viz.* verbal and spatial abilities. An explicit property of this theory is that specific abilities become more *differentiated* with increasing IQ.

The second route to knowledge acquisition is through dedicated processing systems called modules after Fodor (1983). These modules provide complex representations of the world that could not be provided by central processes of thought. The maturation and development of modules is the primary motor of cognitive development but, because their operation is hypothesised to be independent of the speed of the basic processing mechanism, the knowledge they provide is available to all, independently of differences in IQ. For example, savant skills (in otherwise mentally handicapped individuals) are taken as evidence for the postulated independence of modular and IQ-related central processes: Isolated skills in art, music, language, spatial processing, or memory are taken to indicate the functioning of a preserved module, spared by global brain damage that affects predominantly the functioning of the BPM (see Nettelbeck & Young, 1996). This theory has already been used to explain patterns of cognitive functioning found in experimental studies of savant abilities (Anderson, O'Connor, & Hermelin, in press; Smith & Tsimpli, 1995).

The agenda (explaining both the regularities and exceptions) that was set for this theory necessitated that an adequate theory be couched in cognitive or computational terms. Thereafter a synthesis of current data and arguments relevant to the cognitive level of explanation that could accommodate the research agenda was provided by the Minimal Cognitive Architecture. In addition the theory generated a number of new hypotheses about the relationship between intelligence and development. In particular, the theory proposes that individual differences in intelligence and developmental changes in intelligence lie, in the main, on different dimensions of intelligence (see Chapter Seven). Further, the major processing variable underlying the individual differences dimension, speed of processing, is hypothesised to be unchanging during development. But the goal of this theory was broader than the goal of this book. While any consideration of the development of intelligence in my view must still look to the agenda I set for the broader theory, there are likely to be other more specific issues that were not addressed. For example, the architecture represented in Fig. 1.2 makes no explicit reference to the impact of either environmental or genetic variables on knowledge outcomes. Yet a fuller account clearly needs to explain the relationship between these two contributors to developmental change. I would like to know how genes contribute differentially to general and specific abilities and how to represent this within the structure of the theory. More though, I would like to know how genes contribute to the *development* of abilities and how these data might be accommodated by the theory. Yet again, I would like to know in more detail the consequences of specific deficits for the development of intelligence in general and I would like to know what the data on educational interventions imply for the theory. So you see that there are some questions that arise from my own theoretical orientation that predisposed me to seek particular contributions for this book. However, once the contributions are in then it might be that the issues tackled and data presented suggest quite different questions. As I said, research is an iterative process of questions and answers that pulls us forward.

THE STRUCTURE OF THE BOOK

This book represents the next stage in my own iterative process. Having set these original questions and answered most of them, at least to my own satisfaction, can I go back to gather more views and data (in the light of my theory) and come up with the next set of questions that might move the theory forward? Or indeed might the necessary distortion of the field required by my previous agenda be shown to be a sub-optimal view when seen in the light of others' different concerns? We shall see.

For me the questions that we can plausibly seek answers to will emerge out of a number of central issues around which the book is structured, some of which have been presaged in the earlier discussion.

The first issue concerns a much-neglected aspect of scientific explorations in psychology and that is *measurement*. How are we to develop appropriate measures of intelligence and what are the lessons that we can learn from the history of the development of intelligence tests? Our measures of intelligence are still based on a century-old formulation and if we have new cognitive theories can we not come up with new appropriate measures of our constructs? Measurement issues are dealt with in Part One. The second issue is the *genesis* question. Again it seems highly unlikely that we can have an adequate developmental account of intelligence that does not address the differential contributions of genes and environment. This is the central focus of Part Two and is dealt with more obliquely in both the third and fourth parts. Part Three is in many ways the engine of the book because it deals with both the *structure of intelligence* and *models of change*. Here we must tackle the issue of the relationship (if any) between general and specific abilities and how this might change with development. The fourth issue, which is becoming of greater concern for psychology as a whole, is how a general theory of the development of intelligence might be applied to particular cases. This has long been a venerable strategy for research in intelligence—testing the general theory by its ability to account for specific conditions of abnormality. The fourth section on *abnormal development* should throw up some crucial questions for future research.

Now that we have poured over my particular charts of the intellectual domain, it is time for the contributors to speak for themselves.

Dah doo di dah doo.

REFERENCES

Anderson, M. (1992). *Intelligence and development: A cognitive theory*. Oxford, UK: Blackwell.

Anderson, M., O'Connor, N., & Hermelin, B. (in press). A specific calculating ability. *Intelligence*.

Brand, C.R. (1996). *The g factor*. New York: John Wiley & Sons.

Eysenck, H.J. (1988). The concept of "intelligence": Useful or useless? *Intelligence, 12*, 1–16.

Fodor, J.A. (1983). *The modularity of mind*. Cambridge, MA: MIT Press.

Gardner, H. (1983). *Frames of mind: The theory of multiple intelligences*. London: Heinemann.

Gould, S.J. (1981). *The mismeasure of man*. Harmondsworth, UK: Pelican Books.

Gould, S.J. (1996). *The mismeasure of man* (Rev. ed.). Harmondsworth, UK: Pelican Books.

Hendrickson, A.E. & Hendrickson, D.E. (1980). The biological basis for individual differences in intelligence. *Personality and individual differences, 1,* 3–33.

Herrnstein, R.J., & Murray, C. (1994). *The bell curve: The reshaping of American life by differences in intelligence.* New York: Free Press.

Jensen, A.R. (1982). Reaction time and psychometric g. In H.J. Eysenck (Ed.), *A model for intelligence.* Berlin, Germany: Springer-Verlag.

Nettelbeck, T., & Young, R. (1996). Intelligence and savant syndrome: Is the whole greater than the sum of the fragments? *Intelligence, 22,* 49–68.

Smith, N., & Tsimpli, I. (1995). *The mind of a savant: Language learning and modularity.* Oxford, UK: Blackwell.

Spearman, C. (1904). "General intelligence", objectively determined and measured. *American Journal of Psychology, 15,* 201–293.

Thurstone, L.L. (1938). *Primary mental abilities.* Chicago: University of Chicago Press.

PART ONE

The assessment of intelligence in development

CHAPTER TWO

The study of intelligence—the interplay between theory and measurement*

Irene Styles
Murdoch University, Perth, Western Australia

In the history of the physical sciences, the development of theory and the development and application of good principles of measurement have gone hand in hand: each has informed the other. Among many examples is the interpretation of Planck's constant, h, in the formula E=hυ developed by Planck to account for experimental data. Although Planck introduced h of empirical and mathematical necessity, he did not initially know what it might mean at the time and only later did its interpretation lead to a model of the atom with discontinuous energy orbits (Zajonc, 1995). The argument put forward in this chapter is that the interplay between theory and measurement is true, too, for a number of fields of interest in psychology, but that what began as a close and necessary alliance seems to have broken down—that theory and sound principles of measurement in psychology seem to have diverged. This divergence is mirrored in the insistence by many people on the separation of qualitative and quantitative aspects of research, though others, such as Kuhn, have recognised their mutually dependent role in seeking to understand phenomena and develop theory (Kuhn, 1977). It is also argued here that we have at hand the measurement models to enable us to reunite theory and qualitative understanding, with quantification and measurement to their mutual benefit, leading us to new and better understandings of many psychological phenomena.

*The author thanks Professor David Andrich for his comments and suggestions on this chapter and for many interesting conversations over several years on some of the issues raised here.

Since the earliest developments of quantification in the social sciences, the construct of intelligence in the field of psychology has been the most intimately related to measurement. There are two major conceptual approaches to the study of intelligence—one is referred to as the psychometric approach, epitomised by the work of Binet and Simon (1905/1980) and perceived as quantitative, and the other the cognitive-developmental approach, epitomised by the work of Piaget (1970) and perceived as qualitative. In parallel with the perceived divergence between theory and measurement, and in spite of their initial close alliance, many researchers have seen these two approaches as mutually exclusive (for example, de Vries, 1974; de Vries & Kohlberg, 1977), although others have seen them as complementary (Andrich & Styles, 1994; Elkind, 1975). Some of the many similarities between these two conceptual approaches are discussed later, but, to anticipate that discussion, it is noted that Binet and Simon's approach focused on the meaning and interpretation of *correct* responses to a range of relatively complex tasks using single, standard questions, the responses to which the administrator had to assign a mark depending on the quality of the response. The notion of development is evident in the ordering of items according to age and, within age, according to difficulty. Piaget, on the other hand, focused on the construction and development of intelligence through a study of the nature of *incorrect* responses to even more complex tasks using a similar clinical, diagnostic approach, but one in which the administrator had more freedom to probe the respondent's understandings and assign a stage depending on the quality of response. "We have here an examination approaching a clinical examination", wrote Binet and Simon (1905/1980, p. 122). "Piaget's method is the semiclinical interview", states Elkind (editor's introduction in Piaget, 1968). Their methodologies, therefore, were quite similar and certainly more similar to each other than later developments in test construction and administration were to them.

Following a short discussion of some major steps in the history of measurement in psychology which demonstrate the divergence of theory and measurement, a specific latent trait model of measurement, which may serve to close the gap between the two, is described. The power of this model is then illustrated by descriptions of how the model has been used to try to understand some of the major issues of interest in the measurement and theory of intellectual functioning. The foremost issue is the integration of psychometric and cognitive-developmental perspectives, in essence, an integration of quantitative and qualitative conceptions of intellectual functioning which mirrors the concern to integrate measurement and theory. This leads to insights into the question of the dimensionality of the concept of intelligence and the possibility of the occurrence of growth spurts in its development.

EARLY DEVELOPMENTS IN MEASUREMENT

Early attempts to measure intelligence seemed to have assumed that intellectual functioning was manifested in gross physical aspects of human beings. This is evidenced in, for example, the work of Broca who used measures of skull circumference and/or brain volume as indications of intellectual performance (Broca, 1861, cited in Gould, 1981). Galton (often referred to as the father of psychometrics; Duncan, 1984) maintained the link between the physical and the mental in his quantification of non-physical qualities. He included anthropomorphic measures as well as psychophysical measures of sensory discrimination and fine motor performance among his criteria for intelligence in his work on Heredity Genius (Galton, 1884). In the context of the general views of the time, especially the perceived strong biological basis of intelligence and the assumption of genetic causation, coupled with the relative ease of measurement of physical measures, this is not surprising. However, more complex mental measures such as judgement, memory, invention, attention, and language were also explored, by Galton and by others, in the latter half of the last century, as manifestations or indications of intellectual functioning (Spearman, 1927b; Spearman & Jones, 1950). This period was, therefore, a time of transition in theorising about the way in which intelligence may be manifested—from an assumption of physical to an assumption of psychological manifestations as evidence of mental phenomena. However, no matter what type of manifestation was in use, the focus in psychometrics then, as now, was on the variability of performance (and by inference, therefore, variability in underlying characteristics) among individuals.

A major step forward in the development of psychometrics in general, and its application to the field of intelligence in particular, came with the work of Alfred Binet and his colleague, Theodore Simon, in the early years of this century. The development of Binet's thinking was a microcosm of the general trends described previously in that, putting aside his early work on skull measurements (with which he was disenchanted), he developed the first individual mental test of intellectual functioning. This was in response to the French Education Department's need to be able to distinguish children who required special educational attention from those who could benefit from normal classroom provision. Binet and Simon derived the idea of the mental test from a series of questions about specific topics which had been developed by Blin and his student, Demaye, as an aid in diagnosing mental deficiency (Binet & Simon, 1905/1980). The purpose of this development was, ostensibly, to serve a practical situation, but it is clear that Binet and Simon also had theoretical concerns, particularly in regard to the vagueness of the symptoms and signs used to diagnose mental deficiency at the time. Their criticisms mainly concerned the then current use of physical rather than psychological symptoms to distinguish subcategories of abnormality, and the unreliability of gradations of symptoms.

Binet and Simon advocated a new method: Their test was the first attempt at developing a psychological scale which assumes an underlying developmental continuum or latent variable of ability. In accordance with the concept of a continuum, items were ordered according to their difficulties and according to the ages at which children could be expected to answer them correctly. The items could be evaluated and assigned a score relatively independently of the idiosyncratic moods or interests of any individual examiner. Theirs was thus, also, the first attempt at adaptive testing, presenting only those items deemed to be near the intellectual level of the respondent. In addition, scores were allotted to items according to the level or quality of the response, that is, there were "better" and "worse" responses to one item rather than answers simply being judged correct or incorrect. Further, Binet and Simon tried to develop items that were of a general nature to reflect the ability to acquire knowledge (that is, intelligence) rather than testing very specific knowledge that might be acquired by some people as a result of specific teaching and not therefore by others. Because of these psychometric characteristics, performance on the tests could be interpreted accordingly to age norms and could also be used to elucidate and, thereby, fix the categories for mental deficiency. Binet and Simon's work constitutes an example of the close relationship between the development of measurement and theory that existed at that time. Binet and Simon's tests consisted of tasks suitable for age one year to adulthood and, thus, assumed the development of intelligence with age. In addition, implicit in the variety of tasks employed is a general, broad conception of what intelligence is, although its source was not assumed: That is, their view was that measurement should focus on current mental state, or performance, irrespective of different views on the sources underlying that state.

This degree of circumspection was not, alas, heeded by many who followed. Too often the measures obtained from such tests have been assumed to be reflections of an innate, unalterable capacity. Neither of these characteristics is inherent in the concept of quantification of mental functioning (it is not so, either, in the measurement of the concept of height, for example), but an unfortunate interpretation from which the concept and measurement of intelligence is still endeavouring to distance itself.

Through the subsequent development of measures of intelligence, the basic requirements of psychometrics, initiated by Binet and Simon, remained: The tests consisted of collections of items deemed to measure some ability considered important in intellectual functioning, which were ordered in difficulty, age-related, and standardised on large groups of people to provide norms representative of different age and, later, occupational or other diagnostic groups. (See, for example, Terman & Merrill, 1960; Weschler, 1958.)

FUNDAMENTAL CONCEPTIONS OF INTELLIGENCE

Having considered some early attempts to measure manifestations of intelligence, there is a need to return to an earlier stage in the history of psychology to consider some the fundamental theoretical conceptions about the construct of intelligence.

Spearman and Jones (1950) mention "three fundamental doctrines of human ability"—three conceptions of intellectual functioning that have been present in different forms for many centuries. These three are, first, *monarchic*, which views intelligence as a single ability, notably Spearman's general intelligence, *g* (Spearman, 1927a, 1927b), or Cattell's fluid intelligence (Cattell, 1963); second, *oligarchic*, which views intelligence as consisting of several broad factors such as Thurstone's Primary Mental Abilities (Thurstone, 1969) or Gardner's multiple intelligences (Gardner, 1983); and, third, *anarchic*, which views intelligence as consisting of many specific abilities such as Guilford's structure-of-intellect model (Guilford, 1967). Spearman's and Jones' opinion that there is "Truth in each of the great and ancient views" (Spearman & Jones, 1950, p. 13) is a perspective which is also taken in this chapter. Here, also, the perspective is taken that it is a question of scale as to which is suitable in understanding any particular situation. In one context and for one purpose, intelligence may be viewed as monarchic; in another context and for a different purpose, it is more specific. This does not mean that any view will do, but rather that an hierarchical view seems most useful and explanatory: This is in line with Vernon's (1965) and, to a lesser extent, Cattell's (1963) conceptions of intelligence. The hierarchical conception is of importance in considering patterns of growth or development because of the notion of different levels of scale associated with it. Whether intellectual development appears continuous or discontinuous, increasing smoothly or in spurts, will depend on the size of the unit of measurement (that is, the scale) and the length of time between successive measurements. Thus, using a large unit (usually associated with a more general measure) far apart in time will make development look discontinuous compared with using a smaller unit (usually associated with a more specific measure) for measurements closer in time. At a fine level, transitions from one level of performance to another are so small that "spurts" are not noticeable unless studied in that context, that is, with a unit of measurement that would permit their visibility. Using more monarchic measures, spurts tend to be more noticeable because the markers are more general, the unit larger.

Unfortunately, the development of these divergent views of intelligence was based, not on sound principles of measurement, but on the use of a statistical tool which bypasses such principles. This statistical tool was factor analysis in which results are not independent of the population characteristics of a trait in the way, for example, that measures of the length of any object are independent of the lengths of other objects that might be measured (Duncan, 1985; Styles, 1994). This is not to say that statistics cannot inform theory, but that they may do so only if their use follows good measurement. Considering the purposes for which factor analysis has been used, it is probably not too strong a position to take to agree with Duncan that "factor analysis is a failure" (Duncan, 1984, p. 207).

It was Spearman who carried out initial work on factor analysis which was developed further by Thurstone during the 1930s. Considering Thurstone's earlier contribution to the principles of measurement, this was, perhaps, the moment when measurement lost the opportunity to play an equal, powerful role in the development of psychological theorising. Lumsden has characterised Thurstone's work on measurement as "stealing fire from the gods" (Lumsden, 1980, p. 7) for which, as a punishment, he was "chained to factor analysis" (p. 7). In any event, factor analysis rather than measurement took hold, and eventually its techniques were extended and employed in the development of theory not only in the field of intelligence but also in fields such as personality, interests, values, and a whole range of psychological constructs (Duncan, 1984).

FUNDAMENTAL MEASUREMENT

To highlight the consequences for the development of theory, we need to consider the requirements of fundamental measurement (typical of measurements in the physical sciences) and the battle to achieve recognition of and adherence to those requirements by researchers in the social sciences. At this point, it is important to distinguish between assumptions and requirements in measurement—a distinction that has been discussed in detail in Andrich (1989a, 1989b). In adhering to fundamental measurement, the researcher does not simply assume the data operate according to its requirements but rather seeks to develop scales which generate data that reflect the trait in question and meet those requirements. If data do not meet the requirements, then fundamental measurement has not been achieved and further conceptual analysis needs to be done in order to understand the reasons for this failure. This distinction is one that has been missed by many researchers who have the criteria as a weakness of the measurement models which seek to adhere to these requirements.

In the 1920s, Thurstone laid down the theoretical requirements or criteria for measurement in the social sciences: (1) items should be located on a continuum, or scale; (2) the locations of the items should be invariant across different populations who are to be measured by the items; and (3) the locations of items on the continuum should satisfy the requirement of additivity (Andrich, 1978a, 1989a). The first criterion implies that the items reflect an underlying or latent trait which is unidimensional at some level of scale. The second criterion implies the item locations should not be affected by the properties of the people whose responses were used to locate the items on the continuum: The relative order of the items should remain invariant and independent of the people. The third criterion means that a continuum should form an equal-interval scale which provides a consistent unit of measurement across the operating range of the variable of interest. Only then is one justified in adding, multiplying, or performing any other arithmetic operation on the scores.

In the 1950s, Louis Guttman, too, saw the importance of being able to order persons on a single, unidimensional continuum with perfect transitivity (Andrich, 1985). Unfortunately, his formulations were deterministic in nature and not easy to apply in a routine way, and, as a result, they have not been found useful in many situations. During his lifetime, he struggled to turn researchers from the rocks. As it happened, few heeded the warnings from Thurstone's and Guttman's work on measurement: Most were seduced by the inexorable siren song of factor analysis.

RASCH MODELS FOR MEASUREMENT

A measurement model that provides fundamental measurement equivalent to that available in the physical sciences was developed for cognitive variables in the 1960s by the Danish mathematician Georg Rasch (1960/1980, 1961), and clarified for use with attitudinal and other variables by others (for example, Andersen, 1977; Andrich 1978b, 1978c). Rasch models synthesise the key features of Thurstone's requirements for fundamental measurement—invariance, unidimensionality, and additivity—and also provide a probabilistic formulation of the Guttman scale. They are the only modern latent trait models that adhere to the requirements of fundamental measurement (Andrich, 1988).

An interesting historical parallel with Binet's work is that Rasch received the impetus to develop his models when asked to monitor the reading progress of students identified as poor readers. Rasch models arose from the following criteria (Rasch, 1961, p. 332):

The comparison between two stimuli should be independent of which particular individuals were instrumental for the comparison; and it should also be independent of which other stimuli within the considered class were or might also have been compared. Symmetrically, a comparison between two individuals should be independent of which particular stimuli within the class considered were instrumental for comparison; and it should also be independent of which other individuals were also compared, on the same or on some other occasion.

If the data fit the Rasch model, the requirements of fundamental measurement will have been achieved. If different populations have different understandings of the construct, then invariance of parameter estimates will break down. The diagnostics available allow the investigation of the extent of invariance of the construct across items, people, and groups of people and the possible reasons for any breakdown in invariance. Studying the fit and misfit of the data to the model may then lead to a greater understanding of how the variable works and how it works relative to different populations. Using this methodology, the link between measurement and theory is firmly re-established. Rasch models can provide the "measurement properties we must demand if we take measurement seriously" (Duncan, 1984, p. 217).

Mathematical models based on Rasch's work can be used to build measurement scales from either dichotomous or polytomous responses or a combination of the two. Full treatments of the models can be found in Andrich (1988), Rasch (1961), and Wright and Stone (1979) for dichotomous data, and Andrich (1978a, 1978b, 1978d, 1978e, 1985) for polytomous data.

APPLICATIONS OF RASCH MEASUREMENT MODELS IN THE STUDY OF INTELLIGENCE

With the availability of fundamental measurement models and the development of complementary computer programs, we have the opportunity to consider fundamental questions about intelligence and its development that have interested researchers for many years. These questions are conceptually based, with strong implications for the theory of intellectual functioning and all can be advanced by the use of the Rasch models of latent trait theory.

The rest of the chapter describes a series of studies in which the Rasch models were used to address some of these questions and which have been carried out by the author and her colleague over the last 10 years. They include the provision of an equal-interval scale for measurement of non-verbal general intelligence; the investigation of the occurrence of growth spurts in intelligence; the integration of psychometric and cognitive-developmental approaches to intellectual functioning, particularly from an information processing perspective.

Provision of an equal-interval scale of non-verbal, general intelligence

To provide fundamental measurement of general, non-verbal intelligence for a series of studies on the development of intelligence, Andrich and Styles (1994) chose the Raven's Progressive Matrices tests (RPM) for reasons which are discussed next.

Since they were first developed, the RPM have been widely considered the "best of all non-verbal tests of *g*" (Spearman & Jones, 1950, p. 70). Raven, himself, postulated the underlying variable (or latent trait, in modern terminology) to be that of abstract analogical reasoning (Raven, 1940). More recently, Snow, Kyllonen, and Marshalek (1984) also concluded that the Raven's Progressive Matrices test is the purest measure of *g*, and the work of Styles and Andrich with Raven's and Piagetian tasks suggests the same: The RPM tests measure a very general construct of intellectual functioning.

There are several forms of the RPM including the Coloured Progressive Matrices (CPM) (Raven, Court, & Raven, 1977), the Standard Progressive Matrices (SPM) (Raven, Court, & Raven, 1992), and the Advanced Progressive Matrices (APM) sets I and II (Raven, Court, & Raven, 1993), which are aimed at different age groups. These are all similar in format and underlying content—more similar than verbal tests of intelligence tend to be. All items consist of a matrix pattern with a section missing, and six or eight alternative responses, one of which completes the missing section of the matrix. An example which is not one of the test items, but is similar to them, is shown in Fig. 2.1.

The tests have been employed in thousands of studies over the 60 or 70 years of their existence during which technical flaws have been eliminated. Evidence is that the items are stable over a range of socioeconomic groups and between societies with a literary tradition (Raven, 1989). There is also evidence that the items conform to the Rasch model for dichotomous responses (Rasch, 1960/1980).

Another reason for selecting the RPM was that the variable should cover a wide range of level of ability, and therefore be applicable to a wide age range. The RPM provides this because it may be used from about four or five years of age up to and including adulthood. Items increase in difficulty from the CPM through the SPM to the APM and, within each of the forms, the level of difficulty depends on the number of variable elements that have to be coordinated, and the difficulty of the algorithm,

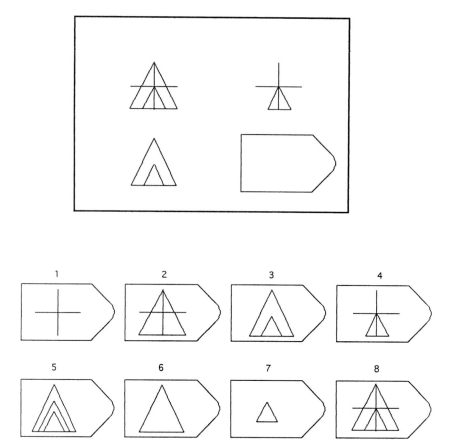

FIG. 2.1   An example of an item similar to a Raven's Progressive Matrices item.

or both (Styles, 1995a). The SPM consists of 5 sets of 12 items each of which employ 5 different algorithms. (According to Raven (cited in Burke, 1958), these are Continuous, Analogies, Progressive alterations, Permutations and Resolution into constituent parts.) By pooling all items from all the scales except set AB from the CPM, and ordering them by difficulty, one large scale of items (108 items altogether) was obtained.

By computerising the items, it was then possible to use a form of computer-adaptive testing whereby respondents began at a point on the continuum estimated to be below their level of ability (two standard deviations below the average for the age group from the published norms) and responded to items until the items became too difficult for them. Details on the administration of the test can be found in Styles (1991). Note the similarity to Binet's administration of his tests—in neither case did children have to respond to all items even within one set of items (as they would in the paper and pencil version of the RPM administered with a traditional measurement perspective in mind): They responded only to those items in the vicinity of their expected level of ability. Targeted testing, as Binet and Simon seem to have understood intuitively, enhances the validity and reliability of responses because it cuts down boredom, frustration, and guessing (Kubinger, 1988) and because the maximum amount of information about a person's ability can be gained from items close to the person's ability.

Rasch first tried his measurement model on data from the Raven's Matrices and concluded they fitted his model. Styles and Andrich's analysis supported this: The RPM conforms to a unidimensional latent trait model with the implication that equal units of measurement can be used across the operating range of the items (Styles & Andrich, 1993).

Investigation of intellectual growth spurts

There have been many studies of intellectual growth, often in conjunction with physical development (for example, Bayley, 1949; Shuttleworth, 1939). In particular, spurts in physical growth have been identified and confirmed (one measure that has been studied in detail is that of height), and it seemed natural to enquire whether something similar could happen as regards intellectual functioning.

Andrich and Styles' (1994) longitudinal study of intellectual growth spurts drew on the two major perspectives on intellectual functioning with which this chapter is concerned—the psychometric and the cognitive-developmental. The first study that is described concentrated on the possibility of intellectual growth spurts using psychometric measures in intellectual functioning. From a psychometric viewpoint, growth spurts would take the form of a relatively rapid quantitative increase in ability estimates on a particular measure at specific chronological ages. The idea of growth spurts is, however, also commensurate with cognitive or stage-developmental theory, that is, a rapid qualitative change of some kind may take place at relatively specific ages. The second study, which is described later in this chapter, sought an integration of these two approaches.

In designing this study, the intention was to overcome the analytical and methodological drawbacks associated with earlier growth studies. First, in order to study intellectual growth, longitudinal studies are preferable to cross-sectional ones: there are no cohort effects and each person acts as his or her own control—the same people are developing all the time. However, longitudinal studies have disadvantages in that they ignore possible cohort effects, they are very time-consuming, and often have high attrition rates (Baltes, Cornelius, & Nesselroade, 1978).

Second, earlier studies often employed a variety of measures of intelligence as persons got older and the tests used were not appropriate across a wide age range. Thus measures across age ranges may reflect different traits and any patterns emerging may be a reflection of a changing latent trait rather than changing levels of ability on the same trait.

Third, in earlier studies, even if one measure was used, the scale was not an equal-interval one, so changes in measures were difficult to interpret. The use of a Rasch model with one kind of test of intelligence, together with a combined longitudinal and cross-sectional design could overcome these weaknesses and allow the investigation of growth patterns. Andrich and Styles (1994) employed this type of design with four cohorts of 8-, 10-, 12-, and 14-year-old children of both sexes over a period of six years. Children were tested on a computerised version of the RPM at six-monthly intervals. Details of the design and testing procedures and discussion of practice and motivational effects are given in Andrich and Styles (1994). In this study, evidence of similarities of patterns across sexes and ages allowed the pooling of results of combined cohorts of boys and girls at overlapping ages.

The statistic used to indicate spurts was change in variance, an idea derived from Epstein's work. Epstein (1974a, 1974b) had reasoned that if there was a characteristic which exhibited a pattern of spurts in growth, and if individuals tended to spurt at different times, then the variance of that characteristic would increase as people became more different from one another and would decrease as the later spurters entered their phase of relatively rapid growth and "caught up" with everyone else. Figure 2.2 shows the change of variance for the RPM as a function of age. An intellectual spurt beginning at about 11 years for both boys and girls is evident. This supports the interpretation Epstein made of data from earlier studies of growth (Epstein, 1974a, 1974b, 1978, 1990) and the interpretation of results in Thatcher, Walker, and Giudice's study (1987), which showed weak spurts in brain growth at about the same age.

Epstein had also identified spurts at 7 years of age and at 13–14 years. Results from Andrich and Styles' study are consistent with this: Evidently, children are coming out of a growth spurt with a maximum some time before age 8, and the "wobble" in the curve at about 13 may indicate a smaller plateau followed by a spurt at that age. The children in the Andrich and Styles study came from quite homogeneous socioeconomic backgrounds and attended the same schools for all of their school lives and hence environmental factors such as educational opportunities, family support and encouragement, and level of nutrition were all likely to be relatively consistent. For this reason, and because some of the children start their intellectual spurt at about 11 and others only at about 14 years of age, a strong maturational, rather than an environmental cause for these

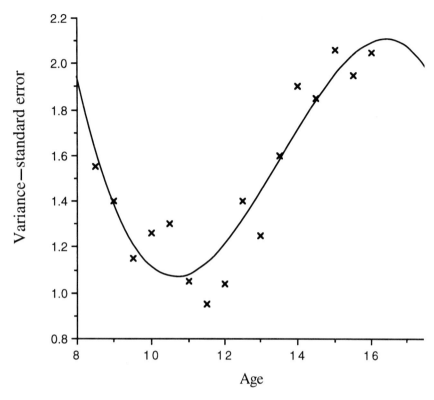

FIG. 2.2   Age against ability variance for males and females combined with third-order polynomial curve fitted.

spurts was postulated. There is no reason that, for example, educational opportunities would directly cause a growth spurt; if it were so, all children would spurt at the same time and if this were so, the pattern of variance would not occur—the variance would remain linear and parallel to the horizontal axis.

However, it is likely that marked variations in environmental factors between individuals could have the effect of delaying or bringing forward the age of onset of a spurt for different children (Andrich & Styles, 1994). It is the view of the author and many others that it must be the case that both genetic and environmental factors contribute to the development and expression of growth (certainly in different amounts in different circumstances) and there is an interplay between the two, their effects being inseparable in most situations. Evidence for the role of maturation is strengthened by Thatcher et al.'s (1987) study and by Epstein's (1974a, 1974b, 1978, 1990) postulation of phrenoblysis (coincident spurts in brain growth and intellectual growth, with skull growth being an index of brain growth) to explain data from growth studies. It is also supported by evidence from one cohort in the Andrich and Styles study which indicates, beyond the possibility of coincidence, the similarity in growth patterns between skull circumference and ability between the ages of 8 and 11 years (Styles, 1995b). These growth patterns are shown in Fig. 2.3.

This is historically interesting because Binet had begun measuring skulls prior to the development of his mental tests, except he used absolute measures instead of rate of change as Styles has done. Further, Spearman (1904, p. 262) commented that "there is a stage of development somewhere near the eleventh year where Intelligence temporarily declines: in connection herewith we have the curious fact that from about eleven to twelve years there appears to ensue a suspension in the growth of children's heads." Both these observations fit the patterns we have found using much more sophisticated designs and measurement methodology

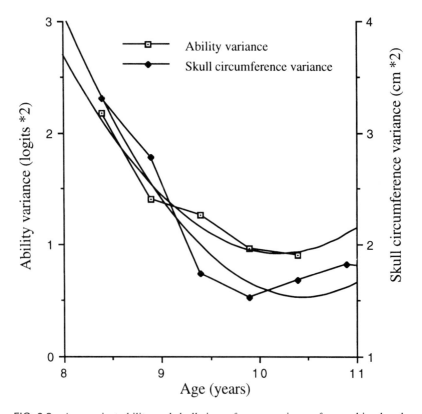

FIG. 2.3   Age against ability and skull circumference variances for combined male and female groups with second order polynomial curves fitted.

and using both group and individual data. Because these findings were incidental to the main purpose of that study, it is intended to carry out a further study devised especially with the aim of checking the relationship between growth in intelligence and rate of change of skull circumference.

Integration of psychometric and cognitive-developmental approaches to intelligence

Most research into the possibility of integrating Piagetian and psychometric approaches has used factor analysis and the results have been interpreted as indicating two distinct intelligences (Carroll, Kohlberg, & de Vries, 1984), with the conclusion that an integration was not possible. More recently, using a similar methodology, Lim (1988) has interpreted results as indicating the two measures (psychometric and Piagetian) he used are reflecting a similar variable, but also a separate "formal reasoning" factor, which, again, constrained the integration of the two approaches.

There has been little work on latent trait approaches to Piaget's work, notable exceptions being the British Intelligence Scales (Ward, 1972), Bond (1993), Andrich and Constable (1984), and Davison, King, Kitchener and Parker (1980). There has been even less work on modern latent trait approaches to the possible integration of psychometric and cognitive-developmental perspectives on intellectual functioning, yet these approaches can hold the key to such an integration. The studies described in the next section investigated this possibility.

Regarding cognitive-developmental responses as psychometric

Comparisons between the psychometric and cognitive-developmental perspectives have been made before and can be found detailed in Elkind (1975) or Styles (1995a), amongst other sources. From an historical point of view, the perspective of the two approaches as complementary is compelling because it was while Piaget worked for Binet that he thought to inspect the consistencies in the types of error children made with the Binet items, rather than simply scoring responses as more or less correct. Substantively, both psychometric and cognitive-developmental views of intelligence accept the essentially adaptive function of intelligence, that changes with age are in the direction of more complexity and stability and that these changes are completed at about the same age—15 years. Methodologically, in both approaches items (or tasks) are matched to age levels and are ordered in difficulty. Thus in both cases the items (or tasks) can be conceived as being on a continuum of increasing difficulty. Piaget, himself, refers to stages thus: "Cognitive stages have a sequential property, that is, they appear in a fixed order of succession" (Piaget, 1970, p. 711).

As noted earlier, Binet was interested in degrees of correctness in responses to well-defined but open-ended tasks, and added scores assigned to these responses across individual items to give a total score which would locate a child on an intellectual continuum. This method clearly has a quantitative emphasis. On the other hand, Piaget was interested in incorrect responses to his tasks and used his classification of the qualitatively different types of reasoning behind the errors in order to locate a child at a stage in a developmental continuum. Binet used many items, Piaget just a few tasks, but both employed relatively complex tasks. Both methodologies employed different tasks for different ages, or a similar but more difficult task across ages or stages. Most subsequent attempts to develop psychometric tests of intelligence diverged from Binet's approach of assessing degrees of correctness of responses and used only dichotomously scored multiple-choice items—a trend that must, also, have hastened the divergence of quantitative and qualitative viewpoints on intelligence. Such dichotomous items (of which the RPM is an example) can be considered as single transition points or thresholds between tasks, whereas Piagetian tasks have graded (polytomous) responses with transition points or thresholds within tasks. In enabling the joint analysis of dichotomous and polytomous responses and their mapping onto the same continuum (with the former responses providing much finer gradations than the latter responses), the Rasch models capture this conceptualisation (Styles & Andrich, 1994).

If the joint scaling of dichotomous (psychometric) and polytomous (cognitive-developmental) tasks is successful in terms of conforming to the measurement model, then it is possible to use such a continuum to investigate: the relationships amongst different items (in this case, the psychometric and cognitive-developmental items); the relationships between the stage thresholds (or transition points between stages) for different items; and the coincidence of stage thresholds with the location of psychometric items on the same continuum. In addition, the persons can be located on the same continuum and their relationship to the items explored. These were the aims of the study described next.

Omitting the sensorimotor period, there are three major Piagetian stages—preoperational (I), concrete operational (II), and formal operational (III)—and the latter two are subdivided into stages IIA and IIB, and IIIA and IIIB, respectively (Inhelder & Piaget, 1958). These stages can be assigned numbers from 0 to 4. The psychometric variable's items are coded as 0 (incorrect) or 1 (correct). Using responses to the RPM from the longitudinal study described earlier, and responses from a subgroup of 60 of the same children on three standard Piagetian tasks—Equilibrium in the

Balance, Chemical Combinations (and its electrical equivalent), and Correlations—Styles and Andrich (1994) employed the Rasch model to show that responses to the RPM and the Piagetian tasks formed a consistent unidimensional scale. This provides evidence for the compatability of the two concepts of intelligence when operationalised by the RPM and by Piagetian tasks and, thereby, also support for the construct of general intelligence. Details of the tests of fit and the administration of the RPM and Piagetian tasks and the rationale for choosing them can be found in Styles and Andrich (1994) and Styles (1995a).

Perhaps of greater interest are the implications of this study for the relationship between quantitative and qualitative conceptions of intelligence. The results of this study are consistent with the interpretation that one is the other, that is, a change in degree (quantitative) is associated with a change in kind (qualitative) and that many small quantitative increments build to a major qualitative change. An example is the major qualitative change that seems to occur between Piagetian stages IIB and IIIA, one which coincides with the change from concrete to formal operations according to Piagetian theory. On the joint continuum, the thresholds between the stages IIB and IIIA for all three Piagetian tasks occur very close together, whereas the thresholds between other stages for the different tasks do not coincide. This pattern indicates that the qualitative change from IIB to IIIA is stable across tasks (Styles & Andrich, 1994). Yet, there are many RPM items on the same continuum in the same region, and these show incremental, quantitative changes. This intimate connection between qualitative and quantitative aspects of the functioning of organisms finds a parallel, too, in the following example from evolutionary biology mentioned by Gould (1991): Structures which function as heat regulators when the ratio of structure size to body size is below a critical point, function as wings when the ratio exceeds that point.

Regarding psychometric responses as cognitive-developmental

We now reverse the process of regarding Piagetian methodology as psychometric and regard psychometric response data in a Piagetian light by interpreting the RPM in terms of Piagetian theory.

Taking advantage of the joint analysis of the RPM and Piagetian tasks further, it is possible to identify and then compare the RPM items that occur in the vicinity of the Piagetian thresholds (transitions between stages), once the algorithms (or processes) necessary to solve the RPM items have been identified and categorised.

Processes can be studied at different levels of scale. From an information processing perspective, at a first-order, fine level of scale there are cognitive processes such as encoding, memorising and recalling, and at a second-order level of scale there are metacognitive processes such as planning, adapting, monitoring, and evaluating. Farnham-Diggory (1972) states three other uses for the term "process": (1) as an algorithm or rule; (2) as an heuristic; and (3) as a logico-mathematical process (the underlying structure of a discipline in the Piagetian sense). These three types would seem to be second- or even third-order processes because they are conglomerates of some of the first-order processes. Further, actually deducing an algorithm rather than merely using one would seem to be a process of even higher order—on a level, perhaps, with the use of the combinatorial and propositional reasoning. It was at this level that the author sought to find similarities between the RPM processes (algorithms) and the Piagetian processes associated with changes in thresholds (or transitions between stages)—with the understanding that it is possible to break these down into more fundamental processes or operations. Perhaps the first-order processes could be referred to as *components* (after Sternberg's terminology; Sternberg, 1985), emphasising their unitary nature as components of higher-order processes. The higher, second-order processes may be referred to as *operations* (a series of components) and the third-order processes, like algorithms, are then *processes*, which are a series of operations.

In order to study the processes involved in the RPM items, a taxonomy was developed to categorise the RPM items according to the major algorithms or processes which underlie successful completion of the items: Details of this taxonomy can be found in Styles (1995a).

One of the major findings was the occurrence at the Piagetian thresholds of RPM items which involved operations distinctly different from those required for the solution of preceding items on the joint continuum. For example, at the major transition point from concrete to formal operations, there appear for the first time in the continuum, RPM items which require a respondent to transform elements of the matrix and recognise at an abstract level what algorithm is operating, rather than the respondent being able to rely on the surface features of the matrix to solve the problem. Piaget refers to this as using logico-mathematical rather than a figurative way of thinking and it is consistent with his description of formal thinking as including an ability to deal with second-order relationships and not being tied to immediate first-order relationships. At the substage threshold from IIA to IIB, the ability to use elementary combinations of elements begins, as evidenced by the types of RPM algorithms that appear on the joint continuum at that threshold for the first time. At the substage threshold from IIIA to IIIB, RPM items requiring the simultaneous operation of transformational operations first appear. The ordering of the RPM items and the coincidence of particular types of items at the

Piagetian thresholds fit well with the notion of an intellect expanding to be able to use more complex, more abstract and, simply, more data.

An unpublished study by Styles which involved asking subjects to think aloud as they solved a selection of RPM items supports the notion that people do use the theoretical solution algorithms identified in the Styles (1995a) study. Some researchers have queried whether analogical reasoning is necessary to solve RPM items, maintaining that some of the RPM items can be solved using perceptual processes only. The ordering of RPM items in this study indicates that "analytical" and "perceptual" items can be mapped onto the same continuum—they are measuring the same variable—with the perceptual items occurring near the beginning, or the easier end of the scale. There is, therefore, a hierarchy of items but it is a hierarchy in terms of both difficulty (a quantitative hierarchy) *and* different processing (a qualitative hierarchy).

This is in agreement with Piagetian theory in which preoperational thinkers are considered to use perceptual cues to reason about situations rather than being aware of "deeper" understandings about the situation. In turn, this is similar to Karmiloff-Smith's microdevelopmental formulation of three phases of task development during the first of which persons use surface, perceptual cues to solve problems and during the second phase of which they tend to rely on internal, theory-based frameworks (Karmiloff-Smith, 1984). Only in the third phase do people use a combination of both—this sequence is what one would expect when a person is faced with an RPM item for the first time. In this case, the person in phase one would remain in that phase for some time before moving to develop theories about the algorithms involved and then eventually would arrive at a correct solution by checking his or her theoretical algorithm against external evidence (that is, whether it fits all aspects of the matrix pattern). In more advanced or older persons, it is likely that the perceptual phase is omitted—such a person realises immediately that there is an algorithm in operation and they seek to understand what it is from the beginning.

One of the implications of this work is that one can estimate Piagetian levels from RPM scores and vice versa. It would be useful to extend this to other Piagetian tasks and psychometric measures.

Errors—Piagetian reasoning and psychometric misunderstandings

In an historical symmetry, just as Piaget focused on the types of reasoning involved in erroneous responses to the Binet items, so it is possible to use the Rasch methodology to study the erroneous responses to RPM items in order to seek correspondences between the reasoning underlying particular RPM errors and Piagetian stages. It is evident that, as in the original Binet test items, some alternative responses to each RPM item are more correct, or closer to the correct response than others, that is, the reasoning processes involved in choosing some alternative responses are closer than others to the processes involved in arriving at the correct solution. Therefore, it is possible to order the alternative responses within one item according to increasing closeness to the correct response, and to assign partial scores to them, thereby making each RPM item more like a Piagetian task—and more like the original Binet items—with different levels of understanding. These alternative responses can then be located, together with responses to other items and Piagetian tasks, on a joint continuum using Rasch methodology for polytomous responses. This allows comparisons to be made between the processes involved in an alternative (erroneous) response to an RPM item, and the reasoning involved in the Piagetian stage at the same point on the continuum. A study which followed these procedures using the APM is described in Styles and Andrich (1996).

Future directions

Opportunities exist to extend investigations to explore the psychometric properties of other measures of intellectual functioning as well as scales from other fields of interest to psychologists from the new perspective offered by measurement models of this type. It is also possible to extend the integration of the two perspectives considered in this chapter to other Piagetian and neo-Piagetian tasks to establish the relationships between the tasks themselves and their relationship to the psychometric variables of interest.

Further, results of these and other studies could be interpreted using an information processing approach, and, hopefully, clarify the hierarchy of processes postulated here. Clearly, the use of modern measurement models can illuminate our theoretical understanding of the construct of intelligence and yet it is only one aspect of the concept. As others have stated, intelligence is not simply cognitive in nature, it is affective and conative as well: it involves emotional, motivational, and volitional aspects. In fact, it is merely for convenience—to try to handle complexity—that we separate these aspects: In practice they are inseparable. The inseparability of emotion, motivation, and rational thinking in human behaviour, the need to erase what Damasio (1994) calls the "Cartesian error", is underscored in current work in the area of neurophysiology and neuropsychology.

As we seek to integrate measurement and theory once more, so we need to integrate theories of intelligence with affective aspects of human cognition: Perhaps the new methodology can provide the tools to achieve this—the promise is there.

REFERENCES

Andersen, E.B. (1977). The logistic model for m answer categories. In W.E. Kempf & B.H. Repp (Eds), *Mathematical models for social psychology* (pp. 59–80). Vienna: Hans Huber.

Andrich, D. (1978a). Relationships between the Thurstone and Rasch approaches to item scaling. *Applied Psychological Measurement, 2*, 451–462.

Andrich, D. (1978b). Scaling attitude items constructed and scored in the Likert tradition. *Educational and Psychological Measurement, 38*(3), 665–680.

Andrich, D. (1978c). A rating formulation for ordered response categories. *Psychometrika, 43*, 357–374.

Andrich, D. (1978d). Application of a psychometric rating model to ordered categories which are scored with successive integers. *Applied Psychological Measurement, 2,* 581–594.

Andrich, D. (1978e). A binomial latent trait model for the study of Likert-style attitude questionnaires. *British Journal of Mathematical and Statistical Psychology, 31*(1), 84–98.

Andrich, D. (1985). An elaboration of Guttman scaling with Rasch models for measurement. In N. Brandon-Tuma (Ed.), *Sociological methodology* (pp. 33–80). San Francisco: Jossey-Bass.

Andrich, D. (1988). *Rasch models for measurement.* Sage University Papers series on quantitative applications in the social sciences, No. 07-068. Beverly Hills, CA: Sage Publications.

Andrich, D. (1989a). Constructing fundamental measurements in social psychology. In J.A. Keats, R. Taft, R.A. Heath, & S.H. Lovibond (Eds). *Proceedings of the XXIVth International Congress of Psychology: 4. Mathematical and theoretical systems* (pp. 17–26). Amsterdam: Elsevier Science Publications, B.V. North Holland.

Andrich, D. (1989b). Distinctions between assumptions and requirements in measurement in the social sciences. In J.A. Keats, R. Taft, R.A. Heath, & S.H. Lovibond (Eds). *Proceedings of the XXIVth International Congress of Psychology: 4. Mathematical and theoretical systems* (pp. 7–16). Amsterdam: Elsevier Science Publications, B.V. North Holland.

Andrich, D., & Constable, E. (1984). *Studying unfolding developmental stage data based on Piagetian tasks with a formal probabilistic model.* Symposium conducted at the annual meeting of the American Educational Research Association, New Orleans.

Andrich, D., & Styles, I. (1994). Psychometric evidence of intellectual growth spurts in early adolescence. *Journal of Early Adolescence, 14*(3), 328–344.

Baltes, P.B., Cornelius, S.W., & Nesselroade, J.R. (1978). Cohort effects in behavioural development: Theoretical and methodological perspectives. *Minnesota Symposium on Child Development, 11*, 1–63.

Bayley, N. (1949). Consistency and variability in the growth of intelligence from birth to eighteen years. *Journal of Genetic Psychology, 75*, 165–196.

Binet, A., & Simon, T. (1980). *The development of intelligence in children.* Nashville, TN, Williams Printing Co. (Original work published 1905)

Bond, T. (1993). *Empirical research and Piagetian theory: Quantitative approaches applied to qualitative theory.* Paper presented at the annual meeting of the Australian Association for Research in Education, Fremantle, Western Australia.

Burke, H.R. (1958). Raven's progressive matrices: A review and critical evaluation. *Journal of Genetic Psychology, 93,* 199–228.

Carroll, J.B., Kohlberg, L., & de Vries, R. (1984). Psychometric and Piagetian intelligences: Toward resolution of controversy. *Intelligence, 8,* 67–91.

Cattell, R.B. (1963). Theory of fluid and crystallised intelligence: A critical experiment. *Journal of Educational Psychology, 54,* 1–22.

Damasio, A.R. (1994). *Descartes' error: Emotion, reason and the human brain.* London: Picador.

Davison, M., King, P.M., Kitchener, K.G., & Parker, C.A. (1980). The stage sequence concept in cognitive and social development. *Developmental Psychology, 16,* 121–131.

De Vries, R. (1974). Relationships among Piagetian, IQ and achievement assessments. *Child Development, 45,* 746–756.

De Vries, R., & Kohlberg, L. (1977). Relations between Piagetian and psychometric assessments of intelligence. In L. Katz (Ed.), *Current topics in early childhood education* (Vol. 1), (pp. 119–137). Norwood, NJ: Ablex.

Duncan, O.D. (1984). *Notes on social measurement.* New York: Russell Sage Foundation.

Duncan, O.D. (1985). Probability, disposition and the inconsistency of attitudes and behaviour. *Synthese, 42,* 21–34.

Elkind, D. (1975). Two approaches to intelligence: Piagetian and Psychometric. In J. Sants & H.J. Butcher (Eds), *Developmental psychology: Selected readings* (pp. 234–257). Penguin Modern Psychology: London.

Epstein, H.T. (1974a). Phrenoblysis: Special brain and mind growth periods: I. Human brain and skull development. *Developmental Psychobiology, 7,* 207–216.

Epstein, H.T. (1974b). Phrenoblysis: Special brain and mind growth periods: II. Human mental development. *Developmental Psychobiology, 7,* 217–224.

Epstein, H.T. (1978). Growth spurts during brain development: Implications for educational policy and practice. In J.S. Chall & A.F. Mirsky (Eds), *Education and the brain: The seventy-seventh yearbook of the National Society for the Study of Education, Pt. II* (pp. 343–370). Chicago: University of Chicago Press.

Epstein, H.T. (1990). Stages in human mental growth. *Journal of Educational Psychology, 82,* 875–879.

Farnham-Diggory, S. (1972). *Cognitive processes in education: A psychological preparation for teaching and curriculum development.* New York: Harper & Row.

Galton, F. (1884). *Hereditary genius.* New York: Appleton.

Gardner, H. (1983). *Frames of mind: The theory of multiple intelligences.* New York: Basic Books.

Gould, S.J. (1981). *The mismeasure of man.* New York: W.W. Norton.

Gould, S.J. (1991). *Bully for brontosaurus: Reflections in natural history.* London: Random Century.

Guilford, J.P. (1967). *The nature of human intelligence.* New York: McGraw-Hill.

Inhelder, B., & Piaget, J. (1958). *The growth of logical thinking from childhood to adolescence.* London: Routledge & Kegan Paul.

Karmiloff-Smith, A. (1984). Children's problem-solving. In H.E. Lamb, A.L. Brown, & B. Rogoff (Eds), *Advances in developmental psychology,* Vol. 3, (pp. 39–90). Hillsdale, NJ: Lawrence Erlbaum Associates Inc.

Kubinger, K.D. (1988). On a Rasch-model-based test for non-computerized adaptive testing. In R. Langeheine & J. Rost (Ed.), *Latent trait and latent class models* (pp. 277–289). New York: Plenum Press.

Kuhn, T.S. (1977). *The essential tension.* Chicago: University of Chicago Press.

Lim, T.K. (1988). Relationships between standardised psychometric and Piagetian measures of intelligence at the formal operations level. *Intelligence, 12*, 167–182.

Lumsden, J. (1980). Variations on a theme by Thurstone. *Applied Psychological Measurement, 4*, 1–7.

Piaget, J. (1968). *Six psychological studies.* New York: Vintage Books.

Piaget, J. (1970). Piaget's theory. In P. Mussen (Ed.), *Carmichael's handbook of child psychology* (pp. 703–732). New York: Wiley.

Rasch, G. (1961). On general laws and the meaning of measurement in psychology. In J. Neyman (Ed.), *Proceedings of the 4th Berkeley symposium on Mathematical Statistics and Probability* (pp. 321–333). Berkeley, CA: University of California Press.

Rasch, G. (1980). *Probabilistic models for some intelligence and attainment tests.* Chicago: University of Chicago Press.

Raven, J. (1989). The Raven progressive matrices: A review of national norming studies and ethnic and socioeconomic variation within the United States. *Journal of Educational Measurement, 26*(1), 1–16.

Raven, J.C. (1940). Matrix tests. *Mental Health, 1*, 10–18.

Raven, J.C., Court, J., & Raven, J.C. (1977). *Coloured progressive matrices.* London: H.K. Lewis.

Raven, J.C., Court, J., & Raven, J. (1992). *Standard progressive matrices: Raven manual section 3.* Oxford, UK: Oxford Psychologists Press.

Raven, J.C., Court, J., & Raven, J. (1993). *Manual for Raven's progressive matrices and vocabulary scales: Section 4. Advanced progressive matrices (sets I and II).* London: H.K. Lewis.

Shuttleworth, F.K. (1939). The physical and mental growth of girls and boys age six to nineteen in relation to age at maximum growth. *Monographs of the Society for Research in Child Development, IV*, 3.

Snow, R.E., Kyllonen, P.C., & Marshalek, B. (1984). The topography of ability and learning correlations. In R.J. Sternberg (Ed.), *Advances in the psychology of human intelligence, Vol. 2* (pp. 47–103). Hillsdale, NJ: Lawrence Erlbaum Associates Inc.

Spearman, C. (1904). General intelligence objectively determined. *American Journal of Psychology, 15*, 201–293.

Spearman, C. (1927a). *The abilities of man, their nature and achievement.* New York: MacMillan.

Spearman, C. (1927b). *The nature of intelligence and the principles of cognition.* London: Macmillan.

Spearman, C., & Jones, L.W. (1950). *Human ability.* London: Macmillan.

Sternberg, R.J. (1985). *IQ: A triarchic theory of intelligence.* Cambridge, UK: Cambridge University Press.

Styles, I. (1991). Clinical assessment and computer-adaptive testing. *International Journal of Man–Machine Studies, 35*, 133–150.

Styles, I. (1994). Psychometric evidence of the relationship between attitude and behaviour. *International Journal of Educational Research, 21*(6), 611–622.

Styles, I. (1995a). *Integrating quantitative and qualitative approaches to intelligence: The relationship between the algorithms of Raven's progressive matrices and Piagetian stages.* Paper presented at the annual conference of the American Educational Research Association, San Francisco.

Styles, I. (1995b). *Evidence of phrenoblysis.* Social Measurement Laboratory, School of Education, Murdoch University, Western Australia.

Styles, I., & Andrich, D. (1993). Linking the standard and advanced forms of the Raven's progressive matrices in both the pencil-and-paper and computer-adaptive-testing formats. *Educational and Psychological Measurement, 53*(4), 905–925.

Styles, I., & Andrich, D. (1994). *Linking psychometric and cognitive-developmental variables of intellectual functioning.* Paper presented at the 23rd international conference of Applied Psychology, Madrid, Spain.

Styles, I., & Andrich, D. (1996). *Information in alternative responses in the Raven's progressive matrices.* Paper presented at the XXVIth International Congress of Psychology, Montreal, Canada.

Terman, L.M., & Merrill, M.A. (1960). *Stanford–Binet intelligence scale: Manual for the third revision, Form L–M.* Boston: Houghton-Mifflin.

Thatcher, R.W., Walker, R.A., & Giudice, S. (1987). Human cerebral hemispheres develop at different rates and ages. *Science, 236,* 1110–1113.

Thurstone, L.L. (1969). *Primary mental abilities.* Chicago: University of Chicago Press.

Vernon, P.E. (1965). Ability factors and environmental influences. *American Psychologist, 20,* 723–733.

Ward, J. (1972). The saga of Butch and Slim. *British Journal of Educational Psychology, 42,* 267–289.

Weschler, D. (1958). *The measurement and appraisal of adult intelligence.* Baltimore, MD: Williams & Wilkins.

Wright, B., & Stone, M.H. (1979). *Best test design.* Chicago: MESA Press.

Zajonc, A. (1995). *Catching the light.* Oxford: Oxford University Press.

CHAPTER THREE

Recent advances and issues in the study of preverbal intelligence

John Colombo
The University of Kansas, Lawrence, USA

Janet Frick
University of Georgia, Athens, USA

INTRODUCTION

Over the course of the past decade, developmental psychologists and psychometricians have been drawn together over a set of findings that show that individual differences in cognitive function during the first year of life are correlated with cognitive function later in childhood and adolescence. These correlations have attracted interest from various disciplines with the behavioural sciences, because they have been seen by some as evidence for continuity from early infancy to adulthood within the domain of intelligence.[1]

Our purpose here is to review and discuss these findings, and to provide some sense of the current state of the field. We will outline what we think are critical lines of investigation into this continuity, and delineate some of the issues under debate within the field at this time. Finally, we will close the

---

[1] It seems to us that the term "intelligence" means different things to different psychologists. To those interested in a general factor (*g*, or "biological intelligence"; Haier, Siegel, Crinella, & Buchsbaum, 1993; Vernon & Mori, 1992), the term seems to be largely reserved for reference only to the underlying principal component that is presumed to contribute to all or many of the sub-tests that comprise the standardised tests. For other, more "modular" theorists, the term is used more as a synonym of "competence" or "skill" (e.g. as in "musical", or "interpersonal" intelligences; Gardner, 1983), or more simply to refer to the aggregate standardised score computed from the sub-tests that comprise the IQ test. Given that our purpose in this chapter is neither to resolve these issues or to take a particular side, we will use terms like "intellectual function" or "cognitive status" when referring to the outcome measures through which developmental continuity is established. We realise that some will find this hedging qualification annoying, and so we apologise in advance.

chapter with commentary concerning the ways in which measures of infant cognition might be best used with respect to both research and practice.

PREDICTION OF CHILDHOOD INTELLIGENCE FROM INFANCY

Discontinuity of intellectual function

Up until about a decade ago, the contention that behavioural manifesta-tions in infancy bore little or no relation to mature intellectual function was a widely accepted tenet within the field of developmental psychology. The derivation of this tenet was not ideologically driven, as it was based on empirical evidence that had accumulated over nearly three-quarters of a century. Once articulated, however, the tenet was held firmly, given that it was in accord with the two major theoretical influences on developmental psychology during the 20th century: behaviourism and Piagetian theory. It is in fact possible to argue that evidence for this position could be traced all the way back to Binet, who included items for infants on the initial forms of his intelligence scales but promptly abandoned them in subsequent revisions (Binet & Simon, 1905, 1908, 1911). One might surmise that he found the pursuit of mental function in infancy to be lacking in promise.

More recently, support for this tenet came from longitudinal research showing that very reliable and well-standardized measures of sensory-motor competence from the first year of life (the Bayley Scales of Infant Development, Gesell Developmental Schedules, the Merrill-Palmer Scales, or the Cattell Scales of Infant Intelligence) predicted no more than 1% to 2% of the variance in IQ later in childhood and adolescence (McCall, 1983; see Table 3.1). This lack of prediction was interpreted as evidence for a fundamental discontinuity in intelligence (broadly defined) from early infancy to later childhood. A corollary of this interpretation was the judgement that the presence of a "general" factor of intelligence from infancy was quite unlikely (McCall, Hogarty, & Hurlburt, 1972).

TABLE 3.1

Predictive Correlations of Standardised Infant Tests with Childhood Intelligence Scores (Low-risk Samples) (adapted from McCall, 1983)

Age in Infancy (months)	Correlation
1 to 6	+0.12
7 to 12	+0.26
13 to 18	+0.35
19 to 30	+0.49

Findings of continuity

A series of studies conducted during the period from the late 1970s through the mid-1980s, however, revealed significant correlations between a different set of infant measures and subsequent intellectual function. These more "cognitive" measures were derived from research techniques designed to investigate the normative course of perceptual function and visual learning during infancy. During the 1970s and 1980s, research conducted with these techniques had contributed chiefly to a reconceptualisation of the human infant as a cognitively competent being (Horowitz & Colombo, 1990). These included both the habituation (Cohen, 1976; Horowitz, Paden, Bhana, & Self, 1972) and paired-comparison paradigms (Fantz, 1956, 1964).

In the habituation technique, repetitive stimulus presentations are made to an infant with the expectation that the infant's attentional responses (e.g. visual fixations) will decline in strength. This decline in attention has been theoretically attributed to cognitive processes that involve the formation of an "engram", or internal representation, of the stimulus presented during the sequence, and the continuing revision of that engram that occurs as a result of comparisons between the engram and the actual stimulus itself (Sokolov, 1963).

While the habituation technique theoretically assesses the acquisition of the engram, the paired-comparison technique presumably measures the cognitive products of that acquisition. This technique involves the exposure ("familiarisation") of a stimulus to an infant for some amount of time, followed by a paired presentation of the familiarised stimulus with a new (i.e. "novel") one. If the length of familiarisation is sufficient, the infant can be observed to exhibit a modest (5–15%) but reliable preference for the novel stimulus given this choice. The novelty preference allows the inferences that the infant remembers which of the two he or she has previously seen, and also that the differences between the novel and familiar stimuli are visually distinguishable.

Beginning in the 1970s, these measures of preverbal cognition were incorporated into longitudinal studies of long-term developmental outcome (e.g. Fagan & McGrath, 1981; Miller, Spiridigliozzi, Ryan, Callan, & McLaughlin, 1980) as alternatives to the traditional standardised tests. To the surprise of many, individual differences in infants' performance in these paradigms were significantly correlated with standardised assessments of cognitive, linguistic, and overall intellectual function later in childhood. The magnitudes of these correlations vary from about 0.30 to about 0.50; even these moderate associations represented a substantial improvement in the degree of prediction afforded by the traditional standardised sensory-motor tests.

The evidence for this prediction from infancy was first collected and summarised in a seminal review by Bornstein and Sigman (1986). These data (and their implications) have been the topic of many summaries and meta-analyses since; the reader interested in the primary literature would be best directed to the reports themselves, or to any number of comprehensive reviews (Colombo, 1993; Colombo & Mitchell, 1990; Fagan, 1984a, 1984b; Fagen & Ohr, 1990; McCall, 1994; McCall & Carriger, 1993; McCall & Mash, 1995; Mitchell & Colombo, 1997; Rose, 1989), as we will not review the primary literature here.

The existence of these correlations rekindled the debate over whether characteristic attributes of intellectual function might be exhibited during infancy and be preserved through later points in the lifespan. As such, they tempered the widely held claim of intellectual "discontinuity" across the early part of the lifespan (McCall, 1983; McCall & Mash, 1995).

Subsequent research revealed that such prediction was not limited to measures of infant cognitive function from habituation and paired-comparison paradigms (see Colombo, 1993). A measure of long-term memory as assessed in the conjugate reinforcement paradigm (Rovee & Rovee, 1969) collected at various points during the first year was shown to account for 16–20% of the variance in three-year intelligence scores (Fagen & Ohr, 1990). Additionally, a technique for measuring infants' ability to learn a predictable spatiotemporal stimulus pattern (the visual expectation paradigm; see Haith, Hazan, & Goodman, 1988) yielded measures of reaction time (DiLalla et al., 1990; Dougherty & Haith, 1993) and anticipation of the pattern (Dougherty & Haith, 1993), both of which are correlated with various subtests of intelligence scales at two and three years of age.

WHAT COGNITIVE PROCESSES MEDIATE PREDICTION?

The finding that some part of the intellectual composite is continuous from early in the lifespan has generated a number of intriguing questions concerning the nature of the origin of these individual differences (Cardon & Fulker, 1991; DiLalla et al., 1990), the induction and malleability of these basic perceptual-cognitive abilities (Bornstein & Tamis-Lemonda, 1994), and what such findings tell us about the nature of human intelligence (Fagan, 1984b). Perhaps the fundamental question concerning this prediction from infancy, however, involves the search for the cognitive function(s) that are responsible for this continuity; this is explored in this section of the chapter.

Obstacles to interpretation

Any attempt to answer this question, however, is complicated by the fact that the infant measures that predict later intellectual status can be conceptualised as both overlapping with, and independent from, one another. The picture is further clouded by the fact that each of the different predictive measures may be interpreted in more than one way. We hope to illustrate these points by explicating two of the predictive infant measures.

Novelty preference. One of the measures for which significant prediction has been observed is the novelty preference. As noted previously, if an infant older than 10 weeks or so is exposed to a two-dimensional visual stimulus for some amount of time, and then given a choice between fixating that previously exposed stimulus or a new one, an advantage in selective fixation to the novel stimulus is typically observed (e.g., Fagan, 1971). This measure is the cornerstone of the Fagan Test of Infant Intelligence (FTII; Fagan & Shepard, 1986/1987); higher infant novelty preferences predict better scores on intellectual assessments later in childhood (e.g. Fagan, Singer, Montie, & Shepard, 1986).

The cognitive component to which this prediction is attributable, however, is unclear. This is because the occurrence of the novelty preference is dependent upon at least three different and conceivably independent cognitive functions: the infant must be able to (1) discriminate the two visual stimuli from one another; (2) recognise which one of those was previously shown; and (3) exhibit the discriminative response of preferring to fixate the novel stimulus. Thus, the requisite components for showing a novelty preference are derived from at least three different domains (sensory/perceptual ability, memory, and motivation). It is worth noting that each domain may be further reduced to simpler cognitive elements.

Habituation. The conceptual analysis of novelty preference, however, pales in complexity when compared to another example, infant visual habituation. Habituation provides for more interpretive difficulty because it can be quantified in many different ways, and there are significant methodological differences in the ways in which habituation sessions are conducted.

Again, as we have noted previously, the habituation techniques involve a repeated presentation of a visual stimulus, and the monitoring of the attention that the infant devotes to it. This attention may be inferred from autonomic measures (e.g. heart rate change), but most commonly, the dependent variable is a behavioural one, such as visual fixation. Attention typically decreases over these repeated presentations, and this decrease is interpreted as a reflection of the infant "learning" the stimulus (Sokolov, 1963).

But how should this learning be quantified? Because habituation occurs across trials, the habituation function has been considered to be a type of learning "curve". As such, it has been popular to derive measures from across the *entire* habituation session, such as the degree of decrement of response across trials (e.g. Bornstein & Benasich, 1986), how quickly the infant reaches asymptotic levels of responding (e.g. DeLoache, 1976), or some measure of the total or per-trial level of response (Bornstein & Tamis-Lemonda, 1994). Since the shape of the habituation function can also vary, qualitative differences in the pattern of habituation have been examined as well (Bornstein & Benasich, 1986; McCall, 1979, 1994). Finally, based on the prospect that the infant may actually "learn" the stimulus at some critical point *before* reaching an habituation criterion, particular salient events during the habituation sequence (such as the longest, or "peak" fixation) have also been examined as being potentially important (Colombo, Mitchell, O'Brien, & Horowitz, 1987).

In addition to a lack of agreement over how habituation may be best quantified, there is significant methodological variance in the way that habituation sessions are conducted (see Colombo, 1993; Colombo & Mitchell, 1990). The stimulus may be presented for some number of predetermined periods of fixed duration, such as 10 trials at 10 seconds each, or 5 trials at 30 seconds each (e.g. Kaplan, Werner, & Rudy, 1988). Alternatively, single successive responses (e.g. fixations) to the stimulus may be monitored, with "habituation" attained when the level of those responses (e.g. the duration of individual fixations) reaches some asymptotic level (Horowitz et al., 1972), relative to the level of response observed earlier in the habituation sequence. Here, variance is introduced because the response (e.g. the "fixation") may be operationalised in different ways (Colombo & Horowitz, 1985), and the asymptotic criterion may be computed in differently (see Bornstein & Benasich, 1986; Colombo et al., 1987). Finally, there is some variance in the mode of stimulus presentation: a single stimulus presented in the centre of the visual field, two paired stimuli presented to the right and left of midline, or left–right presentations on alternating trials.

All of the basic measures derived from habituation (e.g. decrement of fixation, average or longest fixation duration, number of looks to criterion), have been shown to correlate with later intellectual and cognitive function (see Bornstein & Sigman, 1986); steeper decrements, shorter looking durations, and fewer looks to criterion are associated with higher levels of IQ, linguistic competence, and representational sophistication. However, three important things are not clear.

First, researchers do not necessarily agree on the meaning of any *one* of these variables, much less all of them. As an example, consider look duration, a measure that has been investigated at length in our laboratory (e.g. Colombo, Mitchell, Coldren, & Freeseman, 1991). Basic comparator theory (Sokolov, 1963) holds that the duration of a look reflects the rapidity with which the internal representation is matched with the external stimulus; thus long-looking infants are slower processors. On the other hand, however, dual-process theory (Thompson & Glanzman, 1976) holds that the duration of looking may also reflect some aspect of autonomic arousal; thus long-looking infants are more aroused, or more arousable.

Second, even if questions concerning the construct underlying one variable were to be resolved, it is not clear that all of the different habituation variables (decrement, looks to criterion, look duration) necessarily reflect the *same* underlying construct. For example, comparator theory predicts that fixation duration might reflect how quickly the infant acquires an initial representation of the stimulus, while looks to criterion might reflect how quickly the infant becomes completely satiated with the habituation stimulus; both underlying constructs might contribute to the magnitude of decrement.

Third, it appears likely that the interrelations of the different measures may well vary as a function of the procedures used to elicit them. In other words, the methodological diversity in measuring habituation introduces the possibility that the same variable assessed under different procedural conditions may well reflect different constructs (see Colombo & Mitchell, 1990). To resolve these problems, some researchers have picked one metric and stuck with it (e.g. Colombo, Mitchell, & Horowitz, 1988), whereas others have used complex statistical analyses to derive a composite factor from patterns of shared variance (Bornstein & Tamis-Lemonda, 1994; Tamis-Lemonda & Bornstein, 1989).

Candidate processes for mechanisms underlying prediction

Despite the methodological and interpretive jumble that characterises the infant cognition measures, some investigators have seen fit to speculate about the underlying constructs that carry the prediction from infancy to childhood, either from a theoretical or empirical basis. In this section, we will briefly examine some of the more notable of these speculative mechanisms.

Response to novelty. Berg and Sternberg (1985) have implied that an underlying motivational predisposition to novelty mediates this prediction. Theoretically, this proposal is supported by the presumed contribution of the positive response to novelty to adult intelligence (Sternberg, 1985a, 1985b). The response-to-novelty factor has gained recent credibility as an underlying construct from a sizeable literature that shows it as a reliable dependent variable in assessing the effects of frontal brain injury in human subjects (Paradowski, Zaretsky, Brucker, & Alba, 1980; Zola-Morgan, Dabrowska, Moss, & Mahut, 1983; see also Knight, 1984). Furthermore, novelty detection has emerged as an important theoretical factor in some models of the cognitive functions of frontal-limbic pathways (Levine & Prueitt, 1989; Metcalfe, 1993; Roberts & Tarassenko, 1994), and neuroimaging data have been proffered for evidence supporting the existence of novelty detection systems in the brain (Tulving, Markowitsch, Kapur, Habib, & Houle, 1994).

With respect to the prediction from infancy phenomenon, the response-to-novelty mechanism is supported empirically by analyses that suggest that the magnitude of the novelty response (i.e. a preference for novelty beyond that which is sufficient to indicate above-chance responding) may be a predictor of both concurrent cognitive performance in infancy (Colombo et al., 1988) and later intelligence (e.g. Rose, Feldman, & Wallace, 1992). This hypothesis, however, is not supported by the fact that infants' preferences for *familiar* objects (as is typically observed in cross-modal matching tasks; Rose et al., 1992; Rose, Feldman, Wallace, & McCarton, 1989) are also observed to be associated with higher intelligence in later childhood.

Speed of processing.   Shorter fixation durations, the rapid attainment of habituation criteria, and robust novelty preferences under conditions where stimulus exposures are held constant (this is somewhat equivalent to a timed cognitive task) have all been associated with intellectual-cognitive competence later in childhood (Bornstein & Sigman, 1986; Colombo, 1993). Furthermore, infants with more rapid ocular or oculocephalic reaction times also show higher IQ at later ages (DiLalla et al., 1990; Dougherty & Haith, 1993). At face value, all of these measures seem to bear on how quickly an infant is capable of "processing" or learning the stimulus at hand. Furthermore, the fact that at least some of these measures are intercorrelated suggests that there may be a mechanism underlying infant cognitive performance that might be identifiable as a "speed of processing" factor (e.g. Jacobson, Jacobson, O'Neill, Padgett, Frankowski, & Bihun, 1992; Jacobson, Jacobson, Sokol, Martier, & Ager, 1993).

The postulation of a speed-of-processing factor provides a parsimonious vehicle for accounting for continuity in intellectual performance from infancy (see also Anderson, 1992). Indeed, processing speed is thought by many to underlie the principal component identified so often as "biological" or "general" intelligence (i.e. g; see Larson & Alderton, 1992); the correlation between adult measures of processing speed and IQ approximate those observed between the infant measures and later intellectual status (e.g. Vernon, 1987). However, speed of processing must be regarded simply as a descriptive parameter of an information processing system, because it does not suffice as an explanatory mechanism (Colombo & Mitchell, 1990). That is, speed of processing is a mediational construct that must itself be accounted for by more concrete mechanisms in order to be explanatory in any sense. Highly speculative attempts have been made toward this end; for example, it has been posited that individual differences in the rapidity with which infants encode visual displays may be attributed to anything from the developmental status of the thalamic-occipital-parietal pathway (Colombo, 1995a) to simple differences in "knowledge base" that are brought about by stimulative factors in the environment (Colombo, 1995b).

Furthermore, the intercorrelations of these various infant measures clearly indicate that there is far more variance unaccounted for than there is shared; thus, although the "speed" hypothesis is tempting to consider, it cannot be considered as a definitive one at this time.

Memory factors.   Fagen and Ohr (1990) first reported that a measure of infants' long-term retention of an operant contingency was correlated with a battery of standardised intellectual measures at two and three years of age. This finding was important because it bolstered the candidacy of memory as a potential underlying factor in accounting for prediction of intelligence from infancy to childhood. Indeed, the novelty preference, which was among the first measures to show significant prediction of later intellectual status from infancy (Fagan & Singer, 1983), has long been considered largely to be a measure of recognition memory (Fagan & McGrath, 1981).

Aside from the face-validity of the role of memory and memory systems overall in cognitive function (e.g. Carpenter & Grossberg, 1993), the involvement of memory in the link between infant cognition and later intellectual function is supported by findings that novelty preference during the first year was observed to correlate with performance on a spatial memory task during the second year (Colombo, Mitchell, Dodd, Coldren, & Horowitz, 1989). However, individual differences in infant novelty preferences have also been reported to be uncorrelated with measures of recognition memory later in childhood (Fagan, 1984a).

Thus, although the Fagen and Ohr (1990) reports clearly implicate some component of retention in long-term cognitive continuity, the contribution of memory to longer-term continuity is largely unexplored. Furthermore, much like the "speed of processing" construct, the term "memory" has

been applied nonspecifically in this context. Specific memory subcompo-
nents (e.g. encoding, integrity of the engram, or retrieval), have not been
examined in terms of their independent contribution to either concurrent
or lagged infant cognitive status (Colombo, 1993).

Inhibition.   McCall (1994; see also McCall & Carriger, 1993; McCall &
Mash, 1995) has argued for the possibility that inhibitory behavioural
processes may underlie the predictive nature of the infant tests.
Essentially, the proposal is that the infant's ability to inhibit a variety of
ongoing behavioural processes (such as the generic ability to inhibit
fixation, or the ability to inhibit, more specifically, attention to familiar or
irrelevant stimuli or stimulus properties) is a fundamental prerequisite to
competent performance on many, if not all, of the infant tasks that have
been shown to underlie intellectual and cognitive status later in childhood.
McCall (1994) draws support for this contention from the fact that the
inhibition construct is gaining support in both the consideration of adult
IQ (Dempster, 1991; Zacks & Hasher, 1994) and infant attention (e.g.
Johnson, 1990), as well as in behavioural development in other domains
(e.g. Kagan, 1989; see also Gray, 1988). This contention also draws
considerable support from the fact that many of the basic attentional
functions described by Posner and his colleagues (e.g. Posner & Petersen,
1990) are dependent upon the capacity to both engage and *disengage* from
visual stimuli and visuospatial loci. Indeed, recent data from our
laboratory (Frick, Colombo, & Saxon, 1996) suggest that three- and
four-month-olds who exhibit patterns of fixation duration that are longer
than average (recall that long fixation durations have been typically
associated with slower visual processing) are slower to disengage fixation
from a centrally presented stimulus when another, peripherally located
one is presented.
The inhibitory construct has promise, especially because it represents a
construct that transcends information processing and expands the domain
of prediction and continuity to other constructs such as temperament,
social cognition, and physiological integrity. However, there are not much
data available with which to evaluate it definitively at this time.
Additionally, like many of the other candidate processes, it is defined
with little specificity, and as a result, the hypothesis itself may be in need
of some theoretical "pruning". For example, although there would appear
to be considerable validity to the use of inhibition in terms of Posner's
(1992) or Johnson's (1990; Johnson, Posner, & Rothbart, 1991) description
of attentional "disengagement", it is not altogether clear how an infant
comes to judge the irrelevance of a stimulus or stimulus property in the
absence of instruction or knowledge of the experimenter's goal of a
particular task.

Sustained attention. It is widely recognised that multiple processes contribute to the determination of attention in infancy (e.g. Cohen, 1973; Ruff, 1986). Richards (e.g. 1987), among others, has noted that while an infant fixates a stimulus, there is no assurance that the infant is engaged in active processing of that stimulus. As a result, Richards (e.g. 1985, 1994; Richards & Casey, 1990a) has proposed a parsing of visual attention into different "phases", across which the probability of the active stimulus processing varies systematically. The different phases of attention are defined by different normally occurring patterns of heart rate change that occur across the course of the fixation itself. It is proposed that the infant engages in maximal attention and stimulus processing during a 2- to 20-second phase that is characterised by maximum heart rate deceleration, and called "sustained attention".

Although there are no direct studies linking the presence or amount of sustained attention in infancy to later cognitive-intellectual development, sustained attention has been observed to correlate with a number of autonomic and behavioural measures that predict concurrent or lagged cognitive status from infancy, such as vagal tone (Linnemeyer & Porges, 1986), and successful recognition memory performance (Richards & Casey, 1990b). Additionally, particular direct and indirect measures of heart rate, such as heart rate variability, and the extent and coherence of respiratory sinus arrhythmia, are related to shorter fixation durations in 14- and 20-week-old infants (Richards, 1985). Ruff (e.g. 1990) has implicated sustained attention in infants during the second year of life as being important to later cognitive outcome, and has presented data that indirectly suggest that sustained attention may relate to later intellectual status. Given that sustained attention in the adult is presumed to reflect a stable individual characteristic (Berch & Kanter, 1984) that is an integral component of fundamental attentional function (e.g. Posner, 1980), and given that this attentional component is measurable and similarly stable during and across infancy (e.g. Richards, 1989; Ruff, Lawson, Parrinello, & Weissberg, 1990), it is not unreasonable to propose that it may also contribute to the prediction of later cognitive status from infancy.

This possibility, however, raises some interesting issues and paradoxes to be resolved by future research. For example, infants are not easily distractible during periods of sustained attention (Casey & Richards, 1988). However, such immunity to distraction may also be interpreted as a difficulty to disengage; recall that, according to the hypothesis concerning the role of inhibition, one would expect that *facility* in disengagement from a stimulus would be considered to be a positive attribute. Additionally, at face value, research showing advantageous outcomes associated with shorter fixation durations would appear to be at odds with the sustained attention construct, given that episodes of sustained attention would presumably be reflected by the occurrence of longer, not shorter, epochs of fixation. It is possible, however, that longer fixation durations may be composed of longer periods spent in other phases of attention that are not so closely associated with stimulus processing.

One underlying process, or many?

As one might expect, an implicit and fundamental issue in the debate on which factors mediate the prediction of childhood intellectual status from infancy is whether a single factor is responsible for such prediction, or whether a number of factors are involved. This is an important consideration, because the existence of a single factor can in some way be taken to reflect the existence of a general factor of intelligence (i.e. g), and the existence of a single, general intellectual factor from infancy would be an extremely important theoretical development.

The initial suggestions concerning the predictive validity of the infant measures (e.g. Fagan, 1984b) were that, in fact, the infant measures probably tapped some "general" construct that also contributed to more mature forms of intelligence. The argument for this position rests on several points, some rational in nature, others empirical. First, it has been intimated that a general factor solution would be more parsimonious (Colombo, 1993; Fagen, 1995), but the strength of this argument lies with the strength of belief in g itself, and so this is clearly a debatable judgement (Mitchell & Colombo, 1997). Second, it has been suggested that it is more likely that one or perhaps two parameters or components of the information-processing system would be more likely to survive the tumult of growth and change that characterises the first year of life, rather than an entire matrix of abilities (Colombo, 1993). A third argument is based on the fact that the infant measures do not predict well to specific component tasks, but do predict later IQ through larger constructs. For example, Fagan (1984a) found that novelty preference in infancy (which has been conceptualised as a measure of recognition memory) does not correlate with recognition memory performance in childhood, but does correlate with IQ. Additionally Rose, Feldman, Wallace, and Cohen (1991) have presented data that suggest that the predictive validity of novelty preferences is mediated through language abilities.

Colombo (1993) has suggested a two-factor model involving speed of processing and memory as those components underlying prediction of childhood intelligence from infancy (see also Anderson, 1992). This position is supported somewhat by data reported by Rose and Feldman (1995a, 1995b), and by Jacobson et al. (1992). The Jacobson et al. (1992) report is particularly noteworthy, as they collected data on novelty preference, reaction time, and fixation duration from over 100 alcohol-exposed infants, and subjected these data to a factor analysis. Two factors emerged: Fixation duration and reaction time loaded positively on the first factor, and novelty preference loaded significantly on the other (see Table 3.2)

More recent analyses by Jacobson (1995), however, suggest that the factors may be much more independent or specific than had once been believed. In earlier research, Jacobson, Fein, Jacobson, Schwartz, and Dowler (1985) had reported that infant novelty preferences discriminated infants prenatally exposed to polychlorinated biphenyls (PCBs), a toxic substance found in the diets of women who ate fish caught from the industrially polluted Great Lakes of the north-central United States. This finding confirmed the suspicion that exposure to this toxin might have deleterious effects on the cognitive development of these children. Subsequently, Jacobson et al. (1993) found that the reaction-time/fixation duration factor in infants described earlier was significantly related to the alcohol intake of their mothers during pregnancy. That is, mothers who consumed alcohol during pregnancy had children who looked longer and had slower reaction times (reaction time data provided a stronger linear dose-dependent effect); this supported the contention that early alcohol exposure affected centrally mediated speed of processing (Streissguth, Barr, & Sampson, 1990). It was of some note that novelty preference showed no sensitivity to maternal alcohol exposure. Jacobson (1995), however, reported that reanalyses of the 1989 PCB data showed no effects on fixation duration. In other words, PCB exposure affected novelty preference, but not fixation duration; alcohol exposure affected fixation duration, but not novelty preference. Jacobson's (1995) analyses thus indicated that these measures likely tapped different and potentially independent cognitive components.

Likewise, Rose and Feldman (1995a) found significant multivariate relationships between infant visual recognition memory performance at 7 and 11 months of age and a standardised measure of IQ, as well as

TABLE 3.2

Factor Analysis of Infant Fixation Duration, Novelty Preference, Reaction Time, and Visual Anticipations (adapted from Jacobson et al., 1992)

Measure	Factor 1	Factor 2
Postbaseline Reaction Time	0.77	−0.17
Baseline Reaction Time	0.64	−0.17
Fixation Duration (static task)	0.63	−0.20
Fixation Duration (cross-modal task)	0.64	0.43
Novelty Preference	−0.20	0.60
Percent Visual Anticipations	−0.42	0.56

assessments of four specific abilities (language, memory, perceptual speed, and non-verbal spatial abilities) at 11 years of age. A factor extracted from the four specific abilities and the infancy measures could be best characterised as "speed of processing", thus supporting the hypothesised role of that construct. However, they also found that only some of the correlations between the infancy measures and the specific abilities were reduced by partialling 11-year IQ; this suggests that the infancy measures probably represent much more than just speed of processing. Finally, a path analysis suggested that processing speed and memory mediated relationships between infant performance and verbal and spatial abilities, which in turn directly contributed to IQ.

Summary. The possibility that the predictive validity of the infant cognitive measures is carried by a general factor of intelligence, *g*, is still viable. However, the current trend of investigation points to the involvement of multiple factors that mediate the relationship between infant cognition and mature intellectual function. It has been previously estimated that the likelihood of multiple cognitive components surviving from infancy to near-adulthood to be low (Colombo, 1993), but this trend suggests that this previous estimate may be in need of re-evaluation.

ON THE ORIGIN OF INDIVIDUAL DIFFERENCES IN INFANT COGNITION

A basic question in this area concerns the origins of these early individual differences in cognition. Some studies have been designed to examine the degree of genetic influence on these measures; these have yielded generally modest, but positive results indicating that a genetic contribution to early performance is supportable (Benson, Cherny, Haith, & Fulker, 1993; Thompson, 1989; Thompson, Fulker, DeFries, & Plomin, 1986).

Other studies, however, provide the opportunity to examine data on the relations between the infant measures and some assessment of the infant's immediate caretaking environment; the environmental assessment is usually represented by data on the quality of maternal–infant interaction. The primary focus of many of these studies was on how individual differences in infant cognition combined with environmental variables in contributing to ultimate intellectual-cognitive status later in childhood. However, it is possible to examine these studies for evidence of the influence of the infant's environment on performance on these early measures of cognition *per se*. We briefly review these studies here.

In Tamis-Lemonda and Bornstein's (1989) multivariate longitudinal study of infants during the first year of age, maternal interaction did not affect infant cognition at 5 months, but infant cognition at 5 months *did* influence maternal behaviour at 13 months. Characteristics of infants' habituation at 5 months (shorter looking times, shallower slopes and decrements) contributed unique variance to the prediction of representational competence at 13 months. These findings were essentially replicated and extended by a longitudinal study reported by Mitchell, McCollam, Horowitz, Embretson, and O'Brien (1991; see Fig. 3.1). In this study, a large cohort ($N > 200$) of pre-term and full-term infants were studied during the first year and then evaluated for cognitive-intellectual outcome during the second and third years. Data were analysed with a structural equation modelling (SEM) approach. SEM is an advanced correlational technique that combines the features of both factor analysis and path analysis. First, data are collected on several "observed" variables (these are shown as boxes in Fig. 3.1) that are thought to reflect a consistent underlying construct. The variance shared by those observed variables is then extracted; such shared variance is considered to represent a better measure of the construct, and is typically referred to as a "latent variable" (circles in Fig. 3.1). A SEM analysis typically involves several latent variables, and the evaluation of the most likely of several hypothetical models that involve different directional ("causal") associations, or "paths" among those latent variables. This evaluation is conducted using the logic of path analysis, and culminates in a determination of which of the various hypothetical models best "fit" the data in question.

Figure 3.1 shows the best-fitting model of those tested by Mitchell et al. (1991); the significant paths are indicated by single arrows joining latent variables. As is evident from the figure, this best-fitting model did *not* include a path of influence from maternal interaction variables to infant cognition. As Tamis-Lemonda and Bornstein (1989) reported, maternal interaction and early cognitive measures contributed independently to intellectual/cognitive status during the second and third years.

The results of a short-term longitudinal study by Saxon, Frick, and Colombo (1997) provide further support for the suggestion that infant skills and the quality of infant–caretaker interactions follow parallel and seemingly independent developmental paths. This study featured a cross-lagged longitudinal panel design, a method in which (under the right conditions) the directional nature of correlations between two variables can be determined. This is done by measuring the two variables (e.g. X and Y) that may be correlated with each other at two different points in time (1 and 2). If the correlation on the cross-lag from X_{time1} to Y_{time2} significantly exceeds the correlation on the cross-lag from Y_{time1} to X_{time2}, then a conclusion that X causes Y may be warranted. The opposite is true if the size of the correlations on the cross-lags is reversed. We sought to apply this logic to the issue of whether measures of infant fixation duration affected maternal joint attention and styles of attentional recruitment, or

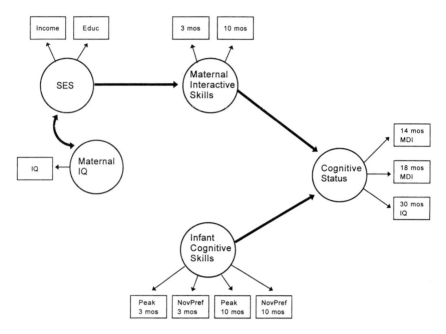

FIG. 3.1 A schematic representation of the best-fitting structural model for the prediction of infant developmental outcome as reported by Mitchell et al. (1991). Path analytic conventions are followed (Loehlin, 1992), such that significant directional paths are indicated by straight lines and non-directional paths by curved ones.

vice versa, by assessing each at both six and eight months of age. Stability was observed for both infants' fixation duration and variables reflecting maternal interactional styles. However, no significant evidence of cross-influence between the maternal and infant variables was observed.

While the studies reviewed to this point indicate little or no relation between measures of infant cognition and the caretaking/maternal environment across time, a few studies have documented concurrent correlations between these two variables. Ruddy and Bornstein (1982) reported that the amount of maternal talking correlated with some parameters of visual habituation at four months of age. Additionally, a study recently published by Bornstein and Tamis-Lemonda (1994) yielded similar results, and extended them to other measures of infant cognition in interesting ways. These investigators observed that fixation duration at five months was predicted by maternal IQ and a measure of visual discrimination taken at two months of age; fixation time was also concurrently correlated with a measure of maternal interaction. Novelty preference was predicted only by maternal IQ, and cross-modal transfer was predicted only by the two-month visual discrimination measure. These results suggest that individual differences on various infant tasks are multiply determined, and they provide further support for the notion that the measures are driven by multiple underlying constructs.

In summary, investigation into the origins of these individual differences in early cognition is just beginning. The extant data on the topic, however, reveal some consistent patterns. First, most show little or no influence of maternal variables on these measures of infant cognition across time; there is some evidence for concurrent relations, but the directionality of this influence is, of course, impossible to determine. Second, these longitudinal studies strongly indicate that individual differences in infant cognition and the stimulative quality of the infant's immediate environment both contribute to the child's ultimate intellectual status; the contribution of these two elements to later intelligence appear to be independent, however.

PERSISTENT ISSUES IN THE LITERATURE

A number of important points are at issue with respect to the measurement of infant cognition and the predictive validity of those measures for mature intelligence. In this section, these points are reviewed briefly with the aim of articulating them clearly as areas for future investigation.

Reliability and prediction

The first of these issues concerns the reliability of the measures. A fundamental psychometric law is that the reliability of any measure (i.e. the degree to which a measure correlates with itself) will limit the degree to which that measure may correlate with other measures. The measures of infant cognition predict significant amounts of variance in later intellectual assessments, despite the fact that the reliabilities of the infant measures are not much higher than the predictive correlations themselves. Indeed, the reliabilities of many of the infant cognition measures are known, and at best, these reliabilities barely exceed +0.50 (Colombo, 1993).

This has two implications, the first of which is positive. From a psychometric point of view, this situation could only arise if nearly all of the "true score" of the infant measures was related to later intellectual function (e.g. McCall, 1994). This implies, in turn, that if the reliability of the infant measures could be improved appreciably, it might be possible to predict a substantial amount of the variance in childhood intellectual function from these infant measures; both Colombo (1993) and McCall and Carriger (1993) have estimated that more than half of this variance could be so accounted for.

The other, more negative, implication is that such "potential" for prediction does not bear on practical application. In other words, the unreliability of these measures is real, and it suppresses the level of actual prediction that they afford. McCall (1994) has implied that, as long as the actual degree of prediction is relatively low, the prediction phenomenon is important only from a theoretical point of view. Attempts to use the infant measures for classifying individuals (e.g. with the Fagan Test of Infant Intelligence) have been criticised because of the lack of reliability (Benasich & Bejar, 1992; but see Fagan & Detterman, 1992).

Our experience, furthermore, suggests that raising the reliabilities of these measures may not be as straightforward as allowing for additional items. Indeed, we recently endeavoured to generate a reliable battery for the assessment of infant look duration, a measure that we have worked with for nearly the last decade (Colombo, et al., 1991; Freeseman, Colombo, & Coldren, 1993; Frick & Colombo, 1996). Data from numerous experiments with three- and four-month-old infants over the last five years had suggested to us that the correlation between any one such assessment of peak look duration with any other one should lie in the range of +0.40 to +0.45. We assumed that we would be able to generate a very reliable assessment of individual differences in looking time with a larger number of items. However, assessments of peak look duration over 20-second accumulation periods with large samples of three-, four-, six-, and eight-month-olds across six different stimuli did not yield the improved levels of reliability that we expected (see Table 3.3).

TABLE 3.3

Internal Consistencies (Cronbach's α) of a six-item Battery for Duration of Peak Look at Different Ages During the First Year

Age	Cronbach's α	N
3 months	0.73	38
4 months	0.51	126
6 months	0.37	65
8 months	0.65	63

Note: three- and four-month-old samples are independent; six- and eight-month-old samples were seen longitudinally. The intercorrelations among the six stimuli used were all positive, and thus in accordance with the assumptions of the calculation of Cronbach's α. The stability of the average peak look duration from six to eight months of age was + 0.39 ($P < .001$; see Saxon et al., 1997, for further details on the longitudinal sample).

Linearity and nonlinearity in prediction

A second issue involves the question of whether prediction from these infants' measures is attributable to meaningful variance across the entire continuum of the measures, or whether such prediction is carried by a portion of the scores involved.

Variability across individuals. For example, it is possible that the actuarial prediction of later cognitive function from the infant scores is attributable to a few individuals in the population. From the incipient reports of the prediction-from-infancy phenomenon, it has been suspected that the prediction may have been carried by only a few individuals within the sample as a whole. For example, the predictive correlations may be due to a few infants who score extremely low (or high) on the early cognition measures, and then who score in a correspondingly extreme way on later tests. This possibility has been discussed at length (see Colombo, 1993, Chap. 4; McCall & Carriger, 1993; Rose et al., 1989), and the current evidence suggests that this is not the case. However, our own work on infant look duration (one of the measures that is predictive of later intelligence; see Rose, Slater, & Perry, 1986; Sigman Cohen, Beckwith, Asarnow, & Parmelee, 1991) is equivocal on this point. We have noted elsewhere that this issue will gain prominence should the measures come into further use for diagnostic and/or clinical purposes (Mitchell & Colombo, 1997).

Variability within individuals. Additionally, it is also possible that prediction for a given individual may be carried by performance on only a few tasks or items (out of many) that the individual has carried out. This second non-linear influence on prediction has not been extensively discussed, but we include it here because it holds promise for further understanding of the predictive nature of these early individual differences.

It is possible that long-term prediction is carried by the tendency of some subjects to exhibit high degrees of variability within their responding across multiple tasks or assessments. To this point, only differences in average levels of responding have been considered as carrying the predictive value of these measures of infant cognition. Although the emphasis on mean levels of responding has a long and successful tradition within the field of psychometrics, it is also feasible that within-subject variability is an important feature of the infant's response on such cognitive tasks.

Intra-individual variability has been proposed as an important para-meter of individual responding within studies of newborn state (Horowitz, Sullivan, & Linn, 1978) and infant autonomic reactivity (e.g. Fox, 1988). In these two contexts, higher variability is considered to be a positive attribute. With respect to the early cognitive measures, however, the opposite interpretation is likely more appropriate. This is because such intra-individual variability on the types of infant tasks used within the prediction literature would likely yield individual difference profiles that have the appearance of being less than optimal. For example, high variability in look duration in an habituation session will most likely be associated with the occurrence of one or more trials of prolonged looking across stimulus presentations, and thus long fixation durations. High variability in responding across a series of novelty preference tasks is likely to depress the overall mean level of response, and thus yield performance that is closer to chance levels of selective fixation. Finally, high variability in reaction time and anticipatory behaviour within the visual expectation paradigm (a procedure in which a predictable spatial sequence of stimuli are presented, and the infants' ocular responses are monitored for simple latency and for anticipatory movements; see Haith et al., 1988) is also likely to influence an individual's mean score toward slower reactions and lower percentages of successful anticipations.

The study of individual differences in variability of performance has already been introduced with respect to the visual expectation paradigm (Dougherty & Haith, 1993). Additionally, we have noted anecdotally that the performance of groups of long-looking infants is typically much more variable than that seen for groups of shorter-looking infants (e.g. Colombo et al., 1991). Furthermore, the possibility that such prediction is carried by individual differences in variability of response (rather than in mean levels of response) might well explain why the infant measures yield predictive correlations that are consistently significant, yet which account for only modest amounts of variance.

Trials and error—the influence of procedural diversity

In an earlier section of this chapter, we discussed procedural variance in the way that many of the infant measures are collected. For example, there are many different ways to conduct an habituation session (Colombo & Mitchell, 1990), and many different ways to assess the infant's response to novelty. The working assumption of many researchers seems to be that the conceptual integrity of the measures being collected remain intact across this procedural diversity. Indeed, these may be safe assumptions, but on the other hand, perhaps a little more caution may be in order. As an example, our early work on the stability and reliability of infant attentional measures suggested that while novelty preferences measured within the paired-comparison paradigm were relatively stable and reliable (Colombo et al., 1988), when novelty preference was operationalised as recovery of fixation to a novel target following habituation, it was not (Colombo et al., 1987). It is entirely possible that subtle differences in the way that measures are collected will greatly affect the comparability of the measures, and the cognitive components or operations that contribute to them.

FUTURE DIRECTIONS AND COMMENTARY

In this final section, we will briefly discuss and comment upon the integration of the basic, fundamental scientific interest that spawned the finding of continuity of mental function from infancy (e.g. Bornstein & Sigman, 1986) and the more applied interests in using that knowledge of continuity for more practical purposes.

Nomothetic findings and idiographic demands—on the best use of measures of early prediction

Interest in the prediction of later intellectual function has naturally provoked a desire to use these infant measures to discern which particular, individual infants are in fact "at risk" for later cognitive or intellectual deficits. Indeed, in the early 1990s, in the course of writing a short volume on the prediction literature (Colombo, 1993, p. 127), both enthusiasm and optimism were expressed for this possibility: "The most obvious direct benefit of these findings is the potential for identification of infants at risk for eventual cognitive deficit. The capacity for specific and sensitive early identification . . . is clearly on the horizon."

Some years later, however, a nagging question remains in evaluating this literature: Can we *really* predict later outcome at the level of the individual? Can we really identify *individual* infants who may be at risk (or at advantage) from these measures?

In examining the literature on prediction, we are aware of only one published report of significant and successful long-term identification of *individual* infants with later cognitive deficits (Fagan et al., 1986). This paper reports on two high-risk samples of infants (N = 62 and 27) tested from three to eight months of life and then followed up at three years of age. We have summarised the data from both samples in Table 3.4. This particular report shows novelty preferences as successfully identifying over 85% of the infants as being normal or disabled on the three-year follow-up. This impressive finding does provide good support for the classification of

TABLE 3.4
Success of the FTII in Predicting Three-year Developmental
Outcome in High-risk Infants (from Fagan et al., 1986)

Predicted Outcome	Actual Outcome		Totals
	Risk	Normal	
Risk	16	8	24
Normal	3	62	65
Totals	19	70	89

Pearson chi-square = 40.2, $P < .001$. Bivariate measures of association: Eta = .67, Phi = .56, Kappa = .66.

individuals from a sample of high-risk infants, but how does this level of
prediction compare to that reported elsewhere in the literature?

Such prediction is typically expressed in terms of bivariate correlations
or regression coefficients, and these correlations vary widely; early reports
included correlations that averaged in the range from +0.40 to +0.50
(Fagan & Singer, 1983), but more recently published work indicates
correlations that range from about +0.30 to +0.40 (e.g. Rose & Feldman,
1995a, 1995b). If we convert the accuracy of classification presented in
Fagan et al. (1986) to a coefficient, the degree of association (depending on
which coefficient is calculated) ranges from 0.56 to nearly 0.70 (see
Table 3.4). Thus, the degree of continuity or prediction necessary to
achieve the success of Fagan et al. (1986) would appear to be much higher
than is typically reported for these measures.

This basic finding brings into question what might constitute the best use
measures of infant cognition. We would contend that, since the success of
these measures is typically reported in terms means of nomothetic,
"actuarial" prediction (i.e. with correlation/regression coefficients), that
such actuarial prediction may not yet be routinely applied to the
idiographic type of prediction of that applies to individual classification.
Until the degree of prediction is improved to the point where greater
certainty exists at the level of the individual, we would propose that the
best use of these infant cognition measures might be as initial outcome
measures in research on particular conditions or manipulations thought to
affect long-term intellectual or cognitive development. Because these
measures capture some portion of the variance in long-term intellectual
outcome from infancy, they can be used to assess the effects of such
conditions during infancy, with some confidence that the effect observed
will translate to actuarial prediction on a longitudinal basis. Numerous
examples of this type of research already exist; these include investigations
of the effects of environmental toxins (e.g. Jacobson et al., 1985), prenatal

substance exposure (e.g. Jacobson et al., 1992, 1993), early nutritional factors in preterm infants (e.g. Carlson & Werkman, 1995, 1996; Werkman & Carlson, 1996), or socioeconomic status (e.g. Colombo & Mitchell, 1990; Mayes & Bornstein, 1995).

The growing evidence that these measures tap a number of cognitive processes that are interrelated in complex ways, however, has some important implications for the choice and implementation of the infant measures for research in this vein. For one, investigators will not be able to choose a single measure in the hope that it will be sensitive enough to detect general, lasting, broad-band cognitive effects. For example, if researchers are investigating the effects of exposure to a particular toxin during infancy, and were to choose only novelty preference tasks for their early cognitive battery, they may well miss significant effects if the effects of that particular toxin were not manifest in recognition memory. Rather, investigators will have to choose one of two strategies in their use of these infant measures. The first of these would be to use multiple measures of infant cognition in order to raise the likelihood that various cognitive components are being assessed; for example, researchers studying the effect of this toxin might include novelty preference, habituation, and visual expectation tasks. The second strategy would be based on specific hypothesised effects that the conditions under study are likely to engender, where investigators would choose the infant measure (or measures) that are most likely to show those specific effects. In keeping with our present example, then, the investigators may review animal models of exposure to this toxin and find that its effects are manifest largely in perceptuo-motor coordination and speed; based on this information, a visual expectation paradigm (which yields individual differences in reaction time and spatiotemporal anticipation) might be the measure of choice.

The future of measuring early cognition still holds considerable promise for a myriad of uses, including identification of specific individuals at risk for later cognitive deficits. Although the field may not be as far along, or moving as quickly as we had at one time hoped, research on potential underlying mechanisms, on procedural variation, and on improving the psychometric of the measures will be critical towards reaching this goal. Furthermore, as noted elsewhere (Mitchell & Colombo, 1997), the measures hold some potential for contributing to our understanding of mature intelligence as well.

REFERENCES

Anderson, M. (1992). *Intelligence and development: A cognitive theory*. Oxford, UK: Blackwell Publishers.

Benasich, A.A., & Bejar, I.I. (1992). The Fagan test of infant intelligence: A critical review. *Journal of Applied Developmental Psychology, 13*, 153–171.

Benson, J.B., Cherny, S.S., Haith, M.M., & Fulker, D.W. (1993). Rapid assessment of infant predictors of adult IQ: Midparent-midtwin analyses. *Developmental Psychology, 29*, 434–447.

Berch, D.B., & Kanter, D.R. (1984). Individual differences. In J.S. Warm (Ed.), *Sustained attention in human performance* (pp. 143–178). New York: John Wiley & Sons.

Berg, C., & Sternberg, R.J. (1985). Response to novelty: Continuity versus discontinuity in the developmental course of intelligence. In H.W. Reese (Ed.), *Advances in child development and behavior* (Vol. 15, pp. 1–47). New York: Academic Press.

Binet, A., & Simon, T. (1905). Sur la necessité d'établir un diagnostic scientifique des états de l'intelligence. *L'Année Psychologique, 11*, 191–224.

Binet, A., & Simon, T. (1908). Le développement de l'intelligence chez les enfants. *Année Psychologique, 14*, 1–94.

Binet, A., & Simon, T. (1911). *A method of measuring the development of the intelligence of young children.* Lincoln, IL: Courier.

Bornstein, M.H., & Benasich, A.A. (1986). Infant habituation: Assessments of short-term reliability and individual differences at five months. *Child Development, 47*, 87–99.

Bornstein, M.H., & Sigman, M.D. (1986). Continuity in mental development from infancy. *Child Development, 57*, 251–274.

Bornstein, M.H., & Tamis-Lemonda, C.S. (1994). Antecedents of information-processing skills in infants: Habituation, novelty responsiveness, and cross-modal transfer. *Infant Behavior and Development, 17*, 371–380.

Cardon, L.R., & Fulker, D.W. (1991). Sources of continuity in infant predictors of later IQ. *Intelligence, 15*, 279–293.

Carlson, S.A., & Werkman, S.H. (1995). Preterm infants fed formula with compared to without docosahexaeonic acid (DNA) have shorter look duration ten months after DNA is discontinued. *Pediatric Research, 37*, 14A.

Carlson, S.A., & Werkman, S.H. (1996). A randomized trial of visual attention of preterm infants fed docosahexaeonic acid until two months. *Lipids, 31*, 85–90.

Carpenter, G.A., & Grossberg, S. (1993). Normal and amnesic learning, recognition, and memory by a neural model of cortico-hippocampal interactions. *Trends in Neurosciences, 16*, 131–137.

Casey, B.J., & Richards, J.E. (1988). Sustained visual attention in infants measured with an adapted version of the visual preference paradigm. *Child Development, 59*, 1514–1521.

Cohen, L.B. (1973). A two-process model of infant visual attention. *Merrill-Palmer Quarterly, 19*, 157–180.

Cohen, L.B. (1976). Habituation of infant visual attention. In T. Tighe & R. Leaton (Eds), *Habituation* (pp. 207–238). Hillsdale, NJ: Lawrence Erlbaum Associates Inc.

Colombo, J. (1993). *Infant cognition: Predicting childhood intelligence.* Newbury Park, CA: Sage.

Colombo, J. (1995a). On the neural mechanisms underlying individual differences in infant fixation duration: Two hypotheses. *Developmental Review, 15*, 97–135.

Colombo, J. (1995b, March). *Some hypotheses about speed of processing in infancy.* Paper presented at the meeting of the Society for Research in Child Development, Indianapolis, IN.

Colombo, J., & Horowitz, F.D. (1985). A parametric study of the infant control procedure. *Infant Behavior and Development, 8*, 117–121.

Colombo, J., & Mitchell, D.W. (1990). Individual and developmental differences in infant visual attention. In J. Colombo & J.W. Fagen (Eds), *Individual differences in infancy* (pp. 193–227). Hillsdale, NJ: Lawrence Erlbaum Associates Inc.

Colombo, J., Mitchell, D.W., Coldren, J.T., & Freeseman, L.J. (1991). Individual differences in infant attention: Are short lookers faster processors or feature processors? *Child Development, 62*, 1247–1257.

Colombo, J., Mitchell, D.W., Dodd, J.D., Coldren, J.T., & Horowitz, F.D. (1989). Longitudinal correlates of infant attention in the paired comparison paradigm. *Intelligence, 13*, 33–42.

Colombo, J., Mitchell, D.W., & Horowitz, F.D. (1988). Infant visual behavior in the paired-comparison paradigm: Test-retest and attention-performance relations. *Child Development, 59*, 1198–1210.

Colombo, J., Mitchell, D.W., O'Brien, M., & Horowitz, F.D. (1987). Stability of infant visual habituation during the first year. *Child Development, 58*, 474–489.

DeLoache, J.S. (1976). Rate of habituation and visual memory in infants. *Child Development, 47*, 145–154.

Dempster, F.N. (1991). Inhibitory processes: A neglected dimension of intelligence. *Intelligence, 15*, 157–173.

DiLalla, L.F., Thompson, L.A., Plomin, R., Phillips, K., Fagan, J.F., Haith, M.M., Cyphers, L.H., & Fulker, D.W. (1990). Infant predictors of preschool and adult IQ: A study of infant twins and their parents. *Developmental Psychology, 26*, 759–769.

Dougherty, T.M., & Haith, M.M. (1993, March). *Relations between manual RT, visual RT, and IQ*. Paper presented at the meeting of the Society for Research in Child Development, Indianapolis, IN.

Fagan, J.F. (1971). Infant recognition memory for a series of visual stimuli. *Journal of Experimental Child Psychology, 27*, 27–34.

Fagan, J.F. (1984a). The intelligent infant: Implications. *Intelligence, 8*, 1–9.

Fagan, J.F. (1984b). The relationship of novelty preferences during infancy to later intelligence and recognition memory. *Intelligence, 8*, 339–346.

Fagan, J.F., & Detterman, D.K. (1992). The Fagan test of infant intelligence: A technical summary. *Journal of Applied Developmental Psychology, 13*, 173–193.

Fagan, J.F., & McGrath, S.K. (1981). Infant recognition memory and later intelligence. *Intelligence, 5*, 121–130.

Fagan, J.F., & Shepard, P.A. (1986/1987). *The test of infant intelligence*. Cleveland, OH: Infantest Corporation.

Fagan, J.F., & Singer, L.T. (1983). Infant recognition memory as a measure of intelligence. In L.P. Lipsitt & C.K. Rovee-Collier (Eds), *Advances in infancy research* (Vol. 2, pp. 31–79). Norwood, NJ: Ablex.

Fagan, J.F., Singer, J., Montie, J., & Shepard, P.A. (1986). Selective screening device for the early detection of normal or delayed cognitive development in infants at risk for later mental retardation. *Pediatrics, 78*, 1021–1026.

Fagen, J.W. (1995). Predicting IQ from infancy: We're getting closer. *Contemporary Psychology, 40*, 19–20.

Fagen, J.W., & Ohr, P.S. (1990). Individual differences in infant conditioning and memory. In J. Colombo & J.W. Fagen (Eds), *Individual differences in infancy* (pp. 155–192). Hillsdale, NJ: Lawrence Erlbaum Associates Inc.

Fantz, R.L. (1956). A method for studying early visual development. *Perceptual and Motor Skills, 6,* 13–15.

Fantz, R.L. (1964). Visual experience in infants: Decreased attention to familiar patterns relative to novel ones. *Science, 146,* 668–670.

Fox, N.A. (1988). Heart rate variability and self-regulation: Individual differences in autonomic patterning and their relation to infant and child temperament. In S. Reznick & J. Kagan (Eds), *Perspectives on behavioral inhibition* (pp. 177–195). Chicago: University of Chicago Press.

Freeseman, L.J., Colombo, J., & Coldren, J.T. (1993). Individual differences in infant visual attention: Four-month-olds' discrimination and generalization of global and local stimulus properties. *Child Development, 64,* 1191–1203.

Frick, J.E., & Colombo, J. (1996). Individual differences in infant visual attention: Recognition of degraded visual forms by 4-month-olds. *Child Development, 67,* 188–204.

Frick, J.E., Colombo, J., & Saxon, T.F. (1996, April). *Long-looking infants are slower to disengage fixation.* Paper presented at the international conference on Infant Studies, Providence, RI.

Gardner, H. (1983). *Frames of mind.* New York: Basic Books.

Gray, J.A. (1988). Behavioural and neural-system analyses of the actions of anxiolytic drugs. *Pharmacology, Biochemistry, and Behavior, 29,* 767–770.

Haier, R.J., Siegel, B.V., Crinella, F.M., & Buchsbaum, M.S. (1993). Biological and psychometric intelligence: Testing an animal model in humans with positron emission tomography. In D.F. Detterman (Ed.), *Current topics in human intelligence* (Vol. 3, pp. 157–170). Norwood, NJ: Ablex.

Haith, M.M., Hazan, C., & Goodman, G. (1988). Expectation and anticipation of dynamic visual events by 3.5-month-old babies. *Child Development, 59,* 467–479.

Horowitz, F.D., & Colombo, J. (1990). Future agendas and directions for infancy research. *Merrill-Palmer Quarterly, 36,* 173–178.

Horowitz, F.D., Paden, L.Y., Bhana, K., & Self, P.A. (1972). An infant control procedure for studying infant visual fixations. *Developmental Psychology, 7,* 90.

Horowitz, F.D., Sullivan, J.W., & Linn, P. (1978). Stability and instability in the newborn infant: The quest for elusive threads. *Monographs of the Society for Research in Child Development, 43,* 29–45.

Jacobson, S.W. (1995, March). *Evidence for speed of processing and recognition memory components of infant information processing.* Paper presented at the meeting of the Society for Research in Child Development, Indianapolis, IN.

Jacobson S.W., Fein, G.G., Jacobson, J.L., Schwartz, P.M., & Dowler, J.K. (1985). The effects of intrauterine PCB exposure on visual recognition memory. *Child Development, 56,* 853–860.

Jacobson, S.W., Jacobson, J.J., O'Neill, J.M., Padgett, R.J., Frankowski, J.J., & Bihun, J.T. (1992). Visual expectation and dimensions of infant information processing. *Child Development, 63,* 711–724.

Jacobson, S.W., Jacobson, J.L., Sokol, R.J., Martier, S.S., & Ager, J.W. (1993). Prenatal alcohol exposure and infant information processing ability. *Child Development, 64,* 1706–1721.

Johnson, M.H. (1990). Cortical maturation and the development of visual attention in early infancy. *Journal of Cognitive Neuroscience, 2,* 81–95.

Johnson, M.H., Posner, M.I., & Rothbart, M.K. (1991). Components of visual orienting in early infancy: Contingency learning, anticipatory looking, and disengaging. *Journal of Cognitive Neuroscience, 3,* 335–344.

Kagan, J. (1989). The concept of behavioral inhibition to the unfamiliar. In J. S. Reznick (Ed.), *Perspectives on behavioral inhibition* (pp. 1–24). Chicago: University of Chicago Press.

Kaplan, P.S., Werner, J., & Rudy, J. (1988). Habituation, sensitization, and infant visual attention. In C. Rovee-Collier (Ed.), *Advances in infancy research* (Vol. 4). Norwood, NJ: Ablex.

Knight, R.T. (1984). Decreased response to novel stimuli after prefrontal lesions in man. *Electroencephalography and Clinical Neurophysiology, 59,* 9–20.

Larson, G.E., & Alderton, D.L. (1992). The structure and capacity of thought: Some comments on the cognitive underpinnings of *g.* In D.K. Detterman (Ed.), *Current topics in human intelligence* (Vol. 2, pp. 141–156). Norwood, NJ: Ablex.

Levine, D.S., & Prueitt, P.S. (1989). Modeling some effects of frontal lobe damage—novelty and perseveration. *Neural Networks, 2,* 103–116.

Linnemeyer, S.A., & Porges, S. (1986). Recognition memory and cardiac vagal tone in 6-month-old infants. *Infant Behavior and Development, 9,* 43–56.

Loehlin, J.C. (1992). *Latent variable models.* Hillsdale, NJ: Lawrence Erlbaum Associates Inc.

Mayes, L.C., & Bornstein, M.H. (1995). Infant information-processing performance and maternal education. *Early Human Development, 4,* 891–896.

McCall, R.B. (1979). Individual differences in the pattern of habituation at 5 and 10 months of age. *Developmental Psychology, 15,* 559–569.

McCall, R.B. (1983). A conceptual approach to early mental development. In M. Lewis (Ed.), *Origins of intelligence* (2nd ed., pp. 67–106). New York: Plenum.

McCall, R.B. (1994). What process mediates prediction of childhood IQ from infant habituation and recognition memory? Speculations on the roles of inhibition and rate of information processing. *Intelligence, 18,* 107–124.

McCall, R.B., & Carriger, M. (1993). A meta-analysis of infant habituation and recognition memory performance as predictors of later IQ. *Child Development, 64,* 57–79.

McCall, R.B., Hogarty, P.S., & Hurlburt, N. (1972). Transitions in infant sensorimotor development and the prediction of childhood IQ. *American Psychologist, 27,* 728–748.

McCall, R.B., & Mash, C. (1995). Infant cognition and its relation to mature intelligence. In G. Whitehurst (Ed.), *Annals of child development* (Vol. 11, pp. 27–56). New York: JAI Press.

Metcalfe, J. (1993). Novelty monitoring, metacognition, and control in a composite holographic associative recall model: Implications for Korsakoff Amnesia. *Psychological Review, 100,* 3–22.

Miller, D., Spiridigliozzi, G., Ryan, E., Callan, M., & McLaughlin, J. (1980). Habituation and cognitive performance: Relationships between measures at four years of age and earlier assessments. *International Journal of Behavioral Development, 3,* 131–146.

Mitchell, D.W., & Colombo, J. (1997). Infant cognition and general intelligence. In J. Kingma & W. Tomic (Eds), *Advances in cognition and education: Vol. 4. Reflections on the concept of intelligence* (pp. 101–118). Greenwich, CT: JAI Press.

Mitchell, D.W., McCollam, K., Horowitz, F.D., Embretson, S.E., & O'Brien, M. (1991, April). *The interacting contribution of constitutional, environmental, and information processing factors to early developmental outcome.* Paper presented at the meeting of the Society for Research in Child Development, Seattle, WA.

Paradowski, W., Zaretsky, H., Brucker, B., & Alba, A. (1980). Recognition of matching tasks and stimulus novelty as a function of unilateral brain damage. *Perceptual and Motor Skills, 51*, 407–418.

Posner, M.I. (1980). Orienting of attention. *Quarterly Journal of Experimental Psychology, 32*, 3–25.

Posner, M.I. (1992). Attention as a neural and cognitive system. *Current Directions in Psychological Science, 1*, 11–14.

Posner, M.I., & Petersen, S.E. (1990). The attention system of the human brain. *Annual Review of Neuroscience, 13*, 25–42.

Richards, J.E. (1985). Respiratory sinus arrhythmia predicts heart rate and visual responses during visual attention in 14 and 20 week old infants. *Psychophysiology, 22*, 101–109.

Richards, J.E. (1987). Infant visual sustained attention and respiratory sinus arrhythmia. *Child Development, 58*, 488–496.

Richards, J.E. (1989). Development and stability of HR-defined visual sustained attention in 14, 20, and 26 week old infants. *Psychophysiology, 26*, 422-430.

Richards, J.E. (1994). Baseline respiratory sinus arrhythmia and heart-rate responses during sustained visual attention in preterm infants from 3 to 6 months of age. *Psychophysiology, 30*, 235–243.

Richards, J.E., & Casey, B.J. (1990a). Development of sustained visual attention in the human infant. In B.A. Campbell, H. Hayne, & R. Richardson (Eds), *Attention and information processing in infants and adults* (pp. 30–60). Hillsdale, NJ: Lawrence Erlbaum Associates Inc.

Richards, J.E., & Casey, B.J. (1990b). *Visual fixation patterns and recognition memory in the paired-comparison paradigm in infants: Effects of attention phases, age, and respiratory sinus arrhythmia.* Unpublished manuscript, Department of Psychology University of South Carolina.

Roberts, S., & Tarassenko, L. (1994). A probabilistic resource allocating network for novelty detection. *Neural Computation, 6*, 270–284.

Rose, S.A. (1989). Measuring infant intelligence: New perspectives. In M.H. Bornstein & N.A. Krasnegor (Eds), *Stability and continuity in mental development: Behavioral and biological perspectives* (pp. 171–188). Hillsdale, NJ: Lawrence Erlbaum Associates Inc.

Rose, S. A., & Feldman, J.F. (1995a, March). *Cognitive continuity from infancy: A single thread or a twisted skein?* Paper presented at the meeting of the Society for Research in Child Development, Indianapolis, IN.

Rose, S.A. & Feldman, J.F. (1995b). Prediction of IQ and specific cognitive abilities at 11 years from infancy measures. *Developmental Psychology, 31*, 685–696.

Rose, S.A., Feldman, J.F., & Wallace, I.F. (1992). Infant information processing in relation to six-year outcomes. *Child Development, 63*, 1126–1141.

Rose, S.A., Feldman, J.F., Wallace, I.F., & Cohen, P. (1991). Language: A partial link between infant attention and later intelligence. *Developmental Psychology, 27*, 798–805.

Rose, S.A., Feldman, J.F., Wallace, I.F., & McCarton, C.M. (1989). Infant visual attention: Relation to birth status and developmental outcome during the first 5 years. *Developmental Psychology, 25*, 560–576.

Rose, D., Slater, A., & Perry, H. (1986). Prediction of childhood intelligence from habituation in early infancy. *Intelligence, 10*, 251–263.

Rovee, C., & Rovee, D. (1969). Conjugate reinforcement of infant exploratory behavior. *Journal of Experimental Child Psychology, 8*, 33–39.

Ruddy, M.G., & Bornstein, M.H. (1982). Cognitive correlates of infant attention and maternal stimulation over the first year of life. *Child Development*, *53*, 183–188.

Ruff, H.A. (1986). Components of attention during infants' manipulative exploration. *Child Development*, *57*, 105–114.

Ruff, H.A. (1990). Individual differences in sustained attention during infancy. In J. Colombo & J.W. Fagen (Eds), *Individual differences in infancy* (pp. 247–270). Hillsdale, NJ: Lawrence Erlbaum Associates Inc.

Ruff, H.A., Lawson, K.R., Parrinello, R., & Weissberg, R. (1990). Long-term stability of individual differences in sustained attention in the early years. *Child Development*, *61*, 60–75.

Saxon, T.F., Frick, J.E., & Colombo, J. (1997). Individual differences in infant visual fixation and maternal interactional styles. *Merrill-Palmer Quarterly of Behavioral Development*, *43*, 48–66.

Sigman, M.D., Cohen, S.E., Beckwith, L., Asarnow, R., & Parmelee, A.H. (1991). Continuity in cognitive abilities from infancy to 12 years of age. *Cognitive Development*, *6*, 47–57.

Sokolov, E. (1963). *Perception and the conditioned reflex*. Oxford, UK: Pergamon.

Sternberg, R.J. (1985a). *Beyond IQ: A triarchic theory of human intelligence*. Cambridge, UK: Cambridge University Press.

Sternberg, R.J. (1985b). *Human abilities: An information processing approach*. San Francisco: W.H. Freeman.

Streissguth, A.P., Barr, H.M., & Sampson, P.D. (1990). Moderate prenatal alcohol exposure: Effects on child IQ and learning problems at age $7\frac{1}{2}$ years. *Alcoholism: Clinical and Experimental Research*, *14*, 662–669.

Tamis-Lemonda, C.S., & Bornstein, M.H. (1989). Habituation and maternal encouragement of attention in infancy as predictors of toddler language, play, and representational competence. *Child Development*, *60*, 738–751.

Thompson, L.A. (1989). Developmental behavioral genetic research on infant information processing: Detection of continuity and change. In S. Doxiadis (Ed.), *Early influences shaping the individual*. New York: Plenum Press.

Thompson, L.A., Fulker, D.W., DeFries, J.C., & Plomin, R. (1986). Multivariate genetic analysis of "environmental" influences on infant cognitive development. *British Journal of Developmental Psychology*, *4*, 347–353.

Thompson, R.F., & Glanzman, D.L. (1976). Neural and behavioral mechanisms of habituation and sensitization. In T. Tighe & R. Leaton (Eds), *Habituation* (pp. 49–94). Hillsdale, NJ: Lawrence Erlbaum Associates Inc.

Tulving, E., Markowitsch, H.J., Kapur, S., Habib, R., & Houle, S. (1994). Novelty encoding networks in the human brain: Positron emission tomography data. *Neuroreport*, *5*, 2525–2528.

Vernon, P.A. (Ed.) (1987). *Speed of information processing and intelligence*. Norwood, NJ: Ablex.

Vernon, P.A., & Mori, M. (1992). Intelligence, reaction times, and peripheral nerve conduction velocity. *Intelligence*, *16*, 273–288.

Werkman, S.H., & Carlson, S.A. (1996). A randomized trial of visual attention of preterm infants fed docosahexaeonic acid until nine months. *Lipids*, *31*, 91–97.

Zacks, R.T., & Hasher, L. (1994). Directed ignoring: Inhibitory regulation of working memory. In D. Dagenbach & T.H. Carr (Eds), *Inhibitory processes in attention, memory, and language* (pp. 241–264). San Diego, CA: Academic Press.

Zola-Morgan, S., Dabrowska, J., Moss, M., & Mahut, H. (1983). Enhanced preference for perceptual novelty in the monkey after section of the fornix but not after ablation of the hippocampus. *Neuropsychologia*, *21*, 433–454.

PART TWO

Behaviour genetics

CHAPTER FOUR

The developmental genetics of intelligence

David Hay
Curtin University of Technology, Perth, Western Australia

INTRODUCTION

Only recently has psychology come to terms with the fact that there can be both genetic and environmental influences on behaviour. The 1970s were the decade of "nature vs. nurture" with two clear and unambiguous camps, totally at conflict with each other and with no compromise (Hay, 1985). By the 1980s this had advanced to "nature and nurture", recognising a place for both determinants of behaviour. The theme of the 1990s is emerging as "nature via nurture", a term originating out of the large Minnesota Study of twins reared apart (McGue et al., in Plomin & McClearn, 1993). There may be quite modest genetic influences on children's behaviour to which adults react; these reactions in turn change the child's behaviour, amplifying the genetic effect. This much more conciliatory view of the determinants of behaviour is indicative of the new ethos.

Circumstances have changed even more with the concept of "the nature of nurture" (Plomin, Owen, & McGuffin, 1994) and the finding that ostensibly environmental variables such as parenting behaviour and amount of TV watched are themselves partly under genetic control. Of course there are many steps between genes and the expression of such behaviours and Rose (1995) sounds a note of caution over how such genetic results may be misconstrued—can children tell their parents "But it's your genes that mean I have to watch so much TV!"

COMMON MISCONCEPTIONS ABOUT GENETICS

While behaviour genetics has advanced considerably in the last 30 years, this has not been reflected in how it is perceived both by many psychologists and by the public (Rose, 1995). Nowhere is this more obvious than in the case of intelligence test performance (Hay, 1990). The situation has been aggravated by the recent text, *The bell curve: Intelligence and class structure in American life* (Herrnstein & Murray, 1994) and the ensuing resurgence of debate over the meaning of intelligence and its aetiology (Jacoby & Glauberman, 1995). Herrnstein and Murray (1994, p. 10) had previously argued a syllogism for the key role of IQ in "success": "because IQ is highly heritable, because economic success in life depends in part on the talents measured by IQ tests, and because social standing depends in part on economic success, it follows that social standing is bound to be based to some extent on inherited differences."

Such a statement gives a pivotal role to the heritability of IQ, although two points should be noted. First, as discussed later, the recent estimates of this heritability are around 0.5 and not nearly as extreme as were being claimed years ago. Second, although the syllogism appears logical and is backed by some evidence, note the use of phrases like "in part" and "to some extent". Even if each of the three steps were individually quite significant, the multiplicative reduction over all three means that the final effect of IQ on social standing may be trivial.

Some common misconceptions have arisen with such extensions of genetics from science to politics. One of these is that genetics means unchangeable. Whether the heritability is 40% or 70% (and most scientific estimates fall in this range) is irrelevant to questions of the extent to which ability can be changed. It is worth reinforcing the message that heritability refers just to the determinants of that behaviour in that population at that point in time (Hay, 1985). It says nothing about changeability with new environmental determinants. A clear and much less contentious example is that of height which has a very high heritability but which has risen considerably in the last few generations with improved nutrition and medical care (Rutter et al., in Plomin & McClearn, 1993). The same goes for behaviour where a very good or a very poor environment can still have a very dramatic effect on behaviour with a large heritability. Certainly heritability may restrict to some extent the response to change—a concept sometimes called the "reaction range"—but considerable scope for variation remains. Heritability refers to the determinants of variability between individuals and not to the performance of an individual or the average of the population.

The second misconception is that genetics is a way of justifying the status quo. For example, if ability and educational success have significant genetic components, then at a very simplistic level this could be interpreted as justification for society's inequalities in educational resources. Genetic inheritance actually implies the opposite. If many genes determine a behaviour, then there is always the possibility that a child from a very disadvantaged background may have a combination of genes enabling him or her to achieve far beyond either of the parents (Hay, 1985). Conversely, highly able parents are no guarantee genetically that their children will be the same. This uncertainty is fundamental to the whole process of meiosis and the creation of sperm and eggs. Indeed the only situation where absolute certainty of transmission of parental status could occur is one where the behaviour is totally determined by the environment and children "inherit" their parents' social advantages or disadvantages rather than their genes.

THE GENETIC DISSECTION OF BEHAVIOUR

But these are public concerns rather than scientific ones. A much more serious misconception for psychology as a discipline is the stereotyping of behaviour genetics as simply being the finding of ever larger estimates of the heritability of IQ (Hay, 1990). In reality, behaviour genetics has moved on to newer and more important questions. The aim of this chapter is to demonstrate that genetic analysis can contribute to an understanding of the development of intelligence (Goldsmith, 1988) and is not simply preoccupied with the heritability of IQ scores. As Plomin and Neiderhiser (1991) emphasise, obtaining reliable estimates of the heritability of intelligence should be seen as the beginning of research and not as the conclusion. One theme of contemporary behaviour genetics (and the focus of this chapter) is "the genetic dissection of behaviour" (Hay, 1985) and the fact that one can acquire unique information about a behaviour through genetic analysis that could not be acquired through even the most exhaustive analysis of the phenotype. The term "phenotype" is used in genetics to define the observed expression of any trait as the compound of genetics and environment, but its implications actually go much further. The phenotype of intelligence is often just perceived as the score on an IQ test, but, as we shall see shortly, such a score can be dissected into a complex of genetic and environmental influences at the level of general ability and specific skills which change during the lifespan.

Yet there is no doubt that so much genetic research has focused on a static view of the traditional IQ score. Critics may argue this focus is because of attempts to use or abuse IQ to support inequality (Hay, 1990) and that may well have been the case in the distant past. My own view is that the reason is pragmatic. As emphasised later, modern behaviour genetics requires data from many individuals, representing many different familial relationships and, as such, behaviour genetic studies tend to be conservative in the behaviours selected for study. At a practical level, if you have 1000 sets of twins who have agreed to spend two hours in your behavioural study, would you spend most of this on some new and relatively untested measures of behaviour or on measures both colleagues and granting bodies are likely to find acceptable? The sheer size, cost, and time involved in such studies makes it difficult for behaviour genetic studies to respond quickly to innovations in psychology and so there has been such emphasis on conservative measures of both intelligence and personality (Eaves, Eysenck, & Martin, 1989).

Although this chapter focuses more on traditional psychometric measures of the components of intelligence test performance than do others in this volume, the methods of analysis and the questions being examined in current studies do show how the discipline is evolving and what could be achieved as the phenotype is broadened. Figure 4.1 (reprinted from Hay, 1985) is one way of viewing how the discipline has changed. The top line in both parts of the figure is the older view. In part (a) genes were viewed as something that exerted a consistent influence over the lifespan, rather than possibly changing during the course of development. In part (b) genes were considered as influencing all aspects of a trait, for example all aspects of intelligence test performance rather than being specific to particular abilities. In practice both genetic and environmental effects may exert influences across many combinations of traits and periods of the lifespan (as shown in the lower part of the diagrams) and one of the key objectives of contemporary behaviour

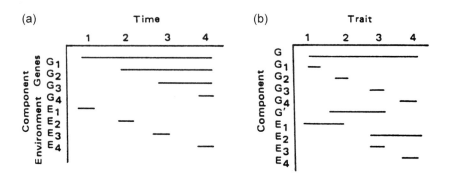

FIG. 4.1   Hypothetical examples of how (a) gene expression may change with time and (b) genetic and environmental effects may contribute to four behavioural traits. G refers to genes having a general effect over all traits, G1 . . . G4 to time or trait specific genes and G′ to genes affecting a pair of traits (from Eaves, 1982). Reprinted with permission.

genetics is to unravel this multiplicity of influences. One point which should be clear is that the genetic and environmental effects need not operate in the same way and thus analysis at the phenotypic level of the relationship between traits at the same time or of the same trait at different times may be misleading.

Deriving from this figure, there are six key questions which arise in contemporary genetic studies of intelligence and its development:

1. Just how good are our estimates of the genetics of intelligence and to what extent are they confounded with the way in which we obtain the data from twins, from adoption studies and other research designs?
2. Are the extent and nature of the genetic influences the same throughout the course of development from infancy to old age?
3. Are fluctuations in performance at different ages nothing more than a reflection of the unreliability of our measures of intelligence?
4. Is there a biological entity called intelligence or are there multiple intelligences? How does the pattern change during development?
5. Just what are the environmental factors and how do they interact with genetic influences during development?
6. Will we ever find a single gene for intelligence and are there clues from neurodevelopmental genetic disorders?

We begin with a general overview of the genetic principles and methodology of all behaviour genetic designs. More comprehensive coverage of behaviour genetics can be found in textbooks such as Plomin, DeFries, McClearn, and Rutter (1996), and a good overview of developmental behaviour genetics including the important areas of animal and evolutionary research is given in Hahn, Hewitt, Henderson, and Benno (1990). The American Psychological Association text (Plomin & McClearn, 1993) has extensive coverage of aspects of intelligence, and the Dahlem Workshop on twins in behaviour genetics (Bouchard & Propping, 1993) gives an insight into current controversies, with much emphasis on cognition. The most ambitious project on the developmental behaviour genetics of cognitive abilities in the broadest sense has been the Colorado Adoption Project (CAP) and the results to date are summarised in two books, one on infancy (Plomin, DeFries, & Fulker, 1988) and one on middle childhood (DeFries, Plomin, & Fulker, 1994). Both these books demand an extensive understanding of the recent developments in statistical methodology for behaviour genetics. One of the easier but comprehensive introductions to this area is in two texts on genetic studies of personality (Eaves et al., 1989; Loehlin, 1992), with a more thorough coverage in Neale and Cardon (1992). Because of the specialised nature of the statistical skills needed in this field, there has developed a tradition of annual workshops aimed predominantly at the postgraduate and post-doctoral level (Boomsma, Martin, & Neale, 1989).

One excellent example of the potential of modern behaviour genetics is in a landmark series of three complementary studies of antisocial personality disorder in a special issue of the *Archives of General Psychiatry on Genetic Epidemiology in Psychiatry*. In introducing these articles, Kendler (1995) and Gershon (1995) point to three issues:

- the same genotype can manifest itself in different ways at different ages;
- the ultimate expression of the genotype may depend upon complex environmental features such as the presence in the family of others with the same condition;
- genetic studies may be the most powerful means of identifying environmental variables.

So it is not just in the area of intelligence that the philosophy and purpose of behaviour genetic analysis is changing. The discipline is advancing so quickly that much inspiration for what could be done in the area of intelligence may come from very different areas of behaviour such as these studies of personality disorders.

HOW DO GENES WORK?

The constant stream of advances in molecular genetics and major initiatives such as the Human Genome Project leads one to believe that we are close to knowing everything about our genes. In fact such research has to date had little impact on work on the genetics of intelligence and perhaps should not have any impact until more is known about the social consequences of the results (Harper, 1995). For example, what should parents and teachers make of a gene which affects a child's IQ score by only two or three points? It is important to realise that most genetic work with behaviour takes a very different emphasis from molecular research. Molecular genetics focuses on the biochemistry of discrete characteristics, features, or one disorders which one either has or has not, an approach called (possibly tongue in cheek) by Plomin, Owen, and McGuffin (1994) the one gene, disorder (OGOD) strategy. This is in contrast to continuous or quantitative characteristics that include most human behaviours as intelligence, personality, social attitudes, and temperament. Even those that appear to be discontinuous such as the diagnosis of schizophrenia can be analysed as a "threshold" character, representing a cut-off along a continuum of liability (Neale & Cardon, 1992).

In contrast to molecular genetics where the focus is on clearly defined genetic sequences, mapped to identified locations on specific chromosomes, research on intelligence has been concerned almost exclusively with polygenic inheritance. ("Poly" refers to the Greek term for "many".) That is, there are assumed to be many genes of small but cumulative effect with some environmental influences as well. Note how different this is from molecular genetics in that we have no idea of the number of genes involved, far less what they do biochemically. We simply hypothesise that for each gene, its alleles (different forms) add or subtract from the overall expression of the character. While this sounds abstract, it has been the formal basis of plant and animal breeding for most of this century and has existed informally since agriculture began. Characteristics as diverse as back fat thickness in pigs and protein content in cereals have been the subject of selective breeding which follows directly from polygenic inheritance. If there are many genes involved, some increasing and others decreasing performance, then we can breed to get all the increasing genes into the one individual. Obviously in humans we are not concerned with selective breeding, but the same genetic principles apply as much to our behaviour as to characteristics of agricultural importance. There have been very successful selective breeding studies in rodents for such behaviours as maze learning (Hay, 1985), but this is a long way from necessarily inferring that this is of any relevance to human intelligence and indeed the conclusions may have been mistakenly applied to the human situation, as discussed later.

The other thing to notice is that polygenic inheritance implies some environmental effects as well, smoothing out distinctions between genotypes (although it says nothing about the magnitude of these environmental effects). The term "heritability" is often used to summarise just what proportion of the total differences between people is due to genetic rather than environmental factors. Thus adult height and weight are both polygenic factors even though weight has a much lower heritability and more scope for environmental influences from our diet and lifestyle.

The distinctions between polygenic and molecular approaches are diminishing. As Goldsmith (1988) explains, one of the key inspirations for strategies in the genetic analysis of behavioural development has been the discovery in molecular genetics that genes are dynamic and may be switched on or off at different stages of development. The classical example of this concerns the different forms of haemoglobin activated prenatally and early in postnatal life to optimise the oxygen-carrying capacity of the blood at these successive and crucial stages of development. We are still a long way from demonstrating this switching in behaviour, but it does offer a whole new way of viewing the role of genes during development.

A further rapprochement is coming with the strategy of quantitative trait loci (QTLs), arguing that even if behaviour is polygenic, some of the genes involved may be of sufficiently large effect that their specific contribution can be identified. Progress to date for intelligence has been modest with few effects of any magnitude being identified (Plomin, Pedersen, Lichtenstein, & McClearn, 1994), but the potential is there. One of the promising results has come from a personality dimension, Novelty Seeking where two separate studies (Benjamin, Li, Patterson, Greenberg, Murphy, & Hamer 1996; Ebstein et al., 1996) using different measures of this behaviour have identified variation in behaviour between individuals differing at the dopamine D4 receptor gene.

HOW DO WE DETERMINE THE HERITABILITY OF ANY BEHAVIOURAL TRAIT?

The word "any" has been deliberately chosen to emphasise one aspect of intelligence as a phenotype. While there can be problems in adequate genetic analysis for some behavioural traits, intelligence test performance is not one of these. This is actually a very important point. Often objections are raised about some if not all aspects of behaviour genetic analysis. Showing that there are valid problems that the analyses can identify with some behaviours but not others is a reassurance that the methods do actually have some merit.

At the same time, a key component to reliable genetic analysis is consistency of results for a particular behaviour across the three main approaches—twin, adoption, and nuclear family studies. It is all too easy to encounter apparently damning critiques of the techniques and data (Kamin, 1974) but so often these just focus on problems specific to each of the three approaches and often to specific studies. But the simple maxim is that three wrongs can make a right. This acknowledges each of the three methods may have significant problems but these are different problems and what really matters is if results are consistent and robust across all three. At least for intelligence, the results are remarkably consistent across the three data sources, with some minor exceptions discussed shortly.

To briefly summarise each of the three approaches. The basis of the twin methodology is that monozygotic (MZ) or identical twins that originate from the splitting of a single fertilised egg will have all their genes in common, whereas dizygotic (DZ) or non-identical twins that originate from the independent fertilisation of two eggs by two sperm in the same cycle have only half their genes in common. At a simplistic level, the comparison of the degree of resemblance in these two groups is some indication of the genetic contribution to behaviour, but obviously the reality is more complex. Issues with the twin study approach have been extensively covered elsewhere (Bouchard & Propping, 1993; Hay, 1985) and it is easy to see there are both biological and social factors which may make them more similar or less similar than their genetic relationship would suggest (Rutter & Redshaw, 1991). Bryan (in Bouchard & Propping, 1993) reviews some of the prenatal and perinatal biological factors that may affect behaviour and behavioural similarities. For example, twins are often premature and obviously both twins in a pair will experience the same degree of prematurity. Some 60–70% of MZ twins are monochorionic, that is they share the same placenta and outer foetal membrane (the chorion). In approximately 15% of cases (Bryan, in Bouchard & Propping, 1993) this can result in a transfusion syndrome, where one twin shunts blood and nutrients into the other twin with a consequent difference in birthweight and mortality. The extent to which chorion type is associated with additional behavioural similarities or differences between MZ twins and impacts upon genetic analysis remains a matter for further research (Rose, 1995; Sokal, Moore, Rose, Williams, Reed, & Christian, 1995). One consistent finding (Spitz et al., 1996) is that monochorionic MZ twins are more similar than dichorionic ones on one measure of spatial ability (Block Design), but the biological mechanism by which this may happen is unclear.

As regards social factors, the key issue is the "equal environments assumption" and the argument that MZ twins are treated more similarly and therefore behave more similarly. Kendler (1993) reviews many lines of evidence against this view, including data from twins where the parents were mistaken about the zygosity of their children. All the evidence points to MZ twins being treated more similarly because they behave more similarly, rather than the converse.

Other approaches to genetics have as many potential flaws, albeit different ones. Thus data from nuclear families confound genetic and environmental factors, in that parents and children share genes and also their environment. So the similarity between parents and offspring or between siblings is often said to represent an upper bound to estimates of heritability. In practice this may not be the case in developmental research where behaviour changes with age and the resemblance of family members may be less, just because they are of different ages.

Apart from twins, the other customary method of dealing with the confound of genes and environment has been through adoption studies where one parent gives the genes and the other the rearing environment. Of course adoption is not as simple as this and Goldsmith (1988, Table 3) summarises some of the key advantages and limitations of adoption and twin approaches to development. Sometimes children are given for adoption because the parents have intellectual disability or severe mental illness and cannot care for them. Sometimes the biological and adoptive parents are matched for education and other variables which can confound genetic analysis. Adopted children are wanted children and thus are often advantaged (DeFries et al., 1994). Adopted children often have scores on IQ tests at least 10 points above those of their siblings who had remained with their biological parents (Rutter et al., in Plomin & McClearn, 1993), and transracial adoptions diminish the differences which have traditionally been reported between ethnic groups (Weinberg, Scarr, & Waldman, 1992) This says less about genetics than about the power of positive environmental influences as these children are placed in particularly positive environments. Locurto (1990) has argued that adoption studies offer the best approach to assessing the malleability of IQ, as children may well be placed in an environment very different from that into which they were born. But there are fundamental problems over the issues of:

"Who is put up for adoption and why?"
"Who is actually adopted?"
"Who adopts them?"
"Which adoptive families participate in studies?"

While these problems do complicate adoption studies, one thing which has been clearly demonstrated is the lack of evidence for genotype-environment interaction (Goldsmith, 1988). A commonly voiced criticism of behaviour genetic analysis is that genes and environment are so strongly enmeshed that their joint effects can never be disentangled (Kamin, 1974). The reason for this criticism is that there is extensive evidence from work with mice and rats for such interaction. Both Hay (1985) and Plomin et al. (1996) review the material, but, basically, differences in the learning ability of genetically distinct rodent strains are influenced by aspects of their environment. Strains may be very different if reared in one environment, whereas this difference is absent if reared another way. (Conversely, the effects of the environment must depend upon the genotype.) The analogy to humans and especially to ethnic groups differences (Herrnstein & Murray, 1994) is obvious and tempting. Where adoption studies become so vital is that they enable children differing in biological endowment to be reared in different environments. While these studies show clear main effects for both genes and environment, no clear evidence has emerged for genotype-environment interaction (Locurto, 1990), raising the question as to why there is such a discrepancy from the animal evidence. One argument (Hay, 1985) derives from experience of commercial breeding in agriculture and is that through their selective breeding or inbreeding, the animals have become much more sensitive to environmental manipulations, enhancing the likelihood of finding such interactions compared with non-inbred species such as humans.

So every approach to polygenic inheritance has serious potential flaws. But there are two encouraging things to note. These are only potential problems and there is a big difference between hypothesising what may complicate the analyses of a given behaviour and actually providing empirical evidence that these effects are so important. Examples would include the failure to find evidence against the equal environments assumption or for genotype-environment interaction. The second and crucial point is that the problems are different for the different relationships. The problems for twin data are different from those for adoption data which in turn are different from those for nuclear family data.

Thus the basic principle is that the methods of analyses developed in the last 25 years examine whether, despite all these problems, the same set of environmental and genetic factors can explain the familial resemblances across the three different approaches to the data. In the past, heritability was calculated separately from each data type, by comparing resemblances in identical and non-identical twins or in adopted compared with non-adopted children. The more recent methods take all the data across a wide range of relationships, specify each relationship in terms of genetic and environmental parameters and mathematically test for consistency of this model of behavioural determinants.

It is easiest to illustrate this with examples. For IQ data on which so much of genetic analysis has been developed, there are few problems, and twin, adoption, and family data come up with the same results. The only exception identified in the very first such analysis (Jinks & Fulker, 1970) is that twins reared apart are more similar than expected because the homes in which they have been placed are fairly similar, reflecting the practices of the adoption agencies. Analyses of more recent and complete data sets (Chipuer, Rovine, & Plomin, 1990) identify a modest role for greater similarity in intelligence test performance between twins as a consequence of being reared together. So psychologists have really been very lucky in that they have based so much of their genetic analyses on a behaviour that shows such a simple and consistent pattern of genetic and environmental influences.

Other behaviours show a phenomenon, called sibling competition or reciprocal interaction. For example, in their study of hyperactivity, Thapar, Hervas, and McGuffin (1995) found the DZ twin resemblance to be much less than expected. The correlation for MZ twin boys was +0.71, compared with −0.22 for same-sex DZ boys, which is much less than the correlation of zero one might expect among children who had never met each other. Their explanation was that the twins are filling different niches in the family, with one being the outgoing and one the more inhibited twin. In contrast for such mental illnesses as schizophrenia, all twins irrespective of zygosity seem to be more similar than could be anticipated from the data on other relationships (McGue et al., 1985).

Ironically, probably the most important single result of these new genetic analyses has been the growing appreciation of the environment within the family (Plomin & Daniels, 1987). Traditionally psychology has focused on those aspects of the environment which are common to and shared by all members of the family. When children share the same parents, they share also the same values, and the same access to opportunities and resources (or the lack of these). What is emerging from the more recent twin and adoption analyses of behaviour is that such influences are of surprisingly small importance for many behaviours and what matters are those aspects of the family environment which make siblings different from each other. We accept differences between first- and second-born children or between boys and girls in the one family, but there seems to be much more to differences within the family than just these. While genetic analyses have identified this is an issue, actual data on what are the within-family factors have been less than productive.

The simplest way to illustrate the magnitude of these effects comes from measures of personality not in twins but in adopted children. Children born to different parents but adopted into the same family at birth are very different in personality by the time they reach adolescence (Plomin & Bergeman, 1991). Despite having shared all this time together, they are no more similar in personality than two people who had never met. If we consider intelligence test performance, then the results are even more striking. Siblings brought up in the same family differ in IQ by 12 points on average, while people picked totally at random differ by only 17 points, indicating just how large differences can be even between those brought up in the same family (Hay, 1985). While differences of this magnitude are consistent with the view that siblings only share half their genes in common, they are less consistent with those who espouse the role of family environment (Hoffman, 1991). Certainly the family may contribute to environmental factors influencing ability, but such factors influence differences between siblings much more than they do similarities. The jury is still out on this issue with Rose (1995) and Hoffman (1991) arguing that the nature of behaviour genetic designs may limit the capacity to identify common environmental effects. For example, unreliability of measurement will be counted as part of environmental differences between siblings, limiting the percentage of variance able to be attributed to their shared environment. Nevertheless, given that such differences within families were not previously the focus of psychology and psychiatry, it is important for developmental research that they are leading to a major rethink of what are the important influences upon children and their development.

Throughout the behaviour genetics literature one encounters the term, the ACE model, which identifies three influences on behaviour, A refers to the additive genetic effects, C to the common or shared environment, and E to the unique or non-shared environment. (It has also been termed the ECH model by Petrill, Thompson, & Detterman, 1995, using the more obvious term H for heritability but this has limitations because it plays down the possibility of non-additive and other more complex genetic effects.) Whatever the letters used, every relationship can be defined in terms of these three. Identical twins share all the A; non-identical twins share half the A. If they are brought up together, they share C and so on. There can be extra influences hypothesised such as specific twin environments and assortative mating, etc. (Neale & Cardon, 1992), but the basic rule is that these are not included if the statistical analysis indicates a simpler explanation is sufficient to explain the patterns of resemblances across the various relationships.

The statistical methodology to achieve such analyses have developed over the same period. The first and very landmark publication (Jinks & Fulker, 1970) used methods that required ability with sophisticated algebraic programs. The obvious difficulty in implementing such methods by scientists more interested in the psychology than the mathematics has led to the widespread use of the LISREL confirmatory factor analysis program which has the facility to test different structural models of the determinants of a behaviour (Eaves et al., 1989) with even more flexible programs becoming available recently such as Mx (Neale & Cardon, 1992) to handle data from more complex or more varied family relationships. While the actual methodology is beyond the scope of this chapter, the logic follows for anyone who has encountered structural equation modelling. LISREL and equivalents have mainly been used in psychology to address measurement models and such questions as the number of latent (underlying) variables needed to define the relationship between observed measures. For those not familiar with this approach, a pertinent and non-genetic analogy would be whether the interrelationship of the subtests of the Wechsler Intelligence Test for Children-III can adequately be explained by a single general factor (g) or whether group and specific factors are needed as well for an adequate statistical fit. The genetic equivalent is to determine the minimum number of parameters needed to define the pattern of similarities across multiple relationships. Thus with the ACE model, if a CE model fits the data, genes (A) are not needed. If an AE model fits, then shared environment (C) is of no significance, etc.

The advantage of this approach is that it can so easily be extended to address fundamental questions about the nature and determinants of behaviour. Figure 4.2 (on p. 93), from Casto, DeFries, and Fulker (1995), applies the ACE model to overall scores on the WISC-R and also to the three contributing Kaufman factors, Verbal Comprehension, Perceptual Organisation, and Freedom from Distractibility. Obviously one is now going beyond the usual phenotypic consideration of the intercorrelations between the three factors and asking what contributed to this correlation— do they share genes or environmental effects (the upper part of the diagram) or are they independent (the lower part), or is the best model some combination of the two? As discussed later, the last is the most appropriate model.

Bigger is better

It should be obvious from this account that contemporary behaviour genetics is much more than testing a few sets of twins and simply comparing the resemblance in identical and non-identical twins. The sophistication of the mathematical analysis is such that very large numbers are needed to accurately estimate the genetic and environmental effects and to be sure that all possible factors are tested. At the same time a wide range of relationships are needed. For example, in our recent work on attention deficit disorder in children (Hay & Levy, 1996; Levy, Hay, McLaughlin, Wood, & Waldman, 1996) we obtained information from some 2400 families with 4–12-year-old twins. Taking their siblings into account as well, over 6000 children were involved. Similarly, the work in Colorado on the development of intelligence has involved interlinked adoption and twin projects, where collecting similar measures at the same age in the various studies has enabled much more powerful and robust genetic analyses (Cardon, Fulker, DeFries, & Plomin, 1992a).

So behaviour genetic studies have become massive exercises involving many scientists. The Colorado Adoption Study is following some 200 families right from the time of adoption until (at present) adolescence. The Louisville Twin Study in Kentucky (Wilson, 1983) and our own LaTrobe Twin Study in Australia (Hay & O'Brien, 1983) have done the same for twins and a similar study is just beginning in the United Kingdom. Twins reared apart are a unique and very special group of people. The Minnesota Study (Bouchard, Lykken, McGue, Segal, & Tellegren, 1990) has now seen over 100 sets and there is similar study in Scandinavia (Pedersen, in Bouchard & Propping, 1993) focusing on the later stages of development (SATSA-Swedish Adoption/Twin Study of Ageing), with separated twins who are now in their 60s and older. They tended to be separated as children because of the death of the mother and the difficulty in those days of economically disadvantaged fathers caring for two young children.

It seems excessive to say that we must throw out many of the earlier studies but that is not far from the truth. Many of the inconsistencies and difficulties with the results of such studies arose from the small size, the lack of adequate sampling of families and the limited range of relationships.

So much time has been devoted to the background of the developmental questions, because it is important to appreciate the changes in methodology. Without the power of the new analytic methods, we simply would not have the capacity to even begin to address these questions.

ARE THE GENETIC INFLUENCES THE SAME THROUGHOUT THE COURSE OF DEVELOPMENT?

There are three ways in which the extent of genetic influences on intelligence test performance may change during development. The first is quite trivial. The adoption and family studies show that children only really begin to resemble their biological parents after the age of three or more, reflecting the fact that we cannot tap into the abilities measured on the tests until that age. There is growing interest in infant intelligence measures, especially in the Colorado Adoption Project, but these are beyond the scope of the present account (Boomsma, in Bouchard & Propping, 1993; Plomin et al., 1988).

The simplistic view is that if genetics are involved in intelligence test performance, then they may well "wear off" as children develop and as they are exposed more and more to environmental influences (Goldsmith, 1988; Loehlin, Horn, & Willerman, 1989). Yet, if anything, the data point in the opposite direction with there being a significant role for shared family environment during childhood, with this influence tapering off into adulthood.

The most comprehensive study is the meta-analysis by McCartney, Harris, and Bernieri (1990) which accumulated the data from many twin studies and found that over the lifespan the MZ twin resemblance rose for IQ (the correlation with age was +0.15) while the DZ dropped (correlation with age -0.25). Continuing the same theme, McGue et al. (in Plomin & McClearn, 1993) emphasise that much of the data on which genetic analyses have been done derive from twins and adopted children under the age of 20. The growing body of data from older adult twins is consistent with a higher heritability (closer to 80% compared with the 50% found in the other studies), but caution must be used in interpreting this figure. Not all twins survive into later adulthood and not all are willing to be involved in research programmes, so that only those who are more similar in behaviour may be willing to participate. This may be a particular issue with studies of that rare group, MZ twins reared apart, where the twin–twin correlation is a direct measure of heritability since they have shared little of the postnatal environment. But McGue et al. argue the higher heritability obtained from this group is a consequence of them being older than twins in most other studies and support this with data from their own cross-sectional study, using a protocol for recruitment and assessment which was consistent across different ages (11 to 88 years). This indicated a uniform rise in the MZ but not the DZ correlation which they explain as a consequence of changes in who determines their environment. In adulthood MZ twins can impose their own environment and may select similar levels of stimulation. In contrast the DZ correlation may decrease because they are no longer being exposed to similar parenting styles. As well as the relative role of genes increasing with age, genes may contribute to the stability of intelligence. In the SATSA study (Plomin et al., 1994) where twins were tested at an average age of 64 and then again three years later, the heritability was over 80% and genes were the major reason for continuity of scores between the two assessments. These results may have to be regarded cautiously since the correlation for DZ twins reared together was consistently very low both on general IQ and on some specific tests such as Digit Span. Further, some differences have been found between comparative genetic and factor analyses of the older adult twins in SATSA compared with a Minnesota sample (Finkel, Pedersen, McGue, & McClern, 1995). Although this may reflect nothing more than methodological differences in how some of the abilities were assessed (Finkel et al., 1995; p. 430), the issue does need to be resolved.

While McGue et al. explain the rise in heritability as a consequence of changes in environmental determinants, a much more exciting possibility is that additional genetic influences come into action as children grow. The definitive studies are still in progress, mainly as part of the various twin and adoption projects in Colorado (Cardon et al., 1992a). Apart from the extra power gained by combining adoption, family, and twin data, a major advantage of these studies is that the same measures have been used in each part of the programme (the Bayley Scales at ages one and two, the Stanford–Binet at three and four, and the WISC-R at age seven). C, the common family environment, tends to be a consistent influence across all the ages and of a similar magnitude in twins as in family and adoption data. (They argue this is because, unlike many other studies, they excluded low birthweight twins where the prematurity may contribute to excess similarity.) E, the nonshared environmental effects, were specific to each age. There was consistent evidence that new genetic influences became obvious at ages two and seven, the latter about the same time children acquire Piagetian conservation skills and when one may expect some reorganisation of their reasoning skills. A separate study based on the Texas Adoption Project (Loehlin et al., 1989) tested children at age 3–14 and again 10 years later. While they admit the range of ages is a problem, it is clear from their results that genetic changes do occur in adolescence and early adulthood, which again makes sense, in that one could expect the hormonal changes associated with puberty to contribute to the switching on of genes.

There is no doubt the data on this topic are less adequate than one would like, because the changes between the tests used at different ages confound the finding of genetic changes—is the difference between younger and older children in both the Colorado and Texas studies a consequence partly of differences between skills tapped in the Stanford–Binet and in the WISC-R? But a key theme needs to be emphasised. While genetics is often portrayed as being the immutable influence on behaviour, here we have the opposite and support for what Goldsmith (1988) has called "the genetic underpinning for biobehavioural relationships". In fact, the new genetics is arguing that intelligence is not fixed and that the traditional IQ score may change more than many psychologists would like to admit. The changes happen not through unreliability of the test or through environmental effects but because new genetic effects come into play. In practical terms, if we were to try to estimate adult IQ from the scores of a young child, should we pay more attention to the scores of their adult relatives rather than to how the young person performs him- or herself?

FLUCTUATIONS IN PERFORMANCE

Are fluctuations in performance at different ages nothing more than a reflection of the unreliability of our measures of intelligence? One of the standard criticisms of intelligence test performance has been that it is so variable and that scores for the one individual fluctuate so much from one test to the other. One of the more unusual consequences of longitudinal twin studies of intelligence has been the realisation that such fluctuations are much more systematic genetically in that they occur at the same stage for different children in the same family. The key study has been the Louisville Twin Study in Kentucky which has followed twins and their single-born siblings from three months of age (Wilson, 1983). No one would deny that performance at such ages does change a lot but what is new is the finding that such changes are systematic and occur at the same time for children of different ages within the one family. In concrete terms, there are cases where both twins may change in performance at the same age. This may well be attributed to specific events in the family impinging upon both twins at the same time (although this would not necessarily explain the greater MZ than DZ similarity). What makes the results so convincing is that their older or younger single-born siblings showed equivalent changes when they were at the same age. Thus it is much easier to explain the changes in terms of genetic programming than simple changes in the environment at or near the time they were assessed.

There is one limitation to such research. While there is no doubt that it is a convincing demonstration of the role of genetics, just what does it mean? Some families will find their children increase in score while others decrease. Why should some children be destined to fluctuate much more in performance than others and what is the genetic mechanism that may underlie this? Yet at least we do have some proven precedent for genetic differences in variability in performance. One of the most common genetic disorders is Down syndrome, and one of the key issues in the assessment and management of young people with this condition is that they are so variable—one day they have acquired a new skill and the next they have lost this, albeit temporarily (Lewis, 1987). Such a variability does not occur with other disorders and is clearly something specific to this chromosomal disorder.

One extension to this approach has been to try to model the actual growth curve of intellectual ability and to examine the extent to which this curve and deviations from it are determined by genetics or environment. Obviously this is a much more difficult task, both psychometrically as one tries to equate measures at various ages and in terms of quantitative genetics as one tries to fit models to complex growth functions (Phillips & Fulker, 1989; Waldman, DeFries, & Fulker, 1992) but it is an important area for future development. The development of new analytic methods that enable the modelling of means as well as measures of resemblance (Boomsma, in Bouchard & Propping, 1993) may significantly advance this approach.

IS THERE A BIOLOGICAL ENTITY CALLED INTELLIGENCE OR ARE THERE MULTIPLE INTELLIGENCES?

Virtually since Psychology developed the concept of "general intelligence" or "*g*", there has been debate as to the existence or adequacy of this view. At a simplistic level, British psychologists have argued much more for "*g*" (Brand, in Bouchard & Propping, 1993), whereas American psychologists have argued much more for separate and relatively independent aspects of ability. Most recently and most publicised has been the view of Gardner (1983, 1992) that there are at least seven types of intelligence, each of which needs different types of intervention and support. With concepts such as musical intelligence, this clearly goes well beyond conventional views of intellectual performance. Gardiner based his idea partly on biological evidence, to do with specific abilities or disabilities in defined genetic disorders or consequences of head injuries, and his ideas remain controversial, though having wide impact on education in the USA. Baker et al. (in Bouchard & Propping, 1993, pp. 92–93) provide a useful discussion of how the differences between *g* and multiple intelligences may not be so great as might appear.

The recent genetic dissections of intelligence test performance give a more definitive view as to whether or not a general intelligence factor exists (Fulker & Cardon, in Bouchard & Propping, 1993). In terms of analysis, this represents an extension of the ACE model to the multivariate situation, as shown in Fig. 4.2, testing models of the covariance between scores on the subtests of the Wechsler Intelligence Scale for Children-revised (WISC-R; Casto et al., 1995) and the Wechsler Adult Intelligence Scale (WAIS; Tambs, Sundet, & Magnus, 1984). The answer is "Yes, no, or maybe"! This does sound confusing but highlights the different determinants of performance. There is clearly some genetic component (A) to general ability (the upper part of the figure), but also genetic influences unique to specific aspects of intelligence (the lower part). Effects of shared family environment (C) vary, with Verbal Comprehension showing both general and specific effects, while growing-up together has no specific

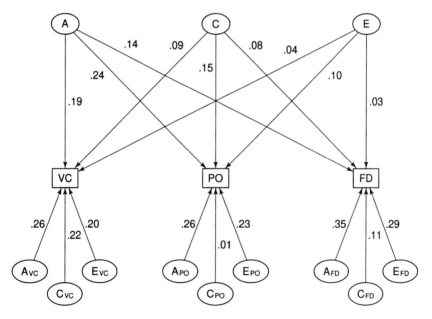

FIG. 4.2 Multivariate model for the variance components of performance on the WISC-R. The general and specific determinants are A (additive genetic), C (common environment), E (non-shared environment); the ability measures are VC (Verbal Comprehension), PO (Perceptual Organisation), FD (Freedom from Distractibility) (from Casto et al., 1995). Variance estimates sum to 1.0 over the general and specific determinants of each ability measure (see Casto et al., for details).

effects on perceptual Organisation. Nonshared factors (E) and influence just specific aspects of performance. This does emphasise the specificity of such effects not just to the one individual in the family but to the one aspect of ability. A slightly different picture emerges when a battery of specific abilities is analysed (Cardon, Fulker, DeFries, & Plomin, 1992b) rather than subtests of conventional intelligence tests such as the WISC-R with less evidence for a general C contribution, although genes continue to operate at the general and specific level. While this complex pattern of general and specific effects may disappoint those who would like a definitive answer one way or the other, this result is consistent with what has until now been such an area of conflict. It does imply that much future research efforts on the unitary concept of ability or on specific abilities may have to incorporate a genetic design.

A more sophisticated approach which incorporates a developmental perspective comes with the "performance differentiation" hypothesis discussed by Cardon and Fulker (1994). Examining the question of whether it is g or its specific components which are stable over time, they consider whether abilities correlate more with each other at the same point in time (the g approach) or more with the same ability at different time points. Using the Colorado twin and adoption data sets discussed previously and measures of four specific abilities (verbal, spatial, perceptual speed, and visual memory), they demonstrated there are general genetic effects on g apparent from the age of three, with genetic effects on specific abilities (both on related measures at the one time and on the same measure across time) becoming more obvious as development proceeds.

One of the newer areas of behaviour genetics has emerged from the question of a general intelligence. Is it possible to find some biological marker that underlies this ability? Thus there has been a growing interest in twin studies of electroencephalograms, of nerve conduction velocity, and of similar indices of what may be fundamental aspects of nervous system function and efficiency (Baker et al., 1991; Ho, Baker, & Decker, 1988; Petrill et al., 1995; Petrill, Luo, Thompson & Detterman, 1996). Although there are not yet any data that could be considered definitive, the whole concept is indicative of the new direction for intelligence research and a change from the tests which have been the basis for assessment over the entire century. The main results have been negative. It sounds reasonable to hypothesise that more biological markers of ability such as evoked potentials, EEGS, and reaction/inspection time measures will have a higher heritability since they may be closer to the biology of intelligence and less affected by the environment, but the results are far from clear. In the most detailed study, the Western Reserve Twin Project that combined conventional intelligence measures with more elementary cognitive tasks in 263 same-sex twin pairs (Petrill et al., 1995, 1996), it was only C, the common family environmental effect, which was common to both sets of measures, while the genetic effects were much less consistent and varied with the measure. Their reaction time measures showed common C effects with psychometric IQ, while the Stimulus Discrimination measures showed genetic overlap.

JUST WHAT ARE THE ENVIRONMENTAL FACTORS AND HOW DO THEY WORK?

A fundamental focus of developmental psychology is the extent to which behaviour and specifically intelligence can be modified by environmental manipulation. Behaviour genetic analysis defines environment by default in that it includes anything that is not categorically assigned to genetics as "environmental". This does actually include any unreliability in the measures and there is a clear dictum "heritability can never exceed reliability". For example, the correlation between identical twins is limited by the tests but often does approach the reliability of the same test given to the one individual at different times.

There are three fundamental problems in identifying environmental effects.

1.   Some effects apply to only a small group of children. For example, a six point IQ difference between children 2 SDs above and below the mean birthweight or between those who were first- or fifth-born (Mascie-Taylor, in Bouchard & Propping, 1993) does not imply that one can infer an explanatory role for these variables in the vast majority of the population falling within these extremes. A distinction must be made between variables which are statistically significant and those that account for a significant proportion of the variation in the population as a whole. As discussed by Mascie-Taylor, there are many examples of the former but few of the latter.

2.   A major distinction must be made between environmental effects which are part of the child's life and those which are part of environmental manipulation. As emphasised at the beginning, behaviour genetics is concerned with the former and says little about the potential impact of the latter except possibly in the area of genotype-environment interaction. To return to an earlier topic, the artificial selection experiments of rats where they were bred for high or low ability to perform in a maze did show genotype-environment interaction, in that the lower-ability rats benefited through exposure to an enriched environment with lots of rat toys and similar. This result was translated to the human situation with very little

critical evaluation—it sounded so right that the most disadvantaged would benefit from environmental intervention. In fact the data are much less optimistic. There is no doubt that a good environment does accelerate performance but there is absolutely no evidence that effects are differential with the less able benefiting more (Hay, 1985; Locurto, 1990).

3. There can be confounding between genetic and environmental effects or what Coon, Fulker, DeFries, and Plomin (1990) call "genetic mediation". As emphasised for many years (Baker, Treolar, Reynolds, Heath, & Martin, 1996; Fulker, 1979; Hay, 1985), measures such as parental socio-economic status, number of books in the home or educational achievement are not purely environmental but partly reflect the parents' intelligence and are thus reflections, however distant of their genotype. (Wadsworth, DeFries, Fulker, & Plomin, 1995 provide a more formal analysis of the genetic overlap between intelligence and academic achievement.)

Coon et al. compared the resemblance between WISC-R scores in seven-year-old children and measures of the home environment provided by adoptive and non-adoptive parents. For the former, any resemblance must be purely environmental while for the latter it may be increased by genetic mediation. On the widely used Family Environment Scale, the relationship to IQ was much higher for the non-adoptive children and correlated also with parental IQ, suggesting this was what was mediating the relationship between the children's IQ and the "environmental" measures.

Thus sorting out what is environmental is actually much more difficult than one would initially imagine.

WILL WE EVER FIND A SINGLE GENE FOR INTELLIGENCE AND ARE THERE CLUES FROM GENETIC DISORDERS?

The fundamental problem in identifying a single gene is finding its location on one of the 23 chromosome pairs. Often we can turn to genetic disorders to give us a clue as to where to start. So the early onset of Alzheimer's disease in people with Down syndrome who have an extra copy of Chromosome 21 gave a clue that a gene contributing to this form of dementia could well be located here. In fact it has turned out to be more complicated (Rose, 1995) and the gene on Chromosome 21 has to do with a protein which is only one contributor to dementia, with additional genes on chromosomes 14 and 19 also contributing. When it comes to intelligence, there are several hundred genetic disorders where intellectual disability is one of the symptoms. But to date we have had very little success in identifying genes for intelligence within the normal range of ability, despite what many of the proponents (and the critics) of the new genetics would have us believe. The main strategy has been through quantitative trait loci (QTLs) and the search for specific DNA markers which may be associated with high or low performance on intelligence tests (Plomin, Pedersen et al., 1994). It should be emphasised that such a search is not for "the" gene for intelligence. Rather it accepts the polygenic view but hypothesises that some of the many genes will be of sufficient magnitude that their location and effects can be identified. Just how many genes may be involved is a matter for debate, especially if some such genes have more than two alleles (Weiss, 1995).

The one gene that holds some promise is not actually a gene at all in the conventional sense. One of the most common genetic causes of intellectual disability in boys and learning disability in girls is Fragile-X syndrome (Rose, 1995). While it obeys some of the genetic laws applying to genes on the X chromosome, it is actually a repeated section of DNA. All of us have some repeats of this sequence, those with the full disorder have over 200 repeats and those at risk of having the disorder have 40–200 repeats.

Fragile-X is important in two other ways which reinforce the emphasis of this chapter in taking behaviour genetics beyond the IQ score. The effects are specific with some aspects of intelligence being much more affected than others and effects may change during development. Our work with Fragile-X families over many years (Hay & Loesch, 1989) has emphasised disparities in their test performance. Often people with the condition would do well on verbal aspects of intelligence (vocabulary, verbal similarities) but did very badly on non-verbal tasks. When asked to complete a paper and pencil maze or put blocks together to form a pattern, often even adults could not do items designed for quite young children. It is not uncommon to see differences of 30 or more IQ points between their verbal and non-verbal performance. In a comparison of Fragile-X and Down syndrome boys matched for verbal abilities, the non-verbal deficits of the Fragile-X were so extreme that they could be considered as a constructional apraxia (Crowe & Hay, 1990). Thus we have one of the few examples of a genetic effect which is relatively specific to a particular aspect of intellectual ability.

At the same time there is growing concern about whether intelligence test performance does decline in people with Fragile-X (Hay, 1994; Zigler & Hodapp, 1991). At a scientific level this is very interesting in that it may imply neurogenetic changes during development, especially at adolescence, the time when the decline in the ability of Fragile-X individuals is being claimed. But the quality of the evidence may be limited by the very nature of the fact that one is dealing with individuals at the lower end of the spectrum of intelligence, where there are practical difficulties in assessment. This is especially when there are more concomitant behavioural problems at this ability level (Goodman, Simonoff, & Stevenson, 1995) and where there are also psychometric issues over the quality and precision of the norms for this group so far from the population mean (Hay, 1994). Often people have been assessed on very different instruments, such as the Bayley Scales in infancy and the WISC-R quite a few years later, and there are many limitations in speaking of a direct comparison of scores on these two measures of "intelligence" (especially in the lower ability area). This is one area of the developmental behaviour genetics of intelligence where a distinction must be drawn between the scientific and the clinical implications of the results—although the evidence may be robust that some decline is seen in the population of individuals with Fragile-X, this is quite different from counselling families that they should expect such a change in their Fragile-X family member, since some will actually improve (Hay, 1994).

IN CONCLUSION

One thing should be noted is that there has been very little discussion of the heritability of intelligence, the extent to which individual differences in ability are genetically determined. It should be clear that behaviour questions have moved to a much more dynamic view of intelligence, concerned about its development and its structure. There are still unanswered questions especially about the extent to which genes affecting intelligence are switched on during development (and this means lifespan development including old age) and about the relationship between conventional measures of intelligence and the more biologically based measures of functioning of the brain and nervous system. Some of the specific ways in which the developmental behaviour genetics of intelligence could develop may include:

More emphasis on lower ability groups with defined genetic disorders. These may not only give a clue as to where to search for QTLs and genetic variation in intelligence in the majority of the population (Plomin & Neiderhiser, 1991), but may also help identify deficits in specific abilities or developmental trajectories. One caveat is the ongoing debate (Detterman & Daniel, 1989; Rose, 1995) over the heritability and the genetic structure of intelligence in the lower IQ groups which may or may not limit the ability to extrapolate from research with this group. Although studies of these defined groups may initially not appear to require the sophisticated genetic modelling, in fact this is not the case and the effects of specific genetic disorders may have to be examined against the polygenic background (Loesch, Huggins, Hay, Gedeon, Mulley, & Sutherland, 1993).

One of the most intriguing issues in developmental behaviour genetics is the extent to which IQ can be increased, and the whole approach of "learning potential" and "dynamic assessment" (Lidz, 1987), which considers not so much the performance on standard intelligence measures, as the extent to which these can be changed with directive intervention. The fact that Fragile-X individuals do not improve as the result of such intervention, whereas people with Down syndrome do (Hay & Loesch, 1989), implies that the generalisability of this approach needs to be evaluated more clearly in terms of the potential clients.

Modelling of the genetic and environmental covariance between intelligence and associated measures.   Reference has already been made to the studies examining the association between intelligence and academic achievement (Wadsworth et al., 1995), but there are many other areas that would warrant consideration of the extent to which the overlap with intelligence reflected genetic or environmental effects. To give one parallel illustration: There has long been debate over the direction of causation between reading problems and Attention Deficit Hyperactivity Disorder, and we have recently been able to demonstrate (Hay & Levy, 1996) that the overlap is largely genetic rather than directional. For example in the case of MZ twins, one can predict their reading disability from their twin's ADHD just as well as from their own. There is no doubt that more needs to be understood about the overlap between ADHD and intelligence, both at a practical as well as a scientific level (Faraone et al., 1993), especially when it comes to understanding the relationship between attentional processing and intelligence.

There are many other areas where this same approach to disorders could benefit the understanding of intelligence. Berman and Noble (1995) have countered the usual view that the specific impairment of visuospatial abilities in chronic alcoholics is a direct consequence of alcohol-related brain damage. They showed that the alcohol-naive sons of these alcoholics demonstrated the same pattern of deficits if they had the particular allele of the D2 dopamine receptor gene which has been associated with alcoholism, albeit controversially (Holden, 1994). That is, the specific cognitive deficit is associated with the gene predisposing to alcoholism rather than to the direct effects of the alcohol.

More awareness of cross-cultural research.   The debate over putative racial differences in intelligence has long scarred behaviour genetics and nothing would be gained by resuming this argument. But with the breakdown of the former Soviet Union, we are now being challenged by a very different approach to the nature of intelligence and sophisticated but different genetic analyses (Bulayeva, Pavlova, Dubinin, Hay, & Foley,

1993). As we have indicated (Hay & Bulayeva, 1993), a considerable challenge exists in developing a *rapprochement* between two such different views but much could be gained in two ways. The Russian conception of functioning of the nervous system may give much inspiration to the growing focus on more direct measures of biological processing of ability, although there is much of a challenge still in understanding the relationship between their measures and conventional Western measures of ability and personality. Second, the ethnic diversity in Russia does lend itself to quite different approaches both to genetic diversity and to an understanding of evolutionary processes in intelligence (Bulayeva et al., 1993) without the connotations associated with the discussion of ethnic differences in the West.

While modern behaviour genetics may not yet have all the answers, it should be clear from this chapter that it now has the right questions and the right methodologies to begin to answer them. Understanding the structure and development of intelligence is going to depend more and more upon genetic methodologies, not so much because of the extent of genetic variation for intelligence but more because of the unique potential provided by such research. As emphasised here, such research is not easy in that it requires large and expensive samples and increasingly sophisticated methodology, but the gains far outweigh the efforts.

REFERENCES

Baker, L.A., Treloar, S.A., Reynolds, C.A., Heath, A.C., & Martin, N.G. (1996). Genetics of educational attainment in Australian twins: Sex differences and secular changes. *Behavior Genetics, 26,* 89–102.

Baker, L.A., Vernon, P.A., & Ho, H.Z. (1991). The genetic correlation between intelligence and speed of information processing. *Behavior Genetics, 21,* 351–368.

Benjamin, J., Li, L., Patterson, C., Greenberg, B.D., Murphy, D.L., & Hamer, D.H. (1996). Population and familial association between the D4 dopamine receptor gene and measures of novelty seeking. *Nature Genetics, 12,* 81–84.

Berman, S.M., & Noble, E.P., (1995). Reduced visuospatial performance in children with the D2 Dopamine receptor A1 allele. *Behavior Genetics, 25,* 45–58.

Boomsma, D.I., Martin, N.G., & Neale, M.C. (1989). Genetic analysis of twin and family data: Structural modeling using LISREL. *Behavior Genetics 19,* 3–161.

Bouchard, T.J., Lykken, D.T., McGue, M., Segal, N.L., & Tellegren, A. (1990). Source of human psychological differences: The Minnesota study of twins reared apart. *Science, 250,* 223–228.

Bouchard, T.J. Jr. & Propping, P. (Eds) (1993). *Twins as a tool of behavioral genetics.* Chichester, UK: Wiley.

Bulayeva, K.B., Pavlova, T.A., Dubinin, N.P., Hay, D.A., & Foley, D. (1993). Phenotypic and genetic affinities among ethnic populations in Daghestan (Caucausus, USSR)—a comparison of polymorphic, neurophysiological and psychological traits. *Annals of Human Biology, 20,* 455–467.

Cardon, L.R., & Fulker, D.W. (1994). A model of developmental change in hierarchical phenotypes with application to specific cognitive abilities. *Behavior Genetics*, *24*, 1–16.

Cardon, L.R., Fulker, D.W., DeFries, J.C., & Plomin, R. (1992a). Continuity and change in general cognitive ability from 1 to 7 years. *Developmental Psychology* *28*, 64–73.

Cardon, L.R., Fulker, D.W., DeFries, J.C., & Plomin, R. (1992b). Multivariate genetic analysis of specific cognitive abilities in the Colorado Adoption Project at age 7. *Intelligence*, *16*, 383–399.

Casto, S.D., DeFries, J.C., & Fulker, D.W. (1995). Multivariate genetic analysis of Wechsler Intelligence Scale for Children-Revised (WISC-R) factors. *Behavior Genetics*, *25*, 25–32.

Chipuer, H.M., Rovine, M., & Plomin, R. (1990). LISREL modelling: Genetic and environmental influences on IQ revisited. *Intelligence*, *14*, 11–29.

Coon, H., Fulker, D.W., DeFries, J.C. & Plomin, R. (1990). Home environment and cognitive ability of 7-year-old children in the Colorado Adoption Project: Genetic and environmental etiologies. *Developmental Psychology*, *26*, 459–468.

Crowe, S., & Hay, D.A. (1990). Neuropsychological dimensions of the Fragile-X syndrome: A test of a hemispheric dysfunction hypothesis. *Neuropsychologia*, *28*, 9–16.

DeFries, J.C., Plomin, R. & Fulker, D.W. (1994). *Nature, nurture during middle childhood*. Cambridge, MA: Blackwell.

Detterman, D.K. & Daniel, M.H. (1989). Correlations of mental tests with each other and with cognitive variables are highest for low IQ groups. *Intelligence 13*, 349–359.

Eaves, L.J. (1982). The utility of twins. In V.E. Anderson, W.A. Hauser, J.K. Perry, &, G.F. Sing (Eds), *Genetic basis of the epilepsies* (p. 249). New York: Raven.

Eaves, L.J., Eysenck, H.J., & Martin, N.G. (1989). *Genes, culture and personality: An empirical approach*. London: Academic Press.

Ebstein, E.B., Novick, O., Umansky, R., Priel, B., Osher, Y., Blaine, D., Bennett, E.R., Nemanov, L., Katz, M., & Belmaker, R.H. (1996). Dopamine D4 receptor (D4 DR) exon III polymorphism associated with the human personality trait of novelty seeking. *Nature Genetics*, *12*, 78–80.

Faraone, S.V., Biederman, J., Lehman, B.K., Spencer, T., Noran, D., Seidman, L.J., Kraus, I., Chen, W.J., & Tsuang, M.T. (1993) Intellectual performance and school failure in children with attention deficit hyperactivity disorder and in their siblings. *Journal of Abnormal Psychology*, *102*, 616–623.

Finkel, D., Pedersen, N.L., McGue, M., & McClearn, G.E. (1995). Heritability of cognitive abilities in adult twins: comparison of Minnesota and Swedish data. *Behavior Genetics*, *25*, 421–431.

Fulker, D.W. (1979). Nature and nurture: Heredity. In H.J. Eysenck (Ed.), *The structure and measurement of intelligence,* (pp. 102–132). New York: Springer.

Gardner, H. (1983). *Frames of mind: The theory of multiple intelligences*. New York: Basic Books.

Gardner, H. (1992). *Multiple intelligences: The theory in practice*. New York: Basic Books.

Gershon, E.R. (1995). Antisocial behavior. *Archives of General Psychiatry*, *52*, 900–901.

Goldsmith, H.H. (1988). Human developmental behavior genetics: Mapping the effects of genes and environments. *Annals of Child Development*, *5*, 187–227.

Goodman, R., Simonoff, E., & Stevenson, J. (1995). The impact of child IQ, parent IQ and sibling IQ on child behavioural deviance scores. *Journal of Child Psychology and Psychiatry, 36*, 409–425.

Hahn, M.E., Hewitt, J.K., Henderson, N.D., & Benno, R. (Eds) (1990). *Developmental behavior genetics: Neural, biometrical and evolutionary approaches.* Oxford, UK: Oxford University Press.

Harper, P.S. (1995). DNA markers associated with high versus low IQ: Ethical considerations. *Behavior Genetics, 25*, 197–198.

Hay, D.A. (1985). *Essentials of behaviour genetics.* Oxford, UK: Blackwell Scientific.

Hay, D.A. (1990). Robertoux and Capron are wrong—behaviour genetics is very relevant to cognitive science. *European Bulletin of Cognitive Psychology, 10*, 637–646.

Hay, D.A., & Bulayeva, K.B., (Eds) (1993). Behavior genetics in Russia. Special issue of *Behavior Genetics 23*, 425–508.

Hay, D.A. (1994). Does IQ decline in fragile-X—a methodological critique. *American Journal of Medical Genetics, 51*, 358–363.

Hay, D.A. & Levy, F. (1996). Differential diagnosis of ADHD. *Australian Educational and Developmental Psychologist, 13*, 71–80.

Hay, D.A., & Loesch, D.Z., (1989). Fragile-X: The new challenge in intellectual disability. In N.S. Bond & D.A.T. Siddle (Eds), *Psychobiology: Issues and applications* (pp. 105–111). Elsevier: North Holland.

Hay, D.A., & O'Brien, P.J. (1983). The La Trobe twin study: A genetic approach to the structure and development of cognition in twin children. *Child Development, 54*, 317–330.

Herrnstein, R.J. & Murray, C. (1994). *The Bell Curve.* New York: The Free Press.

Ho, H.Z., Baker, L.A., & Decker, S.N. (1988). Covariation between intelligence and speed of cognitive processing: Genetic and environmental influences. *Behavior Genetics, 18*, 247–261.

Hoffman, L.W. (1991). The influence of the family environment on personality: Accounting for sibling differences. *Psychological Bulletin, 110*, 187–203.

Holden, C. (1994). A cautionary genetic tale: The sobering story of D2. *Science, 264*, 1696–1697.

Jacoby, R., & Glauberman, N. (Eds) (1995). *The bell curve debate: History documents, opinion.* New York: Times Books.

Jinks, J.L., & Fulker, D.W. (1970). Comparison of the biometrical genetical, MAVA, and classical approaches to the analysis of human behavior. *Psychological Bulletin, 73*, 311–349.

Kamin, L. (1974). The science and politics of IQ. Potomac, MD: Lawrence Erlbaum Associates Inc.

Kendler, K.S. (1993). Twin studies of psychiatric illness: Current status and future directions. *Archives of General Psychiatry, 50*, 905–916.

Kendler, K.S. (1995). Genetic epidemiology in psychiatry: Taking both genes and environment seriously. *Archives of General Psychiatry, 52*, 895–899.

Levy F., Hay, D., McLaughlin, M., Wood, K., & Waldman, I. (1996). Twin-sibling differences in parental reports of ADHD, speech, reading and behaviour problems. *Journal of Child Psychology and Psychiatry, 37*, 569–578.

Lewis, V. (1987). *Development and handicap.* Oxford, UK: Basil Blackwell.

Lidz, C.S. (Ed.) (1987). *Dynamic assessment: An interactional approach to evaluating learning potential.* New York: Guilford.

Locurto, C. (1990). The malleability of IQ as judged from adoption studies. *Intelligence, 14*, 275–292.

Loehlin, J.C. (1992). Genes and environment in personality development. Newbury Park, CA: Sage.

Loehlin, J.C., Horn, J.M., & Willerman, L. (1989). Modeling IQ change: Evidence from the Texas adoption project. *Child Development, 60*, 993–1004.

Loesch, D.Z., Huggins, R., Hay, D.A., Gedeon, A.K., Mulley, J.C., & Sutherland, G.R.· (1993). Genotype-phenotype relationships in fragile-X: A family study. *American Journal of Human Genetics, 53*, 1064–1073.

McCartney, K., Harris, M.J., & Bernieri, F. (1990). Growing up and growing apart: A developmental meta-analysis of twin studies. *Psychological Bulletin, 107*, 226–237.

McGue, M., Gottesman, I.I., & Rao, D.C. (1985). Resolving genetic models for the transmission of schizophrenia. *Genetic Epidemiology, 2*, 99–110.

Neale, M.C., & Cardon, L.R. (1992). *Methodology for genetic studies of twins and families*. Dordrecht, The Netherlands: Kluwer.

Petrill, S.A., Luo, D., Thompson, L.A., & Detterman, D.K. (1996). The independent prediction of general intelligence by elementary cognitive tasks: Genetic and environmental influences. *Behavior Genetics, 26*, 135–147.

Petrill, S.A., Thompson, L.A., & Detterman, D.K. (1995). The genetic and environmental variance underlying elementary cognitive tasks. *Behavior Genetics, 25*, 199–209.

Phillips, K., & Fulker, D.W. (1989). Quantitative genetic analysis of longitudinal trends in adoption designs with application to IQ in the Colorado Adoption Project. *Behavior Genetics, 19*, 621–658.

Plomin, R., & Bergeman, C.S. (1991). The nature of nurture. *Behavioral and Brain Sciences, 14*, 373–427.

Plomin, R., & Daniels, D. (1987). Why are children in the same family so different from one another? *Behavioral and Brain Sciences, 10*, 1–60.

Plomin, R., DeFries, J.C., & Fulker, D.W. (1988). *Nature and nurture during infancy and early childhood*. New York: Cambridge University Press.

Plomin, R., DeFries, J., McClearn, G.E., & Rutter, M. (1996). *Behavioral genetics: A primer* (3rd ed.). New York: W.H. Freeman.

Plomin, R. & McClearn, G.E. (1993). *Nature, nurture and psychology*. Washington, DC: American Psychological Association.

Plomin, R., McClearn, G.E., Smith, D.L., Vignetti, S., Chorney, M.J., Chorney, K., Venditti, C.P., Kasarda, S., Thompson, L.A., Detterman, D.K., Daniels, J., Owen, M., & McGuffin, P. (1994). DNA markers associated with high versus low IQ: The IQ quantitative trait loci (QTL) project. *Behavior Genetics, 24*, 107–118.

Plomin, R. & Neiderhiser, J. (1991). Quantitative genetics, molecular genetics and intelligence. *Intelligence, 15*, 369–387.

Plomin, R., Owen, M.J., & McGuffin, P. (1994). The genetic basis of complex human behaviors. *Science, 264*, 1733–1739.

Plomin, R., Pedersen, N.L., Lichtenstein, P., & McClearn, G.E. (1994). Variability and stability in cognitive abilities are largely genetic later in life. *Behavior Genetics, 24*, 207–215.

Rose, R.J. (1995). Genes and human behavior. *Annual Review of Psychology, 46*, 625–654.

Rutter, M., & Redshaw, J. (1991). Annotation: Growing up as a twin—Twin-singleton differences in psychological development. *Journal of Child Psychology and Psychiatry, 32*, 885–895.

Sokal, D.K., Moore, C.A., Rose, R.J., Williams, C.J., Reed, T., & Christian, J.C. (1995). Intrapair differences in personality and cognitive ability among young monozygotic twins distinguished by chorion type. *Behavior Genetics, 25,* 457–466.

Spitz, E., Carlier, M., Vacher-Lavenu, M.C., Reed, T., Moutier, R., Busnel, M.C., & Roubertoux, P.L. (1996). Long-term effect of prenatal heterogeneity among monozygotes. *European Bulletin of Cognitive Psychology 15,* 283–308.

Tambs, K., Sundet, J.M., & Magnus, P. (1984). Heritability analysis of the WAIS subtests: A study of twins. *Intelligence, 8,* 283–293.

Thapar, A., Hervas, A., & McGuffin, P. (1995). Childhood hyperactivity scores are highly heritable and show sibling competition effects: Twin study evidence. *Behavior Genetics, 25,* 537–544.

Wadsworth, S.J., DeFries, J.C., Fulker, D.W., & Plomin, R. (1995). Cognitive ability and academic achievement in the Colorado Adoption Project: A multivariate genetic analysis of parent–offspring and sibling data. *Behavior Genetics, 25,* 1–15.

Waldman, I.D., DeFries, J.C., & Fulker, D.W. (1992). Quantitative genetic analysis of IQ development in young children: Multivariate multiple regression with orthogonal polynomials. *Behavior Genetics, 22,* 229–238.

Weinberg, R.A., Scarr, S., & Waldman, I.D. (1992). The Minnesota Transracial Adoption Study: A follow-up of IQ test performance at adolescence. *Intelligence, 16,* 117–135.

Weiss, V. (1995). The advent of a molecular genetics of general intelligence. *Intelligence, 20,* 115–124.

Wilson, R.S. (1983). The Louisville twin study: Developmental synchronies in behavior. *Child Development, 54,* 298–316.

Zigler, E., & Hodapp, R.M. (1991). Behavioral functioning in individuals with mental retardation. *Annual Review of Psychology, 42,* 29–50.

CHAPTER FIVE

What twins can tell us about the development of intelligence—a case study

J. Steven Reznick
University of North Carolina, Chapel Hill, USA

Robin Corley
University of Colorado, Boulder, USA

INTRODUCTION

Human beings (and many other vertebrates) exhibit a range of cleverness. This claim is offered without citations but could be supported equally well with various sources of data (e.g. psychological research, historical anecdotes, or Biblical proverbs). Moreover, still within the domain of folk wisdom/folk psychology, there are various ways to speak about cleverness. At one extreme, we make general assessments of an individual's intellectual prowess that span abilities and contexts (e.g. she's a genius, he's a fool). At the other extreme, we notice that an individual may appear more or less clever depending upon the focal ability and the context in which it occurs (e.g. she's great at maths, he never knows what to say).

Psychologists who study intelligence have noticed the distinction between general and specific views, and, from the dawn of interest in the topic, have often been inclined toward championing one view as superior to the other. Spearman (1904) and Stern (1914) viewed intelligence as a unitary general capacity, whereas Thorndike (1914) and Thompson (1919) viewed it as a set of separable abilities. Intelligence as a unitary general capacity has its strengths: principal-components analysis often suggests a single general factor across subtests, neurological mechanisms can be posited that could affect a range of cognitive variables (e.g. density of axonal and dendritic processes, efficacy of synapses, speed of neural conduction), and general intelligence is an effective predictor of various outcomes (e.g. school performance). However, pioneering work by James McKeen Cattell (described in Kendler, 1987), and other more recent efforts to define intelligence, emphasise separable aspects such as linguistic, spatial, and logical-mathematical intelligence (e.g. Gardner, 1983; Guilford, 1967; Sternberg, 1977). These process-oriented constructs offer us some hope of understanding the mechanisms that support our intellectual ability, and as noted previously, can be sensitive to individual patterns of differential performance across ability or context.

One the one hand, it seems obvious to us that there is practical and theoretical utility in defining intelligence as both a general competence and a set of separate abilities. A description of intelligence that does not include unitary and componential views is simply incomplete. However, although unitary conceptualisations of intelligence have well-established utility for clinical screening and predicting educational attainment, they may be less interesting from a developmental perspective. In the following sections, we will address the issue of general versus specific measures of infant intelligence in the second year and suggest a strategy for assessing specific abilities. We will then demonstrate the usefulness of specific abilities by contrasting genetic and environmental influences on general and specific abilities as assessed in a longitudinal twin study at 14, 20, and 24 months. We are particularly interested in the second year because of its many significant transitions in cognitive development. Piaget (1952) posits numerous stage-like changes in ability during the second year (e.g. infants become able to form mental representations of objects or actions that are not perceptually present, to defer imitation, and to find objects that have undergone an invisible displacement). Kagan (1981) and Lewis and Brooks-Gunn (1979) posit the emergence of a sense of self late in the second year. Finally, developmental psycholinguists note linguistic milestones in the second year such as the emergence of two-word combinations, the spurt in productive vocabulary, or the dissociation of receptive and expressive language (Anisfeld, 1984; Bates, Bretherton, & Snyder, 1988; Bloom, 1970, 1973; Nelson, 1973.)

ASSESSING INTELLIGENCE IN INFANTS

The most widely known efforts to observe and describe intellectual behaviours in toddlers emerged in the early decades of the 20th century. The widespread interest in adult intelligence crossed paths with the child study movement, and early intelligence tests were introduced, (for example: the Gesell Test (Gesell, 1925, 1928); the Cattell Mental Test for Infants and Young Children (Catell, 1940/1960); and the Griffiths Scale

(Griffiths, 1954). For a detailed description of this period see Brooks and Weinraub (1976), Colombo (1993), or Dunst (1978).

There might be some utility in an effort to describe the various infant intelligence tests, compare their strengths and weaknesses, and track their success and failure, but that is not our intention here. Rather, we will focus on the infant intelligence test that is generally regarded as the best general measure of early development currently available—the California First Year Mental Scale developed by Nancy Bayley (1933) and now known as the Bayley Scales of Infant Development (BSID; Bayley, 1969). (Note that a second edition of the BSID—the Bayley-II—was introduced in 1993, but the field is still undecided as to its utility; Bayley, 1993) We will claim that the BSID is useful as a general measure of performance, but that there are advantages to a more differentiated approach in which the BSID's cognitive questions are divided into separate, theoretically coherent constructs.

The BSID is composed of items (i.e. specific contexts in which infant behaviour is observed and categorised). These items are grouped into two sets: a set of 81 items that are explicitly motor (e.g. crawling, climbing stairs) and a set of 163 items that are explicitly mental (e.g. response to sound, imitation, visual discrimination, memory, problem solving, language comprehension, and language production). The BSID is a "power test" (Anastasi, 1976): Normative research was conducted to determine the age at which most infants of a particular age respond correctly to each item, and items in the final test are ordered by tenths of months according to this age-based expectation. Raw scores calculated on the basis of the number of passed and failed items are converted into a Psychomotor Development Index (PDI) and a Mental Development Index (MDI), which are normalised standard scores derived from a national stratified sample of normal infants and children. The BSID also provides scales for rating various dimensions of temperament, emotion, and test-taking behaviour.

Intelligence is assessed in the MDI through the use of items that require the child to perform activities that are generally considered intellectual (i.e. thinking, memory, problem solving, categorisation, language, or other mental capacities). However, the main developmentally relevant information in the MDI (and other infant intelligence tests as well) is in the arrangement of test items to reflect a normative chronology of accomplishment in which an individual's performance can be evaluated relative to expectations for same-aged peers. The fact that individual differences in test scores are diagnostic assures the MDI's practical relevance (e.g. to identify children whose mental performance is notably advanced or retarded compared with their peers). However, the MDI is a poor tool for studying developmental function because, to the extent that the MDI items have been chosen appropriately and that the normative data are representative, there should be no general change in MDI scores over time. Some children may show a systematic change in MDI because of emerging poor health, recovery from previous poor health, or other circumstances (e.g. colour blindness would become relevant on the MDI only in late infancy), but, for most normally developing children, the MDI should hover at about the same level over time.

DECOMPOSING THE MDI INTO SPECIFIC MEASURES

Despite the fact that the BSID provides a single score reflecting mental development, Bayley did not conceptualise intelligence as a unitary, general capacity. Rather, she posited the successive emergence of complex mental processes or sets of processes, with each growing out of, but not necessarily correlated with previous processes (Bayley, 1933, 1970). The difficult problem is to identify the set of processes that characterise the intellectual ability of infants at various ages.

Empirical approach

One approach to identifying the processes that characterise an infant's mental ability at a specific age is to factor-analyse BSID Mental Scale items, but there is some question as to how these factors should be interpreted. A factor analysis of the MDI items reveals the items (or sets of items) that are most strongly related to the overall MDI. These items emerge because they evoke individual differences at a particular age: items that are well within or far beyond the child's competence serve no diagnostic purpose. There are two practical implications to this fact. First, a factor analysis of MDI items reveals items that are relevant for diagnosing individual differences among infants at a particular age but not necessarily for detecting the abilities that best characterise the infant in any general sense. For example, by 14 months almost all infants will say "da-da" or its equivalent. This tendency to apply simple names is a salient characteristic of 14-month-olds, but this item generates little variance among that age group so is unlikely to emerge in a factor that reflects individual differences. There is more variability in the 14-month-old's ability to name an object presented by the examiner so this item is likely to be included in a factor. By 24 months the tendency to name things is a salient characteristic of the child, and almost all infants will name an object presented by the examiner. But, because there is no longer variability in the item, it is no longer likely to be included in a factor. Second, the items that compose a factor are drawn from the subset of items that are age appropriate and not the broader set of all possible items. Other items that tap this same ability but that are too hard or too easy will not be administered and cannot participate in the factor. Thus, the set of items on a power test that emerge as a factor are not a factor in the traditional sense of a cluster of related items that are a distinguishable component of a larger group of items. Rather, they are a cluster of related items that are a distinguishable component within the subset of items diagnostic of individual difference and typically administered at a particular age.

Despite these limitations, factor analysis of the MDI can be informative. Hofstaetter (1954) used data on the California First-Year Scale, a forerunner of the BSID, collected longitudinally from 2 months to 18 years in the California Growth Study, and identified a potent but vaguely interpretable factor present between 2 and 21 months labelled "sensori-motor alertness". Cronbach (1967) subsequently questioned Hofstaetter's approach and offered analyses that cautioned against the factoring of age-to-age correlations. Stott and Ball (1965) undertook an extensive age-specific factor analysis of items from the 12-month California First-Year Scale and several other infant intelligence tests, and they identified factors that could be labelled (in contemporary terms) "fine motor", "expressive language", "goal-directed behaviour", and "memory". More recently, Lewis, Jaskir, and Enright (1986) used principal component and oblique factor rotation analysis to generate separate, non-orthogonal factors across MDI items for children tested longitudinally across the first three years of life. Three factors emerged at 12 months and were labelled "means–end", "imitation", and "verbal skill". Four factors emerged at 24 months and were labelled "lexical", "spatial", "verbal symbolic", and "imitation". Burns, Burns, and Kabacoff (1992) reported a factor analysis on MDI items from infants at these same ages but different factors emerged such as "fine motor", "language", and "memory" at 12 months and "language", "form board" (one of the BSID test materials), and "interactive behaviour" at 24 months. Finally, Gyurke, Lynch, Lagasse, and Lipsitt (1992) reported MDI factors labelled "fine motor", "perceptual/motor", and "language" at 12 months and "language", "fine motor", and "problem solving" at 18 months.

The components of early cognitive development that emerge in these factor analyses differ across studies but do suggest that sets of items that reflect individual differences in cognitive ability during the second year can be conceptualised within a general bifurcation into verbal and nonverbal domains. Nonverbal components can be separated further into specific abilities such as memory, imitation, and problem solving. A fine motor component also emerges in several studies.

There is one additional approach to factor analysis of BSID items that would seem to be useful. When the BSID is repeated regularly and frequently, these longitudinal data can be recast to reveal the age at which each child first passes each item. This score has the advantage of allowing any pair of test items to correlate despite differences in the average age at which the items are passed. Bayley (1970) reported a factor analysis on the age of first pass for children tested longitudinally in the Berkeley Growth Study (monthly 1 to 15 months and trimonthly to 36 months) with items drawn from the California First-Year Mental Scale and the California Preschool Mental Scale. Factor analysis revealed 12 factors (6 on each test), but only 7 factors had items assessed in the second year: perceptual interest, vocal communications, meaningful object relations, perceptual discrimination, object relations, memory for forms, and verbal knowledge. Thus, despite the change in technique, the same factors reported earlier emerged. Moreover, the problem stated earlier still remains: The analysis of average age at which the items are passed reveals the set of items that tend to be passed at the same age and not the set of items that measure the same underlying construct.

Theoretical approach

A second approach to defining subsets of related test items is to impose them based upon theoretical considerations. Bayley used this strategy in her initial segregation of the BSID into mental and motor items on the implicit theory that the items within each of these two domains tap abilities that seem similar. Indeed, the recent revision of the BSID (Bayley, 1993) uses theoretical and empirical methodology to subdivide MDI items into four facets: cognitive, language, social, and motor. Other test developers also segregate items. For example, the Gesell Developmental Schedules contain items grouped into the categories: motor behaviour, adaptive behaviour, language behaviour, and personality–social behaviour (Gesell, 1925, 1928) and the Griffiths scale (Griffiths, 1954) is divided into locomotor, personal–social, hearing and speech, hand and eye development, and performance subscales.

Several researchers have proposed schemes for subdividing the mental items of the BSID into theoretically defined subsets. Kohen-Raz (1967), in a study of the scalogram properties of the MDI for infants aged 1–27 months, identified subsets of items, each assumed to measure a definitive function of infant behaviour. These subsets, derived from the work of Gesell, Griffiths, and Piaget, were labelled "eye-hand", "manipulation", "object relation", "imitation/comprehension", and "vocalisation/social contact/active vocabulary". Yarrow, Rubenstein, and Pedersen (1975) used a similar approach, grouping MDI items according to the class of response elicited, the cognitive function tapped, or the most relevant psychological processes. Their analysis included only items relevant for the first year of life, but some similar categories emerged, including "vocalisation and language", "object permanence", "visually directed reaching and grasping", and several categories of motoric ability.

Theoretical subsets can also be defined for MDI items in the second year. Dale, Bates, Reznick, and Morisset (1989) sorted items on the BSID for 20-month-old infants into three subsets with theoretical coherence: items that require expressive language skills, which is related to the Kohen-Raz vocalisation/social contact/active vocabulary subset; items that require receptive language skills, which is related to the Kohen-Raz imitation/comprehension subset; and nonverbal items, which combines elements of the remaining Kohen-Raz subsets. In the present work, we extended the Dale et al. (1989) strategy, and sorted items on the BSID that are typically administered in the second year into subsets with theoretical coherence. Two sets of inherently linguistic items were identified: items that require expressive language skills (e.g. naming objects) and items that require receptive language skills (e.g. pointing to named pictures). Items that were ambiguous in their requirement for language skills (e.g. that required both expressive and receptive language, or that assessed imitation using a linguistic response) were excluded from further analysis. The remaining items (e.g. ringing a bell, attaining a toy with a stick), were combined into a set that was considered non-verbal. Items that had verbal instructions but that could have been solved without comprehension of the instructions (e.g. the experimenter gives the child a broken doll and asks the child to put it together) were considered nonverbal. Table 5.1 lists the BSID items retained for each of the three components.

GENETIC AND ENVIRONMENTAL INFLUENCES ON GENERAL MEASURES OF INFANT INTELLIGENCE

We will compare the usefulness of general and specific measures of infant intelligence by exploring the results that emerge for each measure in an ongoing longitudinal twin study. We will first set the stage by reviewing the literature on genetic and environmental influences on infant intelligence. The idea that intelligence is heritable dates from the ancient Greek philosophers, but it had its most formal modern expression in Darwin's theory of biological evolution (Darwin, 1859) and was studied in detail by Galton (1869/1962; 1883). The importance of environmental influence has a rich philosophical and psychological heritage (e.g. Locke, Helmholtz, Watson—see Kimble, 1993 for a review), but became particularly salient in the context of the plight of institutionalised children (Goldfarb, 1943) and controversy about affecting intelligence through enriching the environment (Goodenough, 1939; Simpson, 1939; Wellman, 1932).

TABLE 5.1
BSID Items in the Language and Non-verbal Composites

| | | *Percentage Correct* | | |
		14 months	*20 months*	*24 months*
Expressive language:				
79	Vocalise 4 syllables	98	100	100
85	Say "da-da" or equivalent	95	100	100
101	Jabber expressively	80	97	98
113	Say 2 words	26	90	98
116	Use gestures to make wants known	82	99	100
124	Name 1 object	8	67	90
127	Use words to make wants known	5	69	91
130	Name 1 picture	6	63	89
136	Say sentence of 2 words	2	35	74
138	Name 2 objects	0	29	70
141	Name 3 pictures	0	29	72
146	Name 3 objects	0	15	53
149	Name 5 pictures	0	12	52
Receptive language:				
89	Respond to verbal request	97	100	100
94	Respond to "no no!"	89	99	100
117	Indicate referent for article of clothing	25	83	95
126	Respond to command re: doll	17	83	96
128	Indicate referents for body parts on doll	6	76	95
131	Find 2 hidden objects identified by name	20	58	71
144	Indicate referent for 2 objects	1	43	78
152	Indicate referent for 3 objects	0	24	60
158	Respond to 2 prepositions	0	15	46
162	Respond to "put 1 block on paper"	0	3	8
163	Respond to 3 prepositions	0	3	20
Non-verbal:				
74	Attend to scribbling	98	100	100
75	Look for fallen spoon	98	100	100
76	Playful response to mirror	98	100	100
77	Retain 2 of 3 cubes	98	100	100
78	Manipulate ball: notice detail	98	100	100
80	Pull string adaptively: secure ring	98	100	100
81	Cooperate in games	97	100	100
82	Attempt to secure 3 cubes	97	100	100
83	Ring bell purposively	97	100	100
86	Uncover toy	98	100	100
87	Finger holes in pegboard	95	100	100
88	Pick up cup: secure cube	98	100	100
90	Put cube in cup on command	98	100	100
91	Look for contents of box	99	100	100
92	Stir with spoon in imitation	98	99	100

Table 5.1 *(cont)*
BSID Items in the Language and Non-verbal Composites

		Percentage Correct		
		14 months	*20 months*	*24 months*
93	Look at pictures in book	99	100	100
95	Attempt to imitate scribbles	92	99	100
96	Unwrap cube	85	99	100
97	Repeat performance laughed at	81	98	100
98	Hold crayon adaptively	96	99	100
99	Push car along	96	99	100
100	Put 3 or more cubes in cup	84	99	100
102	Uncover box	88	99	100
103	Turn pages of book	94	97	100
104	Imitate patting of doll	84	96	98
105	Dangle ring by string	55	92	98
107	Put beads in box	89	99	100
108	Place peg repeatedly	70	100	100
109	Remove pellet from bottle	85	98	99
110	Place round block on board	60	97	100
111	Build tower of 2 cubes	52	95	99
112	Spontaneous scribble	58	90	98
114	Put 9 cubes in cup	55	93	97
115	Close round box	50	91	97
118	Place pegs in 70 seconds	11	96	99
119	Build tower of 3 cubes	10	78	95
120	Place round block on board	33	81	96
121	Place 2 round blocks on board	21	88	97
122	Attain toy with stick	44	90	97
123	Place peg in 42 seconds	5	90	98
125	Imitate crayon stroke	24	83	92
129	Place 2 round and 2 square blocks	5	74	93
133	Mend broken doll marginally	5	44	79
134	Place pegs in 30 seconds	1	68	94
135	Differentiate scribble from stroke	7	62	83
137	Place all objects on board	2	54	85
140	Mend broken doll approximately	1	27	68
142	Place 6 blocks on board	1	53	85
143	Build tower of 6 cubes	0	22	47
147	Imitate vertical and horizontal strokes	1	15	40
151	Imitate placement of items on board	0	25	63
153	Mend broken doll exactly	0	6	34
154	Make train of cubes	0	20	53
155	Place items on board in 150 seconds	0	28	69
156	Place pegs in 22 seconds	0	30	71
157	Fold paper	0	12	32
159	Place items on board in 90 seconds	0	24	65
160	Place items on board in 60 seconds	0	14	55
161	Build tower of 8 cubes	0	5	18

All humans and their close relatives (e.g. the chimpanzee) share the majority of their genome (Vigilant, Stoneking, Harpending, Hawkes, & Wilson, 1991). Genetic variability in behaviour occurs when people carry different alleles of a gene at a particular locus influencing behaviour. Thus, we use the term "genetic influence" to describe variance in the small minority of genes that are polymorphic (i.e. that have different alleles) and that affect behaviour (cf. Wahlsten, 1994).

The relative role of genetic and environmental influence on intelligence might be resolved through analysis of adopted children, for, in this circumstance, the correlation that is usually present between genotype and environment is reduced or absent. Adoption studies indicate that intelligence scores for adopted children are correlated with intelligence scores for biological parents and for adoptive parents—Bouchard and McGue (1981) estimate these correlations as 0.22 and 0.19, respectively, which is roughly half the magnitude of the average correlation between parents and offspring (Bouchard and McGue report a value of 0.42 on the basis of over 8000 pairs). It is difficult to estimate heritability precisely in the adoption design because of problems such as assortative mating, selective placement, and genotype-environment correlation and interaction (see Turkheimer, 1991), but these data converge on the conclusion that, for a wide range of ages, IQ scores are affected by heritable and environmental influences (Plomin, DeFries, & McClearn, 1990). This pattern could change with age. For example, genetic and environmental effects in adoption studies for infants in the second year are relatively weak. Plomin and DeFries (1985) review studies reporting IQ correlations for biological mothers and their adopted away infants, and they report a range of values between −0.01 and 0.09. These studies did not provide correlations between adopted children and adoptive parents so environmental effects cannot be assessed, but the data suggest that genetic effects on general intelligence as revealed by adoption studies are modest during the second year. More recent data are available from the Colorado Adoption Project, which includes longitudinal data from adopted children, their biological parents, their adopted parents, and their adopted siblings. The parent–offspring correlations from this study (for both biological parents pooled) are 0.14 and 0.12 at 12 and 24 months, the parent–adoptee correlations are 0.09 and 0.05, and the nonadopted control correlations are 0.05 and 0.14 (Fulker, DeFries, & Plomin, 1988). The magnitude of these effects is small, but, as Plomin (1986) notes, the genetic relation between parent and offspring requires both heritability and an age-to-age genetic correlation (i.e. genetic variance in infancy must be correlated with genetic variance in adulthood). From this perspective, the parent–offspring correlation, although small, implies significant heritability and genetic correlation.

Twin studies offer a second perspective on genetic and environmental effects on intelligence by comparing monozygotic (MZ) twins to dizygotic (DZ) twins. MZ twins have a 100% chance of sharing any relevant alleles found in their co-twin. DZ twins (and siblings) are considered 50% similar genetically in the sense that there is a 50% chance that relevant alleles can be traced back to a common ancestor. That is, the chance that both twins (or siblings) share a particular allele from their father is $0.5 \times 0.5 = 0.25$, and the chance of sharing an allele from their mother is $0.5 \times 0.5 = 0.25$. These two probabilities sum to 0.50, which reflects the probability of tracing any shared psychologically relevant allele back to a parent (Plomin et al., 1990). In contrast, it is often assumed that twins who are reared together, be they MZ or DZ, have the same degree of shared environment. Under the traditional assumptions of Mendelian genetics, the difference between the MZ twin correlation and 1.0 can be attributed to influences that impinge upon one twin and not the other. This quantity is called unique environment, or nonshared environment, and is labelled "e^2". The difference between the MZ twin correlation and the DZ twin correlation reflects half of the variance that can be accounted for by shared genetic effects (i.e. it is a contrast between pairs sharing 100% of their genes and pairs sharing 50% of their genes). To account for the full genetic effect (labelled "h^2"), the difference between the MZ twin correlation and DZ twin correlation is doubled. Finally, the MZ twin correlation minus the genetic variance reflects the variance that can be accounted for by shared environment. The effect of shared environment is labelled "c^2".

Estimates of heritability and environmental influences can be affected by violations of various assumptions of the behavioural genetic model. However, the most salient impact of violating these assumptions is to complicate the comparison of influences measured with different samples, different instruments, or in different laboratories. For a series of measures collected longitudinally or for similar measures obtained at the same time, the relative magnitudes of MZ–DZ twin differences can provide valuable information about genetic and environmental influences across time and across measure (McGue, Bouchard, Iacono, & Lykken, 1993).

Before we review the data from twin studies, note that some implementations of the adoption design afford a similar analysis. For example, the design used in the Colorado Adoption Project allows a comparison of correlations between adopted siblings, whose shared identity by descent is 0%, and non-adopted siblings, whose genetic similarity is 50% (as explained earlier). The number of pairs is relatively small (between 61 and 82 pairs at 12 and 24 months) but would allow the detection of large effects. Plomin, DeFries, and Fulker (1988) report MDI correlations of 0.37 and 0.03 for nonadoptive versus adoptive pairs at 12 months and correlations of 0.42 and 0.12, respectively, at 24 months. This pattern of correlations suggests strong genetic effects and negligible environmental effects.

The Louisville Twin Study has been an important source of data on the development of MZ and DZ twins. Data from approximately 100 pairs of MZ twins and 100 pairs of DZ twins assessed longitudinally reveals MDI correlations of 0.68 and 0.63 for MZ and DZ twins at 12 months, 0.82 and 0.65 at 18 months, and 0.81 and 0.73 at 24 months (Wilson, 1983). These data suggest h^2 values of 0.10, 0.34, and 0.16, at 12, 18, and 24 months, respectively, and strong effects of shared environment. At 18 months and older, the MZ within-pair variance was significantly less than the DZ within-pair variance. These data support the conclusion that there are significant but modest genetic effects on individual differences in general intelligence as measured using the MDI during the second year. Indeed, the Louisville Twin Study twin correlations for general intelligence at 24 months equal or exceed the values generally reported for adults, which can be quantified as median twin correlations of approximately 0.80 for MZ pairs and 0.60 for DZ pairs (Bouchard & McGue, 1981; Loehlin & Nichols, 1976; McCartney, Harris, & Bernieri, 1990; McGue et al., 1993). The comparison of these values suggests that roughly half of the observed variation in general intelligence in adult humans and older infants is associated with genetic influence. Finally, when data from adopted and non-adopted siblings is combined with longitudinal data from twins, effects of heredity and environment can be estimated using sophisticated path models. Cardon, Fulker, DeFries, and Plomin (1992) and Fulker, Cherny, and Cardon (1993) combined data from children in the Colorado Adoption Project with data from the Twin-Infant Project (DiLalla et al., 1990) and a subset of the subjects described later. They found heritability estimates of 0.51–0.55, and 0.60–0.68 at 12 and 24 months, and shared environment estimates of 0.11–0.12 at 12 months and 0.18 at 24 months.

These findings suggest some heritable influence on general intelligence in the second year although there are discrepancies: Heritability estimates in the Louisville data are low when compared with estimates from the Colorado Adoption Project and the Twin-Infant Project. Also, the pattern of change in the age-specific influence of h^2 is unclear: Some data suggest increasing influence and other data suggest a more variable pattern. Effects of shared environment are also discrepant: Estimates from the Colorado Adoption Project and the Twin-Infant Project are low compared with estimates from the Louisville Twin Study.

GENETIC AND ENVIRONMENTAL INFLUENCES ON SPECIFIC MEASURES OF INFANT INTELLIGENCE

Language

Disorders of speech and language such as developmental dyslexia and stuttering appear to be heritable (DeFries, 1985; Howie, 1981; Lewis, Ekelman, & Aram, 1989; Lewis & Thompson, 1992; Pennington & Smith, 1983; Tallal, Ross, & Curtiss, 1989), but most models of normal language development focus on environmental mediators such as parental input. This environmental orientation predominates despite the fact that correlational studies usually confound environmental influence with genetic influence. For example, Lieven (1978) reports that mothers who are verbally responsive and engage in more dialogue have children who do a great deal of labelling and describing of objects (i.e. a referential style), and Goldfield (1993) reports that mothers who more often label toys during play have children who learn more nouns. Note that these effects could be mediated through the linguistic environment that the mother provides, through aspects of the child that evoke language relevant behavioural tendencies in mothers, or through a heterotypic genetic mechanism that induces infants to prefer nouns and that induces mothers to provide labels.

Huttenlocher, Haight, Bryk, Seltzer, and Lyons (1991) investigated these effects by comparing various indices of language input with growth rates for expressive vocabulary in the second year (defined as a quadratic function fit to each child's spontaneous utterances recorded at two- or four-month intervals). Their findings indicate that mothers who speak more have children who acquire vocabulary faster. Moreover, the relative frequency of specific words in maternal speech is related to the order of acquisition of those words. Huttenlocher et al. argue against child-driven causality: The quality of maternal speech does not change across the second year (also see Nelson & Bonvillian, 1973; Smolak & Weinraub, 1983), and child-driven causality is not a plausible explanation for the effect of word frequency. However, as Huttenlocher et al. note, their results do not preclude the possibility of substantial genetic effects.

The data from adoption studies suggest some genetic effect on early language. Hardy-Brown, Plomin, and DeFries (1981) used a full adoption design to contrast the effects of heredity and environment on language in one-year-old children. Children's communicative performance (defined as the first principal factor across a variety of linguistic measures such as vocalisation, gesture, imitation, and phonological ability) was affected by aspects of the behaviour of their adoptive mother but even more so by the cognitive abilities of their birth mother, suggesting genetic influence on language production in the first year. Hardy-Brown and Plomin (1985) reanalysed these data in comparison with nonadoptive control families and replicated the finding that infant communicative competence is signifi-cantly related to general cognitive ability of the birth mother and not the adoptive parents. This additional analysis also revealed that some maternal language variables (e.g. the tendency to imitate the infant's vocalisations) were related to infant communicative competence in both adoptive and nonadoptive homes, but other maternal language variables (e.g., the frequency of question sentences) were only related in nonadoptive homes. These different patterns of correlation suggest that some aspects of the home environment may be mediated by genetic factors shared by parent and child. Plomin et al. (1988) calculated separate correlations for the Bayley factors reported by Lewis et al. (1986). The verbal scale at 12 months had correlations of 0.22 and 0.21 for non-adoptive and adoptive pairs, which suggested no genetic influence but a moderate effect of shared environment. At 24 months, the factors labelled lexical and verbal, which appear to assess production and comprehension, indicated substantial genetic influence. Finally, Thompson and Plomin (1988) used the Sequenced Inventory of Communication Development to assess language in two- and three-year-old adoptees and found both environmental and genetic effects, with the latter effect increasing with age. The variable analysed by Thompson and Plomin was a combination of expressive and receptive items, but 60% of the items included in the composite were expressive. Thus, the genetic effect on language revealed by adoption studies is primarily an effect on expressive vocabulary, and willingness or ability to communicate.

Twin studies are a second tool for exploring genetic effects on language. This method is potentially problematic because twin language is unique in several ways. One aspect of the "twin situation" is that each twin receives less individually directed parental speech (Bornstein & Ruddy, 1984; Conway, Lytton, & Pysh, 1980; Lytton, Conway, & Sauve, 1977; Stafford, 1987; Tomasello, Mannle, & Kruger, 1986). A second aspect is that twins often participate in three-way conversations in which they may commu-nicate with either the parent or the co-twin (Savic, 1980). Research on twin versus non-twin language is sparse, particularly regarding comparisons during the second year for children speaking English. Moreover, when quantitative differences emerge, they may reflect auxiliary processes such as a tendency to complete each other's utterances (Savic, 1979—for twins learning Serbo-Croatian) or syntactic or semantic adaptations to twin status such as misuse of plurals or pronouns (Malmstrom & Silva, 1986). There is a traditional belief that twin language is developmentally delayed (Day, 1932; McCarthy, 1954), but detailed analysis of twin language reveals some domains in which twins are more advanced than singletons. For example, twins acquire the use of "I" relatively quickly (Savic, 1980).

Claims that twins have delayed language could arise because twins tend to have low birth weight, but data from the Louisville Twin Study suggests that this difference dissipates over time (Wilson, 1977). Moreover, to the extent that both MZ and DZ twins are at risk for low birth weight, delay would not affect estimates of heritability.

The presence of a same-aged sibling certainly alters the linguistic environment, and unique aspects of the twin linguistic environment necessitate some caution in interpreting language data from twins. But, these circumstances do not preclude using twins to contrast genetic and environmental effects on language acquisition. In some sense, the twin situation for learning language can be viewed as a special case of the multi-sibling family context, albeit one in which there is no spacing between two of the siblings.

Twin studies suggest a genetic effect on language in preschool-aged children. Mittler (1969) administered the Illinois Test of Psycholinguistic Abilities to four-year-old MZ and DZ twins. Subtests that measure expressive language (e.g. the Vocal Encoding subtest in which the child is asked to describe simple objects, or the Auditory–Vocal Automatic subtest, which measures inflectional aspects of grammar), revealed significant heritable effects. Subtests that should be sensitive to receptive language (e.g. the Auditory Encoding subtest, which assesses the child's ability to understand the spoken word) suggest no heritable effects. Munsinger and Douglass (1976) administered tests of language compre-hension and the receptive and expressive use of syntactic forms to twin pairs aged 3.5 to 17.5 years, and found large estimates of heritability for all measures. Mather and Black (1984) tested preschool twins (mean age = 4.5 years) on standardised measures of vocabulary comprehension, semantic knowledge, morphology, syntax, and articulation (see Mather and Black for a detailed description of the specific measures) and found significant heritability for comprehension and environmental influence for the other measures. However, note that language comprehension skill has a strong relation to measures of general intellectual ability (e.g. the Peabody Picture Vocabulary Test used by Mather and Black to measure comprehension correlates highly with measures of IQ). In a detailed reanalysis of these data, Locke and Mather (1989) discovered that MZ twin pairs were significantly more likely to mispronounce the same sounds on an articulation test than were DZ twin pairs, who in turn shared more errors than children who were unrelated. Finally, Matheny and Brugge-mann (1972) used the Templin-Darley Screening Test of Articulation with twins four to eight years of age and found greater MZ similarity than DZ similarity for boys.

These studies suggest a genetic effect on expressive language in preschool-aged twins, but we know little about genetic and environmental effects on language in the second year, particularly for receptive skills. Leonard, Newhoff, and Mesalam (1980) explored the phonological development in a single set of identical twins from 19 to 22 months. These data suggest some similarities and differences between twins but do not allow a comparison of genetic and environmental effects. Benson, Cherny, Haith, and Fulker (1993) administered the Sequenced Inventory of Communicative Development at five, seven, and nine months to MZ and DZ twins. They found consistent positive correlations with midparent general intelligence (measured using the Wechsler Adult Intelligence Scale-Revised) for the expressive scale and less consistent results for the receptive scale, but separate MZ and DZ twin correlations were not reported. Cardon and Fulker (1991) reported that a measure of vocalisation ability for this sample at nine months suggested an h^2 of 0.51 and a c^2 of 0.38, both statistically significant.

Non-verbal measures

We know of no literature on genetic or environmental influences on non-verbal ability as defined as performance on the set of MDI questions that do not require language. However, there has been some interest in genetic or environmental influences on specific tasks that measure non-verbal abilities. For example, neural mechanisms have been identified that may account for individual differences in attentiveness (Colombo, 1995), but these mechanisms could be influenced by genetic or environmental effects. The role of genetic mediation of attentiveness has also been addressed using observer report. Matheny (1980, 1983) factor-analysed the Bayley Infant Behaviour Record and found a coherent cluster among items in which the observer noted the child's tendency to remain attentive, responsive, and goal directed during administration of the BSID. Twin data from the Louisville Twin Study indicated that this construct, labelled "task orientation", was significantly heritable at 12, 18, and 24 months. Braungart, Plomin, DeFries, and Fulker (1992) replicated this effect in an analysis of sibling adoption data and twin data, and reported heritability at 12 and 24 months of 0.40 and 0.47, respectively.

THE MACARTHUR LONGITUDINAL TWIN STUDY

The MacArthur Longitudinal Twin Study is an ongoing behavioural genetic investigation of cognitive, social, emotional, and temperamental aspects of behaviour being conducted at the Institute for Behavioral Genetics at the University of Colorado. Four hundred and twenty-one same-sexed twin pairs (equally distributed by sex) were recruited from monthly reports of births from the Colorado Department of Health.

Twins were selected preferentially for higher birth weight (1700g or more) and normal gestational age (34 weeks or more), but some small healthy infants were included. The average birth weight for the sample was 2579g (SD = 469). Birth weights were normally distributed and ranged between 1191 and 4763g. Only 4% of the infants weighed less than 1700g at birth.

Eligible families were invited to participate via a letter, and over 50% accepted. The ethnic distribution of the participating families was 88.5% European-American, 9% Hispanic-American, and 2.5% African-American. The vast majority were two-parent families with both parents somewhat older than the average Colorado parents of newborns (30 years vs. 28 years) and more educated (14.3 years vs. 12.5 years).

We will focus on data from the 408 twin pairs for whom Bayley scores were available at 14, 20, or 24 months. The Bayley was administered at home visits. The first occurred between 13.5 and 15.5 months, the second between 19.5 and 21.5 months, and the third between 23.5 and 26.5 months. Two female examiners visited each home. Examiners were blind to any previous data related to the Bayley MDI. Examiners were not blind to zygosity to the extent that zygosity was determined on the basis of examiner ratings of the twin pair's physical similarity (as will be described later) and was often obvious for DZ twins. However, each examiner was blind to the ratings of zygosity provided by other examiners and to the final zygosity determination, which was defined on the basis of average agreement across raters.

The relatively long test battery (described in full by Emde et al., 1992) and the need to complete all testing in a single visit, necessitated that the twins be tested simultaneously on the MDI. To accomplish this, the examiners worked independently in separate rooms with the twin seated in a high chair. In most cases the mother hovered in the doorway in sight of both twins. In the few cases in which a twin refused to cooperate, the mother held that twin on her lap. If both twins refused to cooperate, the examiners rescheduled the home visit and returned on a subsequent day.

The mental development component of the BSID (Bayley, 1969) was administered with the child seated in a high chair, but a few children sat in a booster seat or in the mother's lap. The test was administered according to standardised procedures, with basal and ceiling levels established to derive the MDI. Items from the expressive and receptive components of the Sequenced Inventory of Communication Development (SICD; Hedrick, Prather, & Tobin, 1975) were administered concurrently with the BSID, but will not be our focus here. Note that the unusual testing configuration and the concurrent administration of SICD items may have affected MDI scores in some general way, but the non-standard test procedure should have the same effect on MZ and DZ twins.

Zygosity of the twins was determined through aggregation of independent tester ratings on the similarity of 10 physical attributes across age. The
attributes were selected on the basis of the diagnostic rules developed by
Nichols and Bilbro (1966). When the features of the pair of twins were
rated consistently as highly similar (i.e. scores of 1 or 2 on a five-point
scale), the classification of MZ was made. When two or more features were
only somewhat similar (i.e. a score of 3) or if one feature was not at all
similar (i.e. score of 4 or 5), the classification of DZ was made. Zygosity of
twin pairs was rated by independent testers at various ages and in various
contexts. The modal number of zygosity ratings per subject was 18. Twin
zygosity was considered unambiguous if there was 85% agreement of the
MZ or DZ classification across all testers at all ages, on the basis of a
minimum of four ratings. The current zygosity distribution for the 408
families is: 210 MZ pairs, 177 DZ pairs, and 21 ambiguous pairs. Data from
the ambiguous pairs were excluded from the present analyses.

Measuring specific constructs

Administration procedures for the BSID dictated that each infant be
tested on items that spanned the infant's range of competence. Thus, all
infants were tested on some items from each construct but no infant was
tested on all items from each construct. To calculate specific scores, we
accepted the logic of the administration procedure and assumed that each
infant would have passed the items on that construct that were not
administered because they were too easy and would have failed the items
on that construct that were not administered because they were too hard.
These assumptions raise some questions but must be accepted because of
practical constraints on testing young children. A child who is required to
respond to a large set of non-challenging items will become fatigued, and a
child who is required to respond to a large set of overly challenging items
will become frustrated. In either case, performance will deteriorate. The
strategy used in this study (i.e. giving infants a score of 1 for items not
administered because they were too easy and a score of 0 for items not
administered because they were too hard) establishes a balance between
the quality and quantity of measurement for each child.

The percentage of infants passing each item at each age is listed in
Table 5.1. To form constructs, items on the BSID that had either 100% or
0% correct at a particular age were eliminated, and percentage correct was
calculated across the items at each age that were classified as relevant to
expressive language, receptive language, or non-verbal ability. Cronbach's
alphas (Cronbach, 1951) were relatively low for the receptive construct,
0.40, 0.65, and 0.66 at 14, 20, and 24 months, respectively, and for the
expressive construct at 14 months (0.52), but were above 0.80 for the non-

verbal construct at each assessment and for expressive language at 20 and 24 months. As would be expected, alpha is lower for constructs based on fewer items: The correlation between alpha and number of items in the construct for expressive and receptive language measures was 0.88. Does lower alpha for the receptive items indicate that this construct has been measured less well? We think not on the basis of various evidence. First, cross-time correlations (listed in Table 5.2) were of comparable magnitude across the specific measures. Second, cross-measure correlations (listed in Table 5.3) indicate that expressive and receptive scores were correlated with the MDI at about the same magnitude at each assessment. Third, previous reports have established the validity of the present measures based on comparisons between mid-twin scores and parent-reported scores for the dyad (see Reznick, Corley, & Robinson, 1997). Finally, the expressive and receptive language scores used here were significantly correlated with scores based on items from the SICD expressive and receptive scales, with correlations ranging between 0.38 and 0.69.

MZ versus DZ twin correlations

As a preliminary approach for identifying genetic and environmental influences, we calculated MZ and DZ intraclass correlations. As indicated in Table 5.4, correlations for MZ and DZ twins were relatively high for the MDI and each of the specific measures, but the magnitude of these correlations, and the relation between MZ and DZ correlations varied across measure and across time. All DZ correlations were significantly above chance, suggesting the presence of genetic and/or environmental effects. MZ correlations were significantly greater than DZ correlations at each age for the MDI, suggesting the presence of genetic effects, and DZ correlations exceeded half the MZ correlations, suggesting shared environmental effects at 20 and 24 months. However, this general

TABLE 5.2
Cross-time Correlations

Variable	14–24 Months	14–20 Months	20–24 Months
BSID MDI	0.44 (646)	0.48 (641)	0.67 (614)
Non-verbal	0.33 (652)	0.38 (653)	0.49 (624)
Verbal expressive	0.32 (651)	0.35 (653)	0.58 (624)
Verbal receptive	0.29 (650)	0.33 (652)	0.49 (623)

Values are Pearson Product Moment correlations with degrees of freedom listed in parenthesis. All correlations are statistically significant, $p < 0.01$.

TABLE 5.3
Correlations Among Dependent Variables at Each Age

	NVB	EXP	REC
14 months:			
BSID MDI	0.86 (747)	0.52 (747)	0.55 (747)
Non-verbal		0.37 (751)	0.40 (751)
Verbal expressive			0.30 (750)
20 months:			
BSID MDI	0.78 (660)	0.71 (660)	0.68 (660)
Non-verbal		0.34 (668)	0.44 (668)
Verbal expressive			0.54 (668)
24 months:			
BSID MDI	0.76 (664)	0.74 (664)	0.68 (663)
Non-verbal		0.42 (668)	0.46 (667)
Verbal expressive			0.51 (667)

Values are Pearson Product Moment correlations with degrees of freedom in parentheses. All correlations are statistically significant, $p < 0.01$.

statement was not true across the specific measures. The non-verbal MDI construct suggested genetic effects at each assessment (i.e. MZ correlations were greater than DZ correlations), but the receptive language measure indicated environmental effects at each assessment (i.e. MZ correlations were comparable to DZ correlations). Expressive language correlations were similar to the pattern for the MDI, suggesting both genetic and shared environmental effects.

Estimating h^2, c^2, and e^2

Univariate estimates of h^2, c^2, and e^2 were computed according to the model described by DeFries and Fulker (1988) and extended by Cyphers, Phillips, Fulker, and Mrazek (1990). The parameters for h^2, c^2, e^2 for each variable at each age are presented in Table 5.5. One-tailed t-tests were used to evaluate the statistical significance of each calculated parameter (i.e. h^2 and c^2) relative to its standard error.

GENETIC AND ENVIRONMENTAL INFLUENCES ON GENERAL AND SPECIFIC ABILITIES

We subdivided the items that comprise the Bayley MDI into three distinct categories and eliminated the few items whose categorisation was ambiguous. The index of expressive language was derived on the basis of

TABLE 5.4
Twin Intraclass Correlations

Variable	14 Months			20 Months			24 Months		
	MZ	DZ	MZ vs. DZ	MZ	DZ	MZ vs. DZ	MZ	DZ	MZ vs. DZ
BSID MDI	0.58** (199)	0.38** (169)	2.46*	0.80** (174)	0.64** (146)	3.18**	0.83** (176)	0.61** (152)	4.56**
Non-verbal	0.54** (202)	0.28** (172)	2.96**	0.63** (179)	0.35** (150)	3.58**	0.67** (178)	0.42** (153)	3.50**
Verbal expressive	0.36** (200)	0.28** (171)	0.86	0.76** (178)	0.58** (150)	3.31**	0.81** (177)	0.55** (152)	4.93**
Verbal receptive	0.38** (200)	0.36** (171)	0.19	0.56** (178)	0.56** (150)	0.00	0.54** (177)	0.50** (152)	0.45

Statistical tests for correlations are one-tailed. Number below correlation is degrees of freedom. Comparison of MZ vs. DZ correlations based on one-tailed z-scores. $* = p < 0.05$; $** = p < 0.01$.

TABLE 5.5

Estimates of Genetic (h^2), Shared Environmental (c^2), and Unique Environmental (e^2) Variance at Each Age

Variable	14 Months			20 Months			24 Months		
	h^2	c^2	e^2	h^2	c^2	e^2	h^2	c^2	e^2
BSID MDI	0.39* (0.18)	0.19 (0.14)	0.42	0.34* (0.15)	0.45* (0.12)	0.21	0.45* (0.15)	0.37* (0.12)	0.18
Non-verbal	0.52* (0.19)	0.02 (0.15)	0.46	0.55* (0.19)	0.07 (0.15)	0.38	0.50* (0.18)	0.16 (0.15)	0.34
Verbal expressive	0.16 (0.19)	0.19 (0.15)	0.65	0.35* (0.16)	0.40* (0.13)	0.30	0.49* (0.16)	0.30* (0.13)	0.21
Verbal receptive	0.02 (0.19)	0.33* (0.15)	0.65	0.002 (0.18)	0.53* (0.15)	0.47	0.08 (0.19)	0.45* (0.15)	0.47

Statistical tests for h^2 and c^2 are one-tailed. Parameter of 0.00 indicates use of constrained model. Number in parenthesis is standard error corrected for double entry. * = $p < 0.05$.

the infant's spontaneous comments and on speech that could be evoked in various contexts in the laboratory and the home. This measure is related to word knowledge, but also taps discourse ability and talkativeness. The index of receptive language was derived on the basis of the child's response to questions and thus reflects knowledge of word reference but also the child's compliance with a request to point to, hand over, or look at a particular stimulus. The non-verbal abilities tapped in the BSID are obviously different from non-verbal aspects of intelligence in adults, but capture a range of non-verbal skills that infants acquire or perfect during the second year, including fine motor coordination, ability to imitate, and ability to use a means–end strategy to solve simple problems.

It is interesting to note that despite the obvious differences among the items in the three partitions, the three specific constructs were consistently correlated, with values ranging between 0.30 and 0.54. A mundane interpretation is that the relation among constructs could be a methodological artifact. That is, in the administration of the BSID, testing ends after a series of failures. If a child performs poorly on one type of item (e.g. non-verbal), testing will end before difficult items in the other categories can be administered, which obviously lowers the potential score on the other categories and causes the three scores to be similar. This would be particularly problematic for an infant who performs poorly on the relatively abundant non-verbal items. In future research, it would be interesting to administer the MDI items separately by category, establishing a basal and ceiling level independently for each category.

An alternative interpretation of the correlation among specific abilities is that although most items have an obvious primary designation, ability in the other domains also influences performance. For example, response on the expressive and non-verbal questions might be enhanced if the infant comprehends what the experimenter is saying. This point has a broader extension: A child who is motivated, attentive, or easy-going would be likely to perform better across the range of items. Finally, to return to an earlier theme, the correlation among separable abilities can be a strong incentive for positing a general aspect of intelligence, which in the present circumstance is exactly the interpretation usually given to the MDI score. The question that remains is whether or not general intelligence as measured by the MDI score helps us understand behavioural development.

The heritability estimates here generally replicate and extend previously reported effects for the present cohort in which expressive and receptive composites were composed of items from the BSID and the SICD (Reznick, Corley, & Robinson, 1997). The twin correlations for receptive language are notably lower in the present study, particularly at 14 months. This change in the correlations affects the statistical significance of some parameter estimates, but the overarching story remains the same.

From the general-intelligence perspective (i.e. if we focus on the MDI), we learn that there is a genetic influence throughout the second year. Shared environment exerts some influence across the second year, but its effect is not statistically significant until 20 months. These findings make intuitive sense, but by the same token, are relatively banal: The assertion that genes and environment both affect behaviour offers little insight into the nature of intelligence and how it develops.

If we look at specific measures of intelligence, we find three strikingly different patterns. Twin correlations for the non-verbal MDI items are notably larger for MZ than DZ twins at each age, producing strong estimates of h^2 (0.50 or greater at each age). This pattern is consistent with conclusions on the basis of the MDI but suggests an even stronger genetic effect for non-verbal cognitive abilities. Also, DZ correlations for the non-verbal measure are notably lower than DZ correlations for the MDI and MZ correlations remain high, which suggests a weaker effect of shared environment.

The strong genetic effect on the non-verbal measure invites the hypothesis that there is a set of fundamental cognitive processes that are language-independent and that unfold during the second year under strong genetic constraints. This construct reflects diverse cognitive abilities such as the child's ability to gather new information, to retain information, to compare new information with existing knowledge, to understand and apply causal principles, and to imitate. Alternatively, or perhaps, additionally, non-verbal performance could reflect traits that might be temperamental such as mastery motivation, persistence, or distractibility. For example, Saudino and Eaton (1995) report genetic effects on activity level in twins younger and older than twins tested here. It seems likely that an extremely active child would perform relatively poorly on the non-verbal items. Whatever the mechanism, the non-verbal construct seems to be the locus of genetic effects on the MDI and is affected only slightly by shared environment.

Age-specific twin correlations for receptive language are large and relatively similar for MZ and DZ twins, which suggests significant shared environmental effects at each age. Children learn to comprehend the language that they are taught, so environmental effects on receptive language are not surprising. Receptive language could be influenced by factors in the shared environment such as the quality and quantity of the language the child hears, or other aspects of parental style such as preferred mode of interaction (e.g. tendency to ask questions; responsiveness vs. intrusiveness) or choice of activities (e.g naming games, book reading). Our data do not allow specification of the environmental mechanisms that affect language, but subsequent work on this topic may be warranted because of the potential usefulness of early interventions that promote language competence. The lack of a genetic effect on receptive language argues against a genetically mediated mechanism whereby some individuals grasp words more quickly than others, at least during the second year.

Age-specific twin correlations for expressive language are moderate at 14 months and are comparable for MZ and DZ twins. Twin correlations are notably larger at 20 months, with increased differences between MZ and DZ correlations at 20 and 24 months. This pattern suggests effects of genetics and shared environment on expressive language late in the second year. The lack of effects at 14 months could be a measurement problem: Expressive language is rare at 14 months and increases dramatically later in the second year. However, this complaint is blunted given that twin correlations at 14 months are moderate and cross-time correlations for the expressive language measure are comparable to the values reported for other measures, which would not be the case if measurement at 14 months were inadequate.

An environmental effect on expressive language is to be expected, given the mechanisms stated previously. For example, Huttenlocher et al. (1991) report that individual differences in infant expressive vocabulary are related to the amount that mothers speak to their infants, and that the age of acquisition for individual words can be predicted by the frequency of those words in maternal speech. The genetic effect on expressive language is more intriguing. Locke (Locke, 1990; Locke & Mather, 1989) has argued for the innateness of phonological development, and previous research with adoptees indicates that communicative performance in the first year defined across measures such as vocalisation, gesture, imitation, and phonological ability is more highly correlated with the birth mother than with the adoptive mother (Hardy-Brown et al., 1981; Hardy-Brown & Plomin, 1985). Communicative competence measures at two and three years also show genetic as well as environmental effects (Thompson & Plomin, 1988). This study bridges the gap between these reports and suggests there is genetic influence on expressive language during the second year as well.

The index of expressive language used in this study reflects both the range of the child's expressive vocabulary and, also, the child's willingness to communicate in the presence of an unfamiliar examiner. Genetics could affect the size of the expressive lexicon. For example, Huttenlocher et al. (1991) suggest that there are genetic influences on the child's capacity to learn from input. However, this interpretation would also suggest genetic effects on receptive language but these effects are weak at 20 and 24 months. Thus, we favour an interpretation in which the genetic effect on expressive language is mediated by temperamental factors. This aspect is particularly salient in the present context because an unwillingness to talk in an unfamiliar situation is related to a heritable temperamental disposition toward shyness and fearfulness (Robinson, Kagan, Reznick, & Corley, 1992) and is more likely among MZ twins (DiLalla, Kagan, & Reznick, 1994). The measure of expressive language used in this study is related to knowledge (e.g. the expressive measure is correlated with the receptive measure), but a considerable amount of variance may be accounted for by other influences such as discourse ability and talkativeness. Further research with twins should assess the competence component of expressive ability, which can be measured using extensive recordings of spontaneous production (e.g. as in Huttenlocher et al., 1991). This aspect of expressive ability can be contrasted with the performance component tapped by the measurement procedures used in this study.

CONCLUSION

General measures of intelligence can be useful as a basis for diagnosis and prediction, but have less utility for the study of development (at least, for the MDI measured during the second year of life). The strategy test makers use for selecting items dictates that a normal individual's score will hover at the same level over time. Moreover, an exploration of genetic and environmental influences on a general measure of intelligence reveals robust but undifferentiated effects (i.e. genes and environment affect scores at most assessments). This *mélange* of influences can be decomposed in the context of specific measures: There is strong genetic influence on non-verbal performance, strong environmental influence on receptive language, and both genetic and environmental influence on expressive language. We believe that this multifaceted approach offers the most interesting view of behavioural development. Additional work is needed to develop valid and reliable measures of separate aspects of infant intelligence and to examine development from this perspective.

The results reported here emerged through collaboration among a group of investigators, including J.C. DeFries, R.N. Emde, and D. Fulker at the University of Colorado; J. Campos at the University of California at Berkeley; J. Kagan at Harvard University; R. Plomin at the Pennsylvania State University; J. Robinson at the University of Colorado Health Services Center; and C. Zahn-Waxler at the National Institute of Mental Health. This research was supported by the John D. and Catherine T. MacArthur Foundation through its Research Network on Early Childhood Transitions.

We thank the families who contributed their time and effort, as well as the many research assistants at the University of Colorado, Harvard University, Yale

University, and The Pennsylvania State University who were involved in data collection, behavioural coding, and data management.

Correspondence concerning this chapter should be addressed to J. Steven Reznick, Psychology Department, CB#3270, University of North Carolina, Chapel Hill, NC 27599-3270; Email: reznick@unc.edu

REFERENCES

Anastasi, A. (1976). *Psychological testing* (4th ed.). New York: Macmillan.

Anisfeld, M. (1984). *Language development from birth to three*. Hillsdale, NJ: Lawrence Erlbaum Associates Inc.

Bates, E., Bretherton, I., & Snyder, L. (1988). *From first words to grammar: Individual differences and dissociable mechanisms.* Cambridge, UK: Cambridge University Press.

Bayley, N. (1933). *The California first year mental scale.* Berkeley, CA: University of California Press.

Bayley, N. (1969). *Manual for the Bayley scales of infant development.* New York: Psychological Corporation.

Bayley, N. (1970). Development of mental abilities. In P.H. Mussen (Ed.), *Carmichael's manual of child psychology* (Vol. I, 3rd ed., pp. 1163–1209). New York: Wiley.

Bayley, N. (1993). *Manual for Bayley scales of infant development* (2nd ed.). San Antonio, TX: Psychological Corporation.

Benson, J.B., Cherny, S.S., Haith, M.M., & Fulker, D.W. (1993). Rapid assessment of infant predictors of adult IQ: Midtwin-midparent analyses. *Developmental Psychology, 29*, 434–447.

Bloom, L. (1970). *Language development.* Cambridge, MA: MIT Press.

Bloom, L. (1973). *One word at a time: The use of single word utterances before syntax.* The Hague, The Netherlands: Mouton.

Bornstein, M.H., & Ruddy, M.G. (1984). Infant attention and maternal stimulation: Prediction of cognitive and linguistic development in singletons and twins. In H. Bouma & D.G. Bouwhuis (Eds), *Attention and performance X: Control of language processes* (pp. 433–445). Hove, UK: Lawrence Erlbaum Associates Ltd.

Bouchard, T.J., Jr., & McGue, M. (1981). Familial studies of intelligence: A review. *Science, 212*, 1055–1059.

Braungart, J.M., Plomin, R., DeFries, J.C., & Fulker, D.W. (1992). Genetic influence on tester-rated infant temperament as assessed by Bayley's Infant Behavior Record: Nonadoptive and adoptive siblings and twins. *Developmental Psychology, 28*, 40–47.

Brooks, J., & Weinraub, M. (1976). A history of infant intelligence testing. In M. Lewis (Ed.), *Origins of intelligence: Infancy and early childhood* (pp. 19–58). New York: Plenum Press.

Burns, W.J., Burns, K.A., & Kabacoff, R.I. (1992). Item and factor analyses of the Bayley Scales of Infant Development. In C.K. Rovee-Collier & L.P. Lipsitt (Eds), *Advances in infancy research* (Vol. 7, pp. 199–214). Norwood, NJ: Ablex.

Cardon, L.R., & Fulker, D.W. (1991). Sources of continuity in infant predictors of later IQ. *Intelligence, 15*, 279–293.

Cardon, L.R., Fulker, D.W., DeFries, J.C., & Plomin, R. (1992). Continuity and change in general cognitive ability from 1 to 7 years of age. *Developmental Psychology, 28*, 64–73.

Cattell, P. (1960). *The measurement of intelligence of infants and young children.* New York: Science Press/Psychological Corporation (Original work published 1940).

Colombo, J. (1993). *Infant cognition: Predicting later intellectual functioning.* Newbury Park, CA: Sage.

Colombo, J. (1995). On the neural mechanisms underlying developmental and individual differences in visual fixation in infancy: Two hypotheses. *Developmental Review, 15,* 97–135.

Conway, D., Lytton, H., & Pysh, F. (1980). Twin–singleton language differences. *Canadian Journal of Behavioral Science, 12,* 264–271.

Cronbach, L.J. (1951). Coefficient alpha and the internal structure of tests. *Psychometrika, 16,* 297–234.

Cronbach, L.J. (1967). Year-to-year correlations of mental tests: A review of the Hofstaetter analysis. *Child Development, 38,* 283–289.

Cyphers, L.H., Phillips, K., Fulker, D.W., & Mrazek, D.A. (1990). Twin temperament during the transition from infancy to early childhood. *Journal of the American Academy of Child and Adolescent Psychiatry, 29,* 392–397.

Dale, P.S., Bates, E., Reznick, J.S., & Morisset, C. (1989). The validity of a parent report instrument of child language at 20 months. *Journal of Child Language, 16,* 239–249.

Darwin, C. (1859). *On the origin of species by means of natural selection or the preservation of favoured races in the struggle for life.* New York: Appleton.

Day, E.J. (1932). The development of language in twins: Vol. I. A comparison of twins and single children. *Child Development, 3,* 179–199.

DeFries, J.C. (1985). Colorado Reading Project. In D.B. Gray & J.F. Kavanagh (Eds), *Biobehavioral measures of dyslexia.* Parkton, MD: York Press.

DeFries, J.C., & Fulker, D.W. (1988). Multiple regression analysis of twin data: Etiology of deviant score versus individual differences. *Acta Geneticae Medicae et Gemeologiae, 37,* 205–216.

DiLalla, L.F., Kagan, J., & Reznick, J.S. (1994), Genetic etiology of behavioral inhibition among two-year-old children. *Infant Behavior and Development, 17,* 401–408.

DiLalla, L.F., Thompson, L.A., Plomin, R., Phillips, K., Fagan, J.F., Haith, M.H., Cyphers, L.H., & Fulker, D.W. (1990). Infant predictors of preschool and adult IQ: A study of infant twins and their parents. *Developmental Psychology, 26,* 759–769.

Dunst, C.J. (1978). The structure of infant intelligence: An historical overview. *Intelligence, 2,* 381–391.

Emde, R., Campos, J., Corley, R., DeFries, J., Fulker, D., Kagan, J., Plomin, R., Reznick, J.S., Robinson, J., & Zahn-Waxler, C. (1992). Temperament, emotion, and cognition at 14 months: The MacArthur Longitudinal Twin Study. *Child Development, 63,* 1437–1455.

Fulker, D.W., Cherny, S.S., & Cardon, L.R. (1993). Continuity and change in cognitive development. In R. Plomin & G.E. McClearn (Eds), *Nature, nurture, and psychology* (pp. 77–97). Washington, DC: American Psychological Association.

Fulker, D.W., DeFries, J.C., & Plomin, R. (1988). Genetic influences on general mental ability increases between infancy and middle childhood. *Nature, 336,* 767–769.

Galton, F. (1883). *Inquiries into human faculty and its development.* London: Macmillan.

Galton, F. (1962). *Hereditary genius: An inquiry into its laws and consequences.* Cleveland, OH: World Publishing Co. (Original work published 1869)

Gardner, H. (1983). *Frames of mind: The theory of multiple intelligences.* New York: Basic Books.

Gesell, A. (1925). *The mental growth of the preschool child.* New York: Macmillan.

Gesell, A. (1928). *Infancy and human growth.* New York: Macmillan.

Goldfarb, W. (1943). Infant rearing and problem behavior. *American Journal of Orthopsychiatry, 13,* 249–265.

Goldfield, B.A. (1993). Noun bias in maternal speech to one-year-olds. *Journal of Child Language, 20,* 85–99.

Goodenough, F.L. (1939). Look to the evidence: A critique of recent experiments on raising the IQ. *Education Methods, 19,* 73–79.

Griffiths, R. (1954). *The abilities of babies: A study in mental measurement.* New York: McGraw-Hill.

Guilford, J.P. (1967). *The nature of human intelligence.* New York: McGraw-Hill.

Gyurke, J.S., Lynch, S.J., Lagasse, L., & Lipsitt, L.P. (1992). Speeded items: What do they tell us about an infant's performance? In C.K. Rovee-Collier & L.P. Lipsitt (Eds), *Advances in infancy research* (Vol. 7, pp. 215–225). Norwood, NJ: Ablex.

Hardy-Brown, K., & Plomin, R. (1985). Infant communicative development: Evidence from adoptive and biological families for genetic and environmental influences on rate differences. *Developmental Psychology, 21,* 378–385.

Hardy-Brown, K., Plomin, R., & DeFries, J.C. (1981). Genetic and environmental influences on the rate of communicative development in the first year of life. *Developmental Psychology, 17,* 704–717.

Hedrick, D.L., Prather, E.M., & Tobin, A.R. (1975). *Sequenced inventory of communication development.* Seattle, WA: University of Washington Press.

Hofstaetter, P.R. (1954). The changing composition of "intelligence": A study in T-technique. *Journal of Genetic Psychology, 85,* 159–164.

Howie, P.M. (1981). Concordance for stuttering in monozygotic and dizygotic twin pairs. *Journal of Speech and Hearing Research, 24,* 317–321.

Huttenlocher, J., Haight, W., Bryk, A., Seltzer, M., & Lyons, T. (1991). Early vocabulary growth: Relation to language input and gender. *Developmental Psychology, 27,* 236–248.

Kagan, J. (1981). *The second year.* Cambridge, MA: Harvard Press.

Kendler, H.H. (1987). *Historical foundations of modern psychology.* Chicago: Dorsey Press.

Kimble, G.A. (1993). Evolution of the nature–nurture issue in the history of psychology. In R. Plomin & G.E. McClearn (Eds), *Nature, nurture, and psychology* (pp. 3–25). Washington, DC: American Psychological Association.

Kohen-Raz, R. (1967). Scalogram analysis of some developmental sequences of infant behavior as measured by the Bayley Infant Scale of Mental Development. *Genetic Psychology Monographs, 76,* 3–21.

Leonard, L.B., Newhoff, M., & Mesalam, L. (1980). Individual differences in early child phonology. *Applied Psycholinguistics, 1,* 7–30.

Lewis, B.A., Ekelman, B.L., & Aram, D.M. (1989). A family study of severe phonological disorders. *Journal of Speech and Hearing Research, 23,* 713–724.

Lewis, B.A., & Thompson, L.A. (1992). A study of developmental speech and language disorders in twins. *Journal of Speech and Hearing Research, 35,* 1086–1094.

Lewis, M., & Brooks-Gunn, J. (1979). *Social cognition and the acquisition of self.* New York: Plenum Press.

Lewis, M., Jaskir, J., & Enright, M.K. (1986). The development of mental abilities in infancy. *Intelligence, 10,* 331–354.

Lieven, E.M. (1978). Conversations between mothers and young children: Individual differences and their possible implications for the study of language learning. In N. Waterson & C. Snow (Eds), *The development of communication: Social and pragmatic factors in language acquisition* (pp. 173–187). New York: John Wiley.

Locke, J.L. (1990). Structure and stimulation in the ontogeny of spoken language. *Developmental Psychobiology, 23,* 621–643.

Locke, J.L., & Mather, P.L. (1989). Genetic factors in the ontogeny of spoken language: Evidence from monozygotic and dizygotic twins. *Journal of Child Language, 16,* 553–559.

Loehlin, J.C., & Nichols, R.C. (1976). *Heredity, environment and personality.* Austin, TX: University of Texas Press.

Lytton, H., Conway, D., & Sauve, R. (1977). The impact of twinship on parent-child interaction. *Journal of Personality and Social Psychology, 25,* 97–107.

Malmstrom, P.M., & Silva, M.N. (1986). Twin talk: Manifestations of twin status in the speech of toddlers. *Journal of Child Language, 13,* 293–304.

Matheny, A.P., Jr. (1980). Bayley's Infant Behavior Record: Behavioral components and twin analyses. *Child Development, 51,* 1157–1167.

Matheny, A.P., Jr. (1983). A longitudinal twin study of stability of components from Bayley's Infant Behavior Record. *Child Development, 54,* 356–360.

Matheny, A.P., Jr., & Bruggemann, C. (1972). Articulation proficiency in twins and singletons from families of twins. *Journal of Speech and Hearing Research, 15,* 845–851.

Mather, P.L., & Black, K.N. (1984). Hereditary and environmental influences on preschool twins' language skills. *Developmental Psychology, 20,* 303–308.

McCarthy, D. (1954). Language development in children. In L. Carmichael (Ed.), *Manual of child psychology* (pp. 492–630). New York: Wiley.

McCartney, K., Harris, M.J., & Bernieri, F. (1990). Growing up and growing apart: A developmental meta-analysis of twin studies. *Psychological Bulletin, 107,* 226–237.

McGue, M., Bouchard, T.J., Jr., Iacono, W.G., & Lykken, D.T. (1993). Behavioral genetics of cognitive ability: A life-span perspective. In R. Plomin & G.E. McClearn (Eds), *Nature, nurture, and psychology* (pp. 59–76). Washington, DC: American Psychological Association.

Mittler, P. (1969). Genetic aspects of psycholinguistic abilities. *Journal of Child Psychology and Psychiatry, 10,* 165–176.

Munsinger, H., & Douglass, A., II. (1976). The syntactic abilities of identical twins, fraternal twins, and their siblings. *Child Development, 47,* 40–50.

Nelson, K. (1973). Structure and strategy in learning to talk. *Monographs of the Society for Research in Child Development, 38* (1–2, Serial No. 149).

Nelson, K., & Bonvillian, J. (1973). Concepts and words in the 18-month-old: Acquiring concept names under controlled conditions. *Cognition, 2,* 435–450.

Nichols, R.C., & Bilbro, W.C. (1966). The diagnosis of twin zygosity. *Acta Geneticae Medicae et Statistica, 16,* 265–275.

Pennington, B.F., & Smith, S.D. (1983). Genetic influences on learning disabilities and speech and language disorders. *Child Development, 54,* 369–387.

Piaget, J. (1952). *The origins of intelligence in children.* New York: Norton.

Plomin, R. (1986). *Development, genetics, and psychology*. Hillsdale, NJ: Lawrence Erlbaum Associates Inc.

Plomin, R., & DeFries, J.C., (1985). *Origins of individual difference in infancy: The Colorado Adoption Project*. New York: Academic Press.

Plomin, R., DeFries, J.C., & Fulker, D.W. (1988). *Nature and nurture during infancy and early childhood*. Cambridge, UK: Cambridge University Press.

Plomin, R., DeFries, J.C., & McClearn, G.E. (1990). *Behavioral genetics: A primer* (2nd ed.). New York: Freeman.

Reznick, J.S., Corley, R., & Robinson, J. (1997). A longitudinal twin study of intelligence in the second year. *Monographs of the Society for Research in Child Development, 62* (1, Serial No. 249).

Robinson, J.L., Kagan, J., Reznick, J.S., & Corley, R. (1992). The heritability of inhibited and uninhibited behavior: A twin study. *Developmental Psychology, 28*, 1030–1037.

Saudino, K.J., & Eaton, W.O. (1995). Continuity and change in objectively assessed temperament: A longitudinal twin study of activity level. *British Journal of Developmental Psychology, 13*, 81–95.

Savic, S. (1979). Mother–child verbal interaction: The functioning of completions in the twin situation. *Journal of Child Language, 6*, 153–158.

Savic, S. (1980). *How twins learn to talk*. New York: Academic Press.

Simpson, B.R. (1939). The wandering IQ: is it time to settle down? *Journal of Psychology, 7*, 351–367.

Smolak, L., & Weinraub, M. (1983). Maternal speech: Strategy or response? *Journal of Child Language, 10*, 369–380.

Spearman, C. (1904). General intelligence objectively determined and measured. *American Journal of Psychology, 14*, 201–293.

Stafford, L. (1987). Maternal input to twin and singleton children: Implications for language acquisition. *Human Communication Research, 13*, 429–462.

Stern, W. (1914). *The psychological methods of testing intelligence*. Baltimore, MD: Warwick & York.

Sternberg, R.J. (1977). *Intelligence, information processing, and analogical reasoning: The componential analysis of human abilities*. Hillsdale, NJ: Lawrence Erlbaum Associates Inc.

Stott, L., & Ball, R. (1965). Infant and preschool mental tests: Review and evaluation. *Monographs of the Society for Research in Child Development, 30* (3, Serial No. 101).

Tallal, P., Ross, R., & Curtiss, S. (1989). Familial aggregation in specific language impairment. *Journal of Speech and Hearing Disorders, 54*, 167–173.

Thompson, G.A. (1919). On the cause of hierarchical order among correlation coefficients. *Royal Society of London, A, 95*, 400–408.

Thompson, L.A., & Plomin, R. (1988). The sequenced inventory of communication development: An adoption study of two- and three-year olds. *International Journal of Behavioral Development, 11*, 219–231.

Thorndike, E. (1914). *Educational psychology, Vol. 3*. New York: Columbia University Press.

Tomasello, M., Mannle, S., & Kruger, A. (1986). Linguistic environment of 1- to 2-year-old twins. *Developmental Psychology, 22*, 169–176.

Turkheimer, E. (1991). Individual and group differences in adoption studies of IQ. *Psychological Bulletin, 110*, 392–405.

Vigilant, L., Stoneking, M., Harpending, H., Hawkes, K., & Wilson, A.C. (1991). African populations and the evolution of human mitochondrial DNA. *Science, 253,* 1503–1507.

Wahlsten, D. (1994). The intelligence of heritability. *Canadian Psychology, 35,* 244–260.

Wellman, B.L. (1932). Some new bases for interpretation of the IQ. *Journal of Genetic Psychology, 41,* 116–126.

Wilson, R.S. (1977). Mental development in twins. In A. Oliverio (Ed.), *Genetics, environment, and intelligence* (pp. 305–336). Alphen aan den Rijn, The Netherlands: Elsevier.

Wilson, R.S. (1983). The Louisville twin study: Developmental synchronies in behavior. *Child Development, 54,* 298–316.

Yarrow, L.J., Rubenstein, J.L., & Pedersen, F.A. (1975). *Infant and environment: Early cognitive and motivational development.* New York: Wiley.

PART THREE

Theories of intellectual development

CHAPTER SIX

The vertical mind—the case for multiple intelligences

Bruce Torff
Hofstra University, Long Island, NY, USA

Howard Gardner
Harvard University Project Zero, Cambridge, MA, USA

HORIZONTAL AND VERTICAL FACULTIES OF THE HUMAN MIND

Playing the guitar, solving a physics problem, throwing a baseball, fixing a car—these are among the challenges of life in a modern industrial society. Elsewhere in the world, people face different yet no less daunting tasks. For example, Trobriand Islanders have an elaborate scheme, one that involves no notation system, for determining ownership of land and for negotiating disputes (Hutchens, 1980). Individuals attaining a high level of competence in these activities can surely be said to be exhibiting intelligent behaviour. The question is: How is the mind set up to handle these diverse chores? Does the mind have a single, centralised system, or a set of separate cognitive mechanisms geared to particular kinds of information or tasks?

Befitting so fundamental a question, there is long-standing and wide-spread debate about the propriety of dividing human intellect into parts. Many disciplines feature "horizontalists" who believe in a single faculty and "verticalists" who favour a set of specialised faculties. In what follows, we describe and argue for a vertical approach: Howard Gardner's (1983/ 1993a) theory of multiple intelligences (hereafter "MI"). We begin with a summary of MI and then compare MI to other vertical faculty theories. In making comparisons among the conceptually diverse verticality theories, we will continue to use the neutral terminology—"horizontal faculties" refer to centralised structures or processes, and "vertical faculties" refer to sets of separate mechanisms (e.g. modules, domains, intelligences).

THE THEORY OF MULTIPLE INTELLIGENCES

In the late 19th century, as psychology struggled to become a scientific discipline in the manner of biology or physics, a heavy premium was placed upon the accumulation of quantitative "hard" data about human behaviour. The emergent "classical" view of human intelligence came to focus on psychometric tests—instruments designed to reveal individual variation in intellectual competence on the basis of numerical score on a standardised instrument.

The theory of multiple intelligences contrasts pointedly with the test-based approach. Concerned the intellectual skills that were never considered in the development of test instruments, Gardner endeavours to account for the wide range of intelligent performances that are valued in different societies. As a result, MI theory is not so much concerned with explaining the results of tests than with accounting for the variety of adult roles (or "end-states") that exist across cultures. MI is an attempt at a comprehensive theory of intellect, one that not only charts the realm of maturation but also addresses educational and cultural issues.

Accordingly, MI theory puts forth a broad definition of intelligence: the ability to solve problems or fashion products that are of consequence in a particular cultural setting or community (Gardner, 1983/1993a). Intelligence is a term for organising and describing human capabilities in relation to the cultural contexts in which those capabilities are developed, used, and given meaning. Drawing on diverse sources of evidence, Gardner defined eight criteria which must be met by a candidate's intelligence. This analysis has yielded a list of eight intelligences. Next we describe the sources of evidence, criteria, and resulting intelligences.

Sources of evidence

Before examining MI's sources of evidence, it is important to note that MI theory is empirical though not "experimental" in the usual sense of the term. It is not the kind of theory that can be proved or disproved by crucial experiment. (It is worth noting that no other theory of intelligence has proved susceptible to such a "thumbs up" evaluation.) The subjective factor analysis on which MI is predicated works by establishing a set of criteria for what constitutes an intelligence. Additional information, experimental or otherwise, could have an impact on the resulting list of intelligences. For example, Rauscher, Shaw, and Ky (1993) has provided evidence that training in music can improve performance on certain spatial tasks. These data are limited at present; however, if replicated and elaborated, these new findings would weaken the claim that spatial and musical intelligences are autonomous and would thus suggest a reconfiguration of the intelligences. Rauscher's work serves as a reminder that MI theory is empirical and is subject to supporting or invalidating evidence. In what follows, we summarise in brief the eight criteria that must be met if candidate ability is to be judged as a human intelligence (Gardner, 1983/1993a).

Potential isolation by brain damage. Gardner finds strong support for MI in studies of once-normal people who have become brain damaged due to stroke or injury. Evidence for autonomy is seen in the sparing or breakdown of a capacity after brain damage. For example, brain-injured musicians may have impaired speech yet retain the ability to play music (aphasia without amusia). In other cases, language is spared and musical ability lost (amusia without aphasia) (Hodges, 1996; Sergent, 1993). That these two abilities can be isolated from each other suggests that music and language are based on relatively autonomous intelligences—"autonomous" in that one cannot predict strength or weakness in one intelligence from strength and weakness in another intelligence, and "relative" in that intelligences make use of some of the same processes (e.g. musical rhythm has mathematical components). In our view, it is unnecessary and misleading to suggest complete autonomy.

The existence of idiots savants, prodigies, and other exceptional individuals. Studies of special populations—prodigies, savants, and other exceptional individuals—also lend support for MI. Prodigies are individuals who show high levels of achievement in a discipline (e.g. chess, music) at a young age but who are unexceptional in other areas. *Savants* are individuals of low attainments, sometimes classified as retarded, who demonstrate remarkable skills in one "island" of ability. For example, an individual may be able to play the piano by ear, perform calculations with large numbers instantly, or draw with great accuracy. Among these special populations, certain capacities operate in isolation from others. The appearance of high-level abilities in people who are otherwise unexceptional suggests that the intelligences involved are relatively autonomous (Winner, 1996). It is noteworthy, however, that *savants* often are skilled in only a small part of a discipline (e.g. there are people who cannot add but can calculate prime numbers). Findings as such suggest that the "core operations" (counting in mathematics, tonal apprehension in music) of the intelligences may be more autonomous, and some of the ancillary operations (such as phrasing in music) are somewhat less autonomous.

Support from experimental psychological tasks. Research in experimental psychology also points to autonomous intelligences. For example, studies in which subjects are asked to carry out two tasks simultaneously indicate that some abilities operate autonomously, whereas others appear to be linked by the same underlying mental operations (Brooks, 1968). Findings such as these suggest that certain musical, linguistic, and spatial information-processing operations are carried out independently.

Support from psychometric findings.   Psychometric findings also provide some support for MI. Gardner has criticised psychometric assessment as taking too narrow a sample of human abilities. Certain abilities within the province of these tests have proven relatively autonomous, however. For example, factor analyses generally support the existence of two "big group" factors—verbal and spatial. Other researchers of intelligence have also put forth a multiple interpretation (Gould, 1996; Guilford, 1967; Thurstone, 1938).

A distinctive developmental history, along with a definable set of end-state performances.   Another source of evidence for an intelligence is a characteristic developmental trajectory leading from basic and universal manifestations to one or more possible expert end-states. For example, spoken language develops quickly and to great competence in normal people. In contrast, while all normal individuals can count small quantities, few progress to higher mathematics even with formal schooling.

An evolutionary history and evolutionary plausibility.   Evolutionary biology is an additional if more speculative source of evidence for MI. Gardner looks for origins of human intelligence in the capacities of species which predate humans. The existence, for example, of bird song suggests the presence of a separate musical intelligence, and there are strong continuities in the spatial abilities of humans and other primates. Other intelligences, such as intrapersonal and linguistic, may be distinctly human.

An identifiable core operation or set of operations.   Each intelligence must have one or more basic information-processing operations or mechanisms which can deal with specific types of input. As a neurally based computational system, each intelligence is activated by certain kinds of internally or externally presented information. The intelligences are not input systems *per se*; rather, the intelligences are potentials, the presence of which allows individuals to activate forms of thinking appropriate to specific forms of content. Hence, MI theory is not inconsistent with an information-processing account of human cognition. Indeed, each intelligence presumably has its distinctive modes of information processing.

Susceptibility to encoding in a symbol system.   An intelligence must also be susceptible to encoding in a symbol system—a culturally created system of meaning which captures and conveys important forms of information (e.g. language or mathematics). The relationship of a candidate intelligence to a cultural symbol system is no accident. The existence of a core computational capacity anticipates the existence of a symbol system which exploits that capacity. "Symbol systems have evolved in just those cases where there exists a computational capacity ripe for harnessing by culture. A primary characteristic of human intelligence may well be its 'natural' gravitation toward embodiment in a symbol system" (Gardner, 1993b, p. 66).

The eight intelligences

These criteria and their attendant sources of evidence converge to support a set of eight candidate intelligences. We now describe these, along with end-states that exemplify them.

1. Linguistic intelligence describes the ability to perceive or generate spoken or written language. Linguistic intelligence is exemplified by poets, lawyers, and journalists.

2. Logical/mathematical intelligence involves using and appreciating numerical, causal, abstract, or logical relations. It is exemplified by mathematicians, scientists, and engineers.

3. Spatial intelligence describes the ability to perceive visual or spatial information (large-scale or more local), to transform and modify this information, and to recreate visual images even without reference to an original physical stimulus. Spatial intelligence is used in visual art, drafting, and navigation.

4. Musical intelligence refers to the ability to create, communicate, and understand meanings made out of sound. It can be seen in musicians and music critics but also outside the musical sphere (e.g. auto mechanics and cardiologists make diagnoses based on careful listening to patterns of sound).

5. Bodily/kinesthetic intelligence involves controlling all or part of one's body to solve problems or fashion products. It can be seen, for example, in athletics, dance, and hiking.

6. Interpersonal intelligence involves the capacity to recognise and make distinctions among the feelings, beliefs, and intentions of other people. Interpersonal intelligence enables people such as Martin Luther King and Mao Zedong to communicate with others and do their work effectively.

7. Intrapersonal intelligence enables individuals to form a mental model of themselves and to draw on the model to make decisions about viable courses of action. Among the core operations are the capacity to

distinguish one's feelings and to anticipate reactions to future courses of action.

8.   Naturalist intelligence involves the ability to understand and work effectively in the natural world (Gardner, 1999). A recent addition to the list of intelligences, naturalist intelligence is exemplified in biologists, zoologists, and naturalists.

Horizontal and vertical faculties

An intelligence has automatic and fast mechanisms at its core, but it also involves slow and contemplative ones. The intelligences grow out of sensory systems, but more than one sensory system can lead into or feed an intelligence (e.g. linguistic intelligence can grow out of audition, vision, gesture; spatial intelligence can draw on visual and kinesthetic information). Since they grow out of sensory systems, intelligences inevitably involve sensory cortical microcircuitry; at the same time, the intelligences themselves involve association or cross-modality cortexes (parietal lobe, frontal lobe), not just primary sensory ones. In essence, the intelligences are involved in higher-level computation as well as sensing and discriminating.

Hence, the intelligences are not, in normal adults, "encapsulated" or "cognitively impenetrable" (that is, cut off from the other modules). The intelligences are loosely coupled and penetrable sets of information-processing devices of which only the core processes are encapsulated.

Vertical faculties that communicate enable MI theory to downplay the need for a prominent central processor or executive. One possibility is that there is no executive at all—the intelligences simply coordinate as is necessary to engage in a task, and the effectiveness of this coordination constrains task performance. It is also possible that there exists a "dumb" executive which coordinates the intelligences but which has little intellectual import in its own right. Gardner has also speculated that intrapersonal intelligence may come to function as an executive, as this intelligence is involved in the individual's self-knowledge and deliberate deployment of knowledge and skill.

Development of the intelligences

The intelligences are universal, in that all normal people exhibit some capacity for each, but there is considerable individual variation in initial profile of intelligences. Individuals begin life with a particular profile of intelligences, and this starting profile will have some influence on the achievements of the individual, but the profile will change in the course of development as a result of the history of experiences in particular cultural contexts.

Combining fast and slow mechanisms, MI draws a distinction between two different kinds of verticality, each with its own developmental path. We call these "early developing" and "later developing" verticality.

"Early developing" verticality. At the core of an intelligence is a computational system (or a set of such systems) activated by a certain kinds of internally or externally presented information. These computational systems form the basis for early developing verticality.

The core processes of the intelligences can be characterised in four ways. First, they are innately specified. The human genome endows normal individuals with a complement of core processes that are present at birth or emerge early in life (Zentner & Kagan, 1996). Second, the core processes are probably sensory-linked—that is, they operate in accordance with particular types of sensory input. For example, the core processes in musical intelligence include mechanisms for tonal discrimination that work only in relation to sensory input from hearing. Third, the core processes are encapsulated—a particular core process does not accept output from other ones. Finally, the core processes are not easily perturbed. It would be difficult to argue, for example, that stereoscopic vision used in spatial intelligence develops over time in the sense that its underlying architecture is altered. Rather, the core processes of the intelligences are unlikely to be significantly changed in the course of normal development.

"Later developing" verticality. "Later developing" verticality refers to a later evolving, prototypically developmental form of verticality, that emerges because of years of practices that correlate with one another. For example, a smoothly operating reading faculty comes about because of the ways in which individuals handle sound and grapheme discrimination and combine sounds and graphemes into chunks. Such a faculty would not be present in individuals in nonliterate cultures, and the development of a reading module depends on the cultural milieu—the domains and disciplines organising the reading-oriented activities that are valued by the ambient culture.

Early in life, the child encounters a world of cultural forms—languages, concepts, roles, values, and so on. Different cultures entail different disciplines or "domains" that require the intelligences to be used in particular ways. The intelligences are transformed and combined in ways that relate directly to the culturally devised activities that the individual is called upon to perform. It is noteworthy that disciplinary activities typically require a combination of intelligences. The concert pianist draws on musical intelligence to be sure, but also on logical-mathematical (interpreting the score), linguistic (following verbal directives in the score and responding to coaching), spatial (orienting one's self to the keyboard), interpersonal (responding to the audience), and intrapersonal (playing expressively) (Torff, 1996). The range of intelligences involved in an activity is often greater than it appears at first sight. It may seem, for example, that mathematicians work solely in the logical-mathematical realm, but they must also draw on interpersonal intelligence to function in the field of mathematics, get their work published, and function smoothly in a university setting.

The activities required in disciplines such as music and mathematics require a blend of intelligences. The fact that several intelligences working in concert are utilised in a single activity underscores that an intelligence is not the same as a domain or discipline. There is no one-to-one correspondence, for example, between musical intelligence and music as a discipline.

Unlike early developing modules, later developing modules draw on multiple sources of sensory input. The concert pianist, for example, relies on not just hearing but also vision (e.g. following the conductor) and touch (responding to the feel of the keyboard). Accordingly, later developing modules are unencapsulated, interconnected sets of information-processing devices. These later emerging forms of verticality may be what is being captured in "parallel distributed processing" systems, which slowly evolve and sometimes reach a stable state of functioning.

In sum, MI draws a distinction between two kinds of verticality with separate developmental paths. Hard-wired into the nervous system, the core processes of the intelligences emerge early in life. These early developing forms of verticality have a distinctive developmental path which features little in the way of sweeping developmental changes or cultural differences. Later developing verticality is very different. Combining various senses and intelligences, later developing vertical faculties emerge in response to the particular demands made by culturally organised activities. As a result, this later developing form of verticality involves significant developmental changes and cultural variation. In order to understand cognitive development, it seems necessary to examine the relations between earlier and later forms of intelligence—as Gardner has done previously with earlier (naive) and later (expert) forms of intuition (Gardner, 1991).

MI's stated aim—to frame an account of human intellect that encompasses the range of intelligent performances seen cross-culturally—raises the issue of how mental abilities in such diverse settings are to be assessed. We remain sceptical that tests provide a suitable window on many human mental abilities. In our view, it is not possible to create a valid "knowledge-free" test to measure the core ability of an intelligence. A central implication of MI theory, then, is the need for "intelligence-fair" assessments which allow participants to engage in real-world activities and use relevant background knowledge to solve problems. Thus, we have joined researchers and educators in developing "performance" assessments (e.g. scoring of participants' work on discipline-based projects) and techniques of "portfolio" assessment (process-tracing collections of participants' work). Alternative assessments enable the intelligences to work in assessment as they do in real-world activity (Gardner, 1993b).

COMPARING MI TO OTHER VERTICAL FACULTY THEORIES

Recent vertical faculty theories emphasise such diverse elements as processing speed and cultural context. The conceptual and methodological diversity of these approaches means that comparing them is no straightforward task (Hirschfeld & Gelman, 1994). At the same time, in our view, any vertical faculty theory confronts a set of issues: (1) description and role of vertical faculties; (2) description and role of horizontal faculties, if any; (3) treatment of cognitive development; and (4) connection to cultural roles.

In this section, we look at these issues to compare MI to contemporary vertical faculty theories. Three lines of such theories have emerged in recent years: (1) the modularity theory of Fodor (with its intellectual indebtedness to Chomsky's 1988 notion of "mental organ"); (2) vertical faculty conceptions of intelligence; and (3) domain-specific approaches to cognitive functioning. In what follows we compare MI to three prominent vertical faculty theories, one from each group. These include models put forth, respectively, by Fodor (1983), Anderson (1992), and Karmiloff-Smith (1992).

Jerry Fodor's "modularity of mind"

Fodor (1983, 1985) has strongly argued for the modularity of mind while retaining an explicit focus on horizontal faculties (Fig. 6.1).

Fodor's model, like Gardner's, represents a challenge to the predominant domain-general approaches found in psychology, linguistics, and elsewhere. However, Fodor and Gardner put forth significantly different notions of vertical faculties. By emphasising input mechanisms, Fodor provides a finer-grained analysis than does MI. In essence, while modules are posited to account for what the nervous system is doing (processing sensory input), intelligences are broader faculties that draw from multiple perceptual systems. The intelligences contain core information-processing mechanisms that are similar to Fodor's modules. However, unlike

Description and role of vertical faculties:
To describe the genetically specified structure of cognition, Fodor posits a set of modules based on input systems: hearing, sight, taste, smell, touch—plus language. Patterned after reflexes, modules are fast-acting, mandatory, automatic, and hardwired. Modules are informationally encapsulated—they do not accept input from each other or from the central processor.

Description and role of horizontal faculties:
A central processor is responsible for higher-order processes of thought ("fixation of belief"). It uses a particular "language of thought" and accepts output from modules and from itself.

Treatment of cognitive development:
Neither the modules nor the central processor "develop" in the sense that there are developmental changes in the structure of cognition. Modules remain fully encapsulated throughout the lifespan. Additional modules (e.g. reading) may emerge.

Connection to cultural rules:
Culturally devised artifacts such as language provide content (and triggering mechanisms) for learning, but cultural products have no effect on underlying cognitive structure.

FIG. 6.1   Fodor's "modularity of mind".

modules, the intelligences are involved in the comparatively slow-acting, deliberate, and reflective processes of thought.

From our perspective, the criteria Fodor establishes for his list of modules seem idiosyncratic. Fodor compiles his list combining logical (e.g. domain-specifying) and empirical (e.g. fast-acting) criteria. If language is a module, why not music as well? MI theory explicitly states eight criteria for an intelligence (restricted to empirical considerations) and seeks to survey the evidence for each candidate intelligence in a systematic manner.

Fodor has argued that theories positing modularity of thought—such as MI—represent "modularity theory gone mad" (Fodor, 1985, p. 27). Indeed, the role of a central system is also a point of disagreement between Gardner and Fodor. Since Fodor's modules are encapsulated, his model requires some mechanism for enabling input from the different modules to be drawn together. Thus, a central processor is necessary for Fodor. MI's appeal to interconnected vertical faculties that need no central processor is implausible, according to Fodor, because there is no "unmonitored, preestablished harmony of the modules" (1985, p. 36). According to this argument, too many modules would be required and the coordination problems would be too difficult.

In contrast, Gardner argues that the intelligences have the potential to account for the range of human cognitive achievements and that it is crucial to account for these achievements using a vertical approach. In arguing against a central processor, Gardner differs with Fodor's interpretation of neuropsychological evidence. Gardner finds ample evidence of patterns of breakdown of capacities that suggests that the capacities are not as equipotential or central as Fodor suggests (e.g. Luria, 1976). Another argument against a central processor involves a non-empirical point. On grounds of parsimony, an analyst should favour one cognitive system over two. A second system makes it necessary to trace two evolutional paths, two forms of hardware, and so on. Twin systems as such involve considerable, and perhaps implausible, theoretical and modelling complications. And the central processor, with its "wisdom", raises the spectre of a homuncular solution to human cognitive complexity.

Before a central processor is invoked, and the attendant theoretical baggage taken on, cognitive scientists ought to examine the extent to which human cognition can be accounted for by a vertical faculty account. Gardner believes that such an enterprise should obviate the need for a central processor. In general, MI works to blur the distinction between modules and central systems. Gardner posits that there are module-like processes at the centre of the intelligences, but there is also some degree of penetration or cross-talk between intelligences. As elements become more susceptible to automatisation (incomprehensible shapes come to be seen as letters), their processing seems encapsulated. But, as elements become the subjects of special scrutiny (the typographer critically compares the fonts) they seem less modular. In place of a dichotomy, there emerges a continuum with relatively modular mechanisms (e.g. pitch discrimination) at one end and relatively isotropic mechanisms (e.g. musical composition) at the other.

Such a continuum points out the need for developmental perspective—another point of friction between Gardner and Fodor. The nativist thesis of *The modularity of mind* (Fodor, 1983) provides little room for developmental change. For Gardner, it is important to trace the evolution of the principal forms of thought from the relatively modular and encapsulated forms of processing, which can be observed in infancy, to the far more open or "isotropic" forms characteristic of mature individuals, and ultimately to later developing verticality. Every intelligence has a developmental history, which after the first year of life involves engagement of the symbol systems of the surrounding culture, and which culminates in the mastery of entire cultural domains by adolescence or thereafter. Thus we may begin life with a proclivity to analyse sounds or to parse phrases in certain ways, but these processes undergo perceptual reorganisation in light of the experiences encountered by the individual over the course of life. A non-developmental account of modularity moves away from what is distinctive about human cognition.

A further consequence of Fodor's stance against development is that cultural factors are posited to have little influence on cognitive activities. Cultural products like language are posited to produce learning (new knowledge) but not cognitive change (alteration in underlying cognitive structure). Fodor assumes that each of his modules simply unfolds, independently of the interpretive frameworks provided by culture. Gardner believes that vertical faculties that are isolated as such are visible only in exceptional cases (e.g. *savants* or autistic children). Even phoneme perception and sensitivity to visual illusions are affected by the kinds of sounds and sights that are present or absent in a particular culture. Fodor, like many nativists, does not deny the triggering effect of the environment. However, he sidesteps the question of how the modules are fashioned by the ambient culture and, indeed, how the entire gamut of human cognitive and cultural achievements can be explained.

The modularity of mind has a somewhat ironic title, because the book attributes all higher-order cognitive activities to centralised processes (Sperber, 1994). Like other recent theories (e.g. Karmiloff-Smith, 1992), MI theory holds that thought, as well as perception, is best explained by vertical processes. MI theory, though admittedly more tentative, has the virtue of suggesting ways of explaining human behaviours that transcend reflexes. Fodor's work has been highly influential, however, and much recent productive domain-specific work (e.g. Carey & Gelman, 1991; Hirschfeld & Gelman, 1994; Keil, 1989; Spelke, 1990) bears the Chomsky/Fodor stamp.

Mike Anderson's theory of intelligence

Anderson (1992) focuses on a single level of explanation, the computational or information-processing level, in an attempt to account for a pattern of findings in the experimental literature on intelligence (Fig. 6.2).

Anderson and Gardner marshal similar sources of evidence—including neuropsychological research, studies of *savants* and prodigies, and psychometric research—but they reach different conclusions. At first blush, Anderson's specific processors appear similar to the intelligences—they are broad-based, slow-acting, unencapsulated, and connected to multiple sources of input. However, a closer look reveals differences between intelligences and specific processors. Beyond the obvious discrepancy between eight faculties and two, there are other incompatibilities. Anderson's specific processor "propositional thought" encompasses language and mathematics, which are handled separately in MI theory. The autonomy of these two faculties is, in our view, supported in

Description and role of vertical faculties:
To account for universal human abilities that show no individual differences, a set of "modules" is posited: perception of 3-D space, language functions, various "constraints on induction" and/or "naive
theories", and possibly others that result from automatisation. To
account for "specific cognitive abilities" that are constrained by the
basic processing mechanism and thus show individual differences,
two "specific processors" are posited: propositional thought (in language and logic) and spatial cognition.

Description and role of horizontal faculties:
To account for *g*, Anderson posits a basic processing mechanism
(BPM). The BPM varies across individuals in speed—increased speed
means more knowledge acquired by specific processors. Individual
variation on intelligence tests stems from differences in knowledge,
the acquisition of which depends on BPM speed.

Treatment of cognitive development:
Intelligence constrains development, in that BPM speed and functioning of specific processors constrain knowledge acquisition. Intelligence does not develop; speed or structure of BPM does not change
over time. Developmental changes in intellectual competence are attributable to addition and elaboration of new modules.

Connection to cultural roles:
Cultural products like language provide content for knowledge acquisition mechanisms used by modules and specific processors. Cultural
participation facilitates the addition and elaboration of new modules
but does not influence the underlying architecture of cognition.

FIG. 6.2   Anderson's "minimum cognitive architecture of intelligence".

the neuroscientific literature. For example, there is evidence that
individuals may lose (through brain injury) the ability to reason in
mathematics but retain language skills, or vice versa (Gardner, 1983/
1993a).

Anderson provides no criteria by which specific processors are
nominated: Specific processors are simply posited to account for a
particular pattern (and interpretation) of findings. The absence of criteria
is significant, in that it allows Anderson's vertical faculties to be justified in
an *ad hoc* manner. For example, specific processors and modules are
proposed because some individuals demonstrate particular cognitive
deficits; elsewhere, Anderson ascribes these disorders to impaired
mechanisms.

The second area of contention between Gardner and Anderson concerns
the notion of modules. Many of the comments made in relation to Fodor's

modules apply as well to Anderson's. Anderson's modules may be similar to the information-processing components that comprise the core of the intelligences. Unlike modules, the intelligences are involved in higher processes of thought; they undergo complex developmental changes; and they are influenced by the cultural environment. Moreover, Anderson's claim that modules show no individual differences lacks evidence. Some modules specified by Anderson (e.g. syntactic parsing) may well show individual differences (Pinker, 1994). We think it unlikely that there are significant systems in which individual variation is nil.

Gardner also differs with Anderson in the need to posit a centralised processor like the BPM, and he has criticised the psychological construct g which Anderson's BPM endeavours to explain. According to Gardner, g is a construct that has been encouraged by use of intelligence tests. However, in a non-testing environment, g would either not exist at all or it would consist of different abilities which correlate with different outcomes. If reliable assessments could be constructed for different intelligences, and these assessments did not rely solely on short answers, often through paper-and-pencil presentations, but instead used the materials of the domain being measured, the correlations that yield g would greatly diminish. Indeed, estimation of g can go up or down depending on the population examined and statistical procedures used (Ceci, 1996; Gould, 1996). From a societal point of view, a focus on g is biased and often unproductive.

Turning to the issue of development, Gardner differs with Anderson's Fodorian position in that cognitive development is limited to the appearance of new modules. According to Gardner, sweeping stage-like change cannot be explained as simple maturations of new modules; if so, all normal people would achieve changes such as the formal operations described by Piaget. Rather, schooling and other aspects of culture strongly affect such development (e.g. Bruner, 1990; Newman, Griffin, & Cole, 1989; Vygotsky, 1978). On a related point, Anderson and Gardner provide somewhat different views of the mechanisms that account for individual differences in intelligence(s) and developmental changes in intellectual competence. Like Anderson, Gardner believes that individual differences in intelligence(s) are inevitably a joint product of genetic factors and experiential ones (although, as noted, Gardner does not share Anderson's view that the genetic influence is constrained primarily by speed). Unlike Anderson, Gardner believes that developmental changes result both because of epigenetic factors (including brain development) and because of experiences with culturally devised systems.

Indeed, the role of cultural factors constitutes the final point of dispute between Anderson and Gardner. Like Fodor, Anderson suggests that cultural explanations have held too much sway in recent years. Laudable as is the pursuit to explain human behaviour at a single level of description (in Anderson's case, the computational level), we are unpersuaded that the question of culture is so easily sidestepped. We take the view that intelligence does not operate in a vacuum; it is influenced by the experience of the individual in particular cultural contexts (Ceci, 1996). Strict adherence to the computational perspective gives Anderson's model a certain coherence but at the cost of failing to account for much of what is interesting about intellectual development and achievements.

Anderson's vertical faculties are posited to explain "exceptions" to the general pattern that supports *g*.   This stance is reminiscent to that of Piaget, who put forth the concept *décalage* as a "fudge factor" to explain observed variations across tasks which appear to contradict the theory of domain-general structures. For many psychologists, *décalage* proved more the rule than the exception. We believe that vertical functions, not centralised processes with attendant fudge factors, ultimately yield the more parsimonious and evolutionarily plausible model of intellectual development.

Annette Karmiloff-Smith's "Representational Redescription" Model

Karmiloff-Smith (1992) has heroically attempted to reconcile Piaget's notion of development with the nativism of Fodor and Chomsky (Fig. 6.3).

Karmiloff-Smith's model has much in common with Gardner's. Each posits a set of vertical faculties in the absence of a prominent central processor (although they present somewhat incompatible sets, as we discuss later). Unlike Fodor (and to lessor extent, Anderson), Karmiloff-Smith and Gardner agree on the importance of development. Furthermore, Gardner concurs with Karmiloff-Smith that at least one strand of development moves in the direction of systems which are increasingly modular. What we are calling "later developing" verticality is consistent with Karmiloff-Smith's notion of modularisation. Finally, Karmiloff-Smith and Gardner share the belief that human intellect must be explained in relation to the ambient cultural context.

In a number of ways, however, Karmiloff-Smith's model is incongruent with the notion of multiple intelligences. There is some overlap in the candidate vertical faculties put forth by Gardner and Karmiloff-Smith—in the areas of language, mathematics, and perhaps psychology (interpersonal intelligence). However, there are some significant differences between Karmiloff-Smith's domains and Gardner's intelligences. An intelligence is a biopsychological construct—the sets of capacities that the species has evolved to realise, given cultural support. A domain is a culturally defined activity or set of activities, which can be arrayed in terms of expertise (Csikszentmihalyi, 1988; Feldman, 1980). A single intelligence can thus be

Description and role of vertical faculties:
To account for observed variation in cognitive development in different content areas, Karmiloff-Smith posits a set of domains—sets of
representations sustaining a particular area of knowledge. Candidate
domains describe the child as linguist, physicist, mathematician, psychologist, and notator.

Description and role of horizontal faculties:
No central processor is discussed; cognition is assumed to have a
fundamentally domain-specific character. However, to account for
observed commonalities in cognitive development across domains,
Karmiloff-Smith posits a universal developmental process, called representational redescription (RR).

Treatment of cognitive development:
Taking a developmental-constructivist perspective, the RR model describes development in terms of three phases of representational
character of knowledge in a domain: (1) implicit; (2) explicit level 1
(not available to verbal report); (3) explicit level 2 (available to verbal
report). Development is seen in terms of two parallel processes: progressive modularisation and progressive explicitation.

Connection to cultural roles:
Culture provides the environment for the constructivist interaction
that drives the process of representational change, but the character
of that change is fundamentally regulated by endogenous factors.
Cultural roles and products are built up on domain-specific cognitive
mechanisms.

FIG. 6.3   Karmiloff-Smith's "representational redescription" model.

activated for various domains and will be mobilised differently in different
societies and different epochs. Conversely, domains involve combinations
of intelligences. The domain of physics, for example, involves primarily
logical-mathematical and spatial intelligences. Physicists also use a wider
range of intelligences in the course of gaining funding, collaborating with
colleagues, and disseminating findings.

A second difference concerns the existence of innately specified
modules. Karmiloff-Smith (1992, p. 5) has written that "development
involves a process of gradual modularisation rather than prespecified
modules". This account differs from the notion of "early developing"
presented earlier, which holds that a set of innately specified and early
developing modules constitute the core processes of the intelligences.

Third, Gardner and Karmiloff-Smith offer contrasting views of the role
of domain-general developmental processes such as representational
description. According to Gardner (1995), the RR model captures an

important process in some domains, but evidence for it is weak in other domains. Gardner believes that the RR model works better for skills that people master over time, like playing the piano or using irregular verbs, than it does for conceptual understandings such as those arrived at by the young physicist, mathematician, or theorist-of-mind. In general, MI downplays the importance of commonalities in information-processing across intelligences. Each intelligence is thought to have a separate, if not unique, developmental history. There may be some overlapping qualities between the various developmental histories, and these would be fruitful to uncover, but it is vital to look as well, and perhaps first, at processes unique to particular intelligences.

Overall, we find much to recommend in Karmiloff-Smith's model. Her stated aim is a laudable one—to specify the processes that account for how vertical faculties develop and interconnect. Whereas we remain unpersuaded that a domain-general model such as RR will turn out to be the most felicitous description of development of domains, or of intelligences, we admire Karmiloff-Smith's attempt to integrate nativist and constructivist approaches to intellectual development.

PLACING MI AMONG VERTICAL FACULTY THEORIES

The most striking aspect to emerge from our survey of recent vertical faculty theories is that MI theory presents the most extreme form of verticality. Among the four theories, only MI opts not to appeal to centralised processes or structures—Fodor and Anderson posit prominent central processing mechanisms, and Karmiloff-Smith puts forth a domain-general developmental process. MI is, in a sense, the radical among the vertical faculty theories. Perhaps appropriately, MI theory also presents the most clearly delineated criteria for selection of candidate vertical faculties.

Full-blown verticality is supported by a number of key features of MI theory. First of all, the intelligences present a qualitatively different analytic unit from other vertical faculty theories. Clearly, the intelligences operate at a "higher" level than the modules modelled after reflexes posited by Fodor and Anderson. There are probably module-like mechanisms at the core of the intelligences, but the intelligences also mediate the higher-order processes of thought, not just the reflexive intelligence built into the hardware. The intelligences function at a biopsychological level, while the domains discussed by Karmiloff-Smith are inherently cultural constructions. It turns out that several intelligences are needed to account for operations lumped together in one domain. The intelligences are reminiscent of "specific processors", but Anderson posits only two of these, and there are competing views of how these faculties work—whereas specific processors are constrained by the basic processing mechanism, intelligences operate under no such constraint. Overall, the intelligences stand alone as a necessary and sufficient set of analytic devices.

As a second consideration, MI posits vertical faculties that are penetrable, intercommunicating, and, in a sense, collaborative. MI thus accounts for the fact that individuals can represent knowledge of something in a number of ways and compare those representations. For instance, the fact that people can encode an experience linguistically or spatially and then compare the results of these encodings is a positive human capacity. MI accounts for this capacity not by resorting to a mysterious executive or homunculus, but by positing that the intelligences are able to communicate. Quite possibly, different intelligences serve as a *lingua franca* for different individuals, much as different sections can take the lead in the performance of a musical work.

MI is sometimes called a "modular theory of central processes" (e.g. Anderson, 1992; Sperber, 1994), apparently to distance the intelligences from lower-level mechanisms like modules. This characterisation is somewhat ironic, given that MI is such a strong statement of verticality. At the same time, we accept the characterisation if it helps to keep the focus on interconnected vertical faculties working in the absence of a prominent horizontal processor.

Third, MI theory provides a unique view of the nature of cognitive development. The nativist Fodor has little interest in development— modules are encapsulated and remain so throughout the life span. Anderson concurs and adds that intelligence is a function of speed (which does not change), and thus cognitive development is limited to the addition of new modules. Karmiloff-Smith offers a more comprehensive developmental view but assumes that development proceeds toward modularisation. Only MI describes development in terms of twin systems. Whereas the early developing core processes of the intelligences probably do not involve significant developmental changes over the lifespan, later developing cognitive skills are highly sensitive to developmental changes, cultural influences, and the individual's own personality, motivation, and goals.

Finally, perhaps MI's most significant contribution (to the vertical faculty movement, at least) is its insistence that human intellect be explained in relation to ambient cultural contexts. MI seriously examines the role played by cultural products in the development of the individual mind. Stepping aside from the assumption that cognitive functioning is fundamentally endogenously regulated, MI is consistent with the developmental theory of Vygotsky (1978; see also Rogoff, 1990). Like Vygotsky's theory, MI endeavours to draw together the universal, genetically specified human potentials (c.f. the "genetic method") with the cultural roles and artifacts that organise activity and guide the development of the individual mind (c.f. the theory of internalisation from a "zone of proximal development").

At the heart of any theory is the explanatory goal of the theorist (with resulting implications for how the theory is constructed and how research proceeds). Fodor's goal is to explain the genetically specified structure of input systems. Anderson attempts to account for a particular pattern of experimental findings obtained largely in the psychometric tradition. Karmiloff-Smith endeavours to reconcile Piaget's horizontalist and constructivist notion of development with Chomskian modularity and nativism.

MI has a rather different set of objectives, ones with parallels to the recent history of research on human memory. Earlier in this century, memory research was dominated by laboratory tasks in which subjects memorised strings of nonsense syllables. In recent decades, researchers became dissatisfied with the limitations of this approach and began to use lengthy and substantive texts, resulting in a reinvigoration of memory research and a reconceptualisation of what memory is (Neisser; 1982; Schacter, 1996). Classic intelligence theory has, in its own way, maintained a focus on something like the nonsense syllables. Research on intelligence has been oriented toward its test instruments, many of the dry, brief, paper-and-pencil variety. In essence, classic intelligence theory has tried to lay intelligence bare, and, in the process, may have obscured much of what is distinctive and human about it.

We suggest that MI has contributed to a kind of reinvigoration of investigations of the intellect, one reminiscent of the changes in memory research. Rather than simply using test instruments to make inferences about human intelligence, MI theory works chiefly in the other direction—from the world back to the theory. Examining the skills demonstrated by, say, rock guitarists and Trobriand islanders, MI attempts to frame an account, based on clear criteria, of the universal intellectual faculties needed—alone and in combination—to carry out these tasks. Directly confronting the complexity of cultural and educational influences, MI attempts to restore range and passion to research on intelligence.

REFERENCES

Anderson. M. (1992) *Intelligence and development: A cognitive theory.* Oxford, UK: Blackwell.

Brooks, L. (1968). Spatial and verbal components of the act of recall. *Canadian Journal of Psychology, 22,* 349–350.

Bruner, J. (1990). *Acts of meaning.* Cambridge, MA: Harvard University Press.

Carey, S., & Gelman, R. (Eds) (1991). *The epigenesis of mind.* Hillsdale, NJ: Lawrence Erlbaum Associates Inc.

Ceci, S. (1996). *On intelligence ... more or less.* Cambridge, MA: Harvard University Press.

Chomsky, N. (1988). *Language and problems of knowledge.* Cambridge, MA: MIT Press.

Czikszentmihalyi, M. (1988). Society, culture, person: A systems view of creativity. In R.J. Sternberg (Ed.), *The nature of creativity* (pp. 325–329). New York: Cambridge University Press.

Feldman, D. (1980). *Beyond universals in cognitive development.* Norwood, NJ: Ablex Publishing.

Fodor, J. (1983). *The modularity of mind.* Cambridge, MA: MIT Press.

Fodor, J. (1985). The modularity of mind. *Behavioral and Brain Sciences, 8,* 1–42.

Gardner, H. (1991). *The unschooled mind.* New York: Basic Books.

Gardner, H. (1993a). *Frames of mind.* New York: Basic Books. (Original work published 1983.)

Gardner, H. (1993b). *Multiple intelligences: The theory into practice.* New York: Basic Books.

Gardner, H. (1995). Green ideas sleeping furiously [Review of S. Pinker, *The language instinct*; A. Karmiloff-Smith, *Beyond modularity*; J. Bruner, *Acts of meaning*]. *New York Review of Books, 42*(5), 32–38.

Gardner, H. (1999). Are there additional intelligences?: The case for naturalist, spiritual, and existential intelligences. In J. Cain (Ed.), *Education: Information and transformation* (pp. 111–132). Englewood Cliffs, NJ: Prentice-Hall.

Gould, S. (1996). *The mismeasure of man* (2nd ed.). New York: Norton.

Guilford, J. (1967). *The nature of human intelligence.* New York: McGraw-Hill

Hirschfeld, L., & Gelman, S. (1994). *Mapping the mind: Domain-specificity in cognition and culture.* Cambridge, UK: Cambridge University Press.

Hodges, D. (1996). Neuromusical research: A review of the literature. In *Handbook of music psychology* (2nd ed.) New York: IMR Press.

Hutchens, E. (1980). *Culture and inference.* Cambridge, MA: Harvard University Press.

Karmiloff-Smith, A. (1992). *Beyond modularity.* Cambridge, UK: Cambridge University Press.

Keil, F. (1989). *Concepts, kinds and cognitive development.* Cambridge, MA: Harvard University Press.

Luria, A. (1976). *Cognitive development: Its cultural and social foundations.* Cambridge, MA: Harvard University Press.

Neisser, U. (1982). *Memory observed.* San Francisco: Freeman.

Newman, D., Griffin, P., & Cole, M. (1989). *The construction zone.* Cambridge, UK: Cambridge University Press.

Pinker, S. (1994). *The language instinct.* New York: Morrow.

Rauscher, F., Shaw, G., & Ky, K. (1993). Music and spatial task performance. *Nature, 365,* 611.

Rogoff, B. (1990). *Apprenticeship in thinking.* Cambridge, MA: Harvard University Press.

Schacter, D. (1996). *Searching for memory.* New York: Basic Books.

Sergent, J. (1993). Music, the brain and Ravel. *Trends in Neurosciences, 16,* 5.

Spelke, E. (1990). Principles of object perception. *Cognitive Science, 14,* 29–56.

Sperber, D. (1994). The modularity of thought. In L. Hirschfeld, & S. Gelman (Eds), *Mapping the mind: Domain-specificity in cognition and culture.* Cambridge, UK: Cambridge University Press.

Thurstone, L.L. (1938). *Primary mental abilities.* Chicago: University of Chicago Press.

Torff, B. (1996). Into the wordless world: Implicit learning and instructor modeling in music. In V. Brummett (Ed.), *Music as intelligence.* Ithaca, NY: Ithaca College Press.

Vygotsky, L. (1978). *Mind in society.* Cambridge, MA: Harvard University Press.

Winner, E. (1996). Gifted children: Myths and realities. New York: Basic Books.

Zentner, M., & Kagan, J. (1996). Perception of music by infants. *Nature, 383,* 5th September, 29.

CHAPTER SEVEN

Individual differences and development—one dimension or two?

Helen Davis
Murdoch University, Perth, Western Australia

Mike Anderson
The University of Western Australia, Perth

INDIVIDUAL DIFFERENCES AND DEVELOPMENT

Individual variation in intellectual performance has been one of the central interests of psychology since its inception. Two major phenomena have been studied extensively. First, people of similar ages vary in how well they perform on intellectual tasks. These within-age differences among individuals are the source of the concept of "IQ". Second, between birth and adulthood, all individuals' intellectual abilities increase. These between-age differences are the source of the concept of "mental age" (MA). Interestingly, however, most research to date has taken place either in the field of individual differences or in the field of cognitive development, with little attempt to relate the one field to the other (Anderson, 1992). In this chapter, we will examine the question of whether within-age and between-age differences in intellectual ability are really just two manifestations of the same phenomenon, corresponding to a single theoretical dimension, or whether there is reason to distinguish between the two kinds of variation and consider them as theoretically separate dimensions. We shall show how the fields of individual differences and development took divergent paths, leaving the question of dimensionality unasked. We shall explore current theories of within- and between-age differences and attempt to draw together evidence to answer the question, and, finally, we shall suggest new directions for future research to bring us nearer to a satisfactory answer. First, however, let us clarify what is meant by the term "dimension".

DIMENSIONALITY—THE ISSUE OF LEVELS OF DESCRIPTION AND EXPLANATION

When discussing the number of dimensions needed to describe a psychological construct, it is important to specify the *level* of description or explanation being investigated. A broad distinction can be made between *measurement* and *theory*. The measurement level is solely concerned with describing and summarising subjects' performance on psychometric tests of intellectual performance. The theoretical level, on the other hand, does not seek to summarise so much as to explain and predict psychometric test performance in terms of psychological constructs external to the tests themselves. The theoretical level can, itself, be divided into a number of levels of explanation in a reductionist hierarchy. These include the metacognitive or strategy level, the cognitive mechanistic level, and the neurophysiological level.

Distinguishing between levels is important for a number of reasons. As we shall see in the following sections, what constitutes a dimension varies depending on which level of description is under discussion. Consequently, the number of dimensions needed to characterise a psychological construct such as intellectual ability may be "level dependent", so unidimensionality at a measurement level may be underlain by multidimensionality at a theoretical level. Thus, in order to avoid confusion, we need to specify which level we are referring to and refrain from moving from level to level without an articulated theory of how they relate to each other. This somewhat abstruse distinction has a very practical consequence. Since the level upon which we choose to focus determines both the kind of empirical studies we conduct and our interpretation of their results, we need to consider the issue of which level offers the most appropriate focus for research, balancing theoretical power against empirical practicality. In the following sections we shall outline the various levels and identify what constitutes a dimension at each of these levels.

The psychometric measurement level

At the level of psychometric measurement, the basic data are individuals' scores on different psychometric tests, and factor analysis plays a central part in our understanding of dimensionality. The goal of factor analysis is to extract the underlying dimensions or "latent traits" expressed in test performance. That is, while intellectual ability is not directly observable from test performance (since different tests designed to measure intellectual ability are not perfectly correlated) factor analytic methods were devised as a filter to separate the theoretically interesting common trends in performance on different tests from task-specific and error variance. At this level, the term "dimension" refers to an intellectual performance factor which is uncorrelated with any other factor.

Examples of dimensions at this level include Spearman's (1927) single factor "g", or general intelligence and Thurstone's (1938) seven or eight "primary mental abilities". Other examples include Cattell's (1963) fluid and crystallised intelligence, and Vernon's (1950) verbal-educational and spatial-mechanical specific abilities.

Clearly, this level of description does not offer an unambiguous model of the dimensions of intellectual ability among same-aged subjects, even before the additional question of developmental change is broached. Differences in interpretation arise due to different sub-tests being included in test batteries, and the use of different factor analytic methods, and there is no a priori reason for favouring one method over another (Gould, 1981). However, it is important not to lose sight of the fact that factor analytic studies do not take place in a theoretical vacuum—sub-tests and factor analytic techniques are selected on the basis of theoretical assumptions about the nature of intelligence, be they explicit or implicit. To discriminate between the different models of intelligence it is necessary to go beyond merely describing patterns in intellectual task data and to generate explicit, testable theories regarding the underlying intellectual ability factors.

Theoretical explanation levels

Metacognition and strategies.   This level is concerned with the methods or strategies that different individuals apply to tasks. Following the analogy between human minds and computers, the metacognitive level refers to the available "software". When a task is reasonably complex, as intellectual tasks tend to be, there is considerable scope for subjects to choose different strategies. Not all strategies will be equally efficient, so individuals may perform well on intelligence tests because they apply more efficient strategies to the tasks. Possibly, such individuals have greater "metacognitive awareness"—they are better at deciding which strategy will be the most efficient. Furthermore, strategy efficiency may interact with subject characteristics such that different subjects may reach their optimal levels of performance using different strategies. Examples of strategic differences include children solving arithmetic problems either finger counting or else retrieving the answer directly from long-term memory (Siegler & Jenkins, 1989), and adults representing task stimuli either verbally or spatially in a mental rotation task (Just & Carpenter, 1985).

Cognitive mechanisms and processing parameters. This level of description is concerned with the parameters of the information-processing system which delimit its efficiency in dealing with large amounts of information. Continuing the computer analogy, the cognitive level corresponds to the "hardware/architecture" of the system, in the sense of what mechanisms the computer has to store, retrieve, and compute data. A dimension at this level would be a system parameter which is orthogonal to all others. Three such system parameters commonly investigated as sources of variation in intellectual ability are the *speed* with which information is encoded and manipulated (Anderson, 1992), the cognitive *capacity* or "workspace" available for the uptake and manipulation of information (Halford, 1993), and *inhibitory ability,* the ability to ignore selectively information that is irrelevant to or that interferes with the task at hand.

The neurophysiological level. This level of explanation invokes theories based on the physical structure and function of the brain. To pursue our computer analogy, this level corresponds to the design of the microcircuitry that the machine is built from (universally the silicon chip, but in days of yore valves or transistors were used). Brains vary from each other on a number of dimensions. Attempts have been made to link such variables as overall brain size, number of synapses, nerve conductivity, and degree of myelination to intellectual performance (e.g. Miller, 1994). Various parameters of the wave-form of subjects' average evoked potentials have been linked to IQ differences and also to differences between older and younger children (Barrett & Eysenck, 1994; Jensen, 1987; Stough, Nettelbeck, & Cooper, 1990).

Relationships between levels of explanation—choosing the optimal level for research

The main benefit arising from considering different explanatory levels is that it allows us to move from simple description of data patterns towards understanding why these data form the patterns they do. In the reductionist hierarchy, the greater the disparity between the levels of the explanatory variables and the phenomena to be explained, the more theoretically interesting their relationship becomes, as it escapes the dead-end of circular reasoning. For example, if only the measurement level is considered then all that can be concluded about the nature of intelligence is that it is "what intelligence tests measure" (Boring, 1923). On the other hand, if we seek to explain measured intelligence in terms of, say, neural conductivity, there is no immediately obvious reason why the two should bear any relation to each other at all, but if they do then the finding offers us insight into why some people perform better on intellectual tasks than others. It also generates many potentially testable predictions and offers us possible explanations for related observations such as the heritability of intelligence (e.g. Bouchard, Lykken, McGue, Segal, & Tellegen, 1990) or why intellectual performance deteriorates as ageing progresses (e.g. Nettelbeck & Rabbitt, 1992; Salthouse & Babcock, 1991).

The benefits of low-level explanations of high-level task performance come at a cost, however. One great difficulty is that of actually measuring low-level phenomena, such as neural conductivity. Beyond this, there lies the complication that it is unlikely that there will be a simple relationship between variables at different levels of description—cognitive speed, for instance, is likely to be the result of the interaction of a large number of neurological variables and only related to intelligence via interactions with other cognitive, metacognitive and environmental variables. As researchers, we need to weigh the costs of focusing on a particular level against the benefits. Given these theoretical and empirical limitations, the cognitive level seems a useful focus for current research, and will be the primary focus of this chapter. It has the benefits of being removed from the level of measured intelligence and thus theoretically powerful while still being relatively accessible to empirical study. Before we review current cognitive theories of intellectual ability, let us see how the fields of individual differences and development came to be separated, and the consequences of their divergence.

THE DIVERGENT PATHS OF INDIVIDUAL DIFFERENCES AND DEVELOPMENT

The study of individual differences took a very different path from the study of cognitive development almost from the outset, with the result that the question of whether between- and within-age differences corresponded to two dimensions or one was never raised. In 1905, Binet set out with the task of developing an instrument to identify children in need of special education. Beginning with the reasonable assumption that intelligence increased with age, he set out to construct a set of age-norms for passing and failing a variety of tasks (Binet & Simon, 1905/1980). From this arose the concepts of mental age (MA) and IQ. To say that a child has a MA of 10 years means that he or she is able to solve problems that the average 10-year-old can solve, but fails those more difficult problems that the average 11-year-old can solve. Classically, IQ is derived from MA by dividing it by the child's chronological age and multiplying the result by 100 (Stern, 1912) and reflects children's intellectual performance relative to peers of the same age.

Binet's focus was to derive an index or measure of intellectual performance. On the other hand, Piaget, employed by Binet to standardise the new intelligence test, became intrigued by the *qualitative* differences between children's performance at different ages. He noticed that younger and older children failing the same items often gave very different incorrect responses, suggesting that quantitative differences in pass/fail scores did not fully characterise the differences between age groups. Such observations were, however, of theoretical rather than practical interest and so the two approaches to the study of children's intellectual ability parted company.

The differences between Binet's and Piaget's approaches had far-reaching consequences, particularly for the issue of whether individual differences and developmental change lie on the same or different dimensions. Binet's interest in quantitative differences between children of different ages led him to focus on quantitative data—the scores of many children on many tests. This sort of data had the advantage of being amenable to (and, indeed, leading to the development of) numerous powerful statistical and mathematical modelling techniques. It also brought to light a number of intellectual tasks which show steady improvement with age, such as digit span and vocabulary. It also (rather obviously) provided a relatively fine-grain metric for comparing children to age-norms so that children in need of special education *could* be identified. The major disadvantage of the psychometric approach was its lack of theoretical basis: None the less, unquestioned assumptions about the nature of intelligence were built into intelligence scales, and items not fitting these assumptions systematically discarded as "poor" items. Thus, intelligence tests are not merely built upon the assumption that within-age differences and between-age differences are unidimensional, but their creators have largely removed any possible counter-evidence. Clearly this limits the utility of psychometric data in answering our question about whether individual differences and development lie on the same or different dimensions.

Piaget's qualitative approach led to intensive rather than extensive research: Relatively few subjects were studied, but the data gathered on them was richer in detail. One strength of this approach was that it was concerned with explaining, rather than simply describing, differences in intellectual performance between age groups and thus focused on *how* children reasoned and the general nature of errors made at different ages. This stimulated the production of much theory about general factors which might account for age differences in performance across a wide range of tasks. The approach also embodied the possibility that between-age differences were not due to the same factors as within-age differences. A major weakness of Piaget's approach, however, was that its primarily qualitative data was less able to make use of the new statistical and modelling techniques. Thus, while it was good at generating theory, it was less good at offering means to test that theory.

At the measurement level alone, the two approaches have traditionally been viewed as either complementary or else mutually exclusive, but essentially incomparable (Andrich & Styles, 1991). To bridge the gap, we need to turn to theory at some other level of description. As it happens, cognitive theories of individual differences and of development have independently reached a point where the comparison of one- and two-dimensional models can be made directly. Let us now examine some such theories for each domain in turn.

COGNITIVE AND METACOGNITIVE THEORIES OF INTELLIGENCE

Individual differences

Theories concerning the nature of adult intelligence abound and do not all agree as to whether intelligence is a single domain-general ability or the sum of multiple specific abilities. For the sake of simplicity, we will focus upon theories which allow that intelligence is general in some sense. We will examine three major theories of what this general factor might be, namely, speed of processing, metacognition and strategies, and inhibition.

Speed and individual differences.   A popular theory among researchers (e.g. Anderson, 1992; Eysenck, 1986; Jensen, 1985; Nettelbeck, 1987) is that speed of information processing is the underlying variable determining intelligence. Given that the cognitive system can only maintain representations for a brief period of time before they decay, faster processors will be able to take in and manipulate more information and more complex information than slow processors. When the information load becomes great enough, some systems will be too slow to be able to process it all, resulting in incomplete processing and, ultimately, errors. Increasing the information load still further will eventually make the task impossible for anyone. The point at which the information load becomes too great for an individual system can be thought of as corresponding to the individual's highest possible level of reasoning. Thus, the *speed* with which an individual can process very simple information should be predictive of their *accuracy* on complex reasoning tasks. Speed has been estimated from reaction time (RT) and inspection time (IT) tasks and, more controversially, from physiological measures such as average evoked potentials (AEP) or neural conductivity. The complexity of the evidence for physiological correlates places it beyond the scope of this chapter, so we shall focus on the more established RT and IT studies, and the reader is referred to Vernon (1993) for a review of physiological research.

Jensen (1982) developed an RT task which systematically varied the amount of information which had to be processed. The task makes use of a special box on which eight small lights with corresponding response buttons are arranged in a semicircle around a "home" key. In the task, participants hold down the home key until one of the lights comes on, at which point they release the home key and press the button corresponding to the light as rapidly as possible. Crucially, the task is so simple that all participants can do it—individual differences in performance lie in speed not accuracy. Decision time (DT), the time elapsing between the light coming on and the subject releasing the home key, is measured separately from movement time (MT), the time from the release of the home key to the pressing of the appropriate response button. By varying how many lights there are to choose from, it is possible to measure simple RT, 2-, 4-, and 8-choice RT. According to Hick's (1952) law, these conditions involve 0, 1, 2, and 3 "bits" of information being processed, respectively. It is found that DT shows a negative correlation with IQ, whereas MT is unrelated (Jensen, 1982). More impressive, however is the degree of slowing that occurs as information load increases. This is calculated as the slope of the linear function relating DT to number of bits of information. Slope is reported to correlate negatively with IQ such that low-IQ participants have steeper slopes, showing that they are not merely slower in absolute terms, but that they become relatively slower to respond the more information they have to deal with. Thus, the task seems to provide compelling evidence for the speed theory.

RT tasks have, nevertheless, been criticised as being inadequate measures of cognitive speed. For example, the task confounds number of choices with amount of visual scanning required, DT still contains a motor component and speed–accuracy trade-offs may occur (Longstreth, 1984).

The IT task was developed in the hope of overcoming some of these problems. In this task, individuals are presented with a simple visual stimulus and asked to make a simple decision (e.g. presented with two lines, they must decide whether they are of the same length or different lengths, then the stimulus is masked). In this task participants are not required to respond quickly. Speed of processing is measured as the exposure duration of the stimulus required for an individual to respond at a predetermined level of accuracy (e.g. 71%, 90%). IT has been found to correlate with IQ up to a level of −0.92 over a wide IQ range, although in IQ groups within the normal range, the correlations have been more modest, generally around −0.50 (Nettelbeck, 1987).

Metacognitive abilities and individual differences.   Sternberg (1983) offers the alternative theory that it is not the speed of *simple* processes which determines ultimate intellectual functioning, but metacognitive control over these processes. Metacognitive components include such things as recognition that a problem exists and the nature of this problem, selecting strategies, deciding how to allocate attentional resources, monitoring task performance, and making use of feedback on task performance. These apply equally to intellectual tasks and to performance on speed measures.

Evidence for the metacognitive theory comes from Sternberg's findings that mathematical models including the metacognitive components believed to be involved in the solution of different reasoning tasks fit performance data better than models without these metacomponents, and that intelligence is correlated with speed parameters associated with the metacognitive components of performance on these reasoning tasks, but not with perceptual speed or response time (such as Jensen's RT task is thought to measure). Thus, according to this theory, variation in intellectual task performance is not determined by speed of processing *per se*, but by the efficiency of the metacomponents that control these basic processes.

One short-coming of this theory is that, in isolation, it borders on being tautological. Essentially, performance parameters on one set of reasoning tasks are used to predict performance on another set of reasoning tasks (IQ tests). Because the tasks which measured metacomponent efficiency in time units were also difficult enough to produce substantial error rates, especially among subjects with slower performance rates, it is not possible to tell exactly what parameter varies among individuals, and claims such as "selection of lower-order components varied" between individuals (Sternberg, 1983, p. 22) remain moot and untestable. The theory does, however, offer us an alternative explanation for the speed/reasoning correlations, and remind us that no task, however simple, is completely immune to the influence of strategies, whether at a highly refined and complex level or at the simple level of "keep watching the place where the stimulus is going to appear".

Inhibition and individual differences.   Dempster (1991) also acknowledges the importance of executive functions such as goal-formation and planning in ultimate reasoning performance, but, unlike Sternberg, links this to inhibition at the lower cognitive mechanism level and goes so far as to suggest that this may be related to frontal lobe function at a neurological level. Dempster does not suggest that inhibition is the only variable underlying individual differences in intellectual performance, but argues that it is an important and much neglected one which plays a significant part in many intellectual tasks.

Neurophysiological evidence suggests that the frontal lobes are responsible for the executive functions of coordinating information from multiple sources, forming goals and planning (Lezac, 1983; Stuss & Benson, 1984). They also exhibit large differences in synaptic density, cortical fissuration, and myelination among individuals (Terry, De Teresa, & Hansen, 1987). Patients with frontal lobe lesions mostly retain specific skills, knowledge and abstract thinking ability, but perform poorly on interference-sensitive tasks: those which include distractors, conflicting cues, response delays, or which consist of multiple trials. Some such tasks are the Wisconsin Card Sorting Test (Milner, 1963), on which individuals sort cards on one dimension (e.g. colour) ignoring all others and then switch to sorting cards on a different dimension (e.g. shape); selective attention tasks such as the Stroop task, in which participants are presented with a list of colour names printed in ink which does not match the colour name and are required to name the ink colour as quickly as possible, ignoring the printed word; and measures of field dependence such as Block Design from the Wechsler intelligence tests (Lezac, 1983). Performance on these tasks is also correlated with IQ, and, developmentally, with age, in the normal population (Dempstcr, 1991).

While speed, inhibition and metacognition have all been suggested as possible causes underlying individual differences in intelligence, it should be apparent that they are not completely independent of each other. Variation in any one of the factors may conceivably affect the measurement of the other factors, so increasing speed or inhibition may result in more efficient metacognition, or equally more efficient metacognition may result in superior performance on speeded tasks or interference-sensitive tasks. A general consensus, however, is that the variable of interest changes with age through childhood, and is consequently unidimensional with respect to individual differences and development. Let us turn our attention now to how these theories and others have been applied to developmental differences in reasoning ability.

Developmental change

A number of different mechanisms have been proposed to account for between-age differences in reasoning ability. Some, such as speed and inhibition, we have already encountered as explanations for within-age differences, but since developmental theorists are, for the most part, different researchers employing different methodologies and invoking different evidence for their claims, it is worth considering these variables again in the developmental context. Other cognitive variables such as capacity, representational redescription, and module maturation have been investigated primarily in the developmental domain, although certain theorists claim that their findings can be applied equally to the realm of individual differences.

Speed and cognitive development. Nettelbeck (Nettelbeck & Wilson, 1985; Hale, 1990, Kail, 1986, 1991a, 1991b; Case, 1985) have all proposed that cognitive speed increases developmentally, giving rise to the development of intellectual performance. Evidence for increasing speed comes from a variety of different tasks and approaches.

Nettelbeck's evidence comes from the finding that inspection time (IT) task performance improves with age. However, the view that decreasing IT (or for that matter RT) means that speed of processing is increasing has been challenged (Anderson, 1986, 1988, and see later). Nevertheless in a number of studies Nettelbeck and colleagues have found consistent age related changes in IT. For example, Nettelbeck and Wilson (1985) conducted a cross-sequential study in which they found that children's IT decreased with age, and that this improvement was not attributable to practice. Furthermore, IT has been found to correlate with MA (Nettelbeck & Wilson, 1994).

Hale (1990) and Kail (1986, 1991a) make use of a technique pioneered by Brinley (1965), which involves plotting children's RT on a variety of tasks and task conditions against adults' RT on those same tasks. The argument is that if the relationship between children's and adults RT across a wide variety of tasks and conditions is linear then the parsimonious conclusion is that children's responses are slowed relative to adults' responses by a single common factor with the slope of the linear functioning giving the degree of slowing. The logic is as follows. We have already seen that RT tasks are not very pure measures of speed. Rather than attempting to devise a single, pure measure, the Brinley technique takes a number of different speed estimates and attempts to distil from them a single global speed measure by a process somewhat analogous to the factor analytic method. The argument runs that RT can be considered to measure the time taken to execute a range of different processes (x, y, z . . .). The factor by which children are slower than adults on each of these processes can be represented as i, j, k . . . Thus, children's RT is the sum of the times taken by each process adjusted by their coefficients ($RT = ix + jy + kz$ . . .). Now, if cognitive processes develop in unison then $i = j = k$ . . . Thus, $RT = i(x + y + z)$. So, if children employ the same processes as adults and all of these processes are subject to the same slowing coefficient, then children's RT on any task condition will be equal to adults' RT on that condition multiplied by i. Taking this a step further, if we plot children's RT on tasks employing a range of different processes against adults' corresponding RT then the data should show a linear relationship with a slope value of *i*. If, on the other hand, different cognitive processes increase their efficiency independently of one another (i.e. development is domain-specific rather than domain-general) then the developmental coefficients (*i*, *j*, *k*) will have different values and no simple linear relationship will be found between children's and adults' RT scores on tasks employing different combinations of processes. Hale (1990) and Kail (1986, 1991a) both found a linear relationship between children's and adults' RT scores, with the *i* coefficient diminishing as the children's age increased, suggesting that speed of processing increases globally with age. Although these analyses typically compare groups differing on chronological, rather than mental, age it is argued that speed is causally related to the latter (Fry & Hale, 1996; Kail, 1995). Taken with the evidence that RT correlates with IQ among adults, the finding that it also becomes faster with age is consistent with a unidimensional model of within- and between-age differences in reasoning ability, with that dimension being speed of processing.

Like Kail, Case (1985) argues that increasing speed is the ultimate driving force behind cognitive development. Unlike Kail, his model of how cognitive development occurs is quite complex. He argues that development comes about as the result of the combination of maturational factors, experience and internal hierarchical reorganisation of concepts. The reorganisation of concepts is limited by speed of processing. Speed increases through the combined effects of brain maturation and practice. Case claims executive processing space (the capacity an individual has for actively processing information, and thus a major limiting factor in reasoning performance) to be the sum of operating space (capacity for manipulating bits of information) and short-term storage space (STSS). He claims that the latter becomes more efficient, leaving more resources free to allocate to the former. The gradual increase in short-term storage efficiency allows progressively more complex concepts to be entertained, as does the periodic reorganisation of concepts into new, more efficient forms which become the basis for the next stage of development. Evidence for Case's theory comes from the ability to predict children's performance on developmental tasks, as well as their ability to profit from instruction, from measures of their STSS.

According to Case, individuals may differ in the rate at which processing efficiency (both general and domain-specific) increases. This individual variation may be due to either biological or cultural-experiential factors. Thus, Case subscribes to the unidimensional model of within- and between-age differences in reasoning since the same explanatory variables are invoked for both within- and between-age differences. At a more subtle level, however, there is some suggestion of multidimensionality. Case suggests that degree of biological maturation is a more important factor in early childhood than it is later on, when experiential factors come to the fore. This is consistent with the notion that a unidimensional model is adequate at a cognitive level, but at a neurological level a multidimensional model would be necessary to accommodate children at different stages of maturation performing at similar levels on reasoning tasks.

Capacity and cognitive development. Halford (1987, 1993) proposes that it is cognitive capacity rather than speed which changes with age. Rather than the continuous growth curve put forward by Kail, Halford's view conforms more to the Piagetian stage-shift conceptualisation of cognitive development. According to Halford, the concepts that individuals can understand and the strategies they are able to employ are limited by the complexity (or number of dimensions) of the representations they are able to construct. Infants are able to represent only a single dimension, whereas by adulthood, individuals are typically able to represent four dimensions. Thus, what makes problems soluble or insoluble for a given age group is the cognitive load they impose. This load may be reduced in some cases by processing information serially or by employing chunking techniques to reduce two or more dimensions to a single dimension, but for every problem there is a minimum number of dimensions which must be represented simultaneously for the problem to be solved. When dimensions of a problem do not vary, problems can be solved by no other method than representing all dimensions simultaneously.

While it is no small matter to measure "capacity" as a resource independent of the knowledge-base that people bring to problem solving (see Navon, 1984), Halford argues that the easy-to-hard procedure developed by Hunt and Lansman (1982) allows us to do so. The logic of this method is to demonstrate that the amount of capacity children have left over when solving an "easy" (low load) version of a task predicts how well they will fare when presented with a "hard" (high load) version of the same task. To this end, Halford, Maybery, and Bain (1986) gave two versions of a transitive inference task involving the use of one and two premises respectively to five-year-old children. The children also performed a secondary task (rehearsing pairs of colour names) while completing the easy transitive inference task. It was found that performance on the secondary task in the dual-task condition (i.e. the measure of left-over capacity) was the only significant predictor of accuracy on the hard version of the transitive inference task when the possible effects of similarity between tasks were statistically controlled. While the transitive inference task has received the most empirical attention, Halford (1987, 1993) discusses the application of the capacity framework to a wide range of developmental tasks.

Implicitly, the capacity theory supports the notion that within- and between-age differences in reasoning ability are attributable to a single, global factor. However, it appears that the variation in capacity responsible for within-age differences in reasoning ability is relatively trivial compared to the great differences in capacity between children of different ages.

Inhibition and cognitive development. Bjorklund and Harnishfeger (1990) propose the theory that it may not be children's central processing speed or capacity increasing with age but the improvement in their inhibitory processes which accounts for the development of their reasoning ability with age. Thus, it is not only the activation of *relevant* information and processes which determines success on reasoning tasks, but also the inhibition of *irrelevant* information and processes (Dempster, 1991). According to Bjorklund and Harnishfeger (1990), available cognitive resources may remain constant with age and what changes is control over what is attended to and what is ignored.

Although we are far from being able to map neurological phenomena directly onto psychological phenomena, our knowledge of the relatively few brain structures which continue to develop between birth and adulthood is not inconsistent with the inhibition theory. First, the process of myelination of neural fibres (which insulates them, reducing lateral leakage of energy) is known to continue until mid-adolescence or early adulthood in some areas of the brain, notably the frontal lobes (Yakovlev & Lecours, 1967), which, as we have already seen, are associated with inhibitory ability. Second, neuronal density in the frontal cortex is known to decrease as children grow older, synaptic density in this region declines between 7 and 16 years of age and the number of synapses per neuron decreases (Huttenlocher, 1993).

Cognitive evidence for the inhibition theory of development comes from many sources. Miller and Weiss (1981), for example, found that while children's memory for task-relevant information increased steadily with age, their memory for task-irrelevant information decreased with age. Younger children are also notoriously harder to keep on-task: they show more task-irrelevant intrusions on certain reasoning and memory tasks (Bjorklund & Harnishfeger, 1990); they are worse at tasks calling for verbal and non-verbal inhibition (Passler, Isaac, & Hynd, 1985); they are more field-dependent (Witkin & Goodenough, 1981); and they have a tendency to explore interesting new stimuli rather than limiting their attention to their task-relevant features (Vliestra, 1982).

The inhibition theory is implicitly consistent with the notion that within- and between-age differences in reasoning ability may be different dimensions. This model allows that quantity of cognitive resources (whether speed or capacity) may remain constant for an individual but may vary among individuals, accounting for IQ differences, while all individuals improve with age in their ability to attend selectively, making optimal use of the resources they have, accounting for developmental change in reasoning performance.

Representational redescription and cognitive development.   Karmiloff-Smith's (1992) theory of representational redescription (RR) is of a rather different flavour from the developmental theories encountered so far, but shares some similarities with Case's hierarchical reorganisation of concepts. This theory uses Fodor's (1983) distinction between "modular" input systems and central systems in a developmental context. Fodorian modules are innate; highly specialised; highly efficient, in that they process complex information very quickly; opaque to conscious scrutiny; inflexible; and mandatory (given their trigger stimulus they cannot be prevented from firing). Central systems are domain-neutral and relatively slow, but have the advantage of being flexible rather than hard-wired. Karmiloff-Smith's theory embeds the interface between modular processing and central processing in a developmental context. She argues, contra Fodor, that modules are not fully specified and operational in infants from birth. Instead, Karmiloff-Smith postulates that modules themselves are the result of an on-going developmental process of modularisation, albeit one based on certain innate attentional biases.

According to Karmiloff-Smith, concepts develop by means of the RR cycle which consists of three phases. The first phase consists of achieving successful performance on a task at a procedural level. In this phase the focus is largely on environmental input information. The resulting representation of the stimulus information is essentially modular: highly specific, implicit, and efficient. In the second phase an explicit representation is formed which is available for central processing: A mini-theory is developed of why the procedure devised in phase 1 works. During this phase, children's focus shifts from external stimuli to their internal representation, which, if the mini-theory is inadequate, may actually lead to a deterioration in performance of the task in question. This first level of explicit representation is much less detailed than the implicit representation, extracting only the key features of the original information to be processed, but because it is accessible to central processes, it can now be manipulated and related to other explicit representations within the domain which have been stored previously. The third phase consists of reconciling internal representations with external data and revising tentative mini-theories as required so that performance resumes its high level.

The result of this process is that, ultimately, the same information is represented in many forms: implicitly, at a level available for intra-domain connections; at a level available for inter-domain connections and conscious reflection; and, finally, at a level where understanding can be expressed verbally. Unlike Case, who argues for increasing *economy* of organisation of knowledge, Karmiloff-Smith stresses the value of having a highly *redundant* set of representations of the same information at different levels: Same-task performance is likely to be most efficient using the implicit representation, but given new tasks in the same or different domains, progressively more abstract representations allow knowledge to be transferred to new situations. RR can also occur in the opposite direction: Information initially represented explicitly (as in formal education settings) is later redescribed in more applicable forms for ready use.

Karmiloff-Smith supports her theory with evidence from children's task performance after they reach behavioural mastery. Taking the Piagetian approach of examining qualitative aspects of individual children's performance on tasks such as drawing pictures, balancing blocks, or counting, she shows that, rather than continuing to use the tried and true method of performing a task, children experiment with different methods, apparently spontaneously "testing" their theories. When tasks are subtly changed, children's continued success is dependent on their possessing representations at an appropriate level of explicitness, and this continuing success is often age related. Notably, children show a U-shaped performance curve on a wide range of tasks and the errors they make reveal an inflexible adherence to an inadequate "theory".

The RR theory of cognitive development stands in contrast to the other developmental theories mentioned so far in that it sees development as being highly domain-specific insofar as *content is* concerned. The *process* of RR is domain-general in the way that learning theory is domain-general, but similarly to learning theory, the RR theory would not predict a child's performance on tasks from one domain to give any indication of how well that child will perform in another domain. Also, the RR process is seen as unchanging with age—applicable to adults and infants alike. So, while this theory falls into the unidimensional basket since it offers the same reason for between- as within-age differences in task performance, it is neutral as to whether parameters of the RR process itself are a source of individual variation in reasoning ability or whether all differences can be accounted for by differences in domain-specific experience.

Module maturation and cognitive development.   Anderson (1992), in his model of cognitive development and intelligence, makes explicit the notion that within- and between-age differences in reasoning ability are due to different dimensions. His theory uses Fodor's (1983) distinction between modules and central processes: Individual differences in speed of central processing are responsible for differences in reasoning power (IQ), whereas differences in reasoning power between age groups are attributed to the maturation of modules. Anderson proposes that there are potentially two different ways of building modules. The first follows the Fodorian notion that modules are of evolutionary advantage to the whole species and, as such, are genetically specified and programmed to come on-line at a particular point in development. The second is more in line with the Karmiloff-Smith idea of modularisation, whereby processes or concepts which are initially represented by central processes become essentially modular (automatic, effort-free, etc.) with practice. The second type of modules would tailor themselves to the sorts of reasoning and problem solving that the individual encountered frequently in his or her particular environment. While modules for such things as a theory of mind or syntactic parsing ability are highly specific, Anderson suggests that a general-purpose processing ability such as inhibition might also be a modular system which develops with age.

The several lines of evidence for this model consist mainly of refutations of the unidimensional model, that is showing that IQ is related to a different process (in Anderson's view this is speed of processing) than that causally related to developmental change. First, the course of the development of certain concepts appears to be highly predictable (e.g. Piaget, 1950) and certain concepts seem to emerge at very much the same age for all individuals of normal IQ (e.g. Slobin, 1979). Second, although there is evidence that RT and IT task performance improve with age, there is also evidence (e.g. Anderson, 1989a, 1989b) that these age differences may have less to do with actual speed of processing than with extraneous variables such as attention and response selection—variables that may be more a function of inhibitory processes than speed *per se* (Anderson, Nettelbeck, & Barlow, 1997).

Unifying individual differences and development—theories and data

Evidently, the cognitive paradigm enables us to develop testable causal theories of intelligence and cognitive development which escape the circularity of defining intelligence as what intelligence tests measure. It is also apparent from the diversity of theories produced that psychology has not yet reached a point of certainty about causal mechanisms for within- or between-age differences in reasoning ability, let alone whether they correspond to one or two dimensions.

Two theories, those of Anderson (1992) and Dempster (1991), take explicit account of both within- and between-age differences in intellectual ability. For Dempster, two cognitive mechanisms determine intellectual performance: activation and inhibition. Activatory processing he associates non-specifically with speed of processing, strategy selection or capacity. Anderson (1992) also invokes two different sorts of mechanism to account for within- and between-age differences, namely, speed of processing and module maturation. In agreement with Dempster he suggests that the capacity to select responses (or its complement, inhibition) is an important component of developmental change (Anderson et al., 1997) and that inhibitory systems would have modular status in his theory, that is they develop independently of IQ. Thus, Dempster's and Anderson's accounts have much in common. Their difference lies in the fact that Dempster's theory is unidimensional—inhibitory processes are related to both IQ and development, whereas Anderson's is multidimensional—speed is aligned with within-age differences (IQ) while the maturation of inhibitory systems accounts for developmental change.

Several theorists who conduct their research primarily into within-age differences or between-age differences comment that their theory could be applied equally well to the other of the two. Nevertheless, as we shall see, we should hesitate to accept this without supporting data which clearly demonstrates that young children and low-IQ subjects show equivalent cognitive performance levels on the same performance parameters of the same tasks. Some such data are available. Sternberg (1983) found that metacomponents were good predictors of both within-age and between-age differences in reasoning ability. The inhibitory tasks Dempster (1991) cites as being sensitive to IQ differences are also sensitive to age. Nettelbeck (1987; Nettelbeck & Wilson, 1985) reports that IT performance is related to both IQ and MA. Notably, however, Anderson's (1989a, 1989b) findings suggested that different *components* of the IT task were differentially sensitive to IQ and MA, so that the cognitive basis for the correlation between IQ and IT was different from the cognitive basis for the correlation between MA and IT. Indeed, Nettelbeck and Wilson (1994) found that the correlation between IT and MA disappeared when chronological age was partialled out, suggesting that the cause of cognitive development might not be increasing speed, but some other age-related variable. These findings highlight a methodological hindrance to finding an answer to the dimensionality question: Performance on a single task, or indeed any performance index, may reflect variance in more than one cognitive variable. Other drawbacks are considered in the following section.

SHORTCOMINGS OF RESEARCH TO DATE

There are a number of shortcomings of the current literature for an attempt to answer the question of whether individual differences and developmental change represent a single dimension of intelligence. First, in many studies task validity is open to doubt—empirical measures purported to index cognitive constructs may not, in fact, be the pure measures hoped of those constructs. When the interpretation of the key measures is in doubt, we cannot take the short-cut approach of combining an individual differences theory with a developmental theory (e.g. Kail claims speed increases with age; Jensen claims that it varies with IQ, so intelligence is unidimensional and underlain by cognitive speed). Second, in some cases, the statistical methods employed are not as compelling as they appear initially. Third, the greatest obstacle to answering the dimensionality question is that it has not until recently been explicitly addressed! We will treat each shortcoming in turn.

Task validity

If we are to take seriously the idea that some basic, knowledge-free, cognitive processing parameter (such as speed or capacity) determines complex, knowledge-rich measured intelligence, then we need to be sure that the empirical variable we choose as our parameter measure really is what it is purported to be. It is relatively uninteresting to find that one complex reasoning task (alleged to measure a fundamental processing parameter) correlates with another (alleged to measure intellectual ability). Yet, the task of devising a pure measure, uninfluenced by knowledge, is no easy feat. Some theorists, such as Kail and Halford, do not attempt to find pure tasks, but seek instead to measure their cognitive variables obliquely, relying on various ingenious methods of statistically filtering their measures: Kail by assuming what is common to a selection of speeded tasks to be speed itself, Halford by attributing the trade-off between two tasks to capacity limitations. Others, such as Dempster, and Bjorklund and Harnishfeger, infer their variables of interest from speed and accuracy measures on particular sorts of task. Still others, such as Case, Jensen, and Nettelbeck, seek to eradicate any knowledge component from their tasks by making them (in Case's case) equally novel for all subjects, or (for Jensen and Nettelbeck) so simple that whatever knowledge was necessary would be possessed by all subjects, however young and uninformed, and thus not be a source of variance. While each of these approaches is legitimate in principle, their concomitant assumptions must be met if they are to produce valid measures in practice.

The success of the first, using oblique measurement techniques, depends on common variance among tasks being attributable only to the cognitive variable of interest. Thus, Kail would have to demonstrate that the only thing that his RT tasks had in common was cognitive speed and not, for example, motor response speed or attention. Similarly, the age differences he found would have to be attributable only to basic cognitive speed and not to differences in, for example, the familiarity of stimuli or task requirements (either reasoning processes or computer task format). In a similar vein, Halford would need to demonstrate that the decline in secondary task performance in his dual-task paradigm was due to the two tasks competing for limited resources and not, for example, to the performance of one task specifically interfering with the performance of the other (Navon, 1984).

For the theorists who wish to measure low-level cognitive variables directly, the first requirement is that they measure low-level variables rather than knowledge and strategy use. The second is that they differentiate their key variable from other potential low-level cognitive variables. A general weakness of direct capacity measures (e.g. backward digit span, the Figural Intersection Test; Chapman & Lindenberger, 1989) is their relative complexity, which provides considerable scope for strategy differences and the confounding factor that stimuli may be more familiar to some individuals than others. As mentioned earlier, Jensen's RT task, despite its apparent simplicity, has been criticised for not being simple enough, being sensitive to various confounding factors, and amenable to different strategies (Longstreth, 1984).

The IT task, too, has been dogged by potential knowledge and strategy interference. In the original two-line discrimination task, some people were found to be using an apparent-motion strategy, whereby on trials where the two lines were of different lengths, when the mask covered them it looked as though the short line "grew". (Notably, however, the correlation between IQ and IT actually *increased* when subjects were prevented from using this strategy; Evans & Nettelbeck, 1993.) For younger subjects, potential sources of variance extraneous to speed of processing include use of the rather obvious strategy of watching the computer screen when a stimulus is about to appear, the ability to concentrate for many trials without succumbing to fatigue, the ability to remember arbitrary response requirements and the ability to respond in the face of uncertainty. Thus, even very simple tasks are not immune to the influence of extraneous factors which need to be taken into account when interpreting findings from these tasks.

Additionally, before one low-level cognitive variable can be granted supremacy, it needs to be distinguished from other low-level variables. Performance on *all* speed, capacity, or inhibition measures is likely to improve if any one of those variables is increased. It is not adequate to argue for the importance of one particular theoretical variable on the basis of the particular empirical unit of measurement used in an experiment (i.e. speeded tasks always generate speed scores, capacity tasks always generate capacity scores, regardless of which theoretical variable is actually changing). This leads us to the second shortcoming of research to date, that statistical methods may be inadequate to decide between unidimensional and multidimensional models.

Statistical and methodological issues

Whether aiming to discover which cognitive variable underlies intelligence, or to choose between one- and two-dimensional accounts of within- and between-age differences, simple correlational findings are of relatively little value as they do not discriminate adequately between models. For example, a simple correlation between RT and IQ is consistent with the notion that speed determines intelligence, but it is equally consistent with the alternative notion that intelligence determines RT task performance, or that a motivational factor which determines performance on intelligence tests also determines performance on RT tasks, to name a few. It is not sufficient to demonstrate that performance on a measure of inhibition or speed covaries with age or intelligence since both speed and accuracy on virtually *any* task increases with age and intelligence. It is necessary to introduce some form of statistical control to demonstrate that differences in reasoning ability can be attributed to the ability to inhibit irrelevant information but not to some other likely contender variable. At the very least, it needs to be shown that, in a pool of covarying tasks, the key measures are able to account for variance in reasoning ability beyond that which is accounted for by any other variables.

Similarly, simple correlations between cognitive variables and age are relatively uninteresting unless it is demonstrated that the key variables correlate even more strongly with MA and to continue to correlate with MA when chronological age is partialled out. Thus, while the correlation is a useful starting point, it is essential that alternative hypotheses which could explain the relationship between the variables be ruled out by statistical control.

The Brinley plot procedure employed by Hale (1990) and Kail (1991a), in which younger children's RT performance is plotted against adults, is also subject to criticism. It is argued that a linear relationship and a slope greater than 1 demonstrates that a single, global factor (speed) accounts for age differences. This interpretation can be undermined by various factors. First, Anderson (1995) has shown using computer simulations that while the logic of the Brinley technique may be sound, it may be of little empirical value since it appears to be insensitive to cases of multi-dimensionality. Second, the RT task conditions sampled must cover a disparate enough range of theoretical cognitive processes that there be some scope for tasks to follow different developmental patterns. (This is analogous to the requirement that variables entered into a factor analysis cover a broad range so that any "general" factor represents a general factor and not a bloated specific factor.) Third, the age range sampled must be wide enough to encompass potential qualitative changes in performance on the tasks sampled.

The last factor brings additional problems. Given that children's cognitive development progresses most rapidly over the early years of life, it is unfortunate that the more theoretically interesting younger children are also the ones who are most likely to have difficulty understanding task instructions and making motor responses. Generally, they are less likely to provide pure data. An associated problem is that the most readily available adult subjects for developmental studies, namely, university students, are likely to have higher IQs than school children, thus confounding development with IQ differences.

Theoretical questions tackled

A serious deficiency in the literature is that the question of whether between- and within-age differences in reasoning ability represent a single dimension or two distinct dimensions has been largely ignored. That there is but one dimension is an implicit a priori assumption traceable back to the pioneering work of Binet and reinforced by the fact that intelligence tests produce both MA and IQ scores from performance on the same set of tasks. Let us recall, however, that from the very beginning, psychometric tests of intelligence have been *designed* to be unidimensional within and between ages. Binet, interested in pragmatics rather than theory, chose age groups as a convenient set of subject groups likely to differ in intellectual ability, and selected sub-scales and items on the basis of their showing monotonic developmental trajectories. Any sub-tests which violated the unidimensional model would have been systematically removed from the test.

The bulk of research to date examines the characteristics of IQ groups only (if it is an individual differences theory being investigated) or age groups only (if it is a theory of cognitive development) and makes virtually no attempt to examine both age and IQ-group differences simultaneously. Thus, there is, at the very least, a need at least to test this assumption of unidimensionality.

Another major obstacle to deciding which of the range of theories of intelligence and cognitive development gives the most adequate account of these phenomena is the lack of empirical research conducted which explicitly pits one theory against another. Most studies have been designed to test how well a single theory accounts for the data. While this approach is a legitimate starting point for a new theory, it has severe limitations. This is especially the case since, as we have seen, there is considerable overlap between the predictions of the various theories we have examined:

Gathering more and more data in support of the notion that capacity increases with age is likely to serve just as well as evidence that speed or inhibition increases with age, unless these alternative interpretations are specifically ruled out.

The converse of this problem is, paradoxically, that the data typically published are not theory-neutral. Speed theories tend to generate speed data, capacity theories capacity data, and because these streams of research develop in relative isolation there is no clear grounds for theory comparison. Without experiments which focus on the *different* predictions made by different theories, there are two major sorts of conclusion unavailable to us. First and most obviously, we cannot tell which, if any, of the range of theories presented is superior to the others. Second, if more than one theory turns out to have significant independent explanatory power, we are in no position to devise more detailed theories of the interactions among cognitive variables, or between cognitive variables and age and IQ.

Therefore, the question of the number of dimensions required to capture within- and between-age differences in intellectual ability cannot yet be answered confidently, given the limitations of the data, statistical methods and research questions to date. However, we must not mistake these limitations for signs of stagnation and futility. On the contrary, the centrality of the question of dimensionality has only recently come to light, and provides exciting new territory to be explored.

CONCLUSIONS

Given that there are as yet a number of constraints on the evidence for the unidimensional versus the multidimensional models, can we draw any tentative conclusions at this stage about the relative merits of these two views? The unidimensional model certainly has the advantage of parsimony on its side, but there is at least preliminary evidence to suggest the two-dimensional model is worth considering. Let us turn now to the findings a theory needs to accommodate.

Findings to be accommodated

First, there is the robust finding that factor analysis of the performance of groups of same-aged subjects on batteries of intellectual tasks yields a general factor. Although there is also evidence of some domain-specificity or division between verbal and spatial tasks, and different factor analytic techniques cause different emphasis to be placed on the general versus specific factors, the general factor is always present, even if only as a second-order factor (e.g. Thurstone, 1938).

The second robust finding is that reasoning ability improves with age, and that this is so across many domains. That is, there seems to be some general sense in which children's ability to reason improves from birth until adulthood. Again, some researchers argue that development is domain-specific rather than domain-general (see Torff and Gardner, Chapter 8 of this volume), and even Piaget concedes that children show a certain degree of "horizontal décalage" or mismatch between their levels of reasoning in various domains. Nevertheless, children's performance on any of a large number of intellectual tasks is highly predictable from their age.

The third finding to be accommodated is that children are not infinitely trainable. While their performance on reasoning tasks can be improved up to a point by extensive practice and instruction, there appear to be thresholds beyond which training cannot improve performance (e.g. Siegler, 1978) and indeed, some cases in which children have been found to be quite actively resistant to instruction (e.g. Wimmer & Hartl, 1991)! What this suggests is that learning alone cannot account for cognitive development. It is also notable that, whereas knowledge or crystallised intelligence (Cattell, 1963) continues to increase throughout adulthood, reasoning or fluid intelligence ceases to develop in late adolescence or early adulthood and may even begin to deteriorate. This, too, is inconsistent with the notion that fluid intelligence increases with age due to learning—there appears to be some sort of maturational component involved.

The fourth finding to be accounted for is that IQ remains relatively stable with age. That is, a child's IQ at four years of age is predictive of their eventual adult IQ (Hindley & Owen, 1978). This suggests that IQ has an existence in its own right as an individual characteristic and not just as a derivation from MA relative to chronological age.

Fifth, among both children and adults, performance on speed tasks so simple as to be virtually knowledge-free correlates surprisingly highly with performance on knowledge-rich intellectual tasks.

The sixth noteworthy finding to be accommodated is that when older and younger children are matched for MA, they show characteristically different performance profiles on IQ sub-tests (Spitz, 1982). Typically, older, lower-IQ children have the advantage on tasks with a high knowledge component, while younger, higher-IQ children have the advantage on tasks which call for abstract reasoning. This suggests that maturational level and IQ each contribute different abilities to MA.

A suggested model of intelligence and development

To accommodate all of the previous points, we suggest the following model. To deal with the findings that IQ is relatively stable across an individual's development, and that MA-matched children achieve their same MA through different strengths and weaknesses, we propose that a two-dimensional model at the cognitive level of explanation is needed to represent within- and between-age differences adequately.

Within-age differences in reasoning ability are attributable to speed of cognitive processing. Speed determines how rapidly information can be taken in and processed. A faster processor would be able to acquire basic knowledge more quickly, and also to entertain more complex thoughts since more items of information could be activated at once before they begin to decay. Thus, the speed parameter determines how complex (and powerful) an individual's representations of stimuli can be, and also the complexity (and power) of strategies they may invoke to perform tasks. This relationship between speed and intelligence is supported by the correlation between simple speed tasks, such as RT and IT, and complex reasoning tasks.

It is our contention, however, that speed does *not* change with age, and thus cannot account for between-age differences in reasoning ability. While performance on RT and even IT tasks appears to improve with age, we attribute this not to changing *cognitive* speed but to such things as increasing motoric response facility and attentional control. Evidence for this comes from the experiment by Anderson (1989a) in which the information load and the response complexity of the IT task were varied. Increasing the information load slowed down the IT of all subjects, young and old, by the same amount. If speed increased with age then it would be expected that increasing the information load would have a multiplicative effect on resultant IT rather than an additive effect—younger children would not only be slower on the standard IT task, but disproportionately slower than older children on the high information load IT task—and this was not found to be the case. Furthermore, younger children were disproportionately slower than older children when the response complexity was increased (i.e. the amount of information to be processed remained constant, but how the child had to respond to that information became more complex). Thus, there is a better case for arguing that it is the ability to deal with the performance aspects of the task rather than cognitive speed itself which increases with age.

We attribute the major between-age differences in reasoning ability to module maturation. These may be modules in the Fodorian sense, for example, modules for phonological encoding, for theory of mind and so forth—processors which are highly efficient at processing highly specific sorts of information which are present in all undamaged members of the human species, and which are genetically programmed to come "on-line" at approximately the same point in development for everyone. Alternatively, it is possible that frontal lobe development represents a type of modular maturation which is more general in purpose. Increasing executive control over flow of attention offers an explanation for the domain-generality of cognitive development which remains theoretically distinct from the variable associated with individual differences in reasoning. A further possibility is that some modules developed are of the Karmiloff-Smith variety, that is, developed in response to a particular recurring problem that the child's environment presents. The content of such modules would vary as environment varied from individual to individual, but the process of modularisation could be expected to covary with age to some extent. Nevertheless, whether domain-general or specific, the modular dimension or dimensions ought to develop independently of IQ.

THE WAY FORWARD

Future research will do much to clarify the nature of within- and between-age differences in intellectual ability, their causes and the interactions between them. However, we have reached a point where new approaches need to be taken and new sorts of question asked, which go beyond the scope of studies to date.

Bearing in mind that, at the psychometric level, tests of intelligence were *designed* to be unidimensional, it may well be possible to create new tests which explicitly measure the dimensions of level of maturation and level of intelligence relative to peers separately. In a similar vein, an obvious finding deserving of further investigation is that of Spitz (1982) that MA-matched children of different chronological ages showed qualitative differences in their performance on IQ tests.

There is a need for researchers in the field to become more exacting in what they allow as evidence for a theory. Reliance on simple correlations of cognitive variables with intelligence or age has provided us with weak support for a multitude of theories and no information about the relative merits of one theory over another. In developmental studies particularly there is a great need for explicitly linking cognitive variables to intellectual development itself rather than merely remarking that they change with chronological age.

Rather than seeking simply to confirm or negate a single model of individual or developmental differences, we need to find ways of explicitly comparing one-dimensional with two-dimensional models, exploiting the different predictions they make, and introducing appropriate statistical controls rather than merely commenting on how well they explain pre-existing data. Examples of innovative statistical techniques helping to answer previously intractable questions can be found in behaviour genetics research, such as the LISREL analyses of Cardon, Fulker, and Joreskög

(1991). Comparing one- and two-dimensional models will entail using both IQ *and* age data to define subject groups so that the two bases for comparison are at least given the opportunity to interact differently with cognitive measures. Our progress will be greatly aided by the routine collection of IQ data in developmental studies.

Investigating the dimensionality of intelligence and development will also call for researchers to be aware of the important distinction between the levels of measurement and theory. As we have seen, unidimensionality at a psychometric measurement level does not imply a corresponding unidimensionality at a theoretical level (whether cognitive or physiological), therefore it is important not to confuse the two. It is important to realise that the construction of measures, whether psychometric or cognitive, is a theoretical process. As Andrich (1988) points out, the very process of constructing a pure measure is theoretically informative. Andrich stresses the importance of discovering how and why items (or tasks or trials) violate the unidimensionality of a scale (or test battery or cognitive task) rather than simply rejecting them without further examination. In the present debate, it would be very informative to find test items and tasks and task parameters which discriminate differentially between MA groups or IQ groups. The key point is that theory determines how measures are constructed just as much as the later use of these measures constitutes evidence for theories—neither represents an absolute truth. The task of future researchers will be to make explicit the theory underlying test construction and to test it.

Thus, in summary, the cognitive paradigm offers new approaches to the question of the dimensionality of intelligence and development which had proven intractable when approached from the psychometric measurement level alone. Although research from cognitive theorists indicates that the question is worth pursuing, there is as yet no irrefutable evidence for either the one-dimensional or the two-dimensional models. Future investigations will need to tackle the dimensionality question directly. There is a current need for studies to bridge the gap between individual differences research and cognitive developmental research in order to develop an adequate model of variation in reasoning performance—a task which cannot be accomplished by either field in isolation.

REFERENCES

Anderson, M. (1986). Inspection time and IQ in young children. *Personality and Individual Differences, 7,* 677–686.

Anderson, M. (1988). Inspection time, information processing and the development of intelligence. *British Journal of Developmental Psychology, 6,* 43–57.

Anderson, M. (1989a). Inspection time and the relationship between stimulus encoding and response selection factors in development. In D. Vickers & P. L.

Smith (Eds), *Human information processing: Measures, mechanisms and models* (pp. 509–516). North Holland: Elsevier Science.

Anderson, M. (1989b). The effect of attention on development differences in inspection time. *Personality and Individual Differences, 10,* 559–563.

Anderson, M. (1992). *Intelligence and development: A cognitive theory.* Oxford, UK: Blackwell.

Anderson, M. (1995). Evidence for a single global factor of developmental change—too good to be true? *Australian Journal of Psychology, 47,* 18–24.

Anderson, M., Nettelbeck, T., & Barlow, J. (1997). Reaction time measures of speed of information processing: Speed of response selection increases with age but speed of stimulation categorisation does not. *British Journal of Developmental Psychology, 15,* 145–157.

Andrich, D. (1988). *Rasch models for measurement.* Newbury Park, CA: Sage.

Andrich, D., & Styles, I. (1991). *Psychometric evidence of intellectual growth spurts in early adolescence.* Paper presented at the annual meeting of the American Educational Research Association, Chicago.

Barrett, P.T., & Eysenck, H.J. (1994). The relationship between evoked potential component amplitude, latency, contour length, variability, zero-crossings, and psychometric intelligence. *Personality and Individual Differences, 16,* 3–32.

Binet, A., & Simon, T. (1980). The development of intelligence in children (E.S. Kite, Trans.). Nashville, TN: Williams. (Original work published 1905)

Bjorklund, D.F., & Harnishfeger, K.K. (1990). The resources construct in cognitive development: Diverse sources of evidence and a theory of inefficient inhibition. *Developmental Review, 10,* 48–71.

Boring, E.G. (1923). Intelligence as the tests test it. *New Republic, 35,* 35–37.

Bouchard, T.J., Lykken, D.T., McGue, M., Segal, N.L., & Tellegen, A. (1990). Sources of human psychological differences: The Minnesota study of twins reared apart. *Science, 250,* 223–228.

Brinley, J.F. (1965). Cognitive sets, speed and accuracy of performance in the elderly. In A.T. Welford & J.E. Birren (Eds), *Behavior, aging, and the nervous system: Biological determinants of speed of behaviour and its changes with age* (pp. 114–149). Springfield, MI: Thomas.

Cardon, L.R., Fulker, D.W., & Joreskög, K.G. (1991). A LISREL 8 model with constrained parameters for twin and adoptive families. *Behaviour Genetics, 21,* 327–350.

Case, R. (1985). *Intellectual development: Birth to adulthood.* Orlando, FL: Academic Press.

Cattell, R.B. (1963). Theory of fluid and crystallised intelligence: A critical experiment. *Journal of Educational Psychology, 54,* 1–22.

Chapman, M., & Lindenberger, U. (1989). Concrete operations and attentional capacity. *Journal of Experimental Child Psychology, 47,* 326–358.

Dempster, F.N. (1991). Inhibitory processes: A neglected dimension of intelligence. *Intelligence, 15,* 157–173.

Evans, G., & Nettelbeck, T. (1993). Inspection time: A flash mask to reduce apparent movement effects. *Personality and Individual Differences, 15,* 91–94.

Eysenck, H. (1986). The theory of intelligence and the psychophysiology of cognition. In R.J. Sternberg & D.K. Detterman (Eds), *What is intelligence: contemporary viewpoints on its nature and definition* (pp. 1–34. Norwood, NJ: Ablex.

Fodor, J.A. (1983). *The modularity of mind: An essay on faculty psychology.* Cambridge, MA: MIT Press.

Fry, A.F., & Hale, S. (1996). Processing speed, working memory, and fluid intelligence: Evidence for a developmental cascade. *Psychological Science, 7,* 237–241.

Gould, S.J. (1981). *The mismeasure of man.* New York: Norton.

Hale, S. (1990). A global developmental trend in cognitive processing speed. *Child Development, 61,* 653–663.

Halford, G.S. (1987). A structure-mapping approach to cognitive development. *International Journal of Psychology, 22,* 609–642.

Halford, G.S. (1993). *Children's understanding: The development of mental models.* Hillsdale, NJ: Lawrence Erlbaum Associates Inc.

Halford, G.S., Maybery, M.T., & Bain, J.D. (1986). Capacity limitations in children's reasoning: A dual-task approach. *Child Development, 57,* 616–627.

Hick, W.E. (1952). On the rate of gain of information. *Quarterly Journal of Experimental Psychology, 4,* 11–26.

Hindley, C.B., & Owen, C.E. (1978). The extent of individual changes in IQ for ages between 6 months and 17 years, in a British longitudinal sample. *Journal of Child Psychology and Psychiatry, 19,* 329–350.

Hunt, E., & Lansman, M. (1982). Individual differences in attention. In R.J. Sternberg (Ed.), *Advances in the psychology of human intelligence.* Hillsdale, NJ: Lawrence Erlbaum Associates Inc.

Huttenlocher, P.R. (1993). Morphometric study of human cerebral cortex development. In M.H. Johnson (Ed.), *Brain development and cognition: A reader* (pp. 112–124). Oxford, UK: Blackwell.

Jensen, A. (1982). Reaction time and psychometric g. In H.J. Eysenck (Ed.), *A model for intelligence* (pp. 93–133). New York: Springer.

Jensen, A. (1985). Techniques for chronometric study of mental abilities. In C.R. Reynolds & V.L. Wilson (Eds), *Methodology and statistical advances in the study of individual differences* (pp. 95–99). New York: Plenum.

Jensen, A.R. (1987). Intelligence as a fact of nature. *Zeitschrift fur Padagogische Psychologie, 1,* 157–169.

Just, M.A., & Carpenter, P.A. (1985). Cognitive coordinate systems: Accounts of mental rotation and individual differences in spatial ability. *Psychological Review, 92,* 137–172.

Kail, R. (1986). Sources of age differences in speed of processing. *Child Development, 57,* 969–987.

Kail, R. (1991a). Developmental change in speed of processing during childhood and adolescence. *Psychological Bulletin, 109,* 490–501.

Kail, R. (1991b). Processing time declines exponentially during childhood and adolescence. *Developmental Psychology, 27,* 259–266.

Kail, R. (1995). Processing speed, memory, and cognition. In F.E. Weinert & W. Schneider (Eds), *Memory, performance and competencies: Issues in growth and development* (pp. 71–88). Mahwah, NJ: Lawrence Erlbaum Associates Inc.

Karmiloff-Smith, A. (1992). *Beyond modularity: A developmental perspective on cognitive science.* Cambridge, MA: MIT Press.

Lezac, M. (1983). *Neurological assessment* (2nd ed.). New York: Oxford University Press.

Longstreth, L.E. (1984). Jensen's reaction-time investigations of intelligence: A critique. *Intelligence, 8,* 139–160.

Miller, E.M. (1994). Intelligence and brain myelination: A hypothesis. *Personality and Individual Differences, 17,* 803–832.

Miller, P.H., & Weiss, M.G. (1981). Children's attention allocation, understanding of attention, and performance on the incidental learning task. *Child Development, 52,* 1183–1190.

Milner, B. (1963). Effects of different brain lesions on card-sorting. *Archives of Neurology, 9,* 90–100.

Navon, D. (1984). Resources—a theoretical soup stone? *Psychological Review, 91,* 216–234.

Nettelbeck, T. (1987). Inspection time and intelligence. In P.A. Vernon (Ed.), *Speed of information-processing and intelligence* (pp. 295–346). Norwood, NJ: Ablex.

Nettelbeck, T., & Rabbitt, P.M. (1992). Aging, cognitive performance, and mental speed. *Intelligence, 16,* 189–205.

Nettelbeck, T., & Wilson, C. (1985). A cross-sequential analysis of developmental differences in speed of visual processing. *Journal of Experimental Child Psychology, 40,* 1–22.

Nettelbeck, T., & Wilson, C. (1994). Childhood changes in speed of information processing and mental age: A brief report. *British Journal of Developmental Psychology, 12,* 277–280.

Passler, M.A., Isaac, W., & Hynd, G.W. (1985). Neuropsychological development of behaviour attributed to frontal lobe functioning in children. *Developmental Neuropsychology, 1,* 349–370.

Piaget, J. (1950). *The psychology of intelligence.* San Diego, CA: Harcourt Brace Jovanovich.

Salthouse, T.A., & Babcock, R.L. (1991). Decomposing adult age differences in working memory. *Developmental Psychology, 27,* 763–776.

Siegler, R.S. (1978). The origins of scientific reasoning. In R.S. Siegler (Ed.), *Children's thinking: What develops?* Hillsdale, NJ: Lawrence Erlbaum Associates Inc.

Siegler, R.S., & Jenkins, E. (1989). *How children discover new strategies.* Hillsdale, NJ: Lawrence Erlbaum Associates Inc.

Slobin, D.I.(1979). *Psycholinguistics.* Glenview, IL: Scott, Foresman.

Spearman, C. (1927). *The abilities of man.* New York: Macmillan.

Spitz, H.H. (1982). Intellectual extremes, mental age, and the nature of human intelligence. *Merrill-Palmer Quarterly, 28,* 167–192.

Stern, W. (1912). *Die psychologische Methoden der Intelligenzprüfung.* Leipzig: Barth.

Sternberg, R.J. (1983). Components of human intelligence. *Cognition, 15,* 1–48.

Stough, C.K., Nettelbeck, T., & Cooper, C.J. (1990). Evoked potentials, string length and intelligence. *Personality and Individual Differences, 11,* 401–406.

Stuss, D.T., & Benson, D.F. (1984). Neurological studies of the frontal lobes. *Psychological Bulletin, 95,* 3–28.

Terry, R.D., De Teresa, R., & Hansen, L.A. (1987). Neocortical cell counts in normal human adults aging. *Annals of Neurology, 21,* 530–539.

Thurstone, L.L. (1938). *Primary mental abilities.* Chicago: University of Chicago Press.

Vernon, P.A. (Ed.) (1993). *Biological approaches to the study of human intelligence.* Norwood, NJ: Ablex.

Vernon, P.E. (1950). *The structure of human abilities.* London: Methuen.

Vliestra, A.G. (1982). Children's responses to task instructions: Age changes and training effects. *Child Development, 53,* 534–542.

Wimmer, H., & Hartl, M. (1991). Against the Cartesian view on mind: Young children's difficulty with own false beliefs. *British Journal of Developmental Psychology*, *9*, 125–138.

Witkin, H.A., & Goodenough, D.R. (1981). *Cognitive styles: Essence and origins.* New York: International Universities Press.

Yakovlev, P.I., & Lecours, A. (1967). The myelogenic cycles of regional maturation of the brain. In A. Minkowski (Ed.), *Regional development of the brain in early life* (pp. 3–70). Oxford, UK: Blackwell.

CHAPTER EIGHT

The development of intelligence includes capacity to process relations of greater complexity

Graeme Halford

University of Queensland, Australia

It has been recognised for a long time that intelligence is very much a matter of processing relations. Spearman (1923) defined intelligence as the education of relations and correlates. Despite this, there has been comparatively little attempt to determine in any systematic fashion precisely what processing of relations entails, the benefits it confers, or the costs it imposes. This situation moved Smith (1989, p. 147) to observe that "despite all the empirical work and the clear importance of relational concepts, there is no unified framework for thinking about their structure and about how they develop". I will argue in this chapter that many of the phenomena with which we have been concerned in the study of cognitive development derive their important and interesting properties from the fact that they entail processing relations. We have not recognised the importance of relations in this context, as in many other contexts, because we have had no clear idea of what relational processing is, or of the properties which are characteristic of it. Therefore it is appropriate to consider first what is meant by processing relations.

PROCESSING RELATIONS

The failure of psychologists to consider systematically the nature of relational knowledge and thought is surprising given that the topic has received a great deal of attention in some other sciences. In Computer

Science, for example, there has been very extensive work on the theory of relational databases (Codd, 1990). Phillips, Halford, and Wilson (1995) have proposed that higher cognitive processes in humans entail processing relations in a way that parallels processing of relational databases. They also argued that structures on which many cognitive models depend, including lists, trees, propositional networks, can be defined in terms of relations.

Some approaches to cognitive development have been concerned with relations, though this has not been explicitly stated. Structural approaches, of which Piaget's is perhaps the most notable, are really based on relations, because mathematically a structure is a set of elements on which one or more relations is defined. Thus structural theories are really theories that depend on the processing of relations. However, despite this, the theory of relational knowledge has not generally been explicitly addressed. This brings us to the question of what a relation is.

A relation can be represented as a binding between a relation symbol R, and one or more arguments, a,b, . . . ,n. Thus, we can write a relation in the general case as R(a,b, . . . ,n). Consider the loves relation, for example John loves Jane. The relation is symbolised by a label, LOVES. The LOVES relation has two slots, a lover and a loved person (or thing), corresponding to the agent and the object (in the technical sense of object). In this case the slots are filled by John and Jane. The fact that John Loves Jane is an instance of the loves relation—it is a *relational instance*. Alternatively, consider the size relation between an elephant and a dog; an elephant is larger than a dog. It is symbolised by the label LARGER. The LARGER relation also has two roles, corresponding to a larger and a smaller entity. The fact that an elephant is larger than a dog is a relational instance. It is an instance of the LARGER relation in which the slots are filled by elephant and dog. The roles are usually said to be the *arguments* of the relation. It is convenient to write relations in predicate calculus format with the predicate-label first, and the arguments in parentheses, thus: LARGER(elephant,dog).

Notice that it is virtually impossible to understand a relation without also knowing about its roles or slots. It seems inconceivable that someone could know what loves means without also knowing that entails a love-agent (the lover) and a love-object (the loved person or thing). Similarly, one could hardly know what the relation "larger" meant without also knowing that it entails relating a larger to a smaller entity. Notice also that one knows about the roles of a relation without necessarily having to consider specific instances. One does not have to know who loves whom to understand what love means. If I said: "Some of the people in this group are in love", you would not have to find out who loved whom to know what the statement meant. The important point that follows from this is that relational knowledge has some degree of content independence. One can understand a relation independently of specific relational instances.

Another property of relational knowledge that is psychologically important is its flexibility. Relations have the property of *omni-directional access*. The knowledge that John loves Jane can be accessed in several ways. I can ask: whom does John love? (Jane) Who loves Jane? (John) What is the relation between John and Jane? (the loves relation). Thus, given any two components of this relation, the third can be retrieved. That is, given the symbol (LOVES) and the first slot filler (John), the second slot filler (Jane) can be retrieved. Given the symbol and the second slot filler, the first slot can be retrieved. Given the slot fillers, the symbol can be retrieved. The retrievals might not always be unique, meaning that sometimes there might be more than one answer. For example, the question "What is the relation between John and Jane" might yield answers such as "loves", "is older than", "is opposite sex to" or even "exploits". The important point however is that at least a candidate answer can be produced in every case. The omni-directional access property of relations is somewhat reminiscent of Piaget's (1947/1950) insistence that higher cognitive processes were more mobile and reversible than more primitive processes. The omni-directional access property of relational knowledge and Piagetian reversibility are certainly not the same concept, but there is an interesting link between them.

Each slot of a relation has a number of potential fillers. Thus the "larger" relation has roles for a larger and a smaller entity, each of which can be filled by any of an infinite number of fillers. Thus we have LARGER(whale,dolphin), LARGER(mountain,mole-hill), LARGER (tree,shrub), etc. Therefore, each slot provides a dimension of variation.

Common relations such as "loves" and "larger" have two slots, or two arguments. In principle, however, relations can have any number of arguments. Relations need not relate only two things, but can relate three, four, or more things. There are also relations that relate one thing, or have only one argument. The number of arguments corresponds to number of dimensions.

Readers with mathematical interests will know that a relation is a subset of a Cartesian product. More formally, an N-ary relation R^n (a,b, . . . n) is a subset of the cartesian product $S_a \times S_b \times S_n$, and is a set of points in N-dimensional space. It is a set of ordered n-tuples {. . . (a,b, . . . n) . . .} such that R(a,b, . . . n) is true. The number of arguments, N, corresponds to the number of dimensions in the space defined by the relation. I will also suggest that the number of dimensions provides a measure of conceptual complexity that is very useful in understanding intelligence. In order to do this I would first like to consider relations with different numbers of arguments in more detail.

Unary relation. A binding between a relation and one argument. The representational space has only one dimension, and the argument can be instantiated in only one way at a time. Unary relations can be interpreted as propositions with one argument, or as variable-constant bindings.

A proposition with one argument can represent a state, such as HAPPY(John), an action, such as RAN(Tom), an attribute, such as BIG(dog), or class membership, such as DOG(Fido). The argument can be instantiated in more than one way; in BIG(dog), "dog" can be replaced by horse, whale, . . . , hippopotamus. The argument therefore resembles a variable, or dimension. A binding between a variable and a constant can also be expressed as a unary relation; e.g. HEIGHT(1-metre).

Binary relations. These are the kind of relation we considered earlier. That is, "loves" and "larger" are binary relations because they each have two arguments, or relate two things. They can be represented as a binding between a relation and two arguments. For example, BIGGER-THAN(-, -) has two arguments, which can represent any pair of objects such that the first is bigger than the second; for example, BIGGER-THAN(dog,mouse).

In terms of sets, a binary relation on a set S is a subset of the Cartesian product $S \times S$ of elements of S. It is a set of ordered pairs $\{(a,b), \ldots \}$ such that R(a,b) holds true. The representational space has two dimensions of variation, and two argument instantiations are possible at once.

A univariate function, $f(a) = b$, is a special case of a binary relation, in which the mappings are unique; it is a set of ordered pairs, (a,b) such that for each a there is precisely one b such that $(a,b \in f)$. A unary operator is a special case of a univariate function; for example, the unary operator CHANGE-SIGN comprises the set of ordered pairs $\{(x, -x)\}$.

More complex variations between components can be represented with binary than with unary relations. The binary relation R(x,y) can represent the way x varies as a function of y, and *vice versa*, neither of which is possible with unary relations.

Ternary relations. These are perhaps less familiar than binary relations. A good example would be "love-triangle", which necessarily entails three persons, two of whom love a third. The ternary relation LOVE-TRIANGLE(Tom,John,Wendy) has three arguments, comprising two lovers and a loved-person.

A ternary relation can be represented as a binding between a symbol and three arguments. It has three dimensions, and three argument instantiations are possible at once.

A bivariate function is a special case of a ternary relation. It is a set of ordered triples (a,b,c) such that for each (a,b) there is precisely one c such that $(a,b,c \in f)$.

The familiar operations of arithmetical addition and multiplication are ternary relations. Arithmetic addition may be written as the set of ordered triples $\{. \ldots, +(3,2,5), \ldots, +(5,3,8), \ldots, \ldots\}$.

Quaternary relations.   These can be represented as a binding between a relation and four arguments. An example would be proportion; $a/b = c/d$ expresses a relation between the four variables $a,b,c,$ and d. This can be written as PROPORTIONATE(a,b,c,d), where the symbol PROPORTIONATE symbolises the quaternary relation between a,b,c and d. It is possible to compute how any element will vary as a function of the others. With a quaternary relation all the comparisons that are possible with ternary relations can be made, as well as four-way comparisons; the effect on w of variations in $x,y,z,$ the effects on x of variations in $w,y,z,$ and so on.

Quaternary relations can also be interpreted as functions or as operations. A trivariate function is a special case of a quaternary relation. It is a set of ordered four-tuples (a,b,c,d) such that for each (a,b,c) there is precisely one d such that $(a,b,c,d \in f)$.

Quaternary relations may be interpreted as a composition of binary operations. For example $(a + b) \in c = d$ is a quaternary relation.

RELATIONAL COMPLEXITY AND EXPERIMENTAL DESIGNS

It may already have struck the reader that the number of arguments in a relation is analogous to the number of factors in an experimental design. An experimental design can be thought of as a set of relations between independent and dependent variables. A one-way experimental design is equivalent to a binary relation between one independent and one dependent variable. A two-way experimental design is equivalent to a ternary relation, between two independent and one dependent variables, and so on. This is a useful analogy for the argument I will present, because experimental designs with different numbers of factors illustrate the concept of relational complexity. It is clear than experimental designs with more factors permit more complex interactions, but at the cost of more observations (participants) being required. This is analogous to conceptual complexity: Concepts that entail more complex relations, and relate more dimensions, represent greater complexity, but they also impose higher processing loads on performers.

RELATIONAL PROCESSING AND INTELLIGENCE

As mentioned, it is possible to represent most, if not all, human reasoning as processing relations, and this argument is presented in more detail elsewhere (Halford, Wilson, & Phillips, 1998; Phillips et al., 1995). A lot of human reasoning is based on analogical reasoning processes of some kind (Gentner, 1983; Halford, 1993, 1995; Holyoak & Thagard, 1995), and analogies entail mapping one relational structure to another. We will illustrate the point with the Tower of Hanoi puzzle and with transitive inference.

The Tower of Hanoi comprises three pegs and a number of discs. The discs are placed initially on peg A with the largest on the bottom, the next largest above it, and so on. The goal is to move all discs from peg A to peg C, without moving more than one disc at a time, or placing a larger on a smaller disc. To consider the simplest case first, in a two-disc puzzle, in order to shift disc 2 from A to C, it is necessary to first shift disc 1 from A to B. As Halford et al. (1998) point out, this task can be expressed as a relation:

Prior(shift(2,C),shift(1,B)).

Shift is a relation, so shifting 2 to C can be expressed as shift(2,C). Similarly for shifting 1 to B. The goal is to perform a set of moves in order to perform another move. This can be expressed as the higher order relation Prior, the arguments of which are shift; that is Prior(shift(-,-), shift(-,-)).[1] In the more complex three-disc puzzle, in order to shift 3 to C, it is first necessary to shift 2 to B, in order to do which it is necessary to shift 1 to C. There are now three levels of goals, and the corresponding relations are also more complex. Thus the sequence of decisions that are made in the Tower of Hanoi amount to processing a set of relations.

It has been argued elsewhere that the complexity of a move, and the processing load it imposes, can be assessed from the complexity of the relation that has to be processed (Halford et al., 1998). In the Tower of Hanoi the greater difficulty of the first move in the three-disc puzzle (as compared with the simpler two-disc puzzle) corresponds to a more complex relation that has to be processed.

Transitive inferences, such as "Tom is smarter than John, John is smarter than Stan, therefore Tom is smarter than Stan" are made by integrating the premise elements into an ordered triple, with premises elements Tom, John, Stan typically arranged from top to bottom, or left to right (Halford et al., 1995; Sternberg, 1980). This entails integrating two binary relations, contained in the premises, into a ternary relation, which

---

[1] A higher-order relation is a relation that has other relations as arguments.

we can express as "monotonically-smarter-than(Tom, John, Stan)". Processing load should be higher during premise integration, which entails a ternary relation, than during encoding, which entails a binary relation, such as smarter-than(Tom, Stan). This prediction has been confirmed empirically (Halford, Maybery, & Bain, 1986; Maybery, Bain, & Halford, 1986). Notice that once integration has occurred the load becomes lower, because it is only necessary to store the ordered triple "Tom, John, Stan". This imposes a load on the storage component of working memory, but not on the processing component. The essence of transitive inference therefore entails integrating two binary relations, expressed in the premises, into a ternary relation, from which the inference can be "read off".

These examples merely illustrate a point which could be made in much more detail, which is that all higher cognitive processes entail processing relations. Therefore, I agree with Spearman that relations are the essence of intelligence, but of course much more is known now about the processes that intelligent problem solving entails. One fundamental aspect of intelligence is capacity to process information, and relational complexity makes a good metric by which to measure processing capacity.

PROCESSING CAPACITY

Our capacity to process information has been a major issue both in general cognition and in cognitive development. Increase in processing capacity has been the major explanatory factor in neo-Piagetian theories of cognitive development. Processing capacity has been defined in a variety of ways, each of which has been associated with a set of measurement techniques. I have reviewed these elsewhere (Halford, 1993, chap. 3), but the essential ideas can be summarised here. The measurement techniques can be divided into two broad categories, span measures and resource measures. I have argued that span measures may not be appropriate for the measure of processing capacity because they depend wholly or partly on storage, and processing is at least partly distinct from storage. Resource measures reflect the amount of resources allocated to a task. This can be measured by physiological arousal indices such as pupil dilation, or by decrement in a concurrent task that uses the same resource pool. An efficient procedure for this purpose is probe reaction time, that is, response latency to a stimulus occurring concurrently with the primary task. This provides a sensitive measure of processing demands of the primary task, and the probe can be positioned at various points in the course of processing to determine how demand varies over the time course of the task. Brain imaging techniques now provide a useful alternative means of assessing processing resources allocated to a task, and have the added advantage that the neural structures involved can be identified. Resource measures provide a more direct indicator of processing load than span measures, but do not as readily yield a metric of complexity.

Our research has led us to the conclusion that the best metric for processing capacity is the complexity of relations that can be processed in parallel. From an assessment of the literature, supplemented by experiments in our laboratory, we estimate that adult humans can typically process a quaternary relation (Halford et al., 1998). That is, we have a capacity to process four dimensions in parallel. This is a soft limit, in the sense that more complex concepts can be processed, but with high error rates. However for concepts of more than four dimensions the error rate on most occasions would be such that performance would be no better than chance. As noted earlier, neural nets naturally tend to be characterised by soft limits.

It is obviously necessary for humans to process concepts more complex than four dimensional, so some way has to be found for humans to live within their cognitive limitations. The two processes that permit this are conceptual chunking and segmentation.

Conceptual chunking

This is the "collapsing" or recoding of concepts into fewer dimensions. A conceptual chunk is similar to a mnemonic chunk, except that it consists of relations as well as items. In a mnemonic chunk, items may be compressed into a single unit. For example, C,A,T becomes a chunk by combining the three letters to form a single word CAT.

We can illustrate conceptual chunking using the concept of velocity, defined as $V = st^{-1}$. The relation between velocity, distance and time is three dimensional, and would be implemented by a rank 4 tensor product. However velocity can be expressed as a single dimension, such as the position of a pointer on a dial; VELOCITY(60 kph). In this single dimensional representation, no relation is defined between velocity, distance and time. If we want to compute (say) the way velocity varies as distance increases and time decreases, we must return to the three-dimensional representation. Thus, conceptual chunks save processing capacity, but the cost is that some relations are not represented, and become temporarily inaccessible. There is also a psychological factor which limits chunking, because experience is required in which there is a constant mapping of elements into chunks.

Chunked concepts can be combined with further dimensions to represent higher level concepts. For example, treating velocity as a single dimension, we can now define acceleration, $A = (V_2 - V_1)t^{-1}$. Acceleration also can be chunked, and then Force (F) can be defined as F = MA (where

M = mass). In this way we can bootstrap our way to higher and higher level concepts, without ever exceeding four dimensions processed in parallel.

The general principles   have been defined by Halford et al. (1998) and are:

(a) a chunk functions as a single entity, symbol or argument in a relation;
(b) no relations can be represented between items within a chunk;
(c) relations between the chunk and other items, or other chunks, can be represented.

Segmentation

This is breaking tasks into steps which do not exceed processing capacity, and which are processed one at a time. It depends on the development of serial processing strategies, such as those which we all use for long addition and multiplication operations. When we add (say) 4897 + 8259 we break the task down into a series of small steps each of which is small enough not to overload processing capacity.

What then happens when processing capacity is exceeded? One reason for the unpopularity of processing capacity as a concept is the misconception that it implies "brick walls", so that all processing must cease when capacity is overloaded. In fact, however, there is no such sudden termination of cognitive processes; and a person who has insufficient capacity for the task in hand has three options (Halford, 1993; Halford et al., 1998):

1.   The concept can be chunked to a lower dimensional representation. This will only be possible if appropriate chunks have been learned or can be constructed, and it results in loss of ability to represent relations between chunked entities.

2.   The task can be segmented into smaller steps that are performed serially. This, however, requires a strategy, autonomous planning of which depends on the participant's ability to represent relations in the task.

3.   The participant can default to a lower level representation. This is analogous to performing an experiment with (say) a three-way design, then analysing the data by a series of two-way ANOVAS. Just as the analysis would lead to recovery of most of the relevant data in the experiment (all main effects and two-way interactions would be recovered), the performance would probably be correct in most respects. However, just as the hypothetical experimenter would miss the three-way interactions,

our hypothetical performer could not reason about high level relations in the task. The next question concerns the development of processing capacity.

DEVELOPMENT OF PROCESSING CAPACITY

I propose that processing capacity develops by gradually increasing the complexity of relations that can be represented. The empirical justification for this claim is extensive, and is considered in detail elsewhere (Halford, 1989, 1992, 1993; Halford et al., submitted). My purpose here is to summarise the type of development that occurs, and consider its main characteristics. I will illustrate cognitive performances typical of each level of complexity, and indicate approximate age norms by which it is usually exhibited. I have suggested elsewhere (Halford, 1993) that the phenomena which Piaget (1947/1950) attributed to stages correspond, albeit in very approximate fashion, to levels of relational complexity. The levels of relational complexity, from unary to quaternary, are shown, together with the Piagetian stages to which they approximately correspond, in Fig. 8.1. We will consider each level of complexity in turn, with respect to the age at which it is typically attained, and the conceptual abilities that are characteristic of it. First, however, the nature of the age norms in general should be discussed.

There is no suggestion that each level of complexity is mastered suddenly, or that all instances of a given level are acquired synchronously. These are attributes of Piagetian stages (at least by some accounts of Piaget), and they are sometimes assumed to be characteristic of relational complexity theory. However it should be clear that relational complexity makes no such assumptions, because it naturally postulates a soft limit, as we have already seen. It is also proposed that the proportion of children who can operate at each level would increase gradually with age, in accordance with a biological growth function. Thus processing capacity corresponds to a soft limit, and is subject to individual differences. A given level of capacity will be attained at different ages by different individuals. The observed ages represent medians, and a given level of complexity does not occur suddenly, or at the same time for all individuals.

Attainment of a given level of capacity does not occur synchronously for all content domains. Each level of complexity comprises a potentially infinite variety of concepts. For example, there is potentially an infinite number of concepts that have the complexity of a binary relation, similarly for ternary relations, and so on. The acquisition of any specific concept will depend, not only on development of the relevant capacity, but on experience. Thus cognitive development is experience driven, with

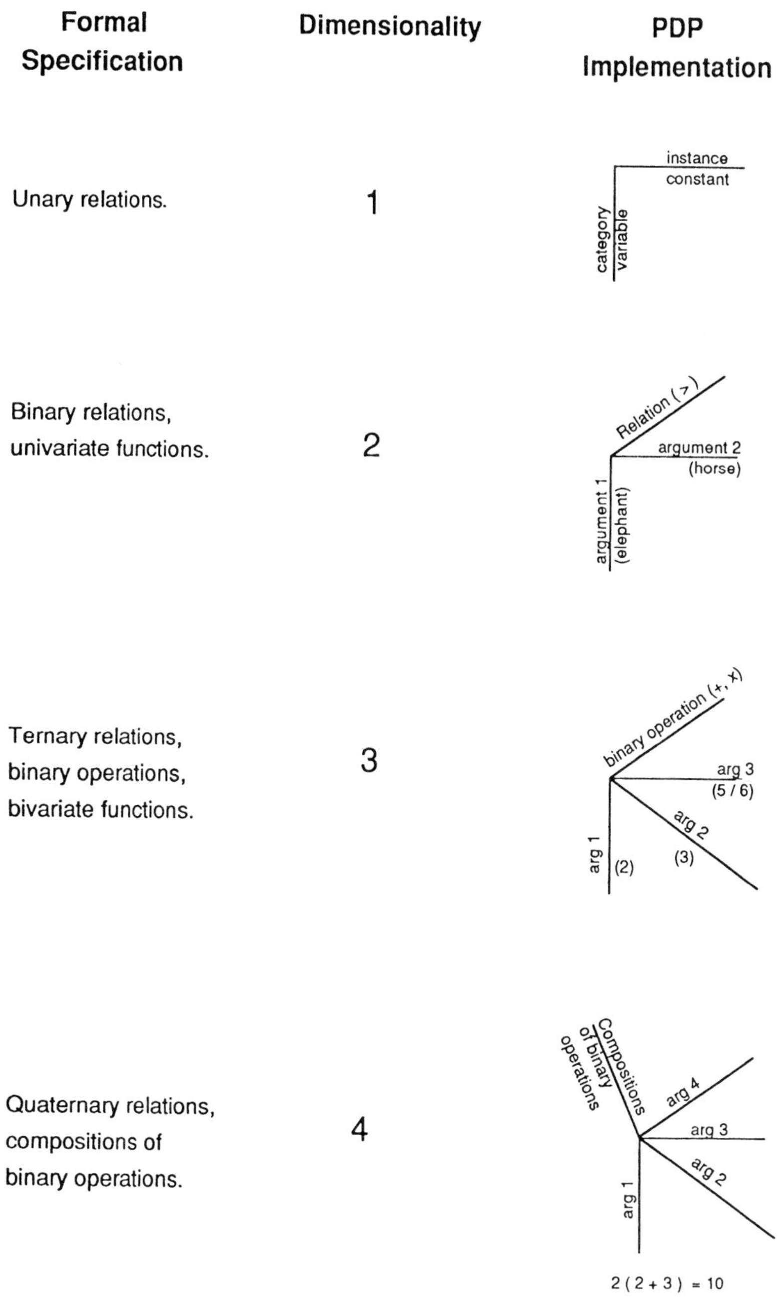

Formal Specification	Dimensionality	PDP Implementation
Unary relations.	1	
Binary relations, univariate functions.	2	
Ternary relations, binary operations, bivariate functions.	3	
Quaternary relations, compositions of binary operations.	4	

FIG. 8.1   Relations from unary to quaternary, showing dimensionality, approximate Piagetian stage, and schematic version of neural net representation.

capacity serving only an enabling role. The function of experience, and of learning mechanisms, has been considered in detail elsewhere (Halford, 1980, 1993, 1995; Halford et al., 1995).

This point cannot be over-emphasised because there is a popular misconception that capacity theory necessarily precludes any role for experience. This misconception arises because of a tendency to use simplistic dichotomies, as though theories have to be either capacity theories or experience theories. In fact no contemporary theory known to me is a non-experience theory, because a theory which had no role for experience would be so obviously inadequate that it could never be taken seriously.

In fact my theoretical position has always had a role for experience (Halford, 1980, 1982, 1993; Halford & Fullerton, 1970). Given that experience must be important the issue is whether there is a role for capacity. The alternatives therefore are not capacity versus experience, and attempts to dichotomise the issue in this way only causes confusion, and leads to futile controversy. The alternatives are experience without any role for capacity, or experience with a role for capacity. This may not seem as appealing as a simple dichotomy, but it is far more realistic, and is much more likely to lead to fruitful research. The evidence that I have assembled elsewhere (Halford 1982, 1989, 1993) overwhelmingly favours the latter alternative. Furthermore it is clear that capacity and experience interact, so the effect of experience is modified by the capacity of the child. With these provisos I would like to outline the typical ages of attainment of each level of relational complexity, based on existing evidence considered in more detail elsewhere (Halford 1989, 1993).

Unary relations   appear to be typically attained at about one year of age. Cognitive performances at this level include simple categories, defined by one attribute such as the category of large things, or the category of triangles. This level also includes categories defined by a collection of attributes that can be represented as a single chunk, such as the category of dogs.

Variable-constant bindings are also unary relations, an example being the well-known A not-B error (Wellman, Cross, & Bartsch, 1986), which can be thought of as requiring ability to treat hiding place as a variable. That is, when an infant has repeatedly retrieved an object from hiding place A, then continues to search for it at A despite having just seen it hidden at B, the infant is treating the hiding place as a constant. However, if hiding place were represented as a variable this perseveration would be overcome. Thus the fact that the A not-B error disappears at about one year is consistent with ability to represent unary relations at that time. This implies that ability to construct representations equivalent to unary relations probably develops at approximately one year of age. We would therefore predict that other performances which require this level of representation, should first appear at this time. There should be a general ability to represent variables as distinct from constants. In general, the observations which Piaget attributed to the preconceptual stage appear to require representations that are equivalent to unary relations.

Binary relations appear to be typically attained at about two years. These include all the common relations such as larger, heavier, nicer, faster, and a myriad others. They correspond to Piaget's observation that in the intuitive stage children process one (binary) relation at a time.

Ternary relations are typically observed at a median age of about five years. Well-known examples include transitivity and class inclusion, but there are many other concepts that belong to this level, including conditional discrimination, the transverse pattern task, the negative pattern task, dimension checking in blank trials task, and many more (Halford, 1993).

Performance on these tasks has been one of the most controversial topics in cognitive development (Bryant, 1989; Bryant & Trabasso, 1971; Halford, 1989, 1992, 1993; Halford et al., 1998; Pears & Bryant, 1990). I cannot present the evidence again here, and the point seems certain to remain in dispute for some time. However, I believe it a fair summary, albeit one that is rather reluctantly accepted, that these tasks are performed readily by children over five years of age, but cause considerable difficulty below this age. In a broad sense, this level of processing corresponds to Piaget's concrete operational stage, which can be conceptualised as ability to process binary operations, or compositions of binary relations (Halford, 1982, 1993; Sheppard, 1978).

Quaternary relations appear to be first mastered at about 11 years of age. Concepts that entail this level of complexity include understanding the balance scale, proportion, and ability to reason about relations between fractions, as well as understanding concepts such as distributivity, that are based on compositions of binary operations. In a broad sense this level of processing corresponds to Piaget's formal operations stage, which entails relations between binary operations (Halford, 1993).

The purpose of presenting these age norms is not to categorise children as having this or that capability, even though I believe the practical value of that information is often underestimated in the current climate where cognitive development has been dominated by the pursuit of precocity. The point of the material in this section is to shed light on the kind of intellectual ability that develops in children. In other words, we want to know what develops when intelligence develops.

However, to understand the underlying processes of intelligence in greater depth we want to know how relations are represented and processed. Our recent modelling work on neural nets has yielded some useful insights into the demands of different levels of relational complexity. We will summarise this work in the next section.

NEURAL NET REPRESENTATION OF RELATIONS

Neural nets have many advantages as models of human psychological functions, because they are closer to the way neurons interact than are most other models, even though the match between neural nets and actual neural functions is still far from exact (Smolensky, 1988). Neural nets tend to provide natural explanations for some basic psychological phenomena including automatic generalisation and discrimination, graceful degradation, regularity detection, and prototype formation. They have also provided effective models of a number of psychological processes in the field of perception, learning, and language.

Neural nets also arguably have some shortcomings as models of higher cognitive processes, and have been criticised for alleged inability to match the properties of symbolic processes (Fodor & Pylyshyn, 1988). They are also sometimes seen as unduly restricted to an associationist conception of psychological processes.

Although this issue is too complex to be discussed in detail here, certain points should be made. The first is that neural nets are not restricted to associative processing, but certain types of nets can process explicit relations, and can model higher cognitive processes, including those involved in reasoning. Neural nets that have these properties have been developed by Smolensky (1990), by Phillips (1994) and by Halford et al. (1994), based on outer (tensor) products of vectors, and by Plate (1995) based on circular convolution.

The second point is that neural nets have the property of graceful saturation, which provides a natural basis for modelling capacity limitations. Suppose we have a set of items to store on a set of neural units. We will assume distributed representation, that is, that each item is distributed over the whole set of units, so each item will be stored as a vector of activation values over the set of units (Rumelhart & McClelland, 1986). The items will be stored by adding the representations (computing the vector sum). As the number of items increases, the representation becomes less distinct, and retrieval of information from the representation is subject to greater error. This effect occurs gradually as more items are added, and corresponds to the property of graceful saturation. Human processing capacity has a similar property, in that it is not like a container that holds a fixed number of elements. That is, human capacity is not like adding books to a bookshelf, where additions continue to be made readily until the shelf is full, when we suddenly find no more can be added. Human capacity does not suddenly "fill up" in this way, but is characterised by a soft limit, with performance degrading gradually as the limit of capacity is approached. This graceful saturation property is well captured by neural nets.

In order to understand the role of neural nets in the development of intelligence we first have to examine the way relations can be represented. A neural net representation of a binary relation, such as LARGER-THAN is shown in Fig. 8.2.

In order to represent (say) the fact that an elephant is larger than a dog, we need to represent four things. These are:

1. The relation symbol, or label, LARGER-THAN.
2. The first argument, elephant.
3. The second argument, dog.
4. The binding of the symbol to the arguments.

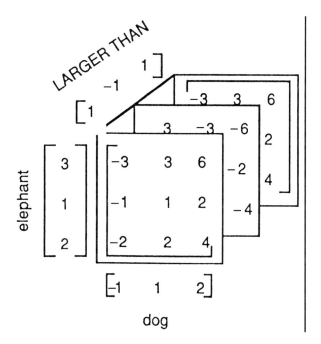

FIG. 8.2   Neural net representation of relation LARGER-THAN(elephant,dog), based on outer product of vectors representing symbol and arguments.

In our representation, a vector is used to represent the symbol, LARGER-THAN, and another vector is used to represent each argument. In this example, there is a vector representing arguments *elephant* and *dog*. The symbol-argument binding, that is, the fact that an elephant is larger than a dog, is represented by the tensor product of the three vectors, as shown in Fig. 8.2. Actually, each of the units in the vectors representing "larger than", "elephant", and "dog" is connected to one of the tensor product units in the interior of the figure, but the connections are not shown because they would make the figure too cluttered. The activations on these units effectively code the relation between the vectors.

This representation permits information about the relation to be recovered, and implements the omni-directional access property of relations discussed earlier (Halford et al., 1994, 1998). Given the symbol and an argument we find possible cases of the second argument; e.g. given the symbol "larger-than" and "elephant" the representation permits retrieval of things (such as dogs) that are smaller than elephants. This is equivalent to asking "What is smaller than an elephant?" The retrieval is achieved by activation spreading from the units representing the symbol (larger-than) and the argument (elephant), through the binding units, to the units representing the second argument (dogs, etc.). The activation is multiplied by the activations in the binding units, which effectively code the relation. Alternatively, given the arguments, the symbol can be found, equivalent to asking what is the relation between elephant and dog. Again, this is achieved by activation spreading from the units representing the arguments, through the binding units, to the units representing the symbol.

Because LARGER-THAN is a binary relation, with two arguments, it is represented by a rank 3 tensor product, that is, one with three vectors. However more complex concepts are represented by structures with more vectors. The representation of transitivity requires a rank 4 tensor product, as shown in Fig. 8.3.

Given that transitive inferences are made by organising premise information into an ordered set of three elements, the core of the transitivity concept is a ternary relation. That is, transitivity is a relation with three arguments, corresponding to a,b,c or top, middle, bottom, depending on the particular instantiation.

Consequently, it has to be represented by a tensor product of higher rank than a binary relation, such as LARGER-THAN. A tensor product of higher rank imposes a higher processing load, because the number of tensor product units increases exponentially with the number of vectors, and the number of connections increases accordingly. The PDP model therefore provides a natural basis for the increase in processing load that is observed with more complex concepts such as transitivity.

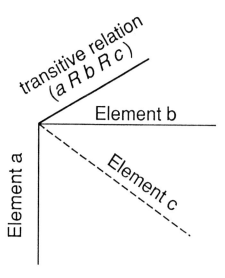

FIG. 8.3   Neural net representation of transitivity.

The representation of unary, binary, ternary, and quaternary relations, as defined by Halford et al. (1998) is shown schematically in the right column of Fig. 8.1. In general, the number of vectors is one more than the dimensionality. Thus unary relations (one-dimensional) are represented by a tensor product of two vectors, binary relations (two-dimensional) by a tensor product of three vectors, and so on.

A unary relation corresponds to category membership, variable-constant binding, and object-attribute binding, two of which are shown in Fig. 8.1. To represent category membership (such as that Fido, etc. are dogs), one vector (shown vertically in Fig. 8.2) represents the category label DOG. The other vector would represent the instances (Fido, etc.). Representations of different dogs would be superimposed on this set of units. Thus vectors representing each known dog would be superimposed, so the resulting vector would represent the central tendency of the person's experience of dogs. It would represent the person's prototype dog. However the representations of the individual dogs can still be recovered. Questions such as "are Chihuahuas dogs?", or "tell me the dogs you know?" can be answered by accessing the representation. Note that the representation is one dimensional because if one component is known, the other is determined. Thus if the argument vector represents a Labrador, the other vector must be "dog". Similarly, if the symbol vector represents "dog", the argument vector must represent one or more dogs.

The representation of ternary relations entails four vectors, one representing the symbol, and three representing arguments. This is also shown schematically in Fig. 8.1. The familiar binary operations of addition and subtraction belong to this level. One vector represents the operation (+ or ×) while two others represent the addends (multiplicands), and the fourth vector represents the sum (product). Note that if you know three of these, the fourth is determined; e.g. if you know the numbers are 2,3,5 you know the operation is addition; if you know the numbers 2,?,5, and the operation is addition, you know the missing number is 3, and so on. (Readers interested in neural nets might note that there is no catastrophic forgetting when addition and multiplication are superimposed on a rank 4 tensor product.)

Representation of a quaternary relation requires five vectors, which are also shown in Fig. 8.1. The particular example illustrates the representation of a composition of two binary operations, $2(2 + 3) = 10$. The symbol vector represents the fact that a combination of multiplication and addition are being represented, while the other vectors represent the four arguments.

The most important point which emerges from this representation is that the computational cost of a representation increases exponentially with dimensionality. The number of units increases exponentially with rank of the tensor product which, as noted above, is one more than dimensionality. Computational cost corresponds, in human terms, to processing load. Thus the implication is that processing load is naturally higher for relations of higher complexity. Putting it another way, intelligence incurs a computational cost, or imposes a processing load, that varies with the complexity of relations being processed. This naturally raises the question of the limits of human information processing capacity. We have suggested elsewhere (Halford, 1993; Halford et al., 1998) that the limits can best be defined in terms of the complexity of relations that can be processed in parallel.

THE DEVELOPMENT OF INTELLIGENCE

An impression of what develops as intelligence develops can be gained from inspecting the right-hand side of Fig. 8.1. It can be seen that what develops is the number of dimensions that can be processed at any point in time (in parallel). This development would come about by dividing a representation into more dimensions, then forming connections between all the resulting dimensions. It is a matter of forming links between more variables. Thus what develops is really more highly interconnected neural net representations. In representations of unary relations, any unit in a vector is connected to a unit in only one other vector. With binary relations, any unit is connected to units in two other vectors, in ternary relations to units in three other vectors, and so on. Thus what develops is the nature of the connectivity between representations in neural nets.

The differentiation of neural nets into larger numbers of dimensions is analogous to splitting an experimental design into more independent variables. Suppose, for example, that we take a two-way ANOVA with four levels of one factor and two levels of another, and convert it into a three-factor design with two levels on each factor. We would still have the same number of conditions (eight), but we would have a design capable of producing three-way interaction as well as two-way interactions and main effects. The total number of conditions represented might not change, but the orders of interaction that can occur does change. This corresponds to an increase in the dimensionality of relations that can be represented, because factors in an experimental design are analogous to arguments in a relation, as we saw earlier. Similarly, growth in processing capacity through development is more likely to mean that higher order relations can be represented, rather than that more information can be stored.

Thus the long-standing question of whether processing capacity changes with age can be reformulated. The question becomes, not whether overall capacity changes with age, but whether representations become more differentiated so that concepts of higher dimensionality can be understood. And if this development does occur, as I contend on the basis of extensive evidence that it does, then important new questions arise. Specifically, what are the mechanisms that lead to representations of higher dimensionality? Are they influenced by maturation, and if so what is the mechanism? How does the capacity to represent relations of higher dimensionality modify the influence of experience, and how does experience affect relational representations? These are more than interesting questions. They seem to open up an entirely new era of research, albeit one that has been almost completely ignored.

This theory also links up with evolution of intelligence as a number of authors have pointed out (Halford et al., 1998; Halford & Wilson, 1993; Holyoak & Thagard, 1995). Relations appear to be first represented in explicit form, that is with properties such as predication, omni-directional access, by primates. There is evidence that some monkey species can represent unary relations, whereas the only non-human animals known to represent binary relations are chimpanzees (Premack, 1983). Thus the theory of relational complexity can be linked, not only to the development of intelligence in children, but to the evolution of intelligence in the higher animals.

CONCLUSION

The development of intelligence no doubt has many facets, and it is almost certainly experience-dependent, as I have been at pains to emphasise, not only here but in publications over the last quarter century. However the particular aspect that I have tried to sketch out in this chapter is the reconstruction of neural net representations so that relations of higher dimensionality can be processed. This suggests that there are two areas of research, both much neglected, that could shed a great deal of light on the nature and development of intelligence. The first is the representation and processing of relations. Relations are the generic concept that underlies higher intellectual activity, but we know amazingly little about how relations are processed by humans. The second is the way relations can be processed by neural nets. This also is an area into which researchers are only now beginning to make inroads. However, some insights are opening up which suggest the rewards for these areas of research could be considerable.

REFERENCES

Bryant, P. (1989). Commentary on Halford (1989). *Human Development, 32*(6), 369–374.

Bryant, P.E., & Trabasso, T. (1971). Transitive inferences and memory in young children. *Nature, 232*, 456–458.

Codd, E.F. (1990). *The relational model for database management: Version 2.* Reading, MA: Addison-Wesley.

Fodor, J.A. & Pylyshyn, Z.W. (1988). Connectionism and cognitive architecture: A critical analysis. *Cognition, 28*, 3–71.

Gentner, D. (1983). Structure-mapping: A theoretical framework for analogy. *Cognitive Science, 7*, 155–170.

Halford, G.S. (1980). A learning set approach to multiple classification: Evidence for a theory of cognitive levels. *International Journal of Behavioral Development, 3*, 409–422.

Halford, G.S. (1982). *The development of thought.* Hillsdale, NJ: Lawrence Erlbaum Associates Inc.

Halford, G.S. (1989). Reflections on 25 years of Piagetian cognitive developmental psychology, 1963–1988. *Human Development, 32*, 325–387.

Halford, G.S. (1992). Analogical reasoning and conceptual complexity in cognitive development. *Human Development, 35*, 193–217.

Halford, G.S. (1993). *Children's understanding: The development of mental models.* Hillsdale, NJ: Lawrence Erlbaum Associates Inc.

Halford, G.S. (1995). Commentary on Moshman (1995). *Human Development, 38*, 65–70.

Halford, G.S., & Fullerton, T. (1970). A discrimination task which induces conservation of number. *Child Development. 41*, 205–213.

Halford, G.S., Maybery, M.T., & Bain, J.D. (1986). Capacity limitations in children's reasoning: A dual task approach. *Child Development, 57*, 616–627.

Halford, G.S., Smith, S.B., Dickson, J.C., Maybery, M.T., Kelly, M.E., Bain, J.D., & Stewart, J.E.M. (1995). Modeling the development of reasoning strategies: The roles of analogy, knowledge, and capacity. In T. Simon & G.S. Halford (Eds), *Developing Cognitive Competence: New Approaches to Cognitive Modeling,* Hillsdale, NJ: Lawrence Erlbaum Associates Inc.

Halford, G.S., & Wilson, W.H. (1993). Creativity and capacity for representation: Why are humans so creative? *AISB Quarterly*, *85*, 32–41.

Halford, G.S., Wilson, W.H., Guo, J., Gayler, R.W., Wiles, J., & Stewart, J.E.M. (1994). Connectionist implications for processing capacity limitations in analogies. In K.J. Holyoak & J. Barnden (Eds), *Advances in connectionist and neural computation theory, Vol. 2: Analogical connections* (pp. 363–415). Norwood, NJ: Ablex.

Halford, G.S., Wilson, W.H., & Phillips, S. (1998). *Processing capacity defined by relational complexity: Implications for comparative, developmental, and cognitive psychology. Behavioral and Brain Sciences, 21*.

Holyoak, K.J. & Thagard, P. (1995). *Mental leaps*. Cambridge, MA: MIT Press.

Maybery, M.T., Bain, J.D., & Halford, G.S. (1986). Information processing demands of transitive inference. *Journal of Experimental Psychology: Learning, Memory and Cognition*, *12*, 600–613.

Pears, R. & Bryant, P. (1990). Transitive inferences by young children about spatial position. *British Journal of Psychology*, *81*(4), 497–510.

Phillips, S. (1994). Strong systematicity within connectionism: The tensor-recurrent network. In A. Ram & K. Eiselt (Eds), *Proceedings of the 16th annual conference of the Cognitive Science Society* (pp. 723–727). Hillsdale, NJ: Lawrence Erlbaum Associates Inc.

Phillips, S., Halford, G.S., & Wilson, W.H. (1995). The processing of associations versus the processing of relations and symbols: A systematic comparison. In J.D. Moore & J.F. Lehman (Eds), *Proceedings of the 17th annual conference of the Cognitive Science Society* (pp. 688–691). Pittsburgh, PA: Lawrence Erlbaum Associates Inc.

Piaget, J. (1950). *The psychology of intelligence* (M. Piercy & D.E. Berlyne, Trans.). London: Routledge & Kegan Paul. (Original work published 1947)

Plate, T.A. (1995). Holographic reduced representations. *IEEE Transactions on Neural Networks*, *6*(3), 623–641.

Premack, D. (1983). The codes of man and beasts. *Behavioural and Brain Sciences*, *6*, 125–167.

Rumelhart, D.E. & McClelland, J.L. (1986). *Parallel distributed processing: Explorations in the microstructure of cognition*. Boston, MA: MIT Press.

Sheppard, J.L. (1978). *A structural analysis of concrete operations*. London: Wiley.

Smith, L.B. (1989). From global similarities to kinds of similarities: The construction of dimensions in development. In S. Vosniadou & A. Ortony (Eds), *Similarity and analogical reasoning* (pp. 146–178). Cambridge, MA: Cambridge University Press.

Smolensky, P. (1988). On the proper treatment of connectionism. *Behavioural and Brain Sciences*, *11*(1), 1–74.

Smolensky, P. (1990). Tensor product variable binding and the representation of symbolic structures in connectionist systems. *Artificial Intelligence*, *46*(1–2), 159–216.

Spearman, C.E. (1923). *The nature of intelligence and the principles of cognition*. London: Macmillan.

Sternberg, R.J. (1980). Representation and process in linear syllogistic reasoning. *Journal of Experimental Psychology: General*, *109*, 119–159.

Wellman, H.M., Cross, D., & Bartsch, K. (1986). Infant search and object permanence: A meta-analysis of the A-not-B error. *Monographs of the Society for Research in Child Development*, *51*.

CHAPTER NINE

Neo-interference research and the development of intelligence

Frank N. Dempster and Alice J. Corkill

Cognitive Interference Laboratory, University of Nevada, Las Vegas, Nevada, USA

BACKGROUND

The roots of all modern interference concepts in the study of cognition can be traced to classical interference theory. The father of classical interference theory was G.W. Muller who, along with Schumann, published the first of a series of empirical demonstrations of interference phenomena (Muller & Schumann, 1894). Using techniques that were influenced by Ebbinghaus's pioneering work on verbal learning, Muller and Schumann observed that the learning of a second list of items impaired memory for the first list. For example, items occupying the same serial position on the two lists were often confused. This observation was extended by Muller and Pilzecker (1900) and the phenomenon was called "retroactive inhibition", although later it would often be called "retroactive interference" (cf. Murray, 1976; Schacter, 1982).

An interesting feature of the early literature is that there was much less emphasis on proactive interference than on retroactive interference. In the late 1950s however, the appearance of a paper by Underwood (1957) intensified interest in proactive interference. In that paper, Underwood demonstrated that proactive interference influenced forgetting far more than had previously been believed. This, and subsequent research exploiting the newly minted Brown-Peterson short-term memory paradigm (Peterson & Peterson, 1959), suggested that proactive interference was at least as potent as retroactive interference. This suggestion also squared with the common sense observation that there is normally much more old information available to interfere with new learning (proactive interference) than there is new information available to interfere with old learning (retroactive interference).

In many respects, the contributions of the classical interference theorists were the most remarkable achievements of the verbal learning tradition in psychology, a tradition that focused on the conditions of acquisition, transfer, and retention of verbal (e.g. nonsense syllables, unrelated word lists) material. Two potent sources of interference and a variety of experimental variables that influenced those sources of interference were identified. Two such variables, similarity and degree of learning, were extensively investigated. Similarity, which was manipulated in a variety of ways (e.g. formal, semantic, taxonomic), tended to increase observed amounts of interference. On the other hand, increasing the degree of original learning tended to reduce interference.

As recently as 1960, interference theory was clearly the pre-eminent approach to the study of learning and memory. Soon thereafter, however, classical interference theory began to decline. The problems posed by classical interference theory never completely died out, but the area has undergone a remarkable transformation in just three decades.

There were many reasons for the decline of classical interference theory and the verbal learning tradition; however, questions about its relevance to the phenomena of everyday cognition were undoubtedly a major factor. In contrast to the many demonstrations of proactive and retroactive interference using traditional verbal learning materials and procedures (e.g. list learning), efforts to extend the theory to more realistic materials and methods met with limited success (for a review, see Dempster, 1995). In addition, classical interference theory contributed little to the study of cognitive development and intelligence. In general, this neglect failed to attract researchers seeking explanations for developmental and individual differences on everyday intellectual tasks, including complex thinking and reasoning situations. In the final analysis, classical interference theory faded from the theoretical landscape not so much because it was wrong as it was irrelevant. In the words of one prominent critic, "the experiments of the [classical] interference theorists seem like empty exercises to most of us" (Neisser, 1982, p. 9).

NEO-INTERFERENCE RESEARCH

After a period of nearly three decades in which interference research was not a domiant theme in experimental psychology, such research is staging a comeback. There are, however, some fundamental differences between this new body of work, which we call neo-interference research, and the earlier research that was conducted in the verbal learning tradition. For example, whereas classical interference theory had a strong preference for general principles that applied more or less evenly across individuals and developmental levels, much of this new body of work is focused on developmental and individual differences. In addition, neointerference research has been more successful in making contact with everyday cognition. In fact, much of this new body of work has dealt with complex real-world phenomena that eluded traditional interference theory. Together, these new directions, as well as the findings they have generated, have sharpened our understanding of the nature of intelligence and how it develops.

Along the way, neo-interference research has posed a challenge to traditional explanations of developmental and individual differences, including knowledge-based theories, activation resource theories, and strategy theories. In the next section, we briefly review these theories, outline some of their shortcomings, and indicate how disenchantment with these theories helped stimulate interest in interference concepts. One of our aims in this section is to show how these traditional approaches differ from neo-interference research. Next, we focus on three neo-interference theories: resistance to interference theory, inefficient inhibition theory, and fuzzy-trace theory. Each of these theories uses interference concepts to explain aspects of the development of intelligence. Finally, we turn to specific phenomena within several domains to illustrate the wide scope of neo-interference research. These illustrative domains are search, selective attention, recall, comprehension, and reasoning. We stress that these areas are merely illustrative, not exhaustive. They were chosen to demonstrate the relevance of neo-interference research to the study of the development of intelligence, not to definitively characterise it.

TRADITIONAL THEORIES OF DEVELOPMENTAL AND INDIVIDUAL DIFFERENCES

Knowledge-based theories

At about the time that classical interference theory reached its peak, the dominant themes in cognitive development research grew out of Piaget's work. According to Piaget, the development of intelligence consists of the acquisition and deployment of progressively more adult-like forms of knowledge, such as the understanding that objects are distinct from action and logical operations. Following Piaget's lead, errors in many situations have been attributed either to an absence of knowledge about objects and spatial relationships or to the absence of logical competence. Before long, however, many researchers reported data suggesting that Piaget had underestimated children's intelligence and that children can succeed at an earlier age than predicted when misleading, potentially interfering information is reduced. For instance, Gelman (1969) showed that preconservers (supposedly prelogical children) could "conserve" if they were taught to ignore the irrelevant features of the task, such as changes in size, shape, and colour. Although findings such as these did little at first to temper enthusiasm for Piaget's account of the development of intelligence, they spawned a line of inquiry featuring the hypothesis that performance on many of Piaget's tasks had as much to do with the ability to resist interference as it does with what the child knows (Brainerd & Reyna, 1990; Dempster, 1992).

Nevertheless, knowledge-based explanations of cognitive development are still popular. With few exceptions, however, such as neo-Piagetian accounts of developmental change (e.g. Case, 1991), the emphasis has swung from broad classes of knowledge applicable across a variety of domains (e.g. logical operations) to more local and specialised forms of knowledge, typically referred to as domain-specific or content knowledge (Chi & Ceci, 1987). For example, Carey (1985) has suggested that domain-specific knowledge accounts for most of the performance differences between three-year-olds and adults. Other related developments inspired by the rise of information-processing theories have explained age-related improvements in cognition on the grounds that individuals acquire and implement more powerful skills (e.g. Fischer, 1980), rules (Siegler, 1981), and other specialised forms of knowledge (e.g. Karmiloff-Smith, 1992) as they grow older.

Although content knowledge clearly plays a critical role in developmental changes in domain competence (for a review, see Bjorklund, 1995), the prevailing view is that factors other than the knowledge base are responsible for intellectual development (e.g. Peverly, 1991; Pressley, 1994). Some recent research, for example, has suggested that developmental changes in the accessibility of relevant content knowledge is just as important as the knowledge itself (Bjorklund, 1987). From a neo-interference perspective, the distinction between relevant and irrelevant knowledge, which can impair performance, is crucial. Relevant knowledge can only be applied if irrelevant responses can be inhibited (e.g. Dempster, 1992; Rovee-Collier & Boller, 1995). As Diamond (1991, p. 67) noted, "Cognitive development can be conceived of, not only as the progressive *acquisition* of knowledge, but also as the enhanced *inhibition* of reactions that get in the way of demonstrating knowledge that is already present."

Activation-resource theories

Another approach that once offered a rarely challenged account of the development of intelligence is based on the information-processing concept of excitation or activation resources, such as working memory capacity and information-processing speed. As Brainerd and Reyna (1989, p. 1) observed, the resources hypothesis was for some time "the pre-eminent metatheoretical principle of cognitive development". According to this account, ontogenetic increases in excitation resources, including increased capacity and increased processing speed, make a substantial contribution to the development of intelligence (e.g. Bjorklund, 1987; Halford, 1982; Kail, 1991, 1992).

After an idea has become commonplace it is often re-evaluated, and this has occurred with resource theory. Objections to resource theory fall into two categories, conceptual shortcomings and empirical inconsistencies (for reviews, see Dempster, 1995; Hasher & Zacks, 1988; Reyna & Brainerd, 1991). Conceptual shortcomings include lack of agreement about whether capacity should be viewed as a single pool of general-purpose processing resource or a set of independent resource pools, each tied to different cognitive functions (Navon, 1984). Indeed, a growing body of research casts doubt on the validity of a single, generic pool of resources (Hasher & Zacks, 1988; Kail, 1991, 1993; Martin, Shelton, & Yaffee, 1994). Empirical inconsistencies include the reasoning–remembering independence effect (which we discuss more fully in the section on fuzzy-trace theory), which suggests that solutions to reasoning tasks and memory for information that authorises solutions are not constrained by the same limited-capacity processing resource (Reyna & Brainerd, 1990), and haphazard correlations between indices of capacity utilisation and intellectual performance (Mitchell & Hunt, 1989). In addition, with proper controls for age-related growth in content knowledge, developmental differences in memory span, a traditional measure of capacity, are sharply attenuated (Dempster, 1978). Finally, some evidence suggests that the elderly, who are often viewed as having less working memory capacity than younger adults, are actually able to hold more, not less, information in working memory than younger adults (Zacks & Hasher, 1994).

Although the activation resources construct is still useful, recent work indicates that inhibitory processes, including those that may support resistance to interference, are just as important (for a sample, see various chapters in Dagenbach & Carr, 1994; Dempster & Brainerd, 1995; Howe & Pasnak, 1993). In part, this recent interest in inhibition processes reflects the desire among cognitive psychologists to have their behavioural models consistent with what is known about brain function (e.g. Bjork, 1989; Dempster, 1991, 1992; Harnishfeger, 1995; Lewandowsky & Li, 1995). As neuroscientists have known for some time, communication within the nervous system involves both the excitation and inhibition of neurons (Dagenbach & Carr, 1994). Moreover, one function of inhibition is to control interference (Fuster, 1989). From the perspective of neo-interference theory, age-related changes in the efficiency of inhibition processes may give the appearance of changes in capacity or changes in information-processing speed, by either inhibitory or failing to inhibit irrelevant, potentially interfering, information (Dempster, 1991, 1992; Kail, 1993).

Strategy theories

Although strategies are a form of knowledge, they are neither domain general nor specialised forms of content knowledge (Howe & O'Sullivan, 1990). Although there is some disagreement among researchers concerning the precise definition of strategies, all seem to agree that they are goal-directed information-processing activities, such as elaboration, imagery, rehearsal, organisation, and various counting strategies used to aid task performance. According to advocates of the importance of strategies to cognitive development, performance on memory and reasoning tasks is assumed to be heavily dependent on these forms of "higher cognition", which become increasingly available as the child develops. It is further assumed that the use and regulation of strategies is governed largely by individual differences in metacognition, which refers to a person's understanding of his or her own cognitive abilities (Brown, 1978; Flavell, 1978). Basically, brighter individuals are assumed to be those who possess sufficient metacognition to accurately monitor their task performance and apply appropriate strategies when necessary. Nowhere are strategy theories more prevalent than in the area of memory development, where strategies were once widely believed to be "what develops" (Flavell, 1971; Ornstein, 1978).

While strategic theories have an empirical literature, they have proved less than satisfactory as explanations of memory and cognitive development (for reviews, see Ackerman, 1994; Bjorklund, 1987; Dempster, 1985; Miller, 1994; Reyna & Brainerd, 1991). Research on memory span is a case in point. Much of that work has focused on the contribution of strategic variables to span differences. Developmental differences in strategies such as chunking, grouping, and rehearsal, however, have accounted for only modest amounts of intersubject variability in span (Dempster, 1981; Dempster & Zinkgraf, 1982). Additional findings that have raised doubts about the utility of strategies include the fact that age improvement in the use of organisational strategies often fail to correlate with age improve-ments in recall (Bjorklund, 1985), the absence of improvement in organisational strategies within certain age ranges in which recall improves considerably (Brainerd, Reyna, Howe, & Kevershan, 1991), and the finding that training-induced improvements in organisational strategies do not produce corresponding improvements in recall (DeMarie-Dreblow, 1991). In short, it seems that strategies are neither a necessary nor sufficient cause of developmental differences in memory.

It is not surprising, therefore, that some investigations have shifted theoretical attention away from strategies. This development, which began in the early 1980s, has been referred to as the "basic process" movement (Brainerd, 1990). Its core hypotheses are that developmental and individual differences in memory and reasoning tasks are chiefly due to collateral differences in basic processes and that differences in content knowledge and strategic factors are rooted in these same basic processes (Brainerd & Reyna, 1991; Dempster, 1992).

This movement has led to renewed interest in interference as an important example of basic processes. For instance, having determined that strategies did a poor job of predicting developmental and individual differences in span, Dempster suggested that susceptibility to interference might explain span differences (Dempster, 1981; Dempster & Cooney, 1982). In addition, Dempster (1992) suggested that children's developing capacity for inhibition enables them to acquire increasingly selective higher order knowledge, such as a fully functional concept of compensation which is required for optimal performance in some conservation tasks. Similarly, other researchers have proposed that the development of recall and reasoning are largely controlled by age changes in sensitivity to different forms of interference (Brainerd, 1995; Reyna, 1995). Such proposals have led to some new theoretical frameworks that use the concepts of interference and inhibition to help explain the development of intelligence. Three such theories are discussed next.

NEO-INTERFERENCE THEORIES

These new theoretical frameworks fall into two categories: (1) those that stress interference and the conditions that create interference—resistance to interference theory (Dempster, 1990) and fuzzy-trace theory (Brainerd & Reyna, 1991); and (2) those that stress the inhibition of potentially interfering—task irrelevant information (Bjorklund & Harnishfeger, 1990). These differences, however, are rather superficial. What these approaches have in common is the thesis that many, if not most, cognitive tasks are interference sensitive and that the ability to inhibit potential sources of interference is an important factor in cognitive development. Accordingly, unlike most theories of adult cognition, which tend to be tied to specific paradigms, these three theories seek to explain a wide range of otherwise disparate phenomena.

Resistance to interference theory

Resistance to interference theory arose as a response to the various empirical shortcomings of activation resource and strategy explanations of cognitive development and individual differences (Dempster, 1985, 1991). Subsequently, this framework was applied to cognitive ageing as well (Dempster, 1990). Although this framework was originally focused on memory phenomena, it has been progressively extended to other domains, including comprehension and reasoning. Thus, it represents a step toward a unified theory of diverse expressions of cognitive development, cognitive ageing, and individual differences (for reviews, see Dempster, 1991, 1992, 1993).

Resistance to interference theory is focused on the relevance of the memory representations that people bring to bear on intellectual tasks. In general, the activation of relevant information promotes task performance and the activation of irrelevant information impedes performance. Simply put, resistance to interference refers to the ability to ignore or inhibit irrelevant information. According to the theory, that ability reflects a basic level process that depends for the most part on the frontal lobes of the brain, a system that appears to play a central role in the selection and regulation of behaviour by inhibiting or suppressing stimuli or associations that are not relevant to the task at hand (Fuster, 1989; Luria, 1973). The frontal lobes are also the last region of the brain to develop and the first to show signs of deterioration in later life. Resistance to interference theory, therefore, is a "frontal lobe model" (Kramer, Humphrey, Larish, Logan, & Strayer, 1994). It assumes that resistance to interference is a fundamental feature of the cognitive system (i.e. a psychological primitive), one that cannot be explained in terms of other cognitive processes.

Although Dempster believes that the frontal lobes, which are rich in an inhibitory synaptic transmitter substance, play a major role in "noise" reduction, resistance to interference is not a unitary construct. Rather, he contends that there are at least three separate types of interference, each with its own developmental trajectory. The hypothesised relation between age and sensitivity to interference is shown in Fig. 9.1 for the motor, perceptual, and verbal domains.

As can be seen, there is a stage-like quality to the developing child's sensitivity to interference. Sensitivity to interference is greatest early in life. Such high sensitivity to motor interference would account for infant behaviour on the A-not-B object permanence task, a task that is discussed in a subsequent section of this chapter. Infants appear to "know" that an

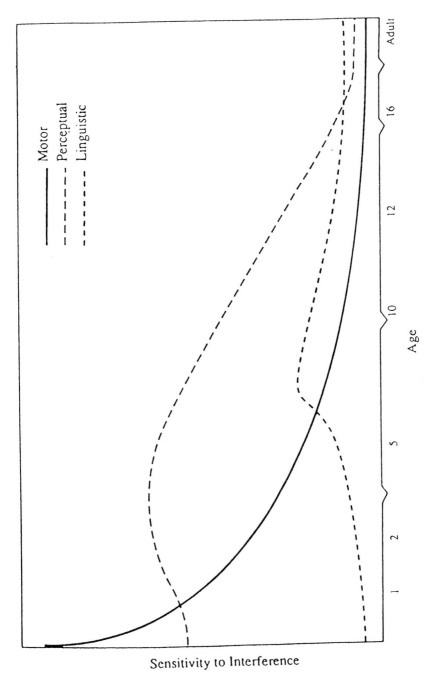

FIG. 9.1 Hypothesised relationship between age and sensitivity to interference.

223

object was hidden at location B, but they cannot suppress the no longer appropriate motor action of reaching toward location A, where the object was hidden on previous trials. Sensitivity to perceptual interference increases slightly early in life and then declines over the school-age years. Thus, perceptual interference is greatest during Piaget's preoperational period when children find it difficult to resist misleading, irrelevant visual and auditory stimuli that are present in measures of field dependence, conservation tasks, and some selective attention tasks. By contrast, sensitivity to verbal/linguistic interference remains relatively constant over development, peaking during early childhood, when language begins to play an increasing role in guiding problem solving (Vygotsky, 1962) and children begin to show interference from word meanings on the Stroop Colour–Word Interference Test (Stroop, 1935).

In some unpublished work, Dempster has attempted to broaden his theory by showing how different cognitive processes (e.g. resistance to interference, activation resources, strategies) work together and how resistance to interference influences the knowledge base. His view is that developmental changes in resistance to motor, perceptual, and verbal forms of interference lead to relatively long-term changes in the knowledge base, including how that knowledge is represented and accessed. Although the details of this feature of the theory have not been worked out, the general idea is that differences in intelligence are largely a function of the way in which information is represented (motorically, perceptually, verbally) and the clarity of those representations. According to Dempster, most memory representations and their connections can be conceived of as containing noise or irrelevant, potentially interfering information. That is, most knowledge representations can be described in terms of a signal-to-noise ratio. In a given situation, the person who activates less noise will perform more intelligently than the person who is more susceptible to interference and who, thus, activates relatively noisy representations.

Inefficient inhibition theory

Inefficient inhibition theory grew out of a need to deal with the empirical challenges to resource theory, although it preserves the notion that working memory capacity increases with age (Bjorklund & Harnishfeger, 1990). Basically, this model is an extension of the activation resources model but it emphasises the role of inhibitory processes. Using the resource metaphor, the model claims that inefficient inhibition clogs storage space with irrelevant information, leaving less of it available for the storage of relevant information including the execution of essential processes.

Central to Bjorklund and Harnishfeger's thesis is the claim that inhibitory processes become more efficient with age (for recent reviews, see Harnishfeger, 1995; Harnishfeger & Bjorklund, 1993). Thus, younger children's working memory space is more likely to be "cluttered" with irrelevant information than the working memory space of older children. This, they propose, could account for intellectual development on a wide range of tasks, including selective attention, memory, and verbal tasks. Consistent with this hypothesis, Harnishfeger and Bjorklund (1993) found that young children's poor memory performance was attributable, in part, to the irrelevant information they remembered. In a series of studies, they reported that in attempting to remember sets of words, younger children produced more intrusions of non-list words in their recall than did older children. Furthermore, the intrusions that the younger children produced were more likely to be task-irrelevant than were the intrusions produced by the older children. According to Harnishfeger and Bjorklund, intrusion errors are made because task-inappropriate information is not inhibited.

Fuzzy-trace theory

Fuzzy-trace theory was motivated largely by findings demonstrating that the relationship between memory and reasoning is more often one of independence or outright competition than one of facilitation. For example, Brainerd and Kingma (1984) modified the standard transitive-inference paradigm ("A is 5 inches long, B is 3 inches long, C is 7 inches long. Which is longer A or C?") by inserting occasional memory probes for adjacent relations ("which is longer, A or B?"). In a series of experiments with children, they found that memory for the premises was independent of reasoning performance. In other words, reasoning accuracy could not be predicted on the basis of memory for the premises.

In order to account for these counter-intuitive findings, Brainerd and Reyna (1990) and Reyna and Brainerd (1990) suggested that people prefer to remember and reason intuitively by processing inexact "fuzzy" memory representations rather than exact "verbatim" representations. Thus, when a reasoning task, such as the previous example, can be accomplished with fuzzy traces (e.g. "C has the most"), performance can progress without the use of verbatim information.

Fuzzy and verbatim traces differ in important ways (for a comprehensive recent review and a response to critiques of fuzzy-trace theory, see Reyna & Brainerd, 1995a, 1995b). First of all, relative to verbatim traces, fuzzy traces are more easily accessed and generally require less effort to use. Also, verbatim traces are more susceptible to interference and forgetting than fuzzy traces. For example, fuzzy-trace theory assumes that output interference, generated by competing information on memory and reasoning tasks is an important source of errors on such tasks. Output interference occurs in two forms: scheduling effects and feedback effects. Scheduling effects are due to the serial nature of response systems. Although people may perform several different cognitive operations simultaneously (that is, in parallel), responses are made serially. This leads to a parallel-to-serial bottleneck at output, or response competition, with the various possible responses competing for priority of execution. Once a response is made (e.g. an item is recalled), off-noise (i.e. irrelevant information) is generated that impedes subsequent performance.

How does fuzzy-trace use interference concepts to help account for the development of intelligence? Fuzzy-trace theory makes specific predictions, some of which have been confimed by research. First of all, there are age differences in gist extraction. Young children's memory is specialised for encoding and processing verbatim information; with age, their ability to extract gist improves and the processing of verbatim traces declines. Second, age differences have been found in sensitivity to output interference, with younger children being more adversely affected than older children and adults. One reason for young children's greater sensitivity to such interference is their reliance on verbatim traces, which are more susceptible to interference than fuzzy traces. Several specific examples of the explanatory power of fuzzy-trace theory are presented in a subsequent section of this chapter.

DOMAINS OF NEO-INTERFERENCE RESEARCH

We now turn to specific phenomena within several developmental domains that illustrate the wide scope and relevance of neo-interference research. These phenomena range from relatively simple processes such as search and selective attention to relatively complex knowledge-rich processes such as comprehension and reasoning.

Search

Young children, especially infants, often fail to search for hidden objects, even under optimal circumstances. Piaget (1954) observed that 8–12-month-old infants will find a hidden object at an initial location (A). However, after several successful searches at A, many infants continue to search there when the object is hidden at a different location (B), even though the displacement is visible and the infant watches as the object is hidden. This error, one of the most extensively studied phenomena in the search literature, is known as the "A not B" error.

Piaget regarded these errors as evidence that the infant's understanding of objects and spatial relationships is fundamentally different than that of adults. According to Piaget, infants search for the object at A because its existence and position in space are linked to or are partially defined by their action; in effect, the object exists as "the object that I find at location A". So, the object remains at disposal in place where the action has made use of it (Piaget, 1954).

More recent research on the "A not B" error has not supported Piaget's formulation. Instead, that work has suggested that infants make these errors, in part, because they are extremely susceptible to the build up of proactive interference from their initial search(es) at location A. For instance, it has been found that infants do not make the "A not B" error unless hiding at location B is preceded by *several* trials of hiding at location A. Further, spatial proximity between A and B increases the incidence of search errors. In addition, a disproportionate number of errors are in the direction of the previously correct location, not just any location. Finally, eye-movement studies have demonstrated that infants seem to "know" the correct location, but they cannot resist the allure of the previously correct location (Dempster, 1993; Diamond, 1991; Diamond, Cruttenden, & Neiderman, 1994).

Although preschool children make fewer errors on search tasks than infants, the errors that they do make often involve the same sort of perseveration. Such errors continue to occur as late as 4½ years of age. Thus, there is a developmental trend from relatively error-prone search during infancy to predominantly error-free search during early childhood; however, the types of errors that are made are remarkably similar. This has been explained on the grounds that the same process—susceptibility to interference—is involved in search errors throughout this age range (Dempster, 1993).

McCall and Carriger (1993) have suggested that individual differences in infants' inhibitory processes may be related to intelligence. A substantial and growing body of evidence indicates that some basic cognitive abilities in infancy (including certain search-like processes) predict childhood intelligence (as measured by IQ) surprisingly well. McCall and Carriger (1993; p. 77) speculate that the mechanism underlying this relationship may be "the disposition to *inhibit* responding to familiar stimuli and to stimuli of minor prominence".

Selective attention

Selective attention is one of the most important functions of cognition. At any given moment, we are normally confronted with multiple stimuli, many of which are irrelevant to the task at hand. Thus, the capacity to ignore irrelevant, potentially interfering information while attending to relevant information is essential for goal-directed behaviour.

Historically, the study of selective attention assumed that the mechanism of attention operates directly on "attended" information (Neill & Valdes, 1996). Until recently, most theories have had little to say about the fate of "ignored" information beyond the assumption of a passive decay process. Now there is a growing literature suggesting that such information is actively suppressed, so that processing of relevant information can proceed without interference. According to this view, selective attention depends on both excitation and inhibition processes; relevant information is identified for further processing and irrelevant background information is identified for suppression (Neill, Valdes, & Terry, 1995). This does not necessarily mean that the initial act of selection is inhibitory. Some data suggest that inhibition does not aid current selection but operates after selection is completed to maintain the distinction between goal-relevant and goal-irrelevant information, once that distinction has been established (May, Kane, & Hasher, 1995; Neill & Valdes, 1996).

Laboratory measures of selective attention index the ability to focus, divide, or maintain attention to target stimuli in the presence of irrelevant stimuli. These include the Stroop test, speeded classification and visual selection tasks, selective listening tasks, and the negative priming paradigm. In the Stroop test, for example, the subject names the colour of ink in which an incongruent word is printed (e.g. the word RED printed in green ink). These naming latencies, which are slower than simply naming colours on a colour chart, are used to estimate the amount of interference from the incongruent word. Thus, the task is a measure of the subject's ability to focus attention on a relevant stimulus dimension (ink colour) and to ignore an irrelevant one (word meaning). As might be expected, then, manipulations designed to increase attention to the word increase the amount of interference (Walley, McLeod, & Weiden, 1994). Although there is still some controversy regarding the mechanism responsible for the interference, much evidence suggests that it is a form of response competition between the irrelevant word and the ink colour (MacLeod, 1991).

It is now well established that children tend to perform more poorly on selective attention tasks than young adults (for reviews, see Davies, Jones, & Taylor, 1984; Lane & Pearson, 1982; Plude, Enns, & Brodeur, 1994). For example, Stroop interference diminishes throughout childhood and into early adulthood (Comalli, Wapner, & Werner, 1962). Similarly, young children are slowed more by irrelevant information than young adults in speeded classification tasks, which require subjects to sort cards according to a relevant dimension in the presence of irrelevant dimensions. Furthermore, these age differences increase as the number of irrelevant dimensions increases (Strutt, Anderson, & Well, 1975).

In general, these results are typical of developmental studies using other interference-sensitive selective attention tasks (Enns & Akhtar, 1989). The ability to listen selectively, that is, to repeat words spoken by one voice in the presence of an irrelevant and potentially distracting voice, also improves during childhood. In a classic developmental study, for example, Doyle (1973) found that intrusions from the distracting message during the selection task decreased greatly between 8 and 14 years. Moreover, there was a positive correlation between the number of intrusions from the unattended message and the number of items from the unattended message subsequently retained among the 8-year-olds, but not among the 14-year-olds. For the latter there was a significant negative correlation between the number of intrusions and the number of items retained from the unattended message. On the basis of these and other data, Doyle concluded that the superior listening performance of older children is not due to a greater ability to filter out distracting material at an early stage of processing, but rather in large part "to an ability to inhibit intrusions from the distracting material during the selection task" (p. 100), a conclusion endorsed by Anooshian and McCulloch (1979).

In the priming paradigm, a currently popular measure of selective attention, two stimuli are presented, with subjects instructed to attend to one and ignore the other. One of the stimuli is then represented for naming. If the represented stimulus is the "ignored" one, naming latencies are longer than those for unrepresented control stimuli. This effect, known as "negative priming", has been, in part, interpreted to mean that the ignored item was suppressed in order to prevent it from interfering with the processing of the target stimulus (cf. Tipper, 1985).

Developmental research using this task has revealed a complicated pattern. Although young children show weakened negative priming effects for item information (Harnishfeger, Nicholson, & Digby, 1993; Tipper, Bourque, Anderson, & Brehaut, 1989; Tipper & McLaren, 1990), young children showed reliable negative priming when the "ignored" location rather than the identity of the ignored stimulus was the target (Tipper & McLaren, 1990). This discrepancy is further complicated by studies showing that negative priming can occur in the absence of measurable interference (for a discussion, see Neill et al., 1995) and that reductions in interference do not necessarily reduce negative priming (Fox, 1995).

In sum, the results of developmental studies are largely consistent with more naturalistic research suggesting that children are more easily distracted by irrelevant stimuli than young adults. This research shows that young children tend to glance away from a task more than older children in the presence of extraneous auditory stimuli (Higgins & Turnure, 1984). Nevertheless, some findings should be viewed with caution. Negative priming studies are a case in point. At the present time the evidence suggests that negative priming is due to more than one mechanism and that it is not always an index of sensitivity to interference (Fox, 1995; May et al., 1995; Neill & Valdes, 1996).

Recall

Free recall is perhaps the most extensively studied of all laboratory memory tasks. It mimics those familiar everyday situations in which we retrieve information from memory without any constraints on the order in which it is accessed (e.g. Name the countries of Europe. Who are your favourite philosophers?). In a typical free-recall design, subjects study a list of words or pictures and then recall as many of them as possible in whatever order they come to mind. The question is, What is that order?

The answer, provided by common-sense and classical memory theories, is that access order is controlled by items' recall difficulty. Since Marbe's work at the turn of the century (Marbe, 1901), items' memory representations have been assumed to vary along a subjective magnitude dimension called memory strength, with stronger items being easier to recall than weaker ones. It has been further assumed that easy-to-recall items with strong representations (e.g. familiar nouns or pictures of common objects) will necessarily come to mind before hard-to-recall items with weak representations (e.g. unfamiliar nouns or pictures of rare objects). Thus, in free recall, items should be accessed in an easier → harder direction. It has been discovered, however, that this prediction is wrong, and the reason seems to be that it fails to take account of the effects of interference.

The access order that has been most commonly observed in experimentation begins with some of the hardest items on a list, then proceeds to the easier items, and returns to some of the harder items at the end of output (Brainerd, Reyna, Howe, & Kevershan, 1991). This harder → easier → harder sequence is called cognitive triage because of its resemblance to the medical procedure of treating the most difficult cases first (see Fig. 9.2).

Although it may be true that items' memory representations vary in strength and that stronger items are easier to recall than weaker ones, it is also true that retrieving and articulating a series of items generates a variety of off-task noise, which is usually called output interference. For instance, recalling the list item "animal" would be expected to generate a number of associations to items that are not on the list (e.g. "dog", "horse", "lion") that are irrelevant to the recall of the remaining items. As such interference accumulates, it impairs subjects' ability to recall further items. This impairment is naturally greater for items with weaker memory representations than for items with stronger representations.

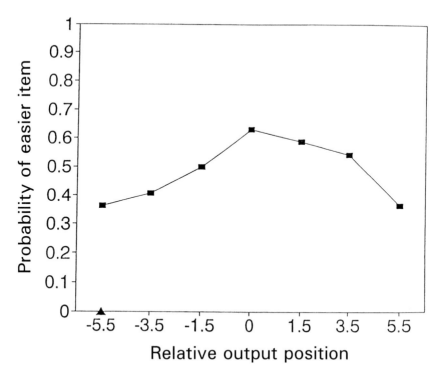

FIG. 9.2   The harder → easier → harder output sequence in free recall. This curve is based on experiments in which subjects studied lists of 12, 16, or 25 words (Brainerd et al., 1990). After each study trial, they were administered a free-recall test. (Recall as many of the words as possible in any order whatsoever.) The X axis is the position of each word that was recalled in an output sequence *relative to the midpoint of that sequence*, with 0 denoting the midpoint. Thus, output positions with negative signs are ones that come before the midpoints of their sequences and unsigned positions are ones that came after. The Y axis is the probability of recalling an easier word at each output position. On any given free-recall test, easier words are ones that were also recalled on the immediately preceding test, whereas harder words are ones that were not recalled on the immediately preceding test. Reprinted with permission of the publisher.

It is this latter fact, that weaker items are more sensitive to the debilitating effects of output interference, that accounts for the harder → easier → harder sequence. Obviously, total recall will be enhanced if subjects first recall some of the hardest items, before much interference has accumulated, and then switch to the easier → harder ordering. In this way, interference has become essential to explaining the dynamics of recall.

This, in turn, has provided developmental researchers with a new heuristic for understanding age differences in the accuracy of recall. For the past quarter-century, those differences have been attributed almost exclusively to ontogenetic changes in metamnemonic knowledge—

specifically, to changes in the ability to use mnemonic strategies such as clustering, rehearsal, and subjective organisation (Schneider & Pressley, 1989). Now, however, there is mounting evidence that changes in the ability to resist the effects of interference are critical to the development of recall.

Cognitive triage is a case in point. The number of items in the initial burst of hard items is a measure of subjects' ability to resist the rapid accumulation of output interference at the start of recall. This number is known to increase with age, as recall accuracy itself is increasing. Crucially, within subjects, the number of hard items in the initial burst is correlated with total recall, and the magnitude of the correlation increases steadily between early childhood and young adulthood (Brainerd, Reyna, Harnishfeger, & Howe, 1993). Though there are other explanations of this phenomenon, including activation-resource and strategic explanations, whenever predictions of each of these explanations have been pitted against predictions of the interference explanation in experimentation, the results have generally favoured interference predictions (for a review, see Brainerd, 1995).

The types of errors that subjects make during recall also support the conclusion that developmental changes in interference sensitivity contribute to age differences in recall. Young children make higher proportions of task-irrelevant recall errors than do older children. That is, young children are much more likely to recall items that were not on the list of to-be-remembered items. The reason seems to be that younger children are less able to suppress the maintenance and retrieval of irrelevant information than older children and adults (Dee-Lucas, 1982; Dempster, 1992; Harnishfeger & Bjorklund, 1993; Harnishfeger & Pope, 1996).

Comprehension

The ability to comprehend written and spoken texts is an important cognitive skill that exhibits sizeable developmental and individual differences (for reviews, see Oakhill, 1993; Perfetti, 1985). Traditional explanations of this variability have emphasised factors such as knowledge base, strategy use, and the capacity and efficiency of working memory (e.g. Bjorklund & Harnishfeger, 1990; Daneman & Blennerhassett, 1984; Oakhill, 1993).

There is, however, an alternative explanation—namely, that these factors may be less crucial than the ability to resist interference. This explanation is based, in part, on evidence that text passages and everyday discourse contain abundant sources of interference. Research has identified seven features of text and narrative discourse that can interfere with comprehension. First, narrative discourse in which there is more than one character and each character is engaged in a variety of activities and relationships, as is often the case, can cause interference when comprehension questions ask for the details of who did what and who was related to whom (Thorndyke, 1977). Second, reading a text that contains multiple arguments to the same predicates produces interference among the predicates. For example, in a study that used a text about Presidents and where they lived, subjects had difficulty learning, for example, that Jefferson, not Washington, lived in Monticello (Thorndyke & Hayes-Roth, 1979). Third, reading material that contains sentences in which two individuals are introduced in the first clause (e.g. Ann predicted that Pam would lose the track race) and one of these two individuals is referred to in the second clause (e.g. but Pam/she came in first very easily) may produce proactive interference unless the subject can effectively suppress the name of the other individual (e.g. Ann). Subjects have greater difficulty suppressing such information following less explicit anaphors (she) than they do following more explicit anaphors (Pam) (Gernsbacher, 1989). Fourth, substantial amounts of interference have been found when the text contains successive, but similar, statements regarding a particular topic, or when two or more related topics are presented in succession (Blumenthal & Robbins, 1977; Dee-Lucas, 1982; Dempster, 1985, 1988; Gunter, Berry, & Clifford, 1981; Gunter, Clifford, & Berry, 1980). Reading about arteries in a chapter on the cardiovascular system, for example, can interfere proactively with comprehension of subsequent material on veins and the latter can interfere retroactively with comprehension of the former. Readers will often thoroughly confuse the two when responding to comprehension questions (Dempster, 1988). Fifth, texts may contain ambiguous messages that have more than one meaning (e.g. "The soldiers took the port"). When irrelevant meanings are activated, comprehension suffers (Hasher & Zacks, 1988; LeFever & Ehri, 1976). Sixth, texts may contain irrelevant peripheral information that can interfere with comprehension of the relevant information (Cotugno, 1981; Willows, 1974). Finally, arithmetic word problems often contain irrelevant information and studies show that the presence of such information, particularly if the irrelevant and relevant information is similar (Littlefield & Reiser, 1993), increases problem difficulty (Kouba, Brown, Carpenter, Lindquist, Silver, & Swafford, 1988; Muth, 1984, 1991). In short, in many cases it appears that comprehension is an interference-sensitive task.

Although developmental data on the relation between resistance to interference and comprehension are in short supply, they are generally consistent with the hypothesis that young children's problems are attributable in part to increased sensitivity to interference. For example, young children have more difficulty ignoring distracting or irrelevant, less informative, material while they are reading than adults (Brown & Smiley, 1978). Young children also suffer from the tendency to carry no-longer-relevant text material into current processing and, in general, to make more inappropriate intrusion errors (Brown, Smiley, Day, Townsend, & Lawton, 1977; Dee-Lucus, 1982). Finally, following the presentation of polysemous words in a biasing sentence context, young children are inefficient in suppressing context-irrelevant meanings (Simpson & Foster, 1986). According to one model of comprehension which has considerable empirical support, failure to suppress irrelevant meanings impairs comprehension by encouraging the formation of new, but misleading, text representations (Gernsbacher & Faust, 1991).

Reasoning

Historically, errors in logical and mathematical reasoning have been attributed either to an absence of logical competence or to an inability to apply that competence (Piaget, 1954). A number of researchers have argued, however, that reasoning errors are more often caused by interference from misleading or irrelevant information (Brainerd, 1979; Dempster, 1992). For instance, the visual properties of stimuli may lead one to "see" a problem incorrectly or the way information is presented may clash with the correct conceptual interpretation of a problem. These interference-based errors can be illustrated by two classic tasks invented by Piaget, conservation and class inclusion.

In conservation, the interference is visual (see Fig. 9.3). The problem involves understanding that if two objects look the same and are equivalent with respect to some quantitative property, the quantitative equivalence is preserved when the visual identity is destroyed. At the top of Fig. 9.3, for example, there are three pairs of objects. The members of each pair are visually identical and equivalent with respect to number (left), quantity (middle), or length (right). At the bottom of Fig. 9.3, visual identities have been destroyed, but quantitative relationships are preserved. Children in the early elementary grades mistakenly conclude that the quantitative relationships have also been destroyed because the objects no longer look the same. Although Piaget thought that this meant that they lack basic logical competence, it has been found that the same children will reason correctly if they are instructed to ignore the misleading visual cues (Brainerd, 1979).

In class inclusion, the interference is conceptual. This task measures children's understanding of the cardinal inclusion principle of set theory—that the cardinal number of a superordinate set is necessarily greater than

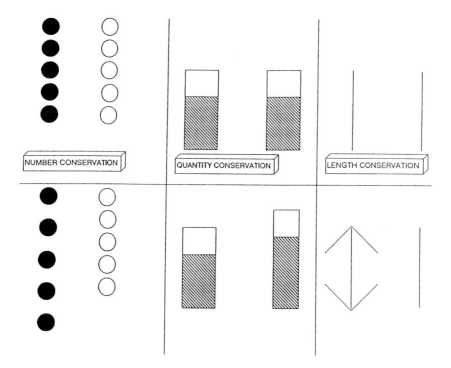

FIG. 9.3 Typical stimulus configurations for number conservation (left panels), quantity conservation (centre panels), and length conservation (right panels). At the beginning of each problem, the two stimuli are perceptually identical and equivalent with respect to the relevant quantitative property (upper panels). The perceptual identity is then destroyed, but in such a way that the quantitative property is unaffected. Questions are then posed to determine whether children understand that the quantitative relationship was conserved. Is there still the same number of black dots as white dots? Do the two glasses still have the same amount to drink? Are the two lines still the same length?

the cardinal numbers of any of its proper subsets. In the standard problem, children are shown an array consisting of two disjoint sets (e.g. 7 cows and 3 horses) that belong to a common superordinate set (e.g. 10 animals). Children are questioned about the relative numerosity of the super-ordinate set and the larger subset: Are there more animals or more cows? Although the answer is self-evident, children in the early elementary grades have difficulty, usually responding "more cows".

The reason is that the nested structure of the two numerical dimensions creates what is called an inclusion illusion (Reyna, 1991). The horizontal dimension, which consists of the numerical values of the disjoint subsets, is conceptually salient and easy to process. This fact interferes with the processing of the critical vertical dimension. Such interference can be removed by stripping the task of conflicting numerical information and posing logically equivalent problems: Are there more people living in San Francisco or in California? Is there more furniture in your living room or in your house? The same children who say "more cows" perform well on problems of this sort, so they apparently understand the principle of cardinal inclusion (Brainerd & Reyna, 1990).

Interference sensitivity has also figured in theoretical explanations of one of the most surprising outcomes of recent research on the development of reasoning, the memory independence effect. With various reasoning problems, the accuracy of solutions has proved to be independent of memory for the information that authorises those solutions. In probability judgement, for example, the problem is to predict what type of element (e.g. red ball, blue ball, green ball) is most likely to be drawn at random from a target sampling space. The answer, of course, is that the most frequent element is likely to be drawn. However, good memory for the relevant frequencies (e.g. 10 reds, 7 blues, 5 greens) does not increase the incidence of correct predictions. Similarly, in a sentence-inference task (e.g. The cage is on the table. The cat is under the cage. Is the cage below the cat?), good memory for critical sentences (The cage is on the table. The cat is under the cage.) does not increase the incidence of correct inferences (The cage is not below the cat.) (Brainerd & Reyna, 1992).

The theory that has been proposed to account for such findings, fuzzy-trace theory, assumes that reasoning does not process verbatim memories of critical problem information (Brainerd & Reyna, 1993; Reyna & Brainerd, 1995a). Instead, gist memories—memories of senses, patterns, and relationships that are extracted from that information—are normally processed during reasoning. In the probability–judgement example, subjects extract numerical gist ("reds are most", "more blues than greens") from the verbatim numbers and use it to make probability judgements ("a red ball should be sampled because reds are most"). In the sentence-inference example, subjects extract spatial gist (cage—top, table—middle, cat—bottom) from the verbatim sentences and use it to make inferences ("the cage cannot be below the cat because the cat is at the bottom").

According to fuzzy-trace theory, reasoning prefers to operate on gist because verbatim memories are more sensitive to interference than is gist. The interference sensitivity of verbatim memories means that they are forgotten more rapidly (e.g. "reds = 10" will be forgotten more rapidly than "reds are most"), which makes gist a more reliable basis for reasoning. Even when verbatim memories have not been forgotten, their greater interference sensitivity makes them harder to retrieve and to process accurately.

SUMMARY

Neo-interference research has its roots in classical interference theory. Compared to the older tradition, however, neo-interference research is broader in scope and much more relevant to everyday cognition. In addition, it is, for the most part, a developmental theory with specific implications for the development of intelligence, a domain that was largely ignored by classical interference theory. Its core feature is the assumption that resistance to interference is a major factor in the development of intellectual competence in a wide variety of interference-sensitive tasks, including search, selective attention, recall, comprehension, and reasoning.

REFERENCES

Ackerman, B.P. (1994). Commentary: The power and limitations of the strategy deficiency model of memory development. *Learning and Individual Differences*, *6*, 357–364.

Anooshian, L.J., & McCulloch, R.A. (1979). Developmental changes in dichotic listening with categorized word lists. *Developmental Psychology*, *15*, 280–287.

Bjork, R.A. (1989). Retrieval inhibition as an adaptive mechanism in human memory. In H.L. Roediger, III & F.M. Craik (Eds), *Varieties of memory and consciousness* (pp. 309–330). Hillsdale, NJ: Lawrence Erlbaum Associates Inc.

Bjorklund, D.F. (1985). The role of conceptual knowledge in the development of organization in children's memory. In C.J. Brainerd & M. Pressley (Eds), *Basic processes in memory development: Progress in cognitive development research* (pp. 103–142). New York: Springer-Verlag.

Bjorklund, D.F. (1987). How age changes in knowledge base contribute to the development of children's memory: An interpretive review. *Developmental Review*, *7*, 93–130.

Bjorklund, D.F. (1995). *Children's thinking* (2nd ed.). Pacific Grove, CA: Brooks/Cole.

Bjorklund, D.F., & Harnishfeger, K.K. (1990). The resources construct in cognitive development: Diverse sources of evidence and a theory of inefficient inhibition. *Developmental Review*, *1*, 48–71.

Blumenthal, G.B., & Robbins, D. (1977). Delayed release from proactive interference with meaningful material: How much do we remember after reading brief prose passages? *Journal of Experimental Psychology: Human Learning and Memory*, *3*, 754–761.

Borkowski, J.G. (1985). Signs of intelligence: Strategy generalization and meta-cognition. In S.R. Yussen (Ed.), *The growth of reflection in children*. New York: Academic Press.

Brainerd, C.J. (1979). Markovian interpretations of conservation learning. *Psychological Review*, *86*, 181–213.

Brainerd, C.J. (1990). Issues and questions in the development of forgetting. *Monographs of the Society for Research in Child Development*, *55* (3–4, Whole No. 222).

Brainerd, C.J. (1995). Interference processes in memory development: The case of cognitive triage. In F.N. Dempster & C.J. Brainerd (Eds), *Interference and inhibition in cognition* (pp. 105–139). San Diego, CA: Academic Press.

Brainerd, C.J., & Kingma, J. (1984). Do children have to remember to reason? A fuzzy-trace theory of transitivity development. *Developmental Review, 4,* 311–377.

Brainerd, C.J., & Reyna, V.F. (1989). Output-interference theory of dual-task deficits in memory development. *Journal of Experimental Child Psychology, 47,* 1–18.

Brainerd, C.J., & Reyna, V.F. (1990). Inclusion illusions: Fuzzy trace theory and perceptual salience effects in cognitive development. *Developmental Review, 10,* 365–403.

Brainerd, C.J., & Reyna, V.F. (1991). Fuzzy-trace theory and children's acquisition of mathematical and scientific concepts. *Learning and Individual Differences, 2,* 27–59.

Brainerd, C.J., & Reyna, V.F. (1992). The memory independence effect: What do the data show? What do the theories claim? *Developmental Review, 12,* 164–186.

Brainerd, C.J., & Reyna, V.F. (1993). Memory independence and memory interference in cognitive development. *Psychological Review, 100,* 42–67.

Brainerd, C.J., Reyna, V.F., Harnishfeger, K.K., & Howe, M.L. (1993). Is retrievability grouping good for recall? *Journal of Experimental Psychology: General, 122,* 249–268.

Brainerd, C.J., Reyna, V.F., Howe, M.L., & Kevershan, J. (1990). The last shall be first: How memory strength affects children's retrieval. *Psychological Science, 1,* 247–252.

Brainerd, C.J., Reyna, V.F., Howe, M.L., & Kevershan, J. (1991). Fuzzy-trace theory and cognitive triage in memory development. *Developmental Psychology, 27,* 351–369.

Brown, A.L. (1978). Knowing when, where, and how to remember: A problem of metocognition. In R. Glaser (Ed.), *Advances in instructional psychology* (pp. 77–165). New York: Halstead Press.

Brown, A.L., & Smiley, S.S. (1978). The development of strategies for studying texts. *Child Development, 49,* 1076–1088.

Brown, A.L., Smiley, S.S., Day, J.D., Townsend, M.A.R., & Lawton, S.C. (1977). Intrusion of a thematic idea in children's comprehension and retention of stories. *Child Development, 48,* 1454–1466.

Carey, S. (1985). *Conceptual change in childhood.* Cambridge, MA: MIT Press.

Case, R. (1991). *The mind's staircase: Exploring the conceptual underpinings of children's thought and knowledge.* Hillsdale, NJ: Lawrence Erlbaum Associates Inc.

Chi, M.T.H., & Ceci, S.J. (1987). Content knowledge: Its role, representation, and restructuring in memory development. In H.W. Reese (Ed.), *Advances in child development and behaviour* (Vol. 20, pp. 91–142). Orlando, FL: Academic Press.

Cohen, G. (1988). Age differences in memory for texts: Production deficiency or processing limitations? In L.L. Light & D.M. Burke (Eds), *Language, memory and aging* (pp. 171–190). New York: Cambridge University Press.

Comalli, P.E., Wapner, S., & Werner, H. (1962). Interference effects of Stroop Color–word Test in children, adulthood, and aging. *Journal of Genetic Psychology, 100,* 47–53.

Cotugno, A.J. (1981). Cognitive controls and reading disabilities revisited. *Psychology in the Schools, 18,* 455–459.

Dagenbach, D., & Carr, T.H. (Eds). (1994). *Inhibitory processes in attention, memory, and language.* San Diego, CA: Academic Press.

Daneman, M., & Blennerhassett, A. (1984). How to assess the listening comprehension skills of prereaders. *Journal of Educational Psychology, 76,* 1372–1382.

Davies, D.R., Jones, D.M., & Taylor, A. (1984). Selective and sustained-attention tasks: Individual and group differences. In R. Parasuraman, R. Davies, & J. Beatty (Eds), *Varieties of attention* (pp. 395–447). New York: Academic Press.

Dee-Lucus, D. (1982, March). *Recall of expository and narrative text.* Paper presented at the annual meeting of the American Educational Research Association, New York.

DeMarie-Dreblow, D. (1991). Relation between knowledge and memory: A reminder that correlation does not imply causation. *Child Development, 92,* 484–498.

Dempster, F.N. (1978). Memory span and short-term memory capacity: A developmental study. *Journal of Experimental Child Psychology, 26,* 419–431.

Dempster, F.N. (1981). Memory span: Sources of individual and developmental differences. *Psychological Bulletin, 89,* 63–100.

Dempster, F.N. (1985). Short-term memory development in childhood and adolescence. In C.J. Brainerd & M. Pressley (Eds), *Basic processes in memory development: Progress in cognitive development research* (pp. 209–248), New York: Springer-Verlag.

Dempster, F.N. (1988). Retroactive interference in the retention of prose: A reconsideration and new evidence. *Applied Cognitive Psychology, 2,* 97–113.

Dempster, F.N. (1990, November). *Resistance to interference: A neglected dimension of cognition.* Paper presented at the annual meeting of the Psychonomic Society, New Orleans, LA.

Dempster, F.N. (1991). Inhibitory processes: A neglected dimension of intelligence. *Intelligence, 15,* 157–173.

Dempster, F.N. (1992). The rise and fall of the inhibitory mechanism: Toward a unified theory of cognitive development and aging. *Developmental Review, 12,* 45–75.

Dempster, F.N. (1993). Resistance to interference: Developmental changes in a basic processing dimension. In M.L. Howe & R. Pasnak (Eds), *Emerging themes in cognitive development. Vol. 1: Foundations* (pp. 3–27). New York: Springer-Verlag.

Dempster, F.N. (1995). Interference and inhibition in cognition: An historical perspective. In F.N. Dempster & C.J. Brainerd (Eds), *Interference and inhibition in cognition* (pp. 3–26). San Diego, CA: Academic Press.

Dempster, F.N., & Brainerd, C.J. (Eds). (1995). *Interference and inhibition in cognition.* San Diego, CA: Academic Press.

Dempster, F.N., & Cooney, J.B. (1982). Individual differences in digit span, susceptibility to proactive interference, and apptitude/achievement test scores. *Intelligence, 6,* 399–416.

Dempster, F.N., & Zinkgraf, S.A. (1982). Individual differences in digit span and chunking. *Intelligence, 6,* 201–213.

Diamond, A. (1991). Neuropsychological insights into the meaning of object concept development. In S. Carey & R. Gelman (Eds), *The epigenesis of mind: Essays on biology and cognition* (pp. 67–110). Hillsdale, NJ: Lawrence Erlbaum Associates Inc.

Diamond, A., Cruttenden, L., & Neiderman, D. (1994). AB with multiple wells: 1. Why are multiple wells sometimes easier than two wells? 2. Memory or memory + inhibition? *Developmental Psychology, 30,* 192–205.

Doyle, A.B., (1973). Listening to distraction: A developmental study of selective attention. *Journal of Experimental Child Psychology, 15,* 100–115.

Enns, J.T., & Akhtar, N. (1989). A developmental study of filtering in visual attention. *Child Development, 60,* 1188–1199.

Flavell, J.H. (1971). First discussant's comments: What is memory development the development of? *Human Development, 14,* 272–278.

Flavell, J.H. (1978). Comments. In R.S. Siegler (Ed.), *Children's thinking: What develops?* (pp. 97–105). Hillsdale, NJ: Lawrence Erlbaum Associates Inc.

Fischer, K.W. (1980). A theory of cognitive development: The control and construction of hierarchies of skills. *Psychological Review, 87,* 477–531.

Fox, E. (1995). Pre-cueing target location reduces interference but not negative priming from visual distractors. *The Quarterly Journal of Experimental Psychology, 48,* 26–40.

Fuster, J.M. (1989). *The prefrontal cortex* (2nd ed.). New York: Raven Press.

Gelman, R. (1969) Conservation acquisition: A problem of learning to attend to relevant attributes. *Journal of Experimental Child Psychology, 7,* 167–187.

Gernsbacher, M.A. (1989). Mechanisms that improve referential access. *Cognition, 32,* 99–156.

Gernsbacher, M.A., & Faust, M.E. (1991). The mechanism of suppression: A component of general comprehension skill. *Journal of Experimental Psychology: Learning, Memory and Cognition, 17,* 245–262.

Gunter, B., Berry, C., & Clifford, B.R. (1981). Proactive interference effects with television news items: Further evidence. *Journal of Experimental Psychology: Human Learning and Memory, 7,* 480–487.

Gunter, B., Clifford, B.R., & Berry, C. (1980). Release from proactive interference with television news items: Evidence for encoding dimensions within televised news. *Journal of Experimental Psychology: Human Learning and Memory, 6,* 216–223.

Halford, G.S. (1982). *The development of thought.* Hillsdale, NJ: Lawrence Erlbaum Associates Inc.

Harnishfeger, K.K. (1995). The development of cognitive inhibition: Theories, definitions, and research evidence. In F.N. Dempster & C.J. Brainerd (Eds), *Interference and inhibition in cognition* (pp. 175–204). San Diego, CA: Academic Press.

Harnishfeger, K.K., & Bjorklund, D.F. (1993). The ontogeny of inhibition mechanisms: A renewed approach to cognitive development. In M.L. Howe & R. Pasnak (Eds), *Emerging themes in cognitive development: Vol. I: Foundations* (pp. 23–49). New York: Springer-Verlag.

Harnishfeger, K.K., Nicholson, S., & Digby, S. (1993, March). *Increasing inhibitory efficiency with age: Evidence for the Stroop task.* Paper presented at the Society for Research in Child Development, New Orleans, LA.

Harnishfeger, K.K., & Pope, R.S. (1996). Intending to forget: The development of cognitive inhibition in directed forgetting. *Journal of Experimental Child Psychology, 62,* 292–315.

Hasher, L., & Zacks, R.T. (1988). Working memory, comprehension, and aging: A review and a new view. In G.H. Bower (Ed.), *The psychology of learning and motivation: Advances in research and theory* (Vol. 22, pp. 193–224). San Diego, CA: Academic Press.

Higgins, T.A., & Turnure, J.E. (1984). Distractibility and concentration of attention in children's development. *Child Development, 55,* 1799–1810.

Howe, M.L., & O'Sullivan, J.T. (1990). The development of strategic memory: Coordinating knowledge, metamemory, and resources. In D.F. Bjorklund (Ed.), *Children's strategies: Contemporary views of cognitive development* (pp. 129–155). Hillsdale, NJ: Lawrence Erlbaum Associates Inc.

Howe, M.L., & Pasnak, R. (Eds). (1993). *Emerging themes in cognitive development: Vol. 1: Foundations.* New York: Springer-Verlag.

Kail, R. (1991). Controlled and automatic processing during mental rotation. *Journal of Experimental Child Psychology, 51*, 337–347.

Kail, R. (1992). Processing speed, speech rate, and memory. *Developmental Psychology, 28*, 899–904.

Kail, R. (1993). The role of a global mechanism in developmental change in speed of processing. In M.L. Howe & R. Pasnak (Eds). *Emerging themes in cognitive development: Vol. 1: Foundations* (pp. 97–119). New York: Springer-Verlag.

Karmiloff-Smith, A. (1992). *Beyond modularity: A developmental perspective on cognitive science.* Cambridge, MA: MIT Press.

Kouba, V.L., Brown, C.A., Carpenter, T.P., Lindquist, M.M., Silver, E.A., & Swafford, J.O. (1988). Results of the fourth NAEP assessment of mathematics: Number, operations, and word problems. *Arithmetic Teacher, 35*, 14–19.

Kramer, A.F., Humphrey, D.G., Larish, J.F., Logan, G.D., & Strayer, D.L. (1994). Aging and inhibition: Beyond a unitary view of inhibitory processing in attention. *Psychology and Aging, 9*, 491–512.

Lane, D.M., & Pearson, D.A. (1982). The development of selective attention. *Merrill-Palmer Quarterly, 28*, 317–337.

LeFever, M.M., & Ehri, L.C. (1976). The relationship between field independence and sentence disambiguation ability. *Journal of Psycholinguistic Research, 5*, 99–106.

Lewandowsky, S., & Li, S.-C. (1995). Catastrophic interference in neural networks. Causes, solutions, and data. In F.N. Dempster & C.J. Brainerd (Eds), *Interference and inhibition in cognition* (pp. 330–361). San Diego, CA: Academic Press.

Littlefield, J., & Reiser, J.J. (1993). Semantic features of similarity and children's strategies for identifying relevant information in mathematical story problems. *Cognition and Instruction, 11*, 122–188.

Luria, A.R. (1973). *The working brain: An introduction for neuropsychology*, New York: Basic Books.

MacLeod, C.M. (1991). Half a century of research on the Stroop effect: An integrative review. *Psychological Bulletin, 109*, 163–203.

Marbe, K. (1901). *Experimentell-psychologisch untersuchungen uber das utriel.* Leipzig: Englemann.

Martin, R.C., Shelton, J.R., & Yaffee, L.S. (1994). Language processing and working memory: Neuropsychological evidence for separate phonological and semantic capacities. *Journal of Memory and Language, 33*, 83–111.

May, C.P., Kane, M.J., & Hasher, L. (1995). Determinants of negative priming. *Psychological Bulletin, 118*, 35–54.

McCall, R.B., & Carriger, M.S. (1993). A meta-analysis of infant habituation and recognition memory performance as predictors of later IQ. *Child Development, 64*, 57–79.

Miller, P.H. (1994). Individual differences in children's strategic behaviour: Utilization deficiencies. *Learning and Individual Differences, 6*, 285–308.

Mitchell, D.B., & Hunt, R.R. (1989). How much "effort" should be devoted to memory? *Memory and Cognition, 17*, 337–348.

Muller, G.E., & Pilzecker, A. (1990). Experimentelle beitrage zur Lehre vom gedachtmis [Experimental contributions to the study of memory]. *Zeitschrift fur Psychologie, Erganzunosband, 1,* 1–288.

Muller, G.E., & Schumann, F. (1894). Experimentelle beitrige zur unterschung des gedachtmisses. *Zeitschrift fur Psychologie, 6,* 81–90.

Murray, D.J. (1976). Research on human memory in the nineteenth century. *Canadian Journal of Psychology, 30,* 201–220.

Muth, D.K. (1984). Solving arithmetic word problems: Role of reading and computational skills. *Journal of Educational Psychology, 76,* 205–210.

Muth, D.K. (1991). Effects of cueing on middle-school students' performance on arithmetic word problems containing extraneous information. *Journal of Educational Psychology, 83,* 173–174.

Navon, D. (1984). Resources—A theoretical soup stone? *Psychological Review, 91,* 216–234.

Neill, W.T., & Valdes, L.A. (1996). Facilitatory and inhibitory aspects of attention. In A.F. Kramer, M. Coles, & G.D. Logan (Eds), *Converging operations in the study of visual selective attention* (pp. 77–138). Washington, DC: American Psychological Association.

Neill, W.T., Valdes, L.A., & Terry, K.M. (1995). Selective attention and the inhibitory control of cognition. In F.N. Dempster & C.J. Brainerd (Eds), *Interference and inhibition in cognition* (pp. 207–261). San Diego, CA: Academic Press.

Neisser, U. (Ed.). (1982). *Memory observed: Remembering in natural contexts.* San Francisco: Freeman.

Oakhill, J. (1993). Children's difficulties in reading comprehension. *Educational Psychology Review, 5,* 223–237.

Ornstein, P.A. (1978). *Memory development in children.* Hillsdale, NJ: Lawrence Erlbaum Associates Inc.

Perfetti, C.A. (1985). *Reading ability.* New York: Oxford University Press.

Peterson, L.R., & Peterson, M.J. (1959). Short-term retention of individual verbal items. *Journal of Experimental Psychology, 59,* 193–198.

Peverly, S.T. (1991). Problems with the knowledge-based explanation of memory and development. *Review of Educational Research, 61,* 71–93.

Piaget, J. (1954). *The construction of reality in the child.* New York: Basic Books.

Plude, D.J., Enns, J.T., & Brodeur, D. (1994). The development of selective attention: A life-span overview. *Acta Psychologica, 86,* 227–272.

Pressley, M. (1994). Embracing the complexity of individual differences in cognition: Studying good information processing and how it might develop. *Learning and Individual Differences, 3,* 259–307.

Reyna, V.F. (1991). Class inclusion, the conjunction fallacy, and other cognitive illusions. *Developmental Review, 11,* 317–336.

Reyna, V.F. (1995). Interference effects in memory and reasoning: A fuzzy-trace theory analysis. In F.N. Dempster & C.J. Brainerd (Eds), *Interference and inhibition in cognition* (pp. 29–61). New York: Academic Press.

Reyna, V.F., & Brainerd, C.J. (1990). Fuzzy processing in transitivity development. *Annals of Operations Research, 23,* 37–63.

Reyna, V.F., & Brainerd, C.J. (1991). Fuzzy trace theory and children's acquisition of mathematical and scientific concepts. *Learning and Individual Differences, 3,* 27–59.

Reyna, V.F., & Brainerd, C.J. (1995a). Fuzzy-trace theory: An interim synthesis. *Learning and Individual Differences, 7,* 1–75.

Reyna, V.F., & Brainerd, C.J. (1995b). Fuzzy-trace theory: Some foundational issues. *Learning and Individual Differences, 7,* 145–162.

Rovee-Collier, C., & Boller, K. (1995). Interference or facilitation in infant memory? In F.N. Dempster & C.J. Brainerd (Eds), *Interference and inhibition in cognition* (pp. 61–104). San Diego, CA: Academic Press.

Schacter, D.L. (1982). *Stranger behind the engram: Theory of memory and the psychology of science.* Hillsdale, NJ: Lawrence Erlbaum Associates Inc.

Schneider, W., & Pressley, M. (1989). *Memory development between 2 and 20.* New York: Springer.

Siegler, R.S. (1981). Developmental sequences within and between concepts. *Monographs of the Society for Research in Child Development, 46* (whole No. 189).

Simpson, G.B., & Foster, M.R. (1986). Lexical ambiguity and children's word recognition. *Developmental Psychology, 22,* 147–154.

Stroop, J.R. (1935). Studies of interference in serial verbal reactions. *Journal of Experimental Psychology, 18,* 643–662.

Strutt, G.F., Anderson, D.R., & Well, A.D. (1975). A developmental study of the effects of irrelevant information on speeded classification. *Journal of Experimental Child Psychology, 20,* 127–135.

Thorndyke, P.W. (1977). Cognitive structures in comprehension and memory of narrative discourse. *Cognitive Psychology, 9,* 77–110.

Thorndyke, P.W., & Hayes-Roth, B. (1979). The use of schemata in the acquisition and transfer of knowledge. *Cognitive Psychology, 11,* 82–106.

Tipper, S.P. (1985). The negative priming effect: Inhibitory priming by ignored objects. *The Quarterly Journal of Experimental Psychology, 37A,* 571–590.

Tipper, S.P., Bourque, T.A., Anderson, S.H., & Brehaut, J.E. (1989). Mechanisms of attention: A developmental study. *Journal of Experimental Child Psychology, 48,* 353–378.

Tipper, S.P., & McLaren, J. (1990). Evidence for efficient visual selectivity in children. In J.T. Enns (Ed.), *The development of attention: Research and theory* (pp. 197–210). Amsterdam: Elsevier/North-Holland.

Underwood, B.J. (1957). Interference and forgetting. *Psychological Review, 64,* 49–60.

Vygotsky, L.S. (1962). *Thought and language.* Cambridge, MA: MIT Press.

Walley, R.E., McLeod, B.E., & Weiden, T.D. (1994). Increased attention to the irrelevant dimension increases interference in a spatial Stroop task. *Canadian Journal of Experimental Psychology, 48,* 467–494.

Willows, D.M. (1974). Reading between the lines: Selective attention in good and poor readers. *Child Development, 45,* 408–415.

Zacks, R.T., & Hasher, L. (1994). Directed ignoring: Inhibitory regulation of working memory. In D. Dagenbach & T.H. Carr (Eds), *Inhibitory processes in attention, memory, and language* (pp. 241–264). San Diego, CA: Academic Press.

PART FOUR

Accelerated and decelerated development

CHAPTER TEN

Savant syndrome—rhyme without reason

Ted Nettelbeck
University of Adelaide, Australia

INTRODUCTION

What is savant syndrome? What can the investigation of this curious capability reveal about the nature and development of intelligence? An answer to the first question is fairly straightforward. Briefly, a savant is an individual who demonstrates exceptional skills within relatively narrowly defined areas but whose general intellectual functioning is nevertheless markedly sub-average. However, an answer to the second question is much more a matter of interpretation, so that it depends on to whom the question is addressed. Gardner (1983), for example, has concluded that the existence of such cases, together with evidence that identifiable brain damage can severely impair some cognitive functioning while leaving other activities unscathed, proves that intelligence is not a unitary construct. Most psychologists who work in this field would agree that intelligence is not unitary. However, Gardner goes on to argue a position that a majority do not, in fact, agree with. In short, this is that, because intelligence is not unitary, a single score expressing it cannot be useful. He discounts the theoretical relevance of a general intelligence factor, concluding that IQ as commonly measured has very limited utility (although he acknowledges that it may have some implications in educational settings). This is both because such tests typically yield a single composite score but also because they sample a limited range of linguistic, logical, and spatial accomplishments. Gardner argues that human abilities cover a much broader

247

spectrum than these and are therefore better defined theoretically in terms of several independent intelligences. These include musical, bodily-kinaesthetic and interpersonal, social abilities, as well as the familiar educationally oriented areas. Others (Howe, 1989; Smith & Tsimpli, 1995) have agreed that cases of savant syndrome expose the impossibility of usefully assigning a single IQ score to an individual, so that the notion of a general intelligence factor (g), as proposed initially by Spearman (1904) is theoretically unproductive (Howe, 1990).

A different perspective recognises the limitations of IQ, particularly for instances where wide variation across different abilities exists, but argues that to ignore the paramount importance of g for most cases is to "throw out the baby with the bath water" (Nettelbeck & Young, 1996).

In one sense Gardner is revisiting the debate about the nature of intelligence, which Spearman, Thurstone, and others had during the first half of this century (Sternberg, 1981). This was essentially a psychometric matter, in terms of how best to interpret the factor analysis of test results, whereas Gardner has drawn on a variety of sources to support his conclusions, such as evidence for localisation of brain function, observations about cultural differences, and instances of extreme ability. However, in the end his theory does amount to a return to the oligarchic doctrine of faculties, which was rejected by Spearman (1923) because it could not accommodate clear evidence for some kind of general intelligence. Gardner raises some challenging questions, not the least being how to account for savant accomplishments, whereby skills at a remarkably high level coexist with general levels of functioning consistent with an intellectual disability. However, his theory does not appeal to those who are convinced that an adequate theory must account for psychometric g. The position taken here is that g is of considerable theoretical importance, although allowing that of itself it provides an insufficient explanation for intelligence, and recognising that the relevance of IQ is constrained by a good many caveats.

Although interest in savant syndrome has a very long history (Foerstl, 1989), O'Connor and Hermelin, together with other colleagues, were the first to apply formal experimental methods to the assessment of cognitive processes underpinning the full range of different savant skills. Their published account of savant syndrome began in the early 1980s (e.g. Hermelin & O'Connor, 1983) and has now expanded to more than 20 articles spanning a decade and a half. They started from the premise that IQ incorporates a general factor, so that exceptionally superior performance in one area by someone with a low IQ must mean that this activity is largely independent of g. This conclusion poses problems, however. General intelligence is so-called because it is generally held to influence all mental activities. This assumption is explicit in theories which conceptualise intelligence as hierarchically organised. O'Connor & Hermelin also recognised that a simple hierarchical solution, whereby all forms of specific abilities are supported by a general capability (e.g. Vernon, 1971), cannot cope with savant syndrome where, by definition, highly developed cognitive skills are divorced from a low, sub-average general capability. Moreover, if some cognitive activities are independent from g, why is it that all persons with an intellectual disability do not do the kinds of things that savants do? These are matters to which we will return in due course.

Following the direction set by O'Connor and Hermelin, Nettelbeck and Young (1996) have argued that any theory of intelligence that neglects the critical importance of g is inadequate. Savant cases inform theory because they illustrate that some cognitive processes that support specific learning, memory, and decision making can operate at unusually high levels, but without transfer to more general areas of cognitive functioning, which may actually be deficient. Thus, far from defining the nature of different kinds of intelligence, as proposed by Gardner (1983), cases of savant syndrome actually help to clarify what intelligence is not. Despite the fact that these or similar processes must inevitably be contributors to intelligent cognitive activities, they do not of themselves constitute intelligence. Nettelbeck and Young acknowledge that intelligence—defined in common-sense terms as reflecting problem-solving capacities and adaptability—is not unitary. However, following Spearman (1927), they insist that an adequate theory of intelligence must incorporate not only specific and relatively independent abilities, but also a general ability which, for the vast majority of people, affects a very wide array of cognitive functions to some extent. Thus, a theory of intelligence must be able to account for everyone—majority and exceptional cases alike.

The next section emphasises the theoretical importance of a general construct for intelligence. In the sections that follow savant syndrome is described in terms of modular functioning, which relies in particular on sound long-term memory, which in the most proficient cases is associated with a talent for specific activities. It is acknowledged from the outset that this theoretical formulation is largely speculative, derived from specific assumptions about the nature of human cognition, but in the absence of direct evidence. The implications of this position for an improved theoretical understanding of intelligence are then discussed. In particular, consideration is given to how Anderson's (1992) cognitive model for the development of intelligence might be modified to improve the account which it provides for the nature of intelligence. Finally, the implications that these matters pose for childhood development and for cognitive changes associated with ageing are discussed.

THE IMPORTANCE OF A GENERAL INTELLIGENCE FACTOR

A very substantial body of evidence supports the proposition that the general factor g, defined in terms of performance on psychometric tests, is related to some as yet unidentified feature of the brain which is involved in those mental activities deemed by common sense to be intelligent (Brody, 1992; Carroll, 1993; Kline, 1991). The g factor encompasses a much wider range of activities than is typically sampled in an IQ test, including laboratory tasks with low knowledge requirements which are conceptually and methodologically strikingly different from psychometric tests (Jensen, 1985; Neisser et al., 1996; Vernon, 1987). None the less, well-designed tests in wide use, like the Standford-Binet or the Wechsler Scales, do provide a composite IQ which is strongly correlated with g (Kline, 1991).

This factor is reasonably stable, both in terms of different psychometric batteries used to derive it and across time. On average, individual differences in IQ change little across middle childhood to early adolescence (Moffitt, Caspit, Harkness, & Silva, 1993), despite markedly increasing mental capacities during this period. Adult differences are similarly relatively stable, despite cognitive changes that tend to accompany ageing beyond middle life (Horn, 1987). Although there is considerable debate about the relative influences of environmental, cultural, and genetic factors, particularly under circumstances involving wide socioeconomic divergence, there is now widespread agreement that g reflects a significant genetic component (Brody, 1992; Kline, 1991; Neisser et al., 1996). This finding is consistent with the proposition that g reflects in part some innate, biological characteristic of the brain.

The general factor predicts real life circumstances other than test performance that, by common consensus, require intelligence. Thus, g predicts to some significant extent performance in situations involving activities that, on the face of it, have little in common with the content of items in IQ tests. Of most relevance to debate about the construct validity of IQ tests, g predicts academic achievement and post-educational accomplishments such as job performance and income moderately well (Neisser et al., 1996).

That g can be demonstrated to have acceptable construct validity and therefore to be of some relevance to an understanding of intelligent behaviour does not mean that it *causes* or is largely responsible for academic achievement or social status or work success. Despite recent highly publicised opinions to this effect (Brand, 1996; Herrnstein & Murray, 1994), g is most plausibly regarded as important but still only one of many personal and socio-cultural factors which can shape social outcomes. Nor does acknowledging that there is an appreciable genetic contribution to g within populations require that we accept any genetic influence to widely recognised group IQ differences. On the contrary, current consensus does not support this interpretation (Neisser et al., 1996).

Other issues also serve to constrain interpretation of *g*. As Sternberg (1988) has pointed out, *g* is probably culturally relative; and the so-called "Flynn effect" (after Flynn, 1987), which is that IQ has increased at an average rate of about three points each decade since the middle of this century to the present, confirms that IQ may be subject to change depending on social or educational factors or perhaps even the type of test used. The causes for the Flynn effect are not yet understood but his finding does underscore the need for caution when interpreting IQ. Moreover, it reinforces recognition that we do not at present understand the nature of *g*. The *g* factor obviously cannot provide a complete explanation for intelligence because factor analysis has consistently established a number of relatively independent abilities that contribute to variance in performance on batteries of IQ-type tests. There is also theoretical debate about whether *g* is unitary (e.g. Horn & Cattell, 1966; Undheim, 1981) or whether it even exists other than as a mathematical manifestation of specific independent processes operating within a single system (Detterman, 1982, 1986).

However, neither relatively crude measurement procedures nor uncertainty about the relative importance of genetic and environmental influences, nor our current incapacities to explain the nature of *g*, renders *g* scientifically useless (Nettelbeck, 1990). The *g* derived by factor analysis from a wide battery of tests will generally explain as much or more variance in test performance than can be explained by adding contributions from various special factors (Carroll, 1993; Kline, 1991) and, most importantly, as outlined earlier, *g* does provide explanatory power. Therefore, taking full account of the various constraints on the interpretation of IQ that have been acknowledged here, it still remains the case that a single composite IQ score does provide useful knowledge about the vast majority of those taking such tests, the questions posed by savants and other exceptional individuals notwithstanding. Attempts to explain intelligence solely or largely in terms of independent abilities seek to diminish the relevance of *g*; but no-one has yet succeeded in designing tests for specific abilities that did not correlate with tests for other cognitive functions. Thus, a reasonable conclusion is that *g*—and ultimately those processes responsible for *g*—must be included as substantive when theorising about intelligence. Given this, Hermelin and O'Connor (1983) were right; savant skills must be relatively independent of *g*—these activities are not intelligent. Yet whatever mental processes support savant performance by way of accumulating knowledge, storing, and retrieving it efficiently, drawing inferences based on that knowledge, and so on, these kinds of activities certainly appear to be consistent with age-old intuitions about what constitutes intelligence. This is clearly a contradiction that requires resolution.

WHAT IS SAVANT SYNDROME?

Individuals who display isolated but exceptional skills, despite overall low IQ, have often been called "idiots-savants"—a term generally credited to the late 19th-century physician J. Langdon Down, although Spitz (1995) has raised doubts about this attribution. However, the terms "savant syndrome" and "savant" are now thought to be preferable (Treffert, 1989). This terminology avoids the pejorative sense now commonly attached to "idiot"—and in any case that term implied a much lower level of mental functioning (e.g. IQ < 25) than characterises savants, among whom IQ generally exceeds 50–60 (Hoffman 1971).

Savants are rare—somewhat less than 1% within the population of persons with an intellectual disability. Males significantly outnumber females (approximately 6:1; Hill, 1978). Incidence among persons with autism is higher at about 10% (Rimland, 1978); but not all savants are autistic (O'Connor & Hermelin, 1991b).

Savants differ considerably in the levels of skills developed, and Treffert (1989) has suggested that "prodigious" and "talented" levels can be distinguished. The former term is reserved for those very rare individuals whose skills are so exceptional that few people can match them. "Talented", on the other hand, is suggested for those relatively more frequent cases where the skill is certainly well above the general low level of functioning that the individual shows in other areas but is none the less consistent with the accomplishments of many non-disabled persons. This distinction excludes "splinter skills", i.e. levels of performance in the same kinds of activities taken up by savants but that, although marginally above the general level of functioning of that person, would not be considered remarkable in the absence of disability. Splinter skills are fairly common among autistic people.

These three categories do provide a system for ordering skill level for comparison purposes but at the present time there is no reliable means for quantifying such skills. Thus, such classification is unlikely to be very reliable. Interested experts would probably agree about outstanding prodigious cases and also about relative rankings within a given area of skill (Young, 1995 includes a discussion of reliability in this regard). However, comparisons across different kinds of skill are much more difficult. And it is by no means clear whether the skills shown by prodigious savants represent the upper extreme of a continuum of skills or a discrete category. The latter possibility is something to which we will return in the section on "Talent".

A remarkable characteristic of savant syndrome is that the skills are found only within a narrow range of activities. Savant and splinter skills are limited to music, arithmetic, and occasionally more complex mathematics such as the identification of prime numbers, calendrical calculation (naming the day of the week on which a given date will fall or has fallen), artistic ability, mechanical dexterity, fine sensory discriminations, memory for relatively trivial facts within a narrowly proscribed field (but with individual interests attached to a bewilderingly wide range, e.g. post codes, telephone numbers, capital cities, street names, public bus routes, train/transport timetables, states of the US according to order of admission/alphabetical order/area/population, etc., location and types of crane on the city skyline, sporting results, and so on), and linguistic representations. This last ability most commonly involves recall or reproduction of language, either written or spoken, with skills extending to superior reading ability and even the ability to translate between languages, but without real comprehension of the content of materials involved. However, there is one instance in the literature of an exceptional multilingualist (whose primary language is English) who can read, write, communicate and translate in 17 or more languages, with fluency in about a dozen, including a number that are represented in alphabets other than the Latin-based one used in English (O'Connor & Hermelin, 1991b; Smith & Tsimpli, 1995). This man's performance on ability tests that are relatively independent from verbal abilities has consistently been low and indicative of an intellectual deficiency. Despite this, however, his level of understanding for linguistic materials is remarkably good. The implications of this case for a model of intelligence will be considered in a later section.

That savant skills cluster within such a small range of activities demonstrates that these skills are not random occurrences. As Anderson (1992) observed, savant syndrome cannot be ignored by theorists about intelligence on the grounds that such cases are idiosyncratic—for example, a genetic accident that results in a unique brain structure which therefore has no theoretical relevance. On the contrary, as Gardner (1983) has observed, the activities demonstrated by savants appear to be universals, so that whatever processes give rise to these activities are presumably also universals.

In areas usually associated with artistic creativity, such as music and graphic art, savants have often been observed to have "mechanical technique", characterised by low levels of expressiveness and emotional involvement. O'Connor and Hermelin (1987a) have speculated that intelligence may interact with IQ-independent skills, with higher aesthetic qualities dependent on higher IQ. However, although this may generally be so, there are apparent exceptions. For example, there have been occasional but well-documented cases of painters, sculptors, and graphic artists with markedly debilitating intellectual disabilities but whose works have been widely acknowledged by experts and patrons of art to be original and therefore to reflect creativity (O'Connor & Hermelin, 1987a; Sacks, 1995; Selfe, 1977; Treffert, 1989). Thus, that genuinely creative qualities may characterise savant skills, yet without the advantage of even low-to-average IQ, poses a theoretical contradiction which requires a solution. This issue is addressed further in a later section.

In the past it has frequently been assumed that most savants develop only one skill. However, there is now evidence to suggest that this is not correct and that the acquisition of multiple skills is common, at least among autistic savants (Duckett, 1976; Rimland, 1978; Young, 1995). It is possible that multiple skills are grouped because similar psychological processes are involved. For example, Rimland (1978) has noted that musical and memory skills are frequently combined in autistic savants. Young (1995) found that music and mathematics frequently occurred together, as did art and calendrical calculation, but she also observed a wider range of combinations than has been reported previously. The acquisition of more than one skill was not related to IQ but was predicted to a statistically significant extent by the property of prodigiousness; i.e. those cases whose major skills were rated as the most accomplished tended to be those who displayed multiple skills. This outcome may reflect Young's rating method, which limited prodigiousness to cases involved with either music or art. In the next section it is argued that these activities depend in part on both a specific aptitude and on efficient memory functioning. Such individuals may therefore be better equipped to develop skills in more than one area than persons whose skills do not require a special talent beyond good memory.

TOWARDS AN EXPLANATION FOR SAVANT SYNDROME

The most comprehensive body of research in the literature on this topic has been carried out by Hermelin, O'Connor, and their colleagues. They have investigated cognitive processes involved in calendrical calculation (Hermelin & O'Connor, 1986; O'Connor & Hermelin, 1984), musical performance (Hermelin, O'Connor, & Lee, 1987; Hermelin, O'Connor, Lee, & Treffert, 1989; Sloboda, Hermelin, & O'Connor, 1985), graphic artistic skills (Hermelin & O'Connor, 1990a; O'Connor & Hermelin, 1987a, 1987b, 1990), linguistic skills (O'Connor & Hermelin, 1991a), mathematical calculation (Hermelin & O'Connor, 1990b), and memory (O'Connor & Hermelin, 1989).

This body of research has established that a viable explanation for most savant activities will have to acknowledge that they derive from knowledge about structural rules relevant to the particular skill domain. This is an important point because it means that, qualitatively and in general terms, savant skills utilise processes that are the same as those used by normally intelligent, highly skilled individuals. Thus, savant skills cannot adequately be explained in terms of some unique and rigid, memory-based mechanism which is domain-specific and which directly translates input into output. For example, the abilities of a musical savant are not appropriately described metaphorically in terms of a tape recorder. This is not to say that exceptional memory is not involved—it may be, as is argued later. Nor does it exclude an important role that a specific, in-built talent will play in mediating some activities, such as musical performance or graphic art. However, investigations of constraints on the reproduction at the keyboard of previously unknown music by savant pianists have established that errors made are virtually entirely consistent with the structural aspects that define the music. So, for example, embellishment to the melody may be omitted, or the melody altered but only in ways consistent with the prevailing diatonic scale and with the rhythm preserved, or a chord may be inverted so that, while not a literal rendition, harmonic identity is retained (Charness, Clifton, & MacDonald, 1988; Sloboda et al., 1985; Young & Nettelbeck, 1995). Even for atonal music, errors in reproduction have been found to preserve the theoretical structure within which the music is embedded (Young & Nettelbeck, 1995). These findings therefore demonstrate that the musical memory involved is supported by cognitive decisions made on the basis of well-organised and structurally based knowledge about music. These savants "know" how the music that they play "works".

Similar findings hold for other kinds of savant skills. Calendrical calculation, for example, has commonly been assumed to reflect nothing more than a highly developed rote memory for days and dates (Hill, 1978; Horwitz, Kestenbaum, Person, & Jarvik, 1965) but this is probably not a sufficient explanation in most cases. As O'Connor (1989) has pointed out, simple rote memory, i.e. nothing more than rehearsal, is scarcely plausible as an explanation for those individuals whose calculations of dates anytime in the future are accurate. O'Connor and Hermelin (1984) therefore concluded that calendrical calculators have extensive knowledge about calendar regularities and make use of these regularities. Young and Nettelbeck (1994; Young, 1995) found evidence which strongly supported O'Connor and Hermelin's proposition, but pointed out that this did not explain how calculations were made. Their experiments with calendrical calculators found that near-perfect accuracy was limited to a specific epoch that varied across individuals, but was in every case consistent with limits set by commercially available perpetual calendars. For a given individual, performance deteriorated dramatically for dates outside the identifiable range of knowledge. All of the 10 participants in these investigations (see Young, 1995) were highly knowledgeable about the 14 calendar templates which complete the Gregorian system and all were able to match a given year with the correct template, although generally only within the span of commonly available perpetual calendars (generally 1900 to 2100). All participants were also familiar with leap-year rules, identical configurations across certain years and consistencies across months which produced common day–date relationships.

Nettelbeck and Young (1996) argued that this knowledge does provide the basis for calendrical calculation skills; but not in the sense of developing a sophisticated mathematical algorithm to make calculations. Such a strategy could be discounted because most participants had very poor mathematical skills; for each individual the speed of responding was remarkably consistent irrespective of recency or distance of the date and whether a repetition was involved, and in most cases much quicker than would be possible if an algorithm was being used; and participants could solve reverse problems (such as identifying the date for a day located in a given week, month and year) which were unresolvable from such an algorithm. Moreover, Young and Nettelbeck's (1994) analyses of reaction times to calendar solutions found no evidence to support the idea that calendar knowledge (which their participants clearly had) provided the basis for genuine computation. On the contrary, any strategies applied must have been invariant because they were not sensitive to experimental manipulations based on calendar regularities. Nettelbeck and Young (1996) therefore concluded that calendrical calculation depends ultimately on the memorisation of simple rules defining template–year relationships, regularities within years, the occurrence of leap years, and appropriate associated adjustments. To achieve this knowledge base clearly requires more than rote memory; assimilation to a knowledge structure must be involved. However, strategies based on these rules have been thoroughly learned and practised and are applied without flexibility, permitting very rapid, automatic processing. This account can accommodate those cases reported by Hermelin and O'Connor (1986) who can solve problems well into the future, providing that one assumes that they have previously tested years in the future against the 14 templates—something which seems plausible, given the obsessional interest that savants hold for their area(s) of expertise. (This proposition is easily tested; following Young, 1995, it is only necessary to test the ability to match future years with the correct template.)

Initially, at least, some savants may use an anchor date within the year from which to project forwards or backwards, using rules for regularities and simple addition or subtraction to adjust for irregularities (Young, 1995 provides an account of an individual who gave a clear account in these terms). Another suggestion is that solutions can be based on mental imagery of calendars (Howe & Smith, 1988; Sacks, 1985). Within constraints set by the calendar characteristics just outlined, there is obviously opportunity for individual differences in the strategies developed; probably there is no single method that all calendrical calculators use. As Spitz (1995) has pointed out, some procedural rules may even be learned incidentally, without conscious application. However, the development of these skills is clearly dependent upon extensive amounts of practice. Anecdotal accounts of savant skills emerging suddenly at high levels of competence, without much by way of tutoring or practice, can be discounted (see, for example, Miller, 1989; Treffert, 1989 for background information about a widely publicised musical savant). Young (1995) found clear evidence to support the contention that considerable practice and preoccupation over long periods of time with the skill sought is essential for the degree of automation achieved. Continued practice is also necessary to the maintenance of the skill, which will decline otherwise (Treffert, 1989; Young, 1995).

It is probably also the case that an obsessional personality (characteristic of autism although not of itself sufficient to define this condition) contributes to the development of savant skills. Although a recent analysis of family background has found that the families of savants encouraged extensive practice and achievement (Young, 1995), a conducive environment is insufficient without high levels of personal motivation.

Thus far, the proposition is that some kinds of savant skills are explicable in terms of, at the least, good procedural long-term memory (Squire, 1986), which coexists with other markedly deficient cognitive functions, together with the opportunity and willingness to devote sufficient time to practice, so that whatever processes are involved become automatic (Fitts & Posner, 1967; Shiffrin & Schneider, 1977). This account copes well with a good memory for facts, calendrical calculation, and perhaps even for the application of simple arithmetic or of verbal representation characterised by mimicry but without understanding. However, as will be discussed further in a later section, it begs the question as to how, given low g, declarative processes which are dependent on conscious control are transformed into automatic processes. Moreover, it is certainly inadequate for a case such as the polyglot described by Smith and Tsimpli (1995), or for high competence in music, art, mathematics, or mechanics. For these, a special talent is necessary.

Before proceeding further to a discussion of talent, we will now address the question foreshadowed in the Introduction; if savant skills do not require even average levels of g, why are they not more widespread among persons with an intellectual difficulty? Three possibilities are suggested. First, the skills may actually be within the cognitive capabilities of other mentally retarded persons but most lack the persistent personality essential to the long periods of dedicated practice which support skill improvement. This possibility is consistent with what is known about the personalities of savants but is countered by the observation that some 90% of autistic cases—characterised by obsessional tendencies—do not develop savant skills.

Second, if we assume that the low levels of IQ which we are discussing are the consequence of insult to the brain, such damage may most commonly impact on brain processes responsible for general intelligence and for procedural long-term memory alike. According to this option, savants are cases who suffer brain damage but where none the less relevant aspects of long-term memory have somehow been spared—"islets of ability", to use Treffert's (1989) description. In these instances procedural long-term memory would function at least at normal levels, whereas this would not be so for other persons with an intellectual disability. A third possibility is that savant skills represent exceptional talents (which could include memory), again spared the effects of brain damage which results in low general intelligence. These second and third options define savants with mental retardation as having some cognitive processes which are qualitatively different from those of other persons with an intellectual disability.

TALENT

"Talent" is used here to describe an assumed brain capacity that is specialised for a particular kind of knowledge, independent from IQ and capable of operating at an unusually high level. This assumption is consistent with the observations of others (e.g. Gardner, 1983; Howe, 1989, 1990; O'Connor, 1989; Spitz, 1995). Talent may be innate—genetically determined and with potential present from birth. However, the argument presented here requires only that skills involved should be laid down early. It is not assumed that talent is all-or-none. Little is known about this at this point in time and, at least on the basis of psychometric evidence, there is debate about whether in areas such as music, art, and mathematics, specific aptitudes can be reliably identified (Carroll, 1993). None the less, such difficulties notwithstanding, these constructs obviously have age-old standing as everyday concepts and what evidence exists for them supports the contention that individual differences in them are widely distributed. Thus the position taken here is that specific talents exist and they reflect individual differences.

In the light of foregoing discussion, however, it is certainly not assumed that a skill built on talent will develop without effort. O'Connor's (1989) view is that talent is innate and therefore independent of rehearsal. However, the developed skill deriving from the talent requires practice. Nevertheless, in the sense analogous to Horn's (1968) distinction between an early *anlage* function and the *fluid intelligence* that is built on it, some level of talent is held to exist as a precondition for the development of the concomitant skill to high levels. Thus, to answer the question raised in the earlier section about whether prodigious skills are somehow qualitatively different from skills at lower levels, the proposition here is that the highest skills will be achieved in those areas requiring a specific talent. Because a specific aptitude dedicated to a particular knowledge domain is involved, such skills are qualitatively different from all others.

The expression of even prodigious talent does not require comparable levels of competence in other areas of cognition except that memory and motor functions must be capable of sustaining that expression. This is an important point, to which we will return in the next two sections. Throughout their research, O'Connor and Hermelin have emphasised that savant skills are independent from IQ and their results have shown that these skills are isolated from other cognitive functioning. Thus, for example, O'Connor and Hermelin (1990) demonstrated that savant graphic artists had drawing ability far beyond what would be predicted by their IQs, while at the same time they had poor visual recognition for shapes, consistent with low IQs.

According to Judd (1988), high musical competence requires a cluster of skills that defines musical memory. Nettelbeck and Young (1996) have speculated that "perfect pitch" is a good candidate for an essential element underpinning musical memory—a talent without which prodigious savant skills will not develop. Perfect pitch is the ability to identify correctly the pitch of any note in an absolute sense, without any aid from an external source. It is commonly held to be a relatively uncommon innate capacity (Bachem, 1955), although Takeuchi and Hulse (1993) have argued that it is a universal potential, dependent only on appropriate environmental stimulation. These authors point to evidence that accurate absolute pitch perception can be acquired with practice, although only if learning occurs before the child is about four to five years old. Substantial individual differences in accuracy are found, even among those claiming absolute pitch. Whether innate or determined by early learning, absolute perfect pitch is rarely reported among the normal population, even for musicians, whereas published accounts of musical savants suggest that every one of them has virtually error-free absolute pitch (Charness et al., 1988; Miller, 1989; Sloboda et al., 1985; Young & Nettelbeck, 1995). Absolute pitch has also been noted in autistic children without musical achievements and in savants with other skills but not music, emphasising that a talent is a precondition for the emergence of skill, not a sufficient explanation. Thus, even to accept the role of a talent, as proposed here, still leaves the realisation of that potential unaccounted for.

Similarly, O'Connor and Hermelin's (1990) research suggests that there is a specific talent underpinning superior artistic ability. This is the capacity to register and recall visual or tactile detail, resulting in an excellent sense of perspective, and to convert this knowledge into graphic output. This suggestion is consistent with speculation that artistic talent is supported by specific brain structures (Schweiger, 1988). Similarly, Smith and Tsimpli (1995) have deduced that a linguistic lexicon, independent from central cognitive control, is necessary to support the exceptional linguistic talent of their savant case-study. Sacks' (1995) speculation about domain-specific categorical memory, which results directly in an understanding of structures relevant to that domain, provides a general account of how a talent might work in other areas like mathematics or mechanics. Sacks has also pointed out that some forms of exceptional specific memory may be "pathological", in the sense that they are rigidly particular, unlike common recall which is dynamic and reconstructive (Bartlett, 1932). If so, this would account for so-called "photographic" memory.

IMPLICATIONS OF SAVANT SYNDROME FOR A THEORY OF INTELLIGENCE

The argument thus far is that an adequate theory of intelligence will account for a range of specific aptitudes but also for a general factor which produces relative stability in individual differences in IQ more or less across the lifespan, despite the obvious fact that cognitive abilities are age-related during both childhood improvement and decline in late old age. In addition, theory must be able to accommodate savant syndrome which, it has been asserted, reflects well-developed long-term memory processes. These are procedural, restricted to specific tasks and, most commonly, savants are not able to explain with any clarity how they do these things. However the skills are certainly acquired by practice so that, initially, cognitive manipulation of relevant knowledge is necessary. In other words, elaborative rehearsal must be involved during early establishment of the skill. This is the crux of the matter. Theory must hold such effective long-term memory—obviously a cognitive domain which is necessary for normal functioning—to be independent of g and not sufficient for the development of intelligence. Moreover, some complex cognitive abilities relating to activities such as mathematics, multilingualism, music, and art, and developed to even prodigious levels, must be independent of g and not sufficient for the development of intelligence, despite the fact that our culture values these activities and typically holds them to be intellectual pursuits. Finally, some way has to be found to acknowledge the originality that characterises some savant achievements, while at the same time maintaining that such creativity also does not constitute a sufficient condition for the emergence of intelligence.

Anderson (1992) has proposed a model for intelligence that directly addresses some of these issues. The model is shaped by two fundamental ideas. The first is that *acquired knowledge* (the current means of testing intelligence by IQ tests) accumulates from two sources. The second is that the brain is conceptualised in terms of three quite different mechanisms.

Intelligence is defined by knowledge that is acquired by *thinking*. Thinking requires the implementation of general-purpose computational routines that are generated by specific processors. These are dedicated to independent knowledge domains (e.g. verbal-propositional and visual-spatial, consistent with the common distinction between left and right hemispheres, although, in principal, other domains may exist). Individual differences in specific abilities are normally distributed and will therefore contribute to individual differences in intelligence.

The second kind of knowledge is generated by *modules*. Acquisition of modular-derived knowledge does not involve thinking. Following Fodor (1983), modules operate bottom-up (i.e. independent of thought and rapidly). Forms of knowledge provided by modules are also highly specific but are held to be competencies, not abilities. Modules are critically important in an evolutionary sense although, being all-or-none mechanisms, some individuals will lack particular modules. However, they bear no relationship to individual differences in intelligence, even though they require complex computational processes. They are, none the less, responsible for increasing mental age throughout childhood because their availability is ontogenetically determined, with different modules coming on-line at different ages.

The central component of the essential cognitive "architecture" in Anderson's model is the *basic processing mechanism* (BPM). The speed of operation of the BPM constrains output from the specific processors, whatever their latent capabilities, but not output from modules. Because of this overriding function, a general intelligence factor will always be found. A deficient BPM will result in low *g* characterising the capabilities of an individual. However, if the BPM is adequate there is opportunity for differentiation across specific abilities. Finally, basic processing speed does not change with childhood development; it is innately acquired and set from the beginning of life.

Anderson's model is therefore a computer metaphor which reconciles Spearman's (1927) theory with Piagetian theory (e.g. Piaget, 1953). It accounts for increasing mental age, characterised by abrupt discontinuities, but also for stability in IQ; and it accommodates the critical issues of individual differences in specific abilities as well as in general intelligence. Although there is currently keen debate about whether speed of processing improves during childhood (Anderson, Nettelbeck, & Barlow, 1997; Kail, 1991; Nettelbeck & Vita, 1992), this is not critical to the validity of the model which is broadly consistent with the Spearman tradition, equating general intelligence with the efficiency of some biological feature of the brain (e.g. Anderson, 1995; Eysenck, 1987). In fact, an earlier version of the model (Anderson, 1986) was couched in terms of BPM "efficiency" and it is certainly plausible that, whereas reaction times and other speed measures improve during childhood, the fundamental efficiency of an individual's brain is normally unchanging because it is characterised by an inborn potential which determines the range and extent of, for example, neuronal interconnectivity (Anderson, 1995).

How well, then, does Anderson's model cope with savant syndrome? In broad terms, it provides a promising account although considerable fine tuning is necessary. It will be obvious from the foregoing account of different kinds of savant skills that, because these are independent from IQ, savant activities must be modular. According to Anderson (1992), in addition to the modules already described (termed Mark I), there is a second type of module (Mark II), which may be neither complex nor innately specified but is, instead, an elementary information processing routine. His example is an automatic function for retrieving well-rehearsed materials from long-term memory. In these terms, if one accepts that calendrical calculations, or memory for sundry facts, are supported by memory-dependent, highly practised, fairly elementary strategies, then such processes are equivalent to Mark II modules. But where are Mark II modules located and how do they develop? The implication is that highly practised routines eventually become automatic—and there is certainly strong evidence that this is so (e.g. Shiffrin & Schneider, 1977). However, the model must be able to provide an account of how a savant, with a deficient BPM, is able to cope with the relevant processing before automaticity is achieved, when conscious thought is necessary.

The model runs into a similar difficulty when confronting a form of savant syndrome dependent on a specific talent. Artistic skill (visuo-spatial aptitude) illustrates the point, as does music. (Anderson's model does not include these kinds of aptitudes but, because these are areas where individual differences are clearly involved, they would not qualify as modules, as defined by Anderson.) Again, the model requires a means whereby a talent, located within a specific processor and therefore subject to individual variation, can be transformed into a module so that output bypasses the BPM. Anderson's (1992) account of such a case in terms of an intact specific processor with a damaged BPM simply will not work.

Because the manifest output from a specific processor is directly constrained by the BPM, the specific skill and general intelligence must be correlated under this model—not the case with savant syndrome.

Smith and Tsimpli (1995) have drawn attention to the same shortcoming in the model in relation to an account for the performance of their linguist. On the basis of a series of nicely controlled experiments with this man, they were able to demonstrate that, despite his remarkable talent, there are aspects of language beyond his capabilities. Isolation of his limitations revealed that these were conceptual—the consequence of poor evaluative capacities. For example, he is incapable of appreciating a linguistic joke. The basis of his learning of all other languages is an exceptional lexical memory which permits direct transfer from English to a new language on a word-for-word basis. Thus, syntactical errors in another language are consistent with English syntax. Smith and Tsimpli's logical conclusion is that the first language is essentially modular based. In this man's case, the module is intact but it exists together with an impaired central system, which therefore prevents interaction between the module and higher cognitive processes.

This conclusion leads Smith and Tsimpli to suggest a number of important modifications to Anderson's (1992) model. First, they introduce a linguistic lexicon which is interfaced with a conceptual lexicon but functions independently as a module outside of the central cognitive system where the conceptual lexicon is located. Second, they permit thought that is independent from the BPM. This is described as "quasi-modular" to distinguish it from the more constrained modules defined by Fodor (1983); but in Anderson's terms it amounts to direct communication between a specific processor and knowledge, without passing through the BPM. Third, they explicity include an executive function to control the progress of information within the central system. It commonly has been argued that to include an executive is a retrograde step, because introducing an element with paramount responsibilities over others drastically reduces the scientific value of a theory because this function merely becomes another metaphor for "intelligence" or g. The position taken here, however, is that the inclusion of an executive function is inevitable; and, moreover, that it is in principle possible to clarify the nature of control processes by appropriate procedures (e.g. Brewer & Smith, 1984, 1989; Rabbitt, 1981). The fact remains that no theorist since Spearman working in that tradition has been able to avoid some kind of homunculus as an essential quality of human intelligence.

Anderson (1992) did not discuss the problem of an executive, although implicitly this is somehow located in the BPM which is responsible for the general intelligence factor. A different approach to the investigation of the nature of g is offered by Detterman (1982, 1986). Instead of a single element such as the BPM, Detterman suggests that an explanation for the nature of intelligence should be sought in terms of a small number of elements. These are independent, in the sense that they represent idiosyncratic processes, each within a given structure and capacity. However, because all elements combine to form a complex system, the output of any element is influenced by the quality of input from the others. Thus, the performance of each element will be influenced by the other elements and g is a composite of outputs. This model nicely captures the common observation that a particular global quality implied by a given IQ score would rarely, if ever, reflect the same underlying elementary functioning across different individuals. An investigation of these issues by Detterman et al. (1992), in which they operationalised attentional, memory, and control constructs in terms of various parameters from basic chronometric tasks, led them to modify their initial working model by isolating long-term memory from executive control. Whereas the executive function was required for the top-down control of less permanent forms of memory, this was not so for long-term memory. This solution from a different context was therefore similar to that proposed by Smith and Tsimpli (1995).

An integration of these various ideas seems likely to be fruitful. The approach advocated by Detterman et al. (1992) has the capacity to explicate further the nature of g by testing the contribution of independent processes to general intelligence. At the same time, there is no reason at this time to abandon the promise of Anderson's (1992) model which so nicely reconciles specific and general aspects of intelligence within a viable developmental framework. It seems plausible that g might reflect both a general efficiency of brain structures because, for example, of a general capacity for dendritic arborisation resulting in neural networks (Anderson, 1995), and the involvement of common elements within a system as envisioned by Detterman (1982, 1986). And, as recognised by O'Connor and Hermelin (e.g. 1990), and elegantly confirmed by Smith and Tsimpli (1995), an adequate account of how the mind works must include modules, autonomous from general intelligence, subject to individual differences, but capable of highly specialised development in the sense that the skills supported are not only improved by practice but may express an outstanding individuality which would qualify as "original" or "creative".

This issue of creativity in savant skills is a particularly difficult one and it cannot be resolved here. However, Sacks' (1995) suggestion about this is particularly worthy of consideration. Essentially, he distinguishes between two different kinds of creativity; savant artistic ability may achieve originality in the sense of personal expression but no savant with an intellectual disability has ever invented an entirely new way of looking at things. Perhaps, then, as O'Connor and Hermelin (1987a) speculated, this latter higher order of creativity requires a quality of conceptualisation for which at least average levels of general intelligence are a precondition. However, speculation about a floor level in g to sustain higher order creativity obviously begs the question as to how lower orders emerge at all; and the fact is that research has not yet attempted to address this area.

IMPLICATIONS FOR CHILDHOOD DEVELOPMENT AND CHANGES RELATED TO OLD AGE

Speculation here about the nature of memory processes required to account for savant syndrome is consistent with what is currently known about how memory develops, although it must be said that a singular lack of exchange between experimental and psychometric endeavours has left these areas isolated from one another (Carroll, 1993). This is something that should be redressed. It is the case that the account developed here in terms of putative long-term processes can draw on little by way of direct evidence from the study of individual differences registered in the psychometric literature. An adequate investigation which includes both individual differences and developmental aspects of long-term memory is yet to be made. What is available supports requirements for the argument that effective long-term memory should be independent from g and available from a young mental age; but these are certainly hypotheses which define useful direction for future research.

First, research by Rovee-Collier and her colleagues has demonstrated that long-term memory is established at a very early age. Infants as young as three months retain information for periods of several weeks and even months about events involving them (Rovee-Collier, 1990). Second, the psychometric evidence is certainly consistent with Spearman's (1927) assertion that some aspects of long-term memory must be independent of g. The best developed psychometric account of differences in childhood long-term memory is provided by the Horn–Cattell model for intelligence (e.g. Horn, 1987). This includes *long-term storage and retrieval* (TSR) as a broad ability independent from the five other second-order abilities, including the paramount fluid and crystallised abilities. There is no direct evidence linking this factor, which is typically indicated by tests of retention following a delay after learning of minutes or hours or days, with the much longer periods of time envisaged when speculating in the foregoing sections about declarative and procedural processes. However, test data establish TSR as a separate factor by no later than four years of age. Moreover, effective TSR not only emerges at a developmentally early stage during childhood but, on average, capacities are not diminished with old age, as is the case with other intellectual abilities, most notably those requiring speed and fluid reasoning (Horn, 1987).

It is immediately obvious to anyone confronted by a young child with a precocious aptitude for music or art that the development of associated skills follows a very different course from that which applies for common intellectual abilities. Such a child seems to be able to learn whatever techniques are involved much more quickly and with so much less effort than a normal child, even one who has well above average general intelligence. Motor requirements that are daunting to others appear to be relatively trivial for a talented child. Levels of skill achieved early are usually well in advance of mental age development.

According to the definition of talent proposed here, it may be innately determined and, at least in the areas of art and music, available from a very early age. However, while it might most commonly be the case that talent is manifested early, this is not always so. O'Connor (1989) has suggested that talent does not need practice for its potential to be maintained; and this may explain why some individuals can quickly develop very high levels of artistic skill in late adolescence or very early adulthood within a relatively short time frame. In such cases, the talent may lie dormant, only developing when opportunity opens or interest becomes focused. However, in other cases the nature of the talent involved may be qualitatively different, only becoming available for exploitation when the child has reached a given stage of development. This possibility is suggested by Anderson's (1992) discussion of discontinuity in development, with some modules only beginning operation later during childhood, linked to specific age bands.

However, even given enormous potential, practice is essential to the development of manifest skill—and, perhaps even more importantly, it is probably necessary to the maintenance of skill, even though procedural memory skills are typically resistant to forgetting. None the less, strong anecdotal evidence supports the contention that even prodigious savant skills are lost without sustained practice (Treffert, 1989). Presumably, if based on talent, such diminished skill should be recoverable, given further practice. However, particularly later in life it may be a case of "use it or lose it".

An important theoretical issue yet to be resolved is how practice transforms talent into skill if g is low. How are rules assimilated? The specific assumption here is that the skills required behave like a module; they are automatic, do not transfer, and are not accessible to metacognition (Sternberg, 1988). Moreover, whatever learning is involved may be accomplished at a young age and it is consistent with early ontological development. But how this is achieved remains to be determined.

It is important to note also that talent-based skills are not the same as crystallised abilities. The distinction between crystallised and fluid abilities, central to the Horn–Cattell model of intelligence (Horn, 1987), derives from observations about different, average rates of improvement during childhood and decline in old age for different cognitive abilities. Beyond middle age, whereas crystallised abilities (epitomised by language skills) maintain earlier levels and may even improve, fluid abilities—paramount to the quality of intelligence because they are responsible for problem solving—begin to deteriorate. Accessing information to retrieve from long-term memory under speed constraints provides a good example of a fluid ability with marked age effects. A talent-based, well-rehearsed skill may seem analogous to a crystallised ability except in one very important respect. Crystallised intelligence is dependent on fluid intelligence for its manifestation, whereas, as savant syndrome demonstrates, a prodigious talent is not. However, there is a great deal of anecdotal evidence from the lives of great artists and musicians to suggest that, providing one remains active in those areas built on talent, the relevant skills will remain largely unimpaired, even into extreme old age.

It is worthwhile emphasising that, because modular activity is independent from *g*, there are no grounds to expect transfer between modular-based competencies and either specific aptitudes or general ability. Thus, it should not be expected that an emphasis on a traditional educational curriculum will impact on areas such as music and art. In cases where these talents are identified early, there may well be advantages in specific training, dedicated to the talent in question. At the same time, however, it should be recognised that investment in module-based competencies during childhood will not enhance general capabilities. In fact, to focus exclusively on a child's talent in, for example, music or art may be to neglect opportunities relevant to the realisation of general potential. The best interests of even a child who exhibits prodigious talent are therefore probably served by adopting a balanced approach to education.

To this point in time, little is understood about the nature of processes underpinning modular competencies. However, to the extent that the processes involved in one area are similar to or overlap with those in another, transfer between areas should be possible. This was illustrated in the case of the linguist investigated by Smith and Tsimpli (1995), where his competency in all other languages was developed essentially by mapping the foreign vocabularies onto English structures. Among savants, as Young (1995) found, there are many cases with skills developed in more than one area. Common pairings such as mathematics and music, or art and calendrical calculation, may be supported by some common neurological substrate. On the other hand, it may be that cases of multiple skills represent the preservation of more than one discrete module, despite brain damage which reduces general capability. This distinction carries implications for an improved understanding of childhood development and is an issue towards which future research could fruitfully be directed.

Although there is debate about whether different categories of talent are genetically endowed or not, few experts would disagree with the assertion that, individual differences notwithstanding, most children are capable of higher accomplishments in areas such as music, art, or mathematics, if provided with appropriate strategies for learning, particularly from an early age. Thus, even if Smith (1988) has overstated the extent to which superior arithmetical calculating skills are the consequence of rehearsal with appropriate algorithms, there is still a strong case to be made for educational practices in this field which favour mental effort and avoid over-dependence on the electronic calculator. Moreover, to the extent that prodigious performance in any area is influenced by early intervention, this will obviously have implications for early education. As one example, if, as has been asserted here and by others, perfect pitch is an accomplishment likely to promote excellence in musical performance, then Takeuchi and Hulse's (1993) review suggests that its acquisition will be maximised by early training which focuses on absolute qualities of pitch. However, such an approach would require a radical departure from current practices which focus on melodic, harmonic, and rhythmic structures from the outset, i.e. on different relationships between notes.

It seems probable that the subset of savant activities represented here as being essentially feats of memory for facts are in principle accessible to anyone whose long-term memory is not impaired and within normal limits, although prodigious skills derived from talent for music or art would not be. If this is so, then many children should, if they were so motivated, be capable of calendrical calculation or memorising impressive lists of facts. Presumably many do for short periods of time; but do not persist in the face of more pertinent educational and recreational demands. Valentine and Wilding (1994) have pointed to the importance of motivation and practice to the superior memory achievements of those employing mnemonic strategies. On the other hand, these researchers are also convinced that, contrary to assertions that impressive memory is no more than acquired skill, some individuals have an outstanding talent for long-term retention that is not dependent on learned techniques. However, as they point out, research into the development of exceptional long-term memory has scarcely begun. Equally important, testing the limits of normal memory, particularly during early childhood, is an essential area for future theoretical advancement.

SUMMARY

The basic proposition addressed here is that savant skills display "rhyme without reason"; activities are highly accomplished within a narrowly prescribed domain but they are carried out without the degree of thought required to regard them as intelligent. This position is therefore the antithesis of the suggestion that savant accomplishments demonstrate the existence of several different kinds of intelligence. The premise on which this conclusion is based is that a general factor (g) is an integral constituent of human intelligence. Because savants have low IQs—accepted here as representing g—their extraordinary accomplishments cannot rely on g. However, because savant skills are supported by cognitive processes which normally contribute to intelligent activities, these individuals pose a problem for theorists—in effect, how to include general and specific factors within a satisfactory theoretical formulation, while at the same time removing some acknowledged complex activities from higher control.

The solution proposed is that savant skills derive from aspects of long-term memory, which may be associated with a specific talent, and which function as modules. Little is yet known about individual differences in the development of long-term memory abilities. What is already known about savant syndrome does hold broader developmental implications, both within childhood but also for transition into old age. Specifically, module-based competencies and general capabilities may require differential educational attention; if we wish to continue module-based competencies into old age we may need to maintain involvement.

However, the immediate challenge for theory is to explain how procedural long-term memory processes can be developed to high levels of performance without the involvement of comparable levels of g. Anderson's (1992) developmental model for intelligence includes all of the components necessary to achieve this but is as yet insufficiently detailed to provide a satisfactory account of savant skills. A number of suggestions for modifying the model have been made, that integrate ideas from other sources and point to potentially fruitful directions for future research.

REFERENCES

Anderson, B. (1995). G explained. *Medical Hypotheses, 45,* 602–604.

Anderson, M. (1986). Understanding the cognitive deficit in mental retardation. *Journal of Child Psychology and Psychiatry, 27,* 297–306.

Anderson, M. (1992). *Intelligence and development: A cognitive theory.* Oxford, UK: Blackwell.

Anderson, M., Nettelbeck, T., & Barlow, J. (1997). Reaction time measures of speed of processing: Speed of response selection increases with age but speed of stimulus categorisation does not. *British Journal of Developmental Psychology, 15,* 145–157.

Bachem, A. (1955). Absolute pitch. *Journal of Acoustical Society of America, 27,* 110–1185.

Bartlett, F.C. (1932). *Remembering: A study of experimental and social psychology.* Cambridge, UK: Cambridge University Press.

Brand, C. (1996). *The* g *factor: General intelligence and its implications.* Chichester, UK: Wiley.

Brewer, N. & Smith, G.A. (1984). How normal and retarded individuals monitor and regulate speed and accuracy of responding in serial choice tasks. *Journal of Experimental Psychology: General, 113,* 71–93.

Brewer, N. & Smith, G.A. (1989). Development changes in processing speed: Influence of speed-accuracy regulation. *Journal of Experimental Psychology: General, 118,* 298–310.

Brody, N. (1992). *Intelligence* (2nd ed.). San Diego, CA: Academic Press.

Carroll, J. (1993). *Human cognitive ability: A survey of factor analytic studies.* London: Cambridge University Press.

Charness, N., Clifton, J., & MacDonald, L. (1988). Case study of a musical "monosavant": A cognitive psychological focus. In L. Obler & D. Fein (Eds), *The exceptional brain* (pp. 277–293). New York: Guilford.

Detterman, D.K. (1982). Does "*g*" exist? *Intelligence, 6,* 99–108.

Detterman, D.K. (1986). Human intelligence is a complex system of separate processes. In R.J. Sternberg & D.K. Detterman (Eds), *What is intelligence? Contemporary viewpoints on its nature and definition* (pp. 57–61). Norwood, NJ: Ablex.

Detterman, D.K., Mayer, J.D., Caruso, D.R., Legree, P.J., Conners, F.A., & Taylor, R. (1992). Assessment of basic cognitive abilities in relation to cognitive deficits. *American Journal on Mental Retardation, 97,* 251–286.

Duckett, J.M. (1976). *Idiot-savants: Super specialisations in mentally retarded persons.* PhD thesis, University of Texas, Austin.

Eysenck, H.J. (1987). Speed of information processing, reaction time and the theory of intelligence. In P.A. Vernon (Ed.), *Speed of information processing and intelligence* (pp. 21–67). Norwood, NJ: Ablex.

Fitts, P.M. & Posner, M.J. (1967). *Human performance.* Belmont, CA: Brooks/ Cole.

Flynn, J.R. (1987). Massive IQ gains in 14 nations: What IQ tests really measure. *Psychological Bulletin, 101,* 171–191.

Fodor, J.A. (1983). *The modularity of mind.* Cambridge, MA: MIT Press.

Foerstl, J. (1989). Early interest in the idiot savant. *American Journal of Psychiatry, 146,* 566.

Gardner, H. (1983). *Frames of mind: The theory of multiple intelligences.* London: Heinemann.

Hermelin, B., & O'Connor, N. (1983). The idiot savant: Flawed genius or clever Hans? *Psychological Medicine, 13,* 479–481.

Hermelin, B., & O'Connor, N. (1986). Idiot-savant calendrical calculators: Rules and regularities. *Psychological Medicine, 16,* 885-893.

Hermelin, B., & O'Connor, N. (1990a). Art and accuracy: The drawing ability of idiot-savants. *Journal of Child Psychology and Psychiatry and Allied Disciplines, 31,* 217–228.

Hermelin, B., & O'Connor, N. (1990b). Factors and primes: A specific numerical ability. *Psychological Medicine, 20,* 163–169.

Hermelin, B., O'Connor, N., Lee, S. (1987). Musical inventiveness of five idiot-savants. *Psychological Medicine, 17,* 685–694.

Hermelin, B., O'Connor, N., Lee, S., & Treffert, D. (1989). Intelligence and musical improvisation. *Psychological Medicine, 19,* 447–457.

Herrnstein, R.J., & Murray, C. (1994). *The bell curve: Intelligence and class structure in American life.* New York: Free Press.

Hill, A.L. (1978). Savants: Mentally retarded individuals with special skills. In N.R. Ellis (Ed.), *International review of research in mental retardation* (Vol. 9, pp. 277–298). New York: Academic Press.

Hoffman, E. (1971). The idiot savant: A case report and a review of explanations. *Mental Retardation, 9,* 18–21.

Horn, J.L. (1968). Organisation of abilities and the development of intelligence. *Psychological Review, 75,* 242–259.

Horn, J.L. (1987). A context for understanding information processing studies of human abilities. In P.A. Vernon (Ed.), *Speed of information processing and intelligence* (pp. 201–238). Norwood, NJ: Ablex.

Horn, J.L. & Cattell, R.B. (1966). Refinement and test of the theory of fluid and crystallized intelligence. *Journal of Educational Psychology, 57,* 253–270.

Horwitz, W.A., Kestenbaum, C., Person, E., & Jarvik, L. (1965). Identical twin-"idiot savants"—calendar calculators. *American Journal of Psychiatry, 121,* 1075–1079.

Howe, M.J. & Smith, J. (1988). Calendar calculating in "idiot savants": How do they do it? *British Journal of Psychology, 79,* 371–386.

Howe, M.J.A. (1989). *Fragments of genius: The strange feats of idiot savants.* London: Routledge.

Howe, M.J.A. (1990). *The origins of exceptional abilities.* Oxford, UK: Blackwell.

Jensen, A. (1985). The nature of the black–white difference on various psychometric tests: Spearman's hypothesis. *The Behavioural and Brain Sciences, 8,* 193–263.

Judd, T. (1988). The varieties of musical talent. In L.K. Obler & D. Fein (Eds), *The exceptional brain: Neuropsychology of talent and special abilities* (pp. 127–155). New York: Guilford Press.

Kail, R. (1991). Developmental change in speed of processing during childhood and adolescence. *Psychological Bulletin, 109,* 490–501.

Kline, P. (1991). *Intelligence: The psychometric view.* London: Routledge.

Miller, L.K. (1989). *Musical savants: Exceptional skill in the mentally retarded.* Hillsdale, NJ: Lawrence Erlbaum Associates Inc.

Moffitt, T.E., Caspit, A., Harkness, A.R., & Silva, P.A. (1993). The natural history of change in intellectual performance: Who changes? How much? Is it meaningful? *Journal of Child Psychology and Psychiatry, 90,* 152–156.

Neisser, U., Boodoo, G., Bouchard, T.J., Jr., Boykin, A.W., Brody, N., Ceci, S.J., Halpern, D.F., Loehlin, J.C., Perloff, R., Sternberg, R.J., & Urbina, S. (1996). Intelligence: knowns and unknowns. *American Psychologist, 51,* 77–101.

Nettelbeck, T. (1990). Intelligence does exist: A rejoinder to M.J.A. Howe. *The Psychologist, 3,* 494–497.

Nettelbeck, T. & Vita, P. (1992). Inspection time in two childhood age cohorts: A constant or a developmental function? *British Journal of Developmental Psychology, 10,* 189–197.

Nettelbeck, T. & Young, R. (1996). Intelligence and savant syndrome: Is the whole greater than the sum of the fragments? *Intelligence, 22,* 49–68.

O'Connor, N. (1989). The performance of the "idiot-savant": Implicit and explicit. *British Journal of Disorders of Communication, 24,* 1–20.

O'Connor, N., & Hermelin, B. (1984). Idiot-savant calendrical calculators: Maths or memory? *Psychological Medicine, 14*, 801–806.

O'Connor, N., & Hermelin, B. (1987a). Visual and graphic abilities of the idiot savant artist. *Psychological Medicine, 17*, 79–90.

O'Connor, N., & Hermelin, B. (1987b). Visual memory and motor programmes: Their use by idiot-savant artists and controls. *British Journal of Psychology, 78*, 307–323.

O'Connor, N., & Hermelin, B. (1989). The memory structure of autistic idiot-savant mnemonists. *British Journal of Psychology, 80*, 97–111.

O'Connor, N., & Hermelin, B. (1990). The recognition failure and graphic success of idiot-savant artists. *Journal of Child Psychology and Psychiatry and Allied Disciplines, 31*, 203–215.

O'Connor, N., & Hermelin, B. (1991a). A specific linguistic ability. *American Journal on Mental Retardation, 95*, 673–680.

O'Connor, N., & Hermelin, B. (1991b). Talents and preoccupations in idiots-savants. *Psychological Medicine, 21*, 959–964.

Piaget, J. (1953). *The origin of intelligence in the child.* London: Routledge & Kegan Paul.

Rabbitt, P.M.A. (1981). Sequential reactions. In D.H. Holding (Ed.), *Human skills* (pp. 153–175). London: Wiley.

Rimland, B. (1978). Savant capabilities of autistic children and their cognitive implications. In G. Serban (Ed.), *Cognitive defects in the development of mental illness* (pp. 43–65). New York: Brunner/Mazel.

Rovee-Collier, C.K. (1990). The "memory system" of prelinguistic infants. *Annals of the New York Academy of Sciences, 608*, 517–542.

Sacks, O. (1985). The twins. *The New York Review of Books, 32*, 16–20.

Sacks, O. (1995). *An anthropologist on Mars.* Sydney, Australia: Picador.

Schweiger, A. (1988). A portrait of the artist as a brain-damaged patient. In L.K. Obler & D. Fein (Eds), *The exceptional brain: Neuropsychology of talent and special abilities* (pp. 303–309). New York: Guilford Press.

Selfe, L. (1977). *Nadia—A case of extraordinary drawing ability in an autistic child.* London: Academic Press.

Shiffrin, R.M., & Schneider, W. (1977). Controlled and automatic human information processing: II. Perceptual learning, automatic attending, and a general theory. *Psychological Review, 84*, 127–190.

Sloboda, J.A., Hermelin, B., & O'Connor, N. (1985). An exceptional musical memory. *Music Perception, 3*, 155–170.

Smith, N. & Tsimpli, I.M. (1995). *The mind of a savant: Language learning and modularity.* Oxford, UK: Blackwell.

Smith, S.B. (1988). Calculating prodigies. In L.K. Obler & D. Fein (Eds), *The exceptional brain: Neuropsychology of talent and special abilities* (pp. 19–47). New York: Guilford Press.

Spearman, C. (1904). "General intelligence", objectively determined and measured. *American Journal of Psychology, 15*, 201–293.

Spearman, C. (1923). *The nature of "intelligence" and the principles of cognition.* London: Macmillan.

Spearman, C. (1927). *The abilities of man: Their nature and measurement.* London: Macmillan.

Spitz, H.H. (1995). Calendar calculation idiot savants and the smart unconscious. *New Ideas in Psychology, 13*, 167–182.

Squire, L.R. (1986). Mechanisms of memory. *Science, 232*, 1612–1619.

Sternberg, R.J. (1981). The evolution of theories of intelligence. *Intelligence, 5,* 209–230.

Sternberg, R.J. (1988). *The triarchic mind: A new theory of human intelligence.* New York: Viking.

Takeuchi, A.H. & Hulse, S.H. (1993). Absolute pitch. *Psychological Bulletin, 13,* 345–361.

Treffert, D.A. (1989). *Extraordinary people.* London: Bantam Press.

Undheim, J.O. (1981). On intelligence: II. A neo-Spearman model to replace Cattell's theory of fluid and crystallized intelligence. *Scandinavian Journal of Psychology, 22,* 181–187.

Valentine, E. & Wilding, J. (1994). Memory expertise. *The Psychologist, 7,* 405–408. (Original work published 1987)

Vernon, P.A. (Ed.). (1987). *Speed of information processing and intelligence.* Norwood, NJ: Ablex.

Vernon, P.E. (1971). *The structure of human abilities.* London: Methuen.

Young, R. (1995). *Savant syndrome: Processes underlying extraordinary abilities.* PhD thesis, Department of Psychology, University of Adelaide, South Australia.

Young, R. & Nettelbeck, T. (1994). The "intelligence" of calendrical calculators. *American Journal on Mental Retardation, 99,* 186–200.

Young, R. & Nettelbeck, T. (1995). The abilities of a musical savant and his family. *Journal of Autism and Developmental Disorders, 25,* 229–245.

CHAPTER ELEVEN

Attempts to raise intelligence

Herman H. Spitz

Unaffiliated

There are some beliefs that appear so logically obvious they are tantamount to received wisdom, considered not just beliefs but proven facts. For many people one such self-evident fact is that with the proper environmental stimulation from birth an individual's intelligence—by which I mean the communal or "mainstream" concept of general intelligence (Spitz, 1986, p. 5)—can be raised substantially and many kinds of mental retardation prevented. Indeed, with proper training, goes the thinking, intervention at any time of life will produce very satisfactory results. The presupposition without which such thinking is impossible is that intelligence is extraordinarily plastic. The statement that intervention has not yet succeeded in raising intelligence is met with disbelief, or countered by citing "successful" studies (which, I will argue, are clearly flawed), or shrugged off as the application of inadequate procedures. New discoveries and modern methods can now be applied, goes the argument, and the received wisdom confirmed.

Allied with the apparently indisputable nature of the ability to raise intelligence is the human propensity to turn wish into fact. We wish it to be so and therefore we make it so. The idea that we cannot raise intelligence is simply unacceptable.

In order to illustrate these convictions and their remarkable staying power I will critically review an example from the 1960s of a "scientific" experiment that presumably demonstrated how classroom teachers can raise intelligence. We will then fastforward three decades to examine the claims that perpetuate the same underlying doctrine. I hope these examples will serve to alert readers to the fact that such assertions should never be accepted without first examining very carefully and critically the sources on which they are based.

SCHOOL TEACHERS AS PYGMALIONS

There is an ancient myth that Pygmalion, son of Cilix and grandson of Agenor, sculpted an ivory statue with which he fell in love, and lo! Aphrodite was so impressed that he gave the statue life, and she became Pygmalion's wife. George Bernard Shaw's play, *Pygmalion*, is a modern version, a tale of a professor of phonetics who wagered successfully that he could take a flower girl out of the gutter and in six months transform her dreadful diction into proper English, and then pass her off as a duchess at an ambassador's garden party.

Enter science. Following a paper they published in *Psychological Reports* in 1966, Robert Rosenthal and Lenore Jacobson published a book, *Pygmalion in the classroom: Teacher expectation and pupils' intellectual development*, and an article in *Scientific American* (Rosenthal & Jacobson, 1966, 1968a, 1968b), all based on a single experiment. In this modern reincarnation of the ancient myth, teachers took the role of Pygmalion and young pupils were their pliable clay—transformed, in this version, simply by their teachers' expectations. These dramatic results caught the media's fancy and the public soon heard about, believed, and endorsed them. Because the media does not get excited about critiques of dramatic studies, few members of the public ever learned how seriously flawed this study was (e.g. Elashoff & Snow, 1971; Snow, 1969; Thorndike, 1968). In fact, few professionals are familiar with the study's defects.

The study was carried out by a Harvard University social psychologist and a school principal.[1] The research plan was this: In the spring of 1964 the teachers in kindergarten (K) through fifth grade at a south San Francisco school (the "Oak School") serving what the authors described as a lower-class community, were asked to administer (in May, 1964) to their students a test called the Harvard Test of Inflected Acquisition. They were further informed that this test was "purported to be a predictor of academic 'blooming' or 'spurting'" (Rosenthal & Jacobson, 1968a, p. 66). This was untrue, however, because the test they were administering was actually a group intelligence test, the Tests of General Ability (TOGA), which provides a total score and verbal and reasoning sub-test scores and requires no reading or writing because teachers read aloud the question or

---

[1] It is ironic that the senior author had recently pointed out the effects of experimenter bias and expectancy on the results of psychological experiments, and subsequently produced important critiques of a number of studies, including those that claimed to demonstrate remarkable animal performance and animal–human communication.

command and pupils mark their response choices. This charade was intended to have its effect the following autumn, when the pupils had advanced to the next grade where each of 18 teachers from second through sixth grade was given a list of from one to nine children in his or her class and told that those on the list were the students who—based on the results of the Harvard Test—were likely to be "spurters" and therefore likely to show improvement in academic and intellectual performance. In actuality those pupils (the experimental group) were chosen randomly. The rest of the children served as controls. All children were tested again in January 1965, May 1965 (the crucial test for gains), and May 1966. The experiment was confined to only one semester, with additional testing designed to measure duration of effects. The tests were, unfortunately, administered by the teachers. They were scored twice independently by research assistants who did not know to which group the children belonged.

The primary results were experimental-control group comparisons on total and subtest "IQs", as they were called by the authors (I have rounded all scores). Results indicated that from pre-testing in May 1964 to post-testing in May 1965, for all grades combined, the experimental group (N = 65) gained an average of four more IQ points than did the control group (N = 255). However, these results were entirely due to large gains of 15 and 10 IQ points made by the first and second graders respectively (a total of 19 students). No statistically significant effect was found for the other three grades. When calculated separately, only two of the six first and second grades made statistically significant gains in total score, and one of these had only two pupils in the experimental group. When all first and second graders were tested a year later even that effect had disappeared, an example of the fade-out (after large initial gains) commonly found in studies aimed at raising intelligence. But were even the results of the first year valid?

In the first place, as Snow (1969) pointed out, the TOGA has inadequate norms in the age range of the youngest children in the study as well as for children from poor socioeconomic environments. The pretest Reasoning IQs of two of the six control K classes (one slow- and one medium-track class) were deep in the mentally retarded range, with mean IQs of 31 and 47, although these students were not now, nor were they ever suspected of being, mentally retarded. Something was wrong with the use of this test, its administration, or the way the IQs were derived, for even random responding should have produced higher scores.

There were also some unusually high scores. In his critical review of this study, Thorndike (1968) pointed out that, among other things, the six pupils listed as "spurters" in a second-grade class had a mean post-test Reasoning IQ of 150 and an SD of 41. Were they that brilliant? The authors of the study wrote, "The advantage of favourable expectations showed itself more clearly in reasoning IQ [than in verbal IQ]" (p. 77). And they considered it remarkable "that the younger children of even the control group should gain so heavily in reasoning IQ . . . [but] It may be that experiments are good for children even when the children are in the untreated control group" (p. 78). Teachers' expectancies must have powerful effects indeed if they can positively influence students who were not even on the list of potential "spurters".

According to Snow (1969), who requested and received the original data from the authors, "one S with a pre-test reasoning IQ of 17 had post-test IQs of 148, 110, and 112. Another showed reasoning IQs of 18, 44, 122 and 98. In the opposite direction, still another S had successive verbal IQs of 183, 166, 221, and 168, though TOGA does not have norms above 160. Many others are equally strange" (p. 198). Of course one can extrapolate beyond 160 and below 60, but "the manual implicitly discourages use of IQs lower than 60 or higher than 160, which should occur very rarely in any case" (Elashoff & Snow, 1971, p. 27). However, such extrapolations were not uncommon in the Pygmalian study.

After the final testing in June 1966 the true nature of the experiment was explained to the assembled teachers, after which they were interviewed individually. The authors found the teachers' reactions "startling", and with good reason. "While all teachers recalled glancing at their lists, most felt they paid little or no attention to them. Many teachers threw their lists away after glancing at them. Many of the teachers felt there were so many memos coming from the office that first week of school that the list of names was just another list and got no special attention" (Rosenthal & Jacobson, 1968a, p. 154). Of the 72 children originally in the experimental group, the teachers correctly recalled 18 experimental children, but incorrectly recalled 18 control children, as being on their list. There was no difference in the gain scores of those experimental children the teachers correctly recalled or recognised and those they did not. Elsewhere, they wrote that last year's teachers "could not recall accurately, nor even choose accurately from a larger list of names, the names of their own pupils designated as experimental-group children" (p. 69).

Considering all this, did the authors toss the experiment out and try again? Not at all. They simply commented that had they known that their list of names would be treated so casually they would have thought twice about obtaining positive results!

Since teachers paid no attention to the lists and could not even pick out their students from the previous semester who were expected to be "spurters", there could not possibly be any teacher expectancy effect. The only expectancy effect was the experimenters'. In a footnote the authors inform us that this experiment was repeated in two Midwestern schools that drew from a middle-class community. "No expectancy advantage was found . . . [and] now we know for sure that Oak School's results . . . are not universal" (p. 96).

Nevertheless, temporary IQ gains based on 19 experimental students in first and second grades, in a project where the independent variable never existed and where the dependent variable was a group test that was particularly unsuitable for the youngest ages and lowest ability levels, created a myth that grew like Topsy, never mind Pygmalion (despite the fact that it was virtually impossible to replicate the results, although many experimenters—in addition to Rosenthal and his colleagues—tried to do so). Rosenthal has continued to defend the study, often camouflaging the lack of confirming evidence of a Pygmalian effect on *intelligence* by intertwining it with supportive evidence for a Pygmalion effect on *other* attributes. Others joined the debate (e.g. Cronbach, 1975; Wineburg, 1987) and the controversy has continued through the years and shows no sign of ending (Rosenthal, 1995; Snow, 1995). In 1992 the publisher reissued *Pygmalion in the classroom*, unchanged (except to call it a College Edition) and with no response to the critics; indeed, with no indication that there is anything controversial about the study. The dust jacket includes this statement: "Though this study does not tell the parents and students anything *radically* new, it does offer carefully documented evidence of what is going wrong in American classrooms today."

What it does, actually, is tell us what is wrong with American psychology—then and now, because sadly, things have not improved, as we shall see in the next section.

THE MYTH IS PERPETUATED

For my example of current proselytisers of the belief that intelligence can be substantially elevated (it can always be *lowered* by raising children in closets) I could have drawn from an overflowing grab bag of papers and books, but chose rather to confine myself to a short section of a recent paper by an eminent intelligence researcher and theorist. The paper (Sternberg, 1995) was a feature review of *The bell curve* (Herrnstein & Murray, 1994) in a journal sent to all members of the American Psychological Society. This organisation is a growing and prestigious society of psychologists who, dissatisfied with the dominance of clinicians and other applied psychologists in the American Psychological Association, formed an association of psychologists for whom psychology is primarily a science. Consequently we expect that the association's publications, including their reviews, will be scholarly and rigorous.

Robert Sternberg did not think much of the book he was reviewing, and section by section of his review took it to task. In the section on "Modifiability of Intelligence" he expressed puzzlement at Herrnstein and

Murray's conclusion that intervention will not, in the foreseeable future, solve the problems of low intelligence, problems that he believes can be ameliorated by pedagogical and psychological intervention. To give some idea of his conception of the broad limits of modifiability, consider his honest concession that: "Clearly, we cannot now, or perhaps ever, take children who are mentally retarded and turn them into intellectual geniuses" (Sternberg, 1995, p. 259). But of course parents of retarded children would be very happy just to bring them up to average intelligence, and the reviewer was implying that this is a feasible objective. The reason we have not made greater strides, he wrote, is that "programs for teaching intellectual skills are relatively new" (p. 259), some a mere 15 years old. "Even Head Start programs date back only to the 1960s" (p. 259). He could have gone back two centuries, however, to a time when Jean-Marc-Gaspard Itard undertook to civilise the Wild Boy of Aveyron; or to the 1860s when Edouard Séguin developed a detailed teaching programme that was said to educate, improve, and even cure mental retardation; or to 1912 when Maria Montessori described her own teaching methods, originally designed to raise the level of mentally retarded children and still in practice today; or to the many other venerable programmes that failed to achieve what they originally had promised (Spitz, 1986).

The reviewer cited five recent studies that he believes refute Herrnstein and Murray's dismal forecast that intervention will not in the foreseeable future solve the problem of low intelligence. Having done that, and confident that he had made his case, he concluded that there are in fact programmes that have "demonstrated solid and replicable gains" (p. 259). We will now look at the programmes he cited to see whether they support his claims.

The Abecedarian Project

As befits its name (abecedarian pertains to the alphabet and an abecedarian is one who is learning the alphabet or teaches it and other elementary skills), this Project was the first entry in an *Encyclopedia of intelligence* edited by our reviewer, where articles were sequenced not by subject matter but alphabetically. Citing the *Encyclopedia* article (Ramey, 1994), our reviewer asserted that Craig T. Ramey's studies "have repeatedly shown significant and even impressive gains in the order of 8 to 20 points in IQ (after controlling for the effects of maternal mental retardation and home environment)" (Sternberg, 1995, p. 259).

More than a decade ago questions were raised about the Abecedarian Project (Spitz, 1986), and subsequently there was a spirited exchange concerning it, relevant references to which can be found in the final paper of that exchange (Spitz, 1993a). Despite this, the reviewer did not think it necessary to warn readers that not everyone was convinced of the Project's soundness.

To briefly recapitulate the history of the Project, its rationale was that "cultural-familial" mental retardation was causally related to poverty. As the Project director and his colleagues saw it, this type of mental retardation was a "sociocultural" disorder, meaning that most children who were mentally retarded and from poor environments were not born retarded. Rather, their intelligence gradually descended into the mentally retarded range because of the inadequate and confused inputs they experienced as they matured. Their first step, therefore, was to develop a 13-item High Risk Index based on estimates of parent characteristics— such as education level, family income, husband's work record, maternal IQ, and so on—that the Project's leaders believed put a child at risk for mental retardation. The Index was administered to pregnant women at a prenatal clinic. Those whose scores indicated (theoretically) that their children would be at risk, and who agreed to participate, were pair-matched on certain variables and the newborn infant of each pair was then randomly assigned to either an intervention or control group. Starting at an average age of 4.4 months (Campbell & Ramey, 1994) and ending when they entered kindergarten, on every weekday the intervention group was transported to the Project's day care centre where they were given the kinds of experience the Project directors believed were needed to prevent them from becoming mentally retarded.

Because not enough subjects could be obtained in one year, new groups (cohorts) were recruited in consecutive years. Consequently not only was the final total sufficiently large, but also each subsequent year supplied a replication group for any effects found in previous years. Mental ability tests were administered every 3 months through the first 18 months, and thereafter at 6-month intervals. Unfortunately, not all testing was done without the tester knowing to which group a child belonged. "For children up to 60 months, tests were administered with the mother present. Half the children at 36 months were tested by an examiner who was 'blind' to the child's assignment. Practical considerations made it impossible to achieve this for all occasions" (Ramey & Campbell, 1987, p. 134).

There are many misconceptions about the Abecedarian Project. In the first place, pairing the Project with the word "gains" is, at the very least, imprecise, suggesting as it does the raising of intelligence. The Project was never intended to raise intelligence. The intervention group's highest average score on any test was 111 and their lowest was 95, but most of their scores did not deviate greatly from 100 (an average score on intelligence tests). At six months of age their score was 107, and their score at five years of age, shortly after intervention had ended, was 101 (I have rounded all scores). In other words, shortly after day care ended the mean score of the intervention group was actually six points lower than it had been shortly after day care had begun, despite attending the special day care centre eight hours a day, five days a week, fifty weeks a year, for more than four years.

The fuss being made in the media and elsewhere about the Project's intelligence test results concerns the finding that at five years of age the intervention group had a mean score that was seven points higher than the score of the control group (101 compared with 94), and this significant difference was maintained in subsequent years. But neither the media nor our reviewer ever mention that the difference between the intervention and control groups at five years of age was about the same as it had been at six months of age. Nor do they cite the Project director's statement that the difference at six months of age could not have been a function of the intervention: "We found that developmental functions were alterable only after 12 months" (Ramey, Yeates, & Short, 1984, p. 1922).

An abridged summary of the comparative test results shows that at three months of age the intervention (experimental) and control groups did not differ, both having scores of about 95 according to the Project reports. At six months of age the intervention group, which by that time had attended the special day care centre for an average of only 1.6 months, had a mean score of 107 on the Bayley Scales of Infant Development, whereas the control group had a score of 101. By 18 months the differences increased to 18 points on the same test (108 vs. 90). At 36 months the differences were still sizeable (101 vs. 84 on the Stanford-Binet), but by 54 months, the endpoint for the preschool intervention, the differences had started to decrease (101 vs. 91 on the McCarthy Scales of Children's Ability). At 60 months the difference was down to 7 points (101 vs. 94 on the Wechsler Preschool and Primary Scale of Intelligence). At 12 years of age (Campbell & Ramey, 1994) it was down to 5 points (94 vs. 89 on the Wechsler Intelligence Scale for Children—Revised).[2]

During the course of the Project the control group's mean score dropped as low as 84 (at three years of age), but thereafter began to climb, an outcome the Project directors had not expected. Nor was it a propitious outcome as far as the Project was concerned, because the Project's purpose was to prevent mental retardation and they could not prove they had prevented mental retardation unless the control group dropped into the mentally retarded range. The failure of the mean score of the control group to drop to the mentally retarded level renders problematic any

---

[2] Scores given here are for all subjects regardless of whether they later dropped out. Using only scores of those subjects who remained up to 54 months, Martin et al. (1990) reported an even larger difference at six months: 110 vs. 101.

strong claim that the Abecedarian Project prevented mental retardation. It also indicates that the High Risk Index was an invalid measure for predicting mental retardation.

When they entered public school the groups were further partitioned for additional experiments but these had no further differential effect on intelligence test scores and need not concern us here. We can note, however, that at 12 years of age the intervention group had dropped further, to a mean IQ of 94, a 13-point drop from their score at six months of age. The control group's mean at 12 years was 89, a 12-point drop. (Of course comparisons between different tests are never precise, especially when going from infant scales to later intelligence tests. In fact infant scales are poor predictors of an individual's subsequent performance, but I am simply using the procedures followed by the Project, where the concern was the average scores of groups.)

In sum, virtually all the durable effects—that is, the differences remaining at 5 and at 12 years of age—had been achieved by 6 months of age. What happened during those first 1.6 months at the day care centre to produce an effect worth 6 points, whereas an additional 4½ years of massive intervention ended with virtually no additional effect? It seems to me that it is not unreasonable to infer that nothing happened, but rather that some initial difference in the control and intervention groups had (by chance) escaped randomisation, and revealed itself at six months of age.

Another interesting aspect of this study was that the successive cohorts did not replicate each other. In fact there were very large differences between cohorts early in the study. For example, at 12 months of age the second and third intervention cohorts had a mean score of 116, much higher than their control group (104) or any other intervention or control cohort. Not surprisingly the Project publications no longer discussed cohort replication.

There was one serendipitous finding that appears to be quite important. At 54 months a subset of six intervention children whose mothers were mentally retarded had a mean IQ of 95, 22 points higher than the mean of 73 for a subset of six control children who had mentally retarded mothers, even though the two subgroups had not differed at 6 months (Martin, Ramey & Ramey, 1990). Three of the control children were within the mentally retarded range, and another three were in the borderline range. This is too small a sample to make much of without replication, but it warrants further study. Obviously it contributed in a major way to the results of the entire group, and it lends support to the hypothesis of the Milwaukee Project (Garber, Hodge, Rynders, Dever, & Velu, 1991) that sociocultural mental retardation results from being raised by an intellectually limited caregiver. Although the Abecedarian project was inspired by the highly criticised Miwaukee Project, the Abecedarian

Project's position was that sociocultural mental retardation results not from having mothers who are mentally retarded, but rather from being raised in a poor socioeconomic environment (in poverty).

Ramey's (1994) *Encyclopedia* article, cited by Robert Sternberg in his review, made no mention of the typical fade-out of large differences that occurred during the course of the study, and the reviewer repeated Ramey's assertion that the Abecedarian Project had obtained permanent effects in the order of 8 to 20 IQ points when controlling for the effects of maternal mental retardation and home environment. Readers of Sternberg's (1995) review were not told at what age the 8-point and at what age the 20-point advantage for the intervention group occurred (they were at 6 months and 18 months, respectively), nor that the intervention group's advantage at the time of their completion of the special day care centre was only 1 point higher at 4½ years than it had been at 6 months. In his *Encyclopedia of intelligence* article, Ramey (1994) reported that results "indicated that the intensive preschool early intervention significantly prevented intellectual declines into mental subnormality" (p. 2). But this statement referred only to the small group of children who had mentally retarded mothers, not to the group as a whole, a fact that could easily be misunderstood by his readers. Once again we find endorsement for the truism that if you want to know the full story you must expend time and effort in the library reading all the relevant papers. Sometimes it is necessary to obtain the original data, as Snow (1969) did with the Pygmalion study (see also Baumeister & Bacharach, 1996).

Improving performance on the Scholastic Assessment Test (SAT)

According to our reviewer, "Messick and Jungeblut have also shown that substantial gains can be attained on the Scholastic Assessment Test (SAT)" (Sternberg, 1995, p. 259), a test administered to college-bound high school students and used by many colleges and universities as part of their entrance selection process. Messick and Jungeblut (1981) conducted an exhaustive survey of studies aimed at improving SAT scores by coaching. Being honest researchers they would surely have followed wherever the data took them, though just as surely—being affiliated with the Educational Testing Service which develops and administers the SATs—they would not have been pleased had they found that coaching had a very striking effect on SAT scores. They need not have been concerned. After reviewing the available literature, they concluded that there are diminishing returns in coaching effects, especially on the verbal section, because "student contact time required to achieve average score increases much greater than 20 to 30 points [on a 600-point scale range of 200 to 800 points] for both SAT-V and SAT-M rapidly approaches full-time schooling" (Messick & Jungeblut, 1981, p. 191), and consequently "the soundest long-range mode of preparation for the SAT would appear to be a secondary school program that integrates the development of thought with the development of knowledge" (pp. 215–216). In other words, private coaching is equivalent to a good high school program.

We know that all measures of mental ability tap general intelligence to varying degrees and the evidence is good that the SAT is a very good intelligence test, though not presented as such. As a peripheral aspect of a study on auditory masking the SAT was correlated with the Cattell Culture Fair Intelligence Test and, for a sample of 32 students, the correlation turned out to be a surprisingly high 0.81 (Raz, Willerman, Ingmundson, & Hanlon, 1983). The standard deviations (SDs) for the math and verbal sections of the SAT differ somewhat at different times, but when Messick and Jungeblut wrote their review a midpoint average SD of the two scales was about 115. The average gain of 25 points mentioned by Messick and Jungeblut is 22% of 1 SD, equivalent to about 3 IQ points on an intelligence test that has an SD of 15 (as in the Wechsler Scales). Putting in even more time would increase the gain, but at diminishing levels. Of course we have no way of knowing the permanence of this modest improvement.

Students of intervention research speak frequently of "teaching to the test", which means training the intervention group on the types of items they will be tested on, thereby raising test scores without changing general intelligence. As noted later, most critics believe the extraordinary early results of intervention studies that time and again raise undue expectations about each new project is the result, in large part, of teaching to the test. It is unlikely that in most intervention projects teaching to the test is consciously intended, but coaching college students for the SAT—which our reviewer cited as an instance of modifying intelligence—is an unalloyed example of this phenomenon. It is in any case unlikely that the gainers were recognised by their friends as being more intelligent after they took the course than before they enrolled.

Teaching thinking skills

The late Richard Herrnstein—senior author of *The bell curve*, the book our reviewer so soundly condemned—is also, paradoxically, senior author of one of the studies cited by our reviewer as successfully illustrating the modifiability of intelligence. But there it is, nevertheless, a study by Herrnstein, Nickerson, de Sánchez, and Swets (1986) that Sternberg (1995) cited as "another successful study published in a refereed journal" (p. 259).

What Herrnstein and his colleagues set out to do was teach cognitive skills to Venezuelan seventh graders as part of a project initiated by Luis

Alberto Machado, who in 1979 was appointed to the newly created position of Minister (without portfolio) of State for the Development of Intelligence. Machado (1981) believes that the human brain is essentially unchanged since the beginning of mankind's history. Differences between modern humans and their ancestors are related to education and the transmittal of knowledge, and consequently the major factor causing differences in intelligence is in its acquisition. In other words, intelligence must be acquired by learning; people have to be taught to think. So Machado set out to increase the intelligence of all the citizens of Venezuela by teaching them how to develop their intelligence, every day, from kindergarten to college, and to teach parents how to teach their children from the moment they are born. "We are going to transform our people and in so doing, we are going to transform our society" (Machado, 1981, p. 4). The programme was massive, "operating through maternity hospitals, the mass media, schools and universities, the armed forces, and civil service" (Walsh, 1981, p. 640).

Machado enlisted the assistance of psychologists throughout the world, including Reuven Feuerstein of Israel; Edward De Bono, director of the Centre for Study of Thinking Skills in Cambridge, UK; some faculty members at Harvard University; and staff members of the Cambridge, Massachusetts consulting firm of Bolt Beranek and Newman (Spitz, 1986, pp. 193–194). Professor B.F. Skinner, whose work greatly influenced Machado, declared that this programme "will no doubt take its place as one of the great social experiments of this century" (cited by Walsh, 1981, p. 641).

Participating in the Herrnstein et al. study were 463 experimental and 432 control students from families of low socioeconomic status. The students were seventh graders in six schools who averaged 13 years of age. As part of their normal school curriculum, on four days a week (in general) the experimental group took a year-long course that the team had developed "to teach cognitive skills that apply to learning and intellectual performance independently of subject matter, stressing observation and classification, reasoning, critical use of language, problem solving, inventiveness, and decision making" (Herrnstein et al., 1986, p. 1279).

Evaluation was extensive. It included adaptations of three standardised multiple-choice intelligence tests plus "Target Abilities Tests", which were tests designed specifically for this study "along the lines of the course itself, drawing on the skills and processes, but not the content, employed in the lessons" (p. 1282). On all three standardised tests the experimental group gained significantly more than did the control group, though on one of them (the Cattell Culture Fair Intelligence Test) the differential gain was only marginally significant. As might be expected, the experimental group gained much more than did the controls on the specifically designed Target Abilities Test.

For the standardised (though somewhat altered) intelligence tests, results can be transposed via standard deviations to show net gains in IQ of the experimental group relative to controls. They ranged from 1.6 to 6.5 IQ points (Herrnstein & Murray, 1994, p. 400), a result that is at least promising. But they were not promising enough to Herrnstein to dissuade him from joining Charles Murray in writing *The bell curve* where they commented, when discussing this study, that "there was no chance to see if the gain faded out or was reflected in the rest of the students' academic performance, nor can we even guess how much a second or third year of lessons would have accomplished" (Herrnstein & Murray, 1994, p. 400).

One might hazard a guess that Herrnstein became disenchanted with his previous belief in the power of teaching to raise general intelligence. Citing the same two studies as were later cited favourably by Sternberg (1995) in his review of *The bell curve*, Herrnstein and Murray came to a decidedly different opinion than did Sternberg. They concluded that variations in schools, attempts at compensatory education, "and the results of the Venezuelan and SAT coaching efforts all point to the same conclusion: As of now, the goal of raising intelligence among school-age children more than modestly, and doing so consistently and affordably [and, I might add, permanently], remains out of reach" (Herrnstein & Murray, 1994, p. 402).

To close the circle, when a new president was elected in 1984, Luis Alberto Machado lost his position and was replaced by a commissioner who, although she modified his programme, intended to continue the classroom teaching of thinking skills. There is as yet no evidence that the programme has had any effect on the intellectual level of the people of Venezuela.[3]

Teaching students practical intelligence for school

The final purported evidence that intelligence can be successfully and permanently increased is provided by a project in which the reviewer himself was involved (Gardner, Krechevsky, Sternberg, & Okagaki, 1994; Sternberg, Okagaki, & Jackson, 1990). The basic premise of this project was that some students never learn what is expected of them, that is, they do not understand their teachers' "implicit" expectations. If they can learn this unspoken, tacit knowledge—"how to allocate their time in doing homework, how to prepare course papers, how to study for tests, how to talk (and not to talk) to a teacher" (Sternberg et al., 1990, p. 35)—their

---

[3] In 1981, at the time of these studies, I wrote to Raymond Nickerson at Bolt Beranek and Newman, consultants to Machado's project, about a book he and his colleagues were writing on the teaching of thinking skills (Nickerson, Perkins, & Smith, 1985). He replied: "Although some investigators have used intelligence tests for various purposes in their programs, I would not characterize these efforts, as a whole, as efforts to raise intelligence" (R.S. Nickerson, personal communication, 16th November 1981).

chances of success in school will be increased immeasurably. The Yale Practical Intelligence for School (PIFS) curriculum, jointly developed by Yale researchers led by Robert Sternberg and Harvard researchers led by Howard Gardner, was designed to enhance this ability. A theoretical basis for the project was created by joining Sternberg's triarchic theory of intelligence with Gardner's theory of multiple intelligences, a marriage created, in my opinion, more by necessity than by any natural affinity—a marriage of convenience, as it were, although ingenious rationales are given to show how each theory complements the other.[4]

In Phase I of the Practical Intelligence for Schools Project, "affectionately abbreviated PIFS" (Gardner et al., 1994, p. 112), a set of curricula was designed to help students who were deficient in practical school intelligence. It is not easy to describe the curricula from the information given, but it does look to me like the kind of approach given in many self-help and self-improvement books. For example, the following are excerpted from the 44 headings of a course outline for *Managing Tasks*: "Is there a problem? What strategies are you using? A process to help you solve the problem. Planning a way to prevent problems. Breaking habits" (Gardner et al., 1994, p. 114). Similar aids are given for *Managing Yourself* and *Cooperating with Others*, which add up to three kinds of tacit knowledge that the authors believe are essential for students. There is also an *Introduction to Teachers*. Students were from a middle school in a middle income suburb and "the program was administered three days per week over a semester" (Gardner et al., 1994, p. 117).

Evaluation of the results was not made by either examination of school grades or by scores on typical measures of intelligence. There was instead a standardised measure of study habits and attitudes, a standardised inventory of learning and study skills, and scores on the Practical Intelligence Section of the Sternberg Triarchic Abilities Test (unreferenced and presumably unpublished at that time). The experimental group made significant gains relative to the control group on the major tests and on almost all the sub-tests, although on one of the sub-tests—Practical data (quantitative) of the Practical Intelligence section of the Sternberg Triarchic Abilities Test—it was the *control* group that gained significantly more than did the experimental group.

When the programme was tried at a different site (for which no information on socioeconomic status is provided) where it was given once

---

[4] If Gardner's concept of multiple intelligences becomes the predominant concept in intelligence research, efforts would have to be directed at modifying each of the intelligences separately. Using the word intelligence for talents such as running and jumping, or playing an instrument, or painting, or intrapersonal facility dilutes the word irreparably and in my view would be a huge step backward. At this writing the predominant view is that general intelligence and specific talents and abilities coexist.

a week for a year, there was "no pattern of significant gains on the pre- and post-test measures. Hence we do not provide the statistics for this part of the study" (Gardner et al., 1994, p. 118).

This curriculum was labelled the "stand-alone curriculum" because it was taught separately, unintegrated with the classroom material. There was also an aspect of the study in which the PIFS was included in—infused or "slotted into"—the regular school curriculum. To assess this approach the project "developed and piloted evaluation measures for each of the infused measures" and added "classroom observations, teacher observations [and] interviews with teachers and students" (Gardner et al., 1994, pp. 119–120). Needless to say the reader is given no information on the reliability or validity of any of the assessment measures that were "developed and piloted" in this study. In any case, results indicated that the experimental group had reliable gains on most of the assessment measures. Gains were very specific, however; no differences between experimental and control groups emerged when there was an attempt to cut across subject matter. The writers are now embarked on a second, even more ambitious phase of the PIFS programme.

This study from the Yale–Harvard collaboration is, like the SAT coaching studies, a nice example of teaching to the test. But did the gains generalise to improved student grades? We do not know, although that is promised for the upcoming "second phase". Did the gains last? There was no follow-up. Did they generalise to gains on typical intelligence tests? That is irrelevant as far as the authors are concerned, because they are modifying only "practical intelligence". When the authors of *The bell curve* claimed that it is not yet possible to raise intelligence, the indignant reviewer included this study in his catalogue of contrary evidence. Is this study an example of success in raising intelligence? The reader will have to decide.

NAVIGATING THE SHOALS OF EARLY INTERVENTION STUDIES

A puzzle frequently remarked upon is how, after a relatively short period of intervention, an experimental (intervention) group can score an astonishing 20 or 30 points higher on intelligence tests than their controls, only to return to the level of the controls just a few years later—the well-known fade-out effect. (Fade-out often results not simply because the experimental group drops back to the control group but because the control group rises to meet the declining experimental group.) The important thing to remember is that modifying performance on a test is not the same as modifying intelligence. What has been temporarily modified in the early stages of early intervention programmes is performance on a test, not the child's general intelligence. A good intelligence test usually reflects quite adequately what most professionals think of as general intelligence, as derived from a comparison of a child's ability relative to other children the same age. Children in an intervention group can outperform a control group if given extensive instruction and practice on the kinds of items that appear on the test. The younger the children the easier this is, because there are limited kinds of skills that can be tested. When the children mature to new levels of ability and are given tests commensurate with those new levels, previous training on the skills of an earlier stage of development is no longer effective.[5] Furthermore, the new levels require more complex mental skills that for some people are unteachable. Consequently, when the groups are tested at more mature ages a more representative cross section of general intelligence level is once again being sampled.

There are other factors to be aware of, including a temporary increase of about 10 IQ points merely as a result of retesting (Spitz, 1986, pp. 207–208; Zigler, Abelson, Trickett, & Seitz, 1982), but this should affect the control group in equal measure unless somehow the testers become aware of which group they are testing.

In its relatively short history, psychology has often succumbed to wishful thinking. This is especially true of American psychology, which harboured and nurtured the long reign of behaviourism. Although behaviourism is no longer in the ascendancy its legacy lingers on and accounts, to some extent at least, for the persistence of claims that intelligence can be manipulated by pedagogical and psychological techniques. But when, despite everything, the failure to raise intelligence cannot be denied, new approaches are implemented. The IQ test is declared biased or otherwise inadequate, the meaning of intelligence is changed, and many different intelligences are proposed so that everyone can be intelligent in at least something.

The best evidence that intelligence and not just a test score has been raised is real-life performance. School grades should improve significantly, and improved performance should persist and be reflected in the quality of the individual's occupation and the efficiency of performance. Anecdotal accounts of an individual's remarkable increase in intelligence are not enough because the bell-shaped curve not only describes the distribution of intelligence at a single age, it also describes typical changes in intellectual level for the members of any large population: After childhood most people change very little intellectually, some people change somewhat more (either up or down) and a very few increase or decrease dramatically (Spitz, 1986). To be scientifically acceptable, a group of people must be given a prescribed regimen and then followed for decades.

Based on the results over the past two centuries, no one should expect dramatic success very soon, if ever. We do not have a deep understanding

---

[5] Unless of course all students are college students being coached on the SAT, which is not the typical target population for intervention research.

of the nature of intelligence. Most thinking and problem solving occurs outside of awareness (Spitz, 1993b, 1995). What we see is the end result, after which we try to reconstruct the process, often incorrectly. The unconscious processes that are critical for thinking and for solving novel problems cannot be taught; they are, in fact, not yet understood. Until we increase our understanding of the intellectual process and until we utilise this understanding wisely, it is wrong to so casually make what really are extraordinary claims. The ability to increase general intelligence substantially, consistently, and permanently would be an enormous achievement, surely meriting a Nobel award.

How much better will the outcomes of current programmes be when it is an unfortunate fact that, unlike other scientists, psychologists do not progressively build on previous findings and theories? In psychology there are no generally accepted grand theories to anchor progress. Newly minted psychologists simply propose new ideas and perform new experiments, isolated from any long-held theoretical structure. "Unlike mathematics, physics, or biology, it [psychology] is not a cumulative science" (Allport, 1955). Consequently I see no reason to believe that current interventions, unrelated to any progressive development and divorced from any generally accepted grand theory, will be any more effective than previous ones. But whatever progress is made in modifying intelligence can only be made by adhering rigorously to a scientific approach and by advancing in small, incremental steps, with each step building on previous findings. We should constantly remind ourselves that science advances best where there is solid knowledge; it can only be impeded by self-deception based on wishful thinking.

REFERENCES

Allport, G.W. (1955). *Becoming: Basic considerations for a psychology of personality*. New Haven, CT: Yale University Press.

Baumeister, A.A. & Bacharach, V. (1996). A critical analysis of the infant health and development program. *Intelligence*, *23*, 79–104.

Campbell, F.A. & Ramey, C.T. (1994). Effects of early intervention on intellectual and academic achievement: A follow-up study of children from low-income families. *Child Development*, *65*, 684–698.

Cronbach, L.J. (1975). Five decades of public controversy over mental testing. *American Psychologist*, *30*, 1–14.

Elashoff, J.D., & Snow, R.E. (1971). *Pygmalion reconsidered: A case study in statistical inference: Reconsideration of the Rosenthal-Jacobson data on teacher expectancy*. Worthington, OH: Charles A. Jones.

Garber, H.L., Hodge, J.D., Rynders, J., Dever, R., & Velu, R. (1991). The Milwaukee Project: Setting the record straight. *American Journal on Mental Retardation*, *95*, 493–525.

Gardner, H., Krechevsky, M., Sternberg, R.L., & Okagaki, L. (1994). Intelligence in context: Enhancing students' practical intelligence for school. In K. McGilly (Ed.), *Classroom lessons: Integrating cognitive theory and classroom practice* (pp. 105–127). Cambridge, MA: Bradford Books.

Herrnstein, R.J., & Murray, C. (1994). *The bell curve*. New York: Free Press.

Herrnstein, R.J., Nickerson, R.S., de Sánchez, M., & Swets, J.A. (1986). Teaching thinking skills. *American Psychologist, 41*, 1279–1289.

Machado, L.A. (1981). The development of intelligence—a political outlook. *Intelligence, 5*, 2–4.

Martin, S.L., Ramey, C.T., & Ramey, S. (1990). The prevention of intellectual impairment in children of impoverished families: Findings from a randomized trial of educational day care. *American Journal of Public Health, 80*, 844–847.

Messick S., & Jungeblut, A. (1981). Time and method in coaching for the SAT. *Psychological Bulletin, 89*, 191–216.

Nickerson, R.S., Perkins, D.N., & Smith, E.E. (1985). *The teaching of thinking*. Hillsdale, NJ: Lawrence Erlbaum Associates Inc.

Ramey, C.T. (1994). Abecedarian Project. In R.J. Sternberg (Ed.), *Encyclopedia of human intelligence,* Vol. 1 (pp. 1–3). New York: Macmillan.

Ramey, C.T., & Campbell, F.A. (1987). The Carolina Abecedarian Project: An educational experiment concerning human malleability. In J.G. Gallagher & C.T. Ramey (Eds), *The malleability of children* (pp. 127–139). Baltimore, MD: Paul H. Brookes.

Ramey, C.T., Yeates, K.O., & Short, E.J. (1984). The plasticity of intellectual development: Insights from preventive intervention. *Child Development, 55*, 1913–1925.

Raz, N., Willerman, L., Ingmundson, P., & Hanlon, M. (1983). Aptitude-related differences in auditory recognition masking. *Intelligence, 7*, 71–90.

Rosenthal, R. (1995). Critiquing *Pygmalion*: A 25-year perspective. *Current Directions in Psychological Science, 4*, 171–172.

Rosenthal, R., & Jacobson, L. (1966). Teacher's expectancies: Determinants of pupils' IQ gains. *Psychological Reports, 19*, 115–118.

Rosenthal, R., & Jacobson, L. (1968a). *Pygmalion in the classroom: Teacher expectation and pupils' intellectual development*. New York: Holt, Rinehart & Winston. (Reissued as College Edition in 1992)

Rosenthal, R., & Jacobson, L.F. (1968b). Teacher expectations for the disadvantaged. *Scientific American, 218*, 19–23.

Snow, R.E. (1969). Unfinished Pygmalion. *Contemporary Psychology, 14*, 197–199.

Snow, R.E. (1995). Pygmalion and intelligence? *Current Directions in Psychological Science, 4*, 169–171.

Spitz, H.H. (1986). *The raising of intelligence: A selected history of attempts to raise retarded intelligence*. Hillsdale, NJ: Lawrence Erlbaum Associates Inc.

Spitz, H.H. (1993a). Spitz's reply to Ramey's response to Spitz's first reply to Ramey's first response to Spitz's critique of the Abecedarian Project. *Intelligence, 17*, 31–35.

Spitz, H.H. (1993b). The role of the unconscious in thinking and problem solving. *Educational Psychology, 13*, 229–244.

Spitz, H.H. (1995). Calendar calculating *idiots savants* and the smart unconscious. *New Ideas in Psychology, 13*, 167–182.

Sternberg, R.J. (1995). For whom the bell curve tolls. *Psychological Science, 6*, 257–262.

Sternberg, R.J., Okagaki, L., & Jackson, A. (1990). Practical intelligence for success in school. *Educational Leadership*, *48*, 35–39.

Thorndike, R.L. (1968). [Untitled review]. *American Educational Research Journal*, *5*, 708–711.

Walsh, J. (1981). A plenipotentiary for human intelligence. *Science*, *214*, 640–641.

Wineburg, S.S. (1987). The self-fulfillment of the self-fulfilling prophecy. *Educational Researcher*, *16*, 28–37.

Zigler, E., Abelson, W.D., Trickett, P.K., & Seitz, V. (1982). Is an intervention program necessary in order to improve economically disadvantaged children's IQ scores? *Child Development*, *53*, 340–348.

CHAPTER TWELVE

Intellectual development and mental retardation—some continuing controversies

Robert M. Hodapp

UCLA, Los Angeles, USA

Edward Zigler

Yale University, New Haven, CT, USA

INTRODUCTION

Throughout the 20th century, mental retardation and intellectual development have experienced an intertwined history. In 1906, shortly after their development, the new Binet-Simon intelligence tests were brought to America and tried out on residents of the Training School in Vineland, New Jersey. Reporting on the several-year longitudinal study, Henry Goddard (1913a) noted that "the vast majority" of children with mental retardation were not improving in their intellectual levels. Another leader of American mental retardation research, Walter Fernald (1913), considered Goddard's findings "the most significant . . . and the most discouraging that we have ever known" (p. 127).

In addition to IQ tests informing us about mental retardation, persons with mental retardation have historically been used to understand intellectual development. Even in the early years of this century, Goddard's (1913b) study of the Kallikaks and Dugdale's (1910) of the Jukes supposedly demonstrated the effects of genetics on intelligence. Later, Spitz's (1945) studies of orphans adopted at birth supposedly showed the effects of the environment. Even given their weaknesses, these studies demonstrate how persons with below-average intellectual abilities have historically been used as "experiments of nature" in debates over intellectual development. Even today workers examine persons with mental retardation to shed light on intellectual development.

But before considering the modern interplay of mental retardation and intelligence, it seems necessary to briefly overview three debates. These debates are ongoing, and to this day one can find many researchers who support varying sides of each position.

THREE ONGOING DEBATES

Debate #1: Is mental retardation a single entity or are there several different types?

Most modern researchers consider mental retardation a single entity. Granted, these workers feel that persons with mental retardation differ one from another, and that it is sometimes useful to examine persons of different levels of intellectual impairment. In behavioural studies, subjects are routinely divided into those with mild (IQ 55–69), moderate (IQ 40–54), severe (IQ 25–39), and profound (IQ below 25) mental retardation. Researchers have also compared children of different ages, or different types of maladaptive behaviour (e.g. self-injurious behaviours), or other behavioural characteristics. In the main, however, most behavioural workers believe that mental retardation is a single "thing" to be examined.

A second view holds that there are several types of mental retardation. Formally begun by Edward Zigler (1967, 1969) in the late 1960s, this view dates its precursors to the beginning of this century (Burack, 1990) and its recent extension to examinations of the many different types of mental retardation (Dykens, 1995; Hodapp & Dykens, 1994). Although examined more later, the ongoing question is simple: From the standpoint of intellectual development and functioning, are there one or many types of mental retardation?

Debate #2: Is intellectual development in mental retardation "deficited" or "delayed"?

Historically, most mental retardation researchers have felt that all mental retardation is caused by a single defect or deficit. Over the years, a variety of such defects have been proposed. Some involve attentional processes, others inefficient stimulus traces, still others defects in the linguistic mediation of experience. Regardless of the defect chosen, however, each defect theorist argues that development in children with mental retardation differs qualitatively compared to the developmental processes of non-retarded children.

In opposition, other theorists contend that development occurs much as it does in non-retarded children, only more slowly. Children progress through identical stages (e.g. Piagetian stages) and have a similar structure to their intelligence. In addition, by the end of the childhood years, children with mental retardation stop their development at lower levels. The main point, though, is that mental retardation involves a generalised slowing of development, across multiple domains.

For now, we note only that this debate pits a more "specific" (defects) versus a more "global" (overall development) view of how children with mental retardation develop. Are all intellectual processes impaired, or are intellectual impairments mainly due to a single (or small number of) circumscribed defects? Such concerns with specific versus global problems lead us to our third debate.

Debate #3: Is intellectual development "all of a piece" or composed of many, separable components?

In order to examine intellectual development in children with mental retardation, it is necessary to understand the meaning of intelligence itself. But, as many contributors to this book note, the field of intellectual development is beset with the problem of whether intelligence is a single, coherent entity, a jumble of disconnected "little intelligences," or something in between. This issue surfaces in several ways. In examinations of adult IQ test performance, various workers have identified a "g", or general factor in intellectual functioning (Humphries, 1979). Thus, most people who perform fairly well in one area of intelligence (say, visuo-spatial skills) are often fairly proficient at others as well (e.g. verbal skills). While many people perform somewhat better in one area or another, it seems rarely the case that a person who is excellent at one particular skill is utterly hopeless at all others.

Examining much the same adult–IQ data, others disagree, pointing instead to the various "s"—or specific—factors that can be identified in intelligence. From Thurstone's (1938) primary factors on, different workers have disagreed about what these various separate intelligences are and how they should be measured. But the "g" versus "s" debate continues among workers interested in adult intellectual performance.

Analogous debates persist among those interested in children's intellectual development. Here the main proponent of "g" is probably Jean Piaget, with his "*structures d'ensemble*", all-of-a-piece view of intellectual development. Granted, Piaget noted the existence of "horizontal decalages," or higher-level performance on one cognitive task versus another (e.g. conservation of number vs. volume). But Piaget (Piaget & Inhelder, 1969) generally attributed such cross-domain discrepancies to performance, not competence, factors. Piaget generally believed that a child who performed at a certain level in one domain would perform at virtually identical levels in all other cognitive domains.

Recent years have seen a reaction against Piaget's all-of-a-piece views of development. Fodor (1983) has noted that language is a "modular" domain—that is, language constitutes a relatively separate, encapsulated area of functioning. Fodor therefore believes that language has little connection to other domains of functioning (e.g. one's non-linguistic intellectual abilities). Similarly, Gardner (1983, this volume) hypothesises seven different domains of intelligence. In the same way, then, that workers argue about "*g*" versus "*s*" factors in adult intelligence, researchers of children's intelligence argue about the connectedness versus modularity of children's intellectual abilities.

INTELLECTUAL DEVELOPMENT IN CHILDREN WITH MENTAL RETARDATION

With these three debates as background, we now tackle several issues in the intellectual development in children with mental retardation.

Two-group approach

In contrast to the "single-entity" model of mental retardation described previously, most developmentally oriented researchers have been influenced by the "two-group approach" to mental retardation (Zigler, 1967, 1969). This approach notes that persons with mental retardation can be divided into two types. The first type of mental retardation is essentially due to unknown causes. These individuals appear similar to their non-retarded peers—they have no obvious organic insult, have reasonably good health, and otherwise appear "normal". They do, however, have IQs in the range of retardation, generally (not always) in the mildly retarded range. Indeed, these individuals may simply constitute the lower end of the normal, Gaussian distribution of intelligence (Zigler, 1967). Further complicating the issue is the fact that disproportionately more of these individuals are poor, from minority backgrounds, and of low-IQ parents (Hodapp, 1994). Although its exact prevalence rate remains unknown and may differ based on the exact definition of mental retardation (MacMillan, Gresham, & Siperstein, 1993), this group is thought to comprise slightly over half of all persons with mental retardation (Zigler & Hodapp, 1986).

Because the causes remain unknown for this type of mental retardation, Zigler (1967) has considered this group the single greatest mystery in the field of mental retardation. This mystery is further demonstrated by the variety of terms used to describe this group: "familial", "cultural-familial", "sociocultural", and "sociocultural-familial" mental retardation, "retardation due to environmental deprivation", and "non-specific", "idiopathic", and "non-organic" mental retardation. In earlier times, these individuals were even described as having "garden variety" mental retardation. As the above list demonstrates, little agreement exists as to what causes the retardation of these individuals (which we will call *familial* mental retardation).

In the second type of mental retardation, individuals show one or another *organic* cause of their mental retardation. Organic retardation seems to account for slightly less than half of all individuals with mental retardation (Zigler & Hodapp, 1986), and many types exist. Such organic insults can occur before birth (i.e. pre-natally), as in all of the genetic causes of mental retardation. Organic forms can also occur peri-natally, such as the oxygen deprivation that oftentimes accompanies severe prematurity. Finally, a small number of individuals suffer post-natal damage, usually from brain trauma or meningitis. All together, there may be upwards of 750 different types of organic mental retardation (Opitz, 1996).

Recent years have affirmed this basic classification, but with some slight modifications. Concerning the familial or cultural-familial group, most recent reviewers concur that familial mental retardation "appears to be the extreme end of the normal range of IQ scores in the population" (Pike & Plomin 1996, p. 562; see also Simonoff, Bolton, & Rutter, 1996; Thapar, Gottesman, Owen, O'Donovan, & McGuffin, 1994). This conclusion is supported in several ways. First, various adoption studies over the years show that heritability indices average about 0.50. A strong, though not all-encompassing, role therefore exists for genetics in intelligence (as well as for the environment; Plomin & Rende, 1991). Second, sibling studies show differences in the siblings of children with mild versus more severe levels of retardation. Specifically, siblings (as well as parents) of children with mild mental retardation often show lower IQs, implying that many cases of mild mental retardation may be related to the family's generally lower levels of IQ, not to some specific organic insult. In one large-scale study, Broman, Nichols, Shaughnessy, and Kennedy (1987) found that siblings of children with severe mental retardation showed higher IQ scores than did siblings of children with mild mental retardation. Even within the group with severe mental retardation, those children showing clear evidence of central nervous system damage had siblings with higher IQs than did siblings of children without central nervous system involvement. In short, there appear to be two groups of children with mental retardation—those with and those without organic impairment.

And yet, a few caveats are in order. First, mild mental retardation is not synonymous with familial mental retardation. Over the past 20 years, many

organic—mainly genetic—forms of mental retardation have been identified that are associated with mild mental retardation. Individuals with
fragile X syndrome, for example, often show mild mental retardation. In
addition, fragile X syndrome, which often affects other family members, is
a disorder that until two decades ago might have incorrectly been
considered familial mental retardation (Dykens & Leckman, 1990). Partly
as a result of these newly discovered organic causes of mild mental
retardation, the percentage of individuals with familial mental retardation
might be expected to decrease slightly in coming years.

A second modification concerns the organic group. In contrast to 20
years ago, when much less was known about the behaviour of persons with
organic mental retardation, recent research shows that individuals with one
versus another type of organicity may differ (Burack, Hodapp, & Zigler,
1988). These differences involve a variety of developmental characteristics:
intellectual, linguistic, and adaptive strengths and weaknesses (Dykens,
Hodapp, & Leckman, 1994); different chronological ages or tasks that slow
development (Hodapp et al., 1990, Hodapp & Zigler, 1990); and even
propensities to different maladaptive behaviours and psychopathology
(Dykens, 1995). Many aspects of development differ in children with one
versus another organic type of mental retardation. We are therefore
moving beyond a view of mental retardation as a single entity, or even as
only two entities (i.e. familial and organic), to a view that mental
retardation is comprised of numerous different types, many of which show
aetiologically specific developmental characteristics.

Cross-domain relations

Given the move from the two-group approach to a more differentiated
organic group, research has also moved to closer examinations of cross-
domain relations. Early on, Zigler (1969) described what came to be called
the "similar structure" hypothesis. This hypothesis, explicitly applied only
to children with familial mental retardation, noted that children with
familial retardation showed no specific organic defect for their retardation.
With no single organic cause, these children were expected to perform
similarly to non-retarded children of identical mental ages (i.e. MA-
matches) on all intellectual tasks.

With a few exceptions, the similar structure hypothesis has been borne
out for the familial group, at least for one class of intellectual task.
Reviewing 33 studies, Weisz, Yeates, and Zigler (1982) found that children
with familial mental retardation performed the same as MA-matched non-
retarded children. These studies employed a range of Piagetian tasks,
including conservation, role taking, sex identity, relative thinking, moral
judgements, and colour identity. Examining information-processing tasks,

however, the findings seem more mixed. Although children with familial mental retardation and non-retarded MA-matches performed similarly on some information-processing tasks, the children with retardation performed worse than MA-matches on tasks of memory and learning-set formation (Weiss, Weisz, & Bromfield, 1986).

Why this difference between Piagetian and information-processing tasks? Weisz (1990) attributes such poorer performance to motivational issues: Compared to MA-matched non-retarded children, children with familial mental retardation may be less motivated to repeatedly perform a specific memory task on a computer. Conversely, Mundy and Kasari (1990) suggest that children with familial mental retardation may actually be deficited in these areas relative to MA-matches. At the present time, we cannot say for certain which explanation seems best.

Less controversial are the findings and implications of cross-domain studies on children with organic mental retardation. Again examining a variety of comparisons between children with organic mental retardation and MA-matched non-retarded children, Weisz et al. (1982) find that children with organic mental retardation perform worse on many Piagetian tasks.

More recently, however, even this finding has been refined due to new studies of children with different types of organic mental retardation. Consider the distinction between sequential versus simultaneous processing tasks. According to one theory (Das, Kirby, & Jarman, 1975), intelligence can best be divided into sequential processing—tasks involving serial, bit-by-bit processing (e.g. remembering a series of digits)—versus those that involve simultaneous processing—tasks involving Gestalt, holistic processing (e.g. deciphering a line drawing in which some lines are missing). This basic distinction shows itself in groups with different genetic forms of mental retardation. For example, boys with fragile X syndrome show deficits in sequential processing tasks compared to tasks of achievement or simultaneous processing (Dykens, Hodapp, & Leckman, 1987; for a different view of the cognitive deficits in fragile X syndrome, see Hay, this volume). Further, such sequential deficits are not found in every organic group. Comparing children with Down's syndrome versus fragile X syndrome, Hodapp et al. (1992) found that, whereas the fragile X group showed the sequential deficit, the Down's syndrome group did not. In fact, the Down's syndrome group was largely flat or even in their levels of sequential processing, simultaneous processing, and achievement (Pueschel, Gallagher, Zartler, & Pezullo, 1986).

The most striking example of an uneven profile, however, arises in Williams Syndrome. Williams syndrome is a rarely occurring genetic condition that is now known to be caused by a micro-deletion on chromosome 7 (Pober & Dykens, 1996). In addition to a specific "elfin-like" facial appearance, these children seem particularly proficient in many areas of language (and poor in many visuo-spatial skills; Udwin, Yule, & Martin, 1987). For example, many children with Williams syndrome have vocabularies that are several years above their overall mental ages. For instance, one child with an overall mental age of approximately five years was able to understand words such as "peninsula" and "spherical" on a test of receptive vocabulary (Bellugi, Marks, Birhle, & Sabo, 1988). In addition, these children show excellent grammatical and storytelling skills (Reilly, Klima, & Bellugi, 1991). In contrast to children with familial mental retardation—or even to most typically developing children— children with different organic forms of mental retardation show various peaks and valleys to their intellectual profiles (see Hodapp & Dykens, 1996 for a review).

WHAT MENTAL RETARDATION TELLS US ABOUT INTELLECTUAL DEVELOPMENT

In addition to studies of intellectual development in mental retardation, we can also use mental retardation to inform us about intellectual development in general. This process involves using an "experiment of nature", examining children with disabilities to tell us about the "typical" or "usual" processes of development (Hodapp & Burack, 1990). As before, it again makes sense to consider separately children with familial retardation versus those with various organic aetiologies.

Familial versus organic mental retardation—helping to understand the structure of intellectual development

From Zigler's (1969) two-group approach until today's behaviour genetic studies (Pike & Plomin, 1996), familial retardation appears to constitute the lower end of the normal or Gaussian distribution of intelligence. As such, children with familial mental retardation should show similar structures to their intelligence as do non-retarded children of identical MA-levels.

This finding holds true on all Piagetian tasks and on most (maybe not all) information-processing tasks. In short, groups of children with familial mental retardation generally appear flat or even in their intellectual profiles.

In essence, children with familial mental retardation re-affirm the presence of a "g", or general intellectual factor, in children whose retardation does not arise from a single organic impairment. Although any single child with familial retardation—like any typically developing child—

may show certain intellectual strengths and weaknesses, as a group children with familial retardation show a flat or even profile. In many ways, then, these children illustrate the "usual workings" of intelligence, with no area way above or way below any other.

Conversely, the different organic aetiologies show the many ways that certain areas of intelligence can, on occasion, be higher or lower than others. Consider the many different profiles already observed in various mental retardation groups. Boys with fragile X syndrome show higher simultanous processing and achievement skills than sequential processing skills. Children with Down's syndrome, who show no particular strength or weakness in simultaneous processing, sequential processing, or achievement, do show a profile in which they perform better on visual tasks than on auditory tasks (Pueschel et al., 1986). Moreover, this strength in processing visual (as opposed to auditory) information has led Buckley (1995) to advocate teaching sight reading to children with Down's syndrome. Finally, children with Williams syndrome have exceptionally high abilities in grammar and in other aspects of language (Bellugi, Wang, & Jernigan, 1994).

Ultimately, we have come full circle, again discussing both "*g*" and "*s*", the general and specific factors that appear in the intelligence of all persons. Studies of retardation demonstrate both. Groups of children with familial mental retardation, like most non-retarded children, clearly illustrate the general, all-of-a-piece nature of intelligence for most children, most of the time. Children with one or another organic aetiology show that the different intellectual components can, under certain circumstances, diverge widely one from another.

Remaining unresolved issues

To say that both "*s*" and "*g*" exist, and that both can be shown in mental retardation research, begs several questions. These questions—many of which this volume begins to tackle—promise to be the subject of some of the most exciting studies in future years.

A first question is why most children, most of the time, show a general similarity in their performances across different intellectual tasks. Although Piaget's *structures d'ensemble* have been criticised (e.g. Fischer, 1980), no one has yet proposed why, if there are several separable domains of intelligence, these domains generally go together in development. In short, if everything is so separate, why does generally uniform development constitute the rule rather than the exception?

A second issue concerns the domains themselves. Although most modern-day intelligence researchers consider as separable many different domains of intelligence, each disagrees about what constitute the exact domains. Even within children with mental retardation, one can find evidence for several different divisions of intelligence. The sequential–simultaneous distinction seems to work well for children with fragile X syndrome (and for children with Prader-Willi syndrome; Dykens, Hodapp, Walsh, & Nash, 1992). In contrast, Down's syndrome researchers are most excited by the distinction between visual and auditory processing. For children with Down's syndrome, this distinction seems to have a variety of practical consequences, including the teaching of some sight-word reading to approximately 50% of children with Down's syndrome (Buckley, Bird, & Byrne, 1996). In another set of studies, Bellugi et al. (1994) find that, for children with Williams syndrome, the most interesting distinctions involve linguistic processing (of various sorts) and visuo-spatial skills.

A third question concerns the developmental nature of within- and between-domain connections. It may be the case, for example, that diverse intellectual domains are more or less connected at various points during development. To use an example from boys with fragile X syndrome, sequential processing becomes a more pronounced deficit as these children get older (Hodapp, Dykens, Ort, Zelinsky, & Leckman, 1991). Thus, if one were to examine the profile formed by the child with fragile X syndrome's levels in simultaneous processing, sequential processing, and achievement, a "V" would form, with simultaneous processing levels high, sequential processing levels lower, and achievement levels high. With increasing chronological age, however, this "V" becomes more "V-like", as simultaneous processing and achievement skills continue developing, whereas sequential processing skills stay relatively unchanged over time. As a result, an already-existing weakness becomes relatively weaker as the child gets older.

Fourth, and in line with the recent advances in developmental psychopathology (Cicchetti, 1993), one must consider the "costs" of discrepant functioning from one area of intelligence to another. What does it mean for the child with Williams syndrome's everyday functioning to be exceptionally good at language and poor at visuo-spatial skills? What does it mean for the boy with fragile X syndrome to be unable to perform a variety of sequential processing tasks, or the child with Down's syndrome to be superior in receiving visual as opposed to auditory input? Each of these implications remain almost totally unexamined at present.

Two remaining issues—compensations and interventions—also remain relatively unexamined. To what extent do—or can—children with Down's syndrome use their relatively stronger visual-receptive abilities to compensate for their weaker auditory-receptive abilities? To what extent can intervention programmes be developed that play to the child's strengths in intellectual processing abilities? Although a few tentative advances have been made along this front (e.g. the LOGOS and other whole-word reading methods for children with fragile X syndrome; Scharfenaker, Hickman, & Braden, 1991), much more remains to be known.

CONCLUSION

After beginning this chapter with three long-running debates in the fields of mental retardation and intelligence, we end with more questions than answers. At present, however, we can say that children with mental retardation do not constitute a single entity, but that familial retardation seems separate from organic retardation. In addition, organic retardation is itself comprised of numerous distinct aetiologies, many featuring concomitant differences in their behaviours. In addition, mental retardation research again affirms both general and specific factors in intellectual development. How these factors go together, what constitute the specific factors themselves, how specific factors develop and how they coexist with general factors throughout the childhood years—all remain unknown. Similarly, the everyday impacts on adaptive behaviour, compensatory strategies, and interventions related to specific intellectual factors remain generally unexplored for most aetiologies of mental retardation. Thus, while we may have learned quite a bit about the intellectual development of children with mental retardation over the past several decades, much more remains to be discovered. Over the coming years, then, we can be sure that the intertwined history of intellectual development and children with mental retardation will continue.

REFERENCES

Bellugi, U., Marks, S., Birhle, A., & Sabo, H. (1988). Dissociations between language and cognitive functions in Williams syndrome. In D. Bishop & K. Mogford (Eds), *Language development and exceptional circumstances* (pp. 177–189). London: Churchill Livingstone.

Bellugi, U., Wang, P., & Jernigan, T. (1994). Williams syndrome: An unusual neuropsychological profile. In S.H. Broman & J. Grafman (Eds), *Atypical cognitive deficits in developmental disorders*. (pp. 23–56). Hillsdale, NJ: Lawrence Erlbaum Associates Inc.

Broman, S., Nichols, P., Shaughnessy, P., & Kennedy, W. (1987). *Retardation in young children: A developmental study of cognitive deficit*. Hillsdale, NJ: Lawrence Erlbaum Associates Inc.

Buckley, S., Bird, G., & Byrne, A. (1996). Teaching children with Down syndrome to read and write. In L. Nadel & D. Rosenthal (Eds), *Down syndrome: Living and learning in the community* (pp. 158–169). New York: Wiley-Liss.

Buckley, S. (in press). Practical and theoretical issues in literacy. In J. Rondal, L. Nadel, & J. Perrera (Eds), *Down syndrome: Psychological, psychobiological, and socio-educational perspectives*. London: Colin Whurr Publishers.

Burack, J.A. (1990). Differentiating mental retardation: The two-group approach and beyond. In R.M. Hodapp, J.A. Burack, & E. Zigler (Eds), *Issues in the developmental approach to mental retardation* (pp. 27–48). Cambridge, UK: Cambridge University Press.

Burack, J.A., Hodapp, R.M., & Zigler, E. (1988). Issues in the classification of mental retardation: Differentiating among organic etiologies. *Journal of Child Psychology and Psychiatry, 29*, 765–779.

Cicchetti, D. (1993). Developmental psychopathology: Reactions, reflections, projections. *Developmental Review, 13*, 471–502.

Das, J.P., Kirby, J., & Jarman, R.F. (1975). Simultaneous and successive abilities: An alternative model for cognitive abilities. *Psychological Bulletin, 82*, 87–103.

Dugdale, R.L. (1910). *The Jukes: A study in crime, pauperism, disease, and heredity*. New York: Putnam.

Dykens, E.M. (1995). Measuring behavioural phenotypes: Provocations from the "New Genetics". *American Journal on Mental Retardation, 99*, 522–532.

Dykens, E.M., Hodapp, R.M., & Leckman, J.F. (1987). Strengths and weaknesses in the intellectual functioning of males with fragile X syndrome. *American Journal of Mental Deficiency, 92*, 234–236.

Dykens, E.M., Hodapp, R.M., & Leckman, J.F. (1994). *Behavior and development in fragile X syndrome*. Newbury Park, CA: Sage.

Dykens, E.M., Hodapp, R.M., Walsh, K.K., & Nash, L. (1992). Profiles, correlates, and trajectories of intelligence in individuals with Prader-Willi syndrome. *Journal of the American Academy of Child and Adolescent Psychiatry, 31*, 1125–1130.

Dykens, E.M., & Leckman, J.F. (1990). Developmental issues in fragile X syndrome. In R.M. Hodapp, J.A. Burack, & E. Zigler (Eds), *Issues in the developmental approach to mental retardation* (pp. 226–245). Cambridge, UK: Cambridge University Press.

Fernald, W.E. (1913). Discussion of H.H. Goddard's "The improvability of feeble-minded children". *Journal of Psycho-Aesthenics, 17*, 126–131.

Fischer, K. (1980). A theory of cognitive development: The control and construction of a hierarchy of skills. *Psychological Review, 87*, 477–531.

Fodor, J. (1983). *Modularity of mind: An essay on faculty psychology*. Cambridge, MA: MIT Press.

Gardner, H. (1983). *Frames of mind*. New York: Basic Books.

Goddard, H.H. (1913a). The improvability of feeble-minded children. *Journal of Psycho-Aesthenics, 17*, 121–126.

Goddard, H.H. (1913b). *The Kallikak family: A study in the heredity of feeble-mindedness*. New York: Macmillan.

Hodapp, R.M. (1994). Cultural-familial mental retardation. In R. Sternberg (Ed.), *Encyclopedia of intelligence* (pp. 711–717). New York: Macmillan.

Hodapp, R.M., & Burack, J.A. (1990). What mental retardation tells us about typical development: The examples of sequences, rates, and cross-domain relations. *Development and Psychopathology, 2*, 213–225.

Hodapp, R.M., & Dykens, E.M. (1994). Mental retardation's two cultures of behavioural research. *American Journal on Mental Retardation, 98*, 675–687.

Hodapp, R.M., & Dykens, E.M. (1996). Mental retardation. In E.J. Mash & R.A Barkley (Eds), *Child psychopathology* (pp. 362–389). New York: Guilford.

Hodapp, R.M., Dykens, E.M., Hagerman, R.J., Schreiner, R., Lachiewicz, A., & Leckman, J.F. (1990). Developmental implications of changing trajectories of

IQ in males with fragile X syndrome. *Journal of the American Academy of Child and Adolescent Psychiatry*, *29*, 214–219.

Hodapp, R.M., Dykens, E.M., Ort, S., Zelinsky, D., & Leckman, J.F. (1991). Changing patterns of intellectual strengths and weaknesses in males with fragile X syndrome. *Journal of Autism and Developmental Disorders*, *21*, 503–516.

Hodapp, R.M., Leckman, J.F., Dykens, E.M., Sparrow, S., Zelinsky, D., & Ort, S.I. (1992). K-ABC profiles in children with fragile X syndrome, Down syndrome, and nonspecific mental retardation. *American Journal on Mental Retardation*, *97*, 39–46.

Hodapp, R.M., & Zigler, E. (1990). Applying the developmental perspective to individuals with Down syndrome. In D. Cicchetti & M. Beeghly (Eds), *Children with Down syndrome: A developmental perspective* (pp. 1-28). New York: Cambridge University Press.

Humphries, L.G. (1979). The construct of general intelligence. *Intelligence*, *3*, 105–120.

MacMillan, D.L., Gresham, F.M., & Siperstein, G. (1993). Conceptual and psychometric concerns about the 1992 AAMR definition of mental retardation. *American Journal on Mental Retardation*, *98*, 325–335.

Mundy, P., & Kasari, C. (1990). The similar-structure hypothesis and differential rate of development in mental retardation. In R.M. Hodapp, J.A. Burack, & E. Zigler (Eds), *Issues in the developmental approach to mental retardation* (pp. 71–92). Cambridge, UK: Cambridge University Press.

Opitz, J.M. (1996). Historiography of the causal analysis of mental retardation. Paper presented at the 29th annual Gatlinburg Conference on Research and Theory in Mental Retardation and Developmental Disabilities, Gatlinburg, TN.

Piaget, J., & Inhelder, B. (1969). *The psychology of the child*. New York: Basic Books.

Pike, A., & Plomin, R. (1996). Importance of nonshared environmental factors for childhood and adolescent psychopathology. *Journal of the American Academy of Child and Adolescent Psychiatry*, *35*, 560–570.

Plomin, R., & Rende, R. (1991). Human behavioural genetics. *Annual Review of Psychology*, *42*, 161–190.

Pober, B., & Dykens, E.M. (1996). Williams syndrome: An overview of medical, cognitive, and behavioural features. *Child and Adolescent Psychiatric Clinics of North America*, *5*, 929–943.

Pueschel, S.R., Gallagher, P.L., Zartler, A.S., & Pezzullo, J.C. (1986). Cognitive and learning processes in children with Down syndrome. *Research in Developmental Disabilities*, *8*, 21–37.

Reilly, J.S., Klima, E., & Bellugi, U. (1991). Once more with feeling: Affect and language in atypical populations. *Development and Psychopathology*, *2*, 367–391.

Scharfenaker, S., Hickman, L., & Braden, M. (1991). An integrated approach to intervention. In R.J. Hagerman & A.C. Silverman (Eds), *Fragile X syndrome: Diagnosis, treatment, and research* (pp. 327–372). Baltimore, MD: Johns Hopkins Press.

Simonoff, E., Bolton, P., & Rutter, M. (1996). Mental retardation: Genetic findings, clinical implications, and research agenda. *Journal of Child Psychology and Psychiatry*, *37*, 259–280.

Spitz, R.A. (1945). Hospitalism: An inquiry into the genesis of psychiatric conditions in early childhood. *Psychoanalytic Study of the Child*, *1*, 54–74.

Thapar, A., Gottesman, I.I., Owen, M.J., O'Donovan, M.C., & McGuffin, P. (1994). The genetics of mental retardation. *British Journal of Psychiatry, 164*, 747–758.

Thurstone, L.L. (1938). *Primary mental abilities.* Chicago: University of Chicago Press.

Udwin, O., Yule, W., & Martin, N. (1987). Cognitive abilities and behavioural characteristics of children with idiopathic infantile hypercalcaemia. *Journal of Child Psychology and Psychiatry, 28*, 297–309.

Weiss, B., Weisz, J.R., & Bromfield, R. (1986). Performance of retarded and nonretarded persons on information-processing tasks: Further tests of the similar-structure hypothesis. *Psychological Bulletin, 100*, 157–175.

Weisz, J.R. (1990). Cultural-familial mental retardation: A developmental perspective on cognitive performance and "helpless" behaviour. In R.M. Hodapp, J.A. Burack, & E. Zigler (Eds), *Issues in the developmental approach to mental retardation* (pp. 137–168). Cambridge, UK: Cambridge University Press.

Weisz, J.R., Yeates, O.W., & Zigler, E. (1982). Cognitive evidence and the developmental-difference controversy. In E. Zigler & D. Balla (Eds), *Mental retardation: The developmental-difference controversy* (pp. 213–276). Hillsdale, NJ: Lawrence Erlbaum Associates Inc.

Zigler, E. (1967). Familial mental retardation: A continuing dilemma. *Science, 155*, 292–298.

Zigler, E. (1969). Developmental versus difference theories of retardation and the problem of motivation. *American Journal of Mental Deficiency, 73*, 536–556.

Zigler, E., & Hodapp, R.M. (1986). *Understanding mental retardation.* Cambridge, UK: Cambridge University Press.

PART FIVE

Conclusion

CHAPTER 13

Project development—taking stock

Mike Anderson

The University of Western Australia, Perth

DAH DOO DI DAH DOO

Well, what has been gained by the surreptitious hijacking of Bart and his colleagues? What can we learn from the views of the experts in the field about the future of research into the development of intelligence? If nothing else you should by now appreciate the range and richness of research in the field. I had hoped for a comprehensive survey of the field and I have not been disappointed. I had hoped for guidelines for innovative methodologies and research strategies and again I have not been disappointed. Finally, I had hoped that opinions and argument as to where the diverse routes through the field might lead would be forthcoming. And, yes, I have not been disappointed. You may of course choose to not read this chapter because you have already come across the question that takes your fancy and already availed yourself of your methodological armoury. But my last task in Project Development is to try to draw conclusions about the field in general (if you remember from the first chapter it was largely a matter of faith that there is a field at all), and to summarise what, for me, are the major lessons. Finally, I hope to glean a research agenda that may arise anew out of the synthesis of the chapters in the book.

WHAT HAVE WE LEARNED AND WHERE CAN WE GO?

The book was divided into four parts demarcated by the major issues outlined in the first chapter:

1. *Measurement.* The focus here was assessment. Specifically, psychometric assessment of intelligence in children and the correlations of new measures of infant information processing with later IQ.

2. *The genesis question.* The second section introduced examples of the behaviour genetics approach to understanding the development of intelligence. Behaviour genetics serves a useful "first pass" sort of the available data, because where there is distinctive genetic and environmental contributions there is likely to be important distinctions for theories of intelligence.

3. *Structural theories and models of change.* The third section is in many ways the engine room of the book, providing a review of the current major theoretical options for explaining the development of intelligence.

4. *Abnormal development.* Savant syndrome, intervention studies in special education, and views on the nature of mental retardation, can be used as a torch to shed some light on the general processes involved in the development of intelligence and to further our understanding of the constraints of biology on education.

As I explained in the first chapter, the book took on this organisation because of my own theoretical perspective. It may be unsurprising that after reading it I still believe that this structure represents a useful taxonomy of research activity. However, as I hoped, it seems to me that a number of issues have emerged that, although correlated with the original taxonomy, to some extent cut across the structure of the book and appear as threads of arguments in many of the chapters. These issues could form the basis of a new common framework or agreed research agenda. These are: (1) the importance of the relationship between theory and measurement; (2) the relationship between general and specific abilities; (3) the centrality of three information processing constructs: speed, interference (or inhibition), and capacity.

THE RELATIONSHIP BETWEEN MEASUREMENT AND THEORY

What became apparent in the review of the assessment of intelligence in children and infancy was how theory has become divorced from measurement. In Chapter 2, Irene Styles argues that this is largely due to the overuse of factor analysis and its legacy of a lack of theoretical consensus as to the underlying structure of the intelligence. In her view, the move to factor analysis spelled the divorce of the happy scientific marriage of theory and measurement. She implies that Binet would be turning in his grave if he realised where his quantitative approach to a very practical problem (the need to identify the intelligence of children in need of special educational provision) had led.

In the hands of the factor analysts, psychometrics and test development lost sight of the necessary interaction between the development of theories of intelligence and the refinement of measures. Factor analysis was seen as a shortcut whereby relatively crude measures would yield the secrets of the structure of intelligence avoiding the need to develop "purer" measures of the resulting theoretical constructs. Piaget was more interested in what the patterns of errors on standardised tests could tell us about the structure of intelligence. As every student of cognitive development knows this led Piaget in a quite different direction to that taken by psychometricians. Piaget himself and, in the main, his European-based followers stuck to the clinical method—the intensive study of, at most, a few children's performance on tasks designed to illuminate particular constructs in the theory. North American and British Piaget followers (and, indeed, bashers) embraced the methods more common in experimental psychology—developing tasks where some factor could be manipulated in a systematic way and investigating whether predicted interactions between experimental factors (e.g. whether the liquid in a conservation of volume experiment was Coca-Cola or plain water) and age-group could be found on the dependent measure (e.g. judgements of "more" or "less").

Whether the direction taken after Binet was factor analysis or the clinical/experimental method, research did not return to measurement issues. Styles suggests, however, that all is not lost and both Piagetian tasks and intelligence tests can be integrated once more within the same measurement model. For my own part, I agree with Styles' view that the missing ingredient is still the connection between the measures and the theories. While the use of factor analysis may have distracted us from the measurement issues, the development of new measures does depend on the development of new theory. Of course, it may be that some theories are incommensurate. For example, there is little point from one theoretical perspective (that of Spearman and general intelligence) in attempting to devise pure measures of primary mental abilities (Thurstone, 1938) because they do not exist. Similarly, it may be that Piagetian conceptions and the psychometrics underlying individual differences in IQ are incommensurate because they are related to different constructs of intelligence (but see Anderson, 1992 for an attempted integration). However, an integrated theory (that is, the integration of Piagetian and psychometric conceptions of intelligence) should lead in turn to new integrated measures. If Styles is right, therein lies scientific progress.

Styles' central point is well taken and comes home to roost in the summary of research efforts in infant intelligence presented in the chapter by John Colombo and Janet Frick. What we see here is a bold attempt to cut through thickets of correlations between infant information processing measures and later IQ differences. Often constructs taken from infancy research have only a nominal similarity with the same hypothetical constructs used in the studies of cognitive development in young children and studies of adult intelligence ("inhibition" for example). There is certainly almost no correspondence in measures (although it is this that makes the correlations theoretically interesting). In short, there is a serious problem in the theory/measurement relationship. In this context the appearance of the correlation between information processing measures of infant attention and later IQ measures was as fortuitous as it was unexpected and exciting. It was fortuitous because there was no good theoretical reason for supposing there was such a link. The discovery of the correlation was a classic scientific example of flying a kite—given that IQ data was available on children for whom infancy data was available, indeed infancy measures that had not previously been tried, why not have a look? Sometimes kites take off.

The correlation was unexpected precisely because the received wisdom was that there is no correlation. This received wisdom was based on the Piagetian view of the discontinuity of the nature of intelligence from infancy to adulthood and the empirical fact that tests designed to measure infant intelligence (for example, the Bayley test) show no correlation with later IQ differences. That those kinds of tests were themselves based on a Piagetian conception of intelligence which argues for discontinuity in intelligence did not strike anyone as a problem. Probably because, as I have argued elsewhere, the deeper, usually implicit, assumption was that the development of intelligence and individual differences in intelligence are different manifestations of the same underlying cognitive construct (Anderson, 1992).

The correlation was, and is, exciting because it led to the obvious question, why do these measures and not the traditional ones correlate with later IQ? This, in turn, led to a great flurry of new research trying to pin down the cognitive connection. The new research has been done almost entirely by infancy researchers rather than those interested in IQ differences because only they had the requisite methodological skills to work with infants. These researchers came from a tradition that was largely antithetical to regarding IQ as measuring anything of much theoretical import and consequently they knew almost nothing of theoretical developments in the study of adult intelligence. In order to interest the rest of the scientific community in the new data they had to take IQ seriously while maintaining a respectable distance from research that was tainted with the leper's touch. It is no wonder then that the first attempts at theoretical integration were based on "nice" conceptions of intelligence. For example, novelty preference was thought to be correlated with later IQ because intelligence was fundamentally concerned with novelty, curiosity, and non-entrenched thinking (Sternberg, 1981). As this somewhat facile approach quickly petered out it was replaced by navel gazing on the part of infancy researchers who ignored any theoretical formulations of IQ. By picking infant tasks to pieces they attempted to determine what information-processing routines these tasks had in common and that might plausibly be labelled a component of intelligence. This lack of concern with adult individual differences can be seen for example in an otherwise excellent review by McCall (1994), where he favours inhibition as the causal construct explaining the correlation but pays only passing attention to its plausibility as the process underlying IQ differences (in my view a plausibility that approaches zero).

Seen in this light, the efforts of John Colombo over the last few years have been exemplary. Colombo (1993) with considerable courage took IQ-based research seriously and started to ask whether constructs such as g, or the information processing equivalent—speed of information processing—might not be usefully applied to the infancy data. We see in the chapter by Colombo and Frick (Chapter 3) that an initial enthusiasm for a speed of processing explanation for the correlation has cooled under the weight of theoretical complexities and psychometric inadequacies of the infant measures—representing a final twist in our theory/measurement tale.

Theory-neutral behaviour genetics?

David Hay (Chapter 4) has shown us how behaviour genetics methodology can allow us to explore both the genetic and environmental contributions to development and individual differences in a way that can appear theory-neutral as far as structural accounts of intelligence may be concerned. For example, the relatively high heritability of IQ is consistent with both a high heritability of a general factor and with a high heritability of a number of independent factors. Of course, even a behaviour genetics analysis depends ultimately on theory because the data are determined by measurements and the measurements are determined by theory (or at least they should be). However, behaviour genetics can tell us about the genesis of current measures in a way that may constrain theoretical options. For example a theory should be able to explain a number of interesting phenomena discussed by Hay, including the observations that:

- genetic influence increases (rather than decreases) with age;
- within-family differences in both environment and genetics have a greater influence on intelligence than between-family environmental differences;
- new genetic effects exert themselves at different points in development, changing the very nature of intelligence;

- there may be genetic influences on the *variability* (as well as mean levels) in cognitive performance in individuals with intellectual deficits.

Reznick and Corley in Chapter 5 attempt to use behaviour genetics methodology in just this fashion, to cut a way through the complex relationships. In an heroic attempt to pick the bones of the Bayley test clean for its genetic and environmental sources of variance, they hope to shed some light on underlying processes of infant intelligence. But with this very attempt they have shown the limitations of such an approach. Behaviour genetics analysis can only tell us about the variables that form the database for the study. This brings us fair and square back to the measurement problem. Are Bayley-like tests of infant development appropriate measures of the theoretical constructs that are the basis of measures of general and specific abilities in children and adults? But equally, the answer to this question depends on appropriate theory. Clearly behaviour genetics would also benefit from new theory-based measures of intelligence. Quite apart from the measurement issue, behaviour genetics will come into its own when testing well-articulated theories that generate hypotheses about the genetic and environmental sources of variance in its important theoretical constructs (one such construct will concern the continuity or lack thereof between general and specific abilities through development). I have attempted some such thing in making predictions about differing heritabilities of intelligence at above and below average IQ (Anderson, 1993) but the principle could be applied equally well to developmental behaviour genetics.

The need to integrate theory and measurement

What remains clear is that the forest of theories, methodologies, and measures in infant, child, and adult research needs to be severely pruned. Explanations for the correlation must satisfy at least two conditions at once: First, they must be grounded in a plausible information processing basis for the infant data; second, they must be consistent with a well-articulated theory of adult IQ differences. In short, we have to look at both "ends" at once. Finally, it would be ideal if we could devise measures that are theoretically grounded and can be used with equal facility in all age groups. An example might be the use of reflex modification procedures to measure speed of processing in children and adults (Anderson, 1996; Smyth, Anderson, & Hammond, in press). These measures are only recently being tested for their observed relationship with IQ differences, but they provide an example of what might be done in the future if two kinds of theories (infant and adult) can be combined and new measures based on the same theoretical construct can be developed.

GENERAL AND SPECIFIC ABILITIES

In this book the single most pervasive consensus is that theories of the development of intelligence need to accommodate both general and specific abilities. There is one exception to this view. Chapter 6 by Bruce Torff and Howard Gardner argues that there is no requirement either theoretically or empirically to take general intelligence seriously. A major developmental question (whether a "g factor" undergoes developmental change or, on the contrary, whether development is driven by changes in specific abilities) is immediately dispensed with. For Torff and Gardner there are only specific abilities. The developmental dimension of this theory posits that the intelligences "unfold", constrained principally by the cultural context of their operating environment. The approach taken by Gardner (1983) is to be applauded because it represents one of the few attempts to integrate under the one theoretical umbrella a set of diverse phenomena in the development of intelligence. However, the process of evaluating the theory of multiple intelligences has revealed two central problems. The first is that there is no clear programme for empirically testing the theory. It is not at all obvious how these intelligences are to be measured and assessed other than that this should be done in an appropriate cultural context. The second problem is that the theory is alone in denying that there is such a thing as general intelligence and, consequently, is sinking under the weight of evidence to the contrary.

As Ted Nettelbeck points out (Chapter 10), not many would take issue with Torff and Gardner that there is specificity to intelligence, but there is near unanimity that there is generality too. Bob Hodapp and Edward Zigler (Chapter 12) consider that 20 years of research since the launch the developmental versus difference controversy (Zigler & Balla, 1977) has affirmed the centrality of general intelligence in cultural familial mental retardation (it is true they put a different slant on it, of which more later). They also ask why it is, if intelligence truly comes in many varieties, that the mentally retarded develop so consistently across domains and why the profiles of specific abilities are so flat in this group at all stages in development. Contrast the latter with the increasing "V"-shaped developmental profiles of the organic retardation group (where one specific ability lags more and more behind other abilities as development proceeds). As Herman Spitz shows so crushingly in Chapter 11, in the major testing ground of educational interventions in the development of intelligence, namely the attempt to raise the intelligence of the "cultural familial" mentally retarded, rather than there being strong support for a multiple intelligences educational perspective there is strong evidence for an all-pervasive general deficit in intelligence.

Nor is there any comfort for the multiple intelligences theory from the systematic study of one of its cornerstones—*savants*. Nettelbeck captures this elegantly—"far from defining the nature of different kinds of intelligence . . . cases of savant syndrome actually help to clarify what intelligence is *not*" [my italics]. Nettelbeck demonstrates that it is the very constraint of having to accommodate the hypothesis that savants are low in general intelligence that leads to a creativity in hypotheses about the nature of the savant abilities, a creativity that not only pushes our understanding of savants forward but also our understanding of intelligence in particular and cognition in general. So we have the hypothesis that the clusters of savant abilities, including calculation, music, graphic art, memory, and language, may be based, in some cases, on innate talents but all rely on exceptional long-term procedural memory. What follows is a discussion of talent, the role of practice in developing the skill and the tantalising distinction between a practised talent and acquired crystallised abilities. This is then tied in with general developmental theories (for example, that long-term procedural memory may develop early and remain relatively unchanged during the developmental period when there is an explosion in crystallised knowledge) that makes sense of why savants' abilities seem to be manifest early, why many talents can be preserved at peak functioning with relatively little use, whereas crystallised skills show an inexorable decline without high levels of use, and why the development of a talent has a quite different profile to that of "intellectual" skills. It is the very acknowledgement of the reality of general intelligence that transforms savant syndrome from a curiosity to a theoretical challenge.

Many of the key issues identified by David Hay (Chapter 4) for the burgeoning research area of developmental behaviour genetics concern the relationship between general and specific abilities. His review of the literature shows that this field has become very sophisticated in identifying the changing contribution of genes to abilities over the course of development. In particular there is strong evidence to suggest that there are marked changes in genetic contribution at two, around seven, and perhaps also in early adolescence. The first may partly be due to an artifact of the change from Piagetian-based infancy intelligence tests to more Binet-like measures used with pre-schoolers. But this does not mean that it could not also be the case that the nature of intellectual development shifts gear at two, something Piaget long claimed. The advance in our knowledge is that we can pick up some of the genetic contributions to this change. The second is harder to explain away in terms of changes in test format and may reflect real changes in cognitive structure with concomitant changes in the genetic contributions to abilities. Certainly this age is consistent with Piagetian, capacity, and inhibition theories about the change in structure of cognition at this particular age. Even more exciting is the work that suggests that the genetic effects on specific abilities becomes more pronounced with age (Cardon & Fulker, 1994) while, simultaneously, the variance accounted for by general intelligence also increases.

Finally, Hodapp and Zigler in Chapter 12 demonstrate the progress that has been made in understanding the interplay between general and specific abilities in the mentally retarded. As mentioned earlier, they now argue for the pervasiveness of effects on general ability in the cultural-familial mentally retarded. However, it should be said that their concept of general intelligence has important differences with Spearman's psychometric notion. They view generality in terms of the Piagetian conception of domain general cognitive structures and claim strong evidence for the contention that the cultural-familial group exhibit the same structures, albeit later in development and perhaps with a lower ceiling of performance (Weisz, Weiss, & Bromfield, 1986). If we put our psychometric glasses on this makes a "difference" theory of mental retardation, such as that of Spitz (1982), equivalent to the delay or developmental theories if the defect or delay is agreed to be in general intelligence. Consistent with this are the observations made by Hodapp and Zigler that clear specific deficits, say between sequential and simultaneous processing or between linguistic and visuo-spatial, are more obviously found in groups with clear organic mental retardation (Fragile-X and Williams syndrome respectively).

Clearly the way forward must embrace both generality and specificity in intelligence and how this relationship may change during development. But, in the greater scheme of things Gardner's assertions to the contrary has provided an invaluable focus for theoretical debate.

SPEED OF PROCESSING, INHIBITION, AND CAPACITY

The next major issue is, what psychological property or process might lie at the heart of the construct of general intelligence, especially as it relates to developmental change? Three options discussed in Part 3 for the processing basis of a general developmental and individual differences factor are: speed of information processing (see the discussion of Hale and Kail in Davis and Anderson, Chapter 7); processing capacity (Halford, Chapter 8); and interference or inhibition of processing (Dempster and Corkill, Chapter 9). Davis and Anderson argue that because each processing parameter has a different theoretical basis and different methodologies they have rarely, if at all, been pitted against each other as competing explanations for the single factor. What is required is a speed manipulation that can be made independently of an influence on capacity or inhibition (and all the complementary manipulations). But, given the relatively rudimentary theoretical specifications and worse, operational definitions of these constructs, it is hard to see how they can be compared.[1] But if it turns out that these constructs are different manifestations of the same thing (and merely operationalised differently in different experimental procedures), or if it is the case that they are constructs with unique properties, then the way forward diverges. In the former case the way forward is to provide a theoretical formulation of the construct that underlies all three. In the latter case what is needed to advance the field are better theoretical definitions (of speed, of capacity, of inhibition) before they can be contrasted, which is, in effect, more of the same. Maybe it is time to take a punt and find a way of trying to differentiate these possibilities with the array of methods we have in store. What might aid our search and formalise our punt? It is time for some speculation on the way forward.

A WAY FORWARD?

From this short synopsis, wearing my own theoretical lenses it seems to me that the way forward must be to:

1. Reintegrate theory and measurement and in the process evaluate the range of existing theories.
2. Acknowledge that both general and specific abilities exist and move on to tackle the detailed questions of the nature of these constructs and how they are related to individual differences and developmental change.
3. Focus on an integration of the three central constructs (and candidates for the general factor in the development of intelligence) of speed of information processing, capacity, and interference.
4. Take the next step and examine the implications of theory for education.

To try to give examples of how we might make progress on these fronts, I will look first at the relationship between general and specific abilities through simulations of models based on my own theory. Second, I will suggest a possible integration between the three central constructs.

[1] Because operational definitions tie theoretical constructs to specific research methodologies.

THE RELATIONSHIP BETWEEN GENERAL AND SPECIFIC ABILITIES—AN EXERCISE IN MODELLING THEORIES

General intelligence and specific abilities

My own theory of intelligence and development (Anderson, 1992) was outlined in the first chapter (see Fig. 1.2) and again in Chapter 7. In the next section I want to show how a theory that acknowledges the existence of both general and specific abilities can be used to make new predictions about how the balance between these different facets of intelligence might change with development. To do this I will focus on a central aspect of the theory—the view specific abilities become more *differentiated* with increasing IQ and show how this can be brought to bear on the developmental question.

Individual differences dimension—the differentiation hypothesis

Psychometric measures of abilities seem to be more differentiated at higher IQs (Deary & Pagliari, 1991; Deary et al., 1996; Detterman & Daniel, 1989), that is, the general ability factor, g, accounts for less of the individual differences variance. In addition, measures of basic processes have lower intercorrelations above average IQ (Detterman & Daniel, 1989). The theory of the minimal cognitive architecture accommodates this in the following fashion. Faster speed of processing (which can be equated, roughly, with higher IQ) will allow the implementation of more complex specific processor algorithms. Consequently, latent individual differences in the power of specific processors become more manifest at faster speeds of processing, leading to more differentiated specific abilities in higher IQ groups. This prediction carries with it the implication that the source of more differentiated abilities in higher IQ groups is to be found in the differentiation of the specific processors. Consequently, measures of specific processor functioning, for example verbal memory or mental rotation tasks, should show lower intercorrelations in high IQ groups than in low IQ groups.

Developmental dimension—changing or unchanging speed of processing

As we saw in Chapter 7, Kail (1988, 1992) has argued that every specific process undergoes a single global change in speed of processing with development. In the theory of the minimal cognitive architecture, however, speed of processing is taken to be unchanging with development. If we put the individual differences dimension in the form of the differentiation hypothesis together with a developmental dimension we can contrast these two options. This is made possible by simulating the consequences of changing or unchanging speed in simple mathematical models that instantiates the relationship between general and specific abilities. The two models are: (1) the speed of the basic processing mechanism changes with development (global model); and (2) the power of the specific processors change with development but the speed of the basic processing mechanism is unchanging (specific model). What we need these models to do is to generate hypothetical data in the form of both psychometric tests and measures of basic information processing.

Psychometric measures of ability. The relationship between the mechanisms of the theory of the minimal cognitive architecture have been represented mathematically (Anderson, 1992), as follows:

$$SP_m = \ln (BPM_{speed}) \times \ln (SP_l)$$

The manifest power of a specific processor (SP_m) is a function of the natural logarithm of the latent power of the specific processor (SP_l) multiplied by the natural logarithm of the speed of the basic processing mechanism. This equation captures the requisite property of the theory, namely that the constraint of speed of processing on the manifest power of a specific processor decreases as speed increases. Although individuals' speed of processing and latent power of their specific processors are independent (uncorrelated in the population), the manifest power of specific processors will be correlated because of the constraint that an individual's speed of processing imposes on each specific processor.

If we then assume that an intelligence test battery consists of heterogeneous tasks that rely on different loadings of each specific processor's manifest ability, we have a way of predicting patterns of psychometric abilities. For example, given nine different sub-tests in a test battery, graded in their loading on each specific processor, an individual's score may range from:

$$\text{test 1 score} = 0.9 \times SP1_m + 0.1 \times SP2_m \qquad \text{very highly "spatial"}$$

$$\text{test 2 score} = 0.8 \times SP1_m + 0.2 \times SP2_m \qquad \text{highly "spatial"}$$

etc.

to:

$$\text{test 9 score} = 0.1 \times SP1_m + 0.9 \times SP2_m \qquad \text{highly "verbal"}$$

We can then take our estimate of "IQ" as the simple sum of the sub-test scores. The resulting psychometric battery can then be factor analysed and what we find is a smaller percentage of the variance of the resulting scores being due to the g factor in higher IQ groups. In short, this model predicts psychometric differentiation of specific abilities with increasing IQ.

This basic model can be expanded to include a developmental dimension leading to two alternative developmental models. The *global model* is one where the speed of the basic processing mechanism changes with age. The *specific model* is one where the power of the specific processors changes with age but speed of processing is unchanging. Comparing the psychometric consequences of each model is interesting. Simulated data for eight-year-olds and adults show that increasing speed of processing with age (global model) leads to *increasing* differentiation with age. However, changing the power of the specific processors (specific model) *decreases* differentiation with age.

As well as making predictions about psychometric patterns of abilities these models also make predictions about the intercorrelations between measures of speed of processing and the manifest power of the specific processors. For example, I have argued that measures of mental rotation (Just & Carpenter, 1985) and verbal information-processing tasks, such as letter naming (Posner & Mitchell, 1967), could be taken as an index of the manifest power of the specific processors related to spatial and verbal ability respectively. The two developmental models make different predictions concerning the pattern of intercorrelations among such information-processing measures expected at different levels of IQ and at different ages. A property of both models is that the intercorrelations between the mental rotation and the verbal information-processing task will be lower at higher IQ. However, this differentiation is dramatically influenced by development and in different ways for each developmental model. For the global model, there will be increasing differentiation with age, as evinced by lower intercorrelation between the measures of specific processor functioning.

To understand how this works in words instead of by simulation, think of two effects operating in the global model: (1) as speed of processing increases with development the constraint on the specific processors decrease and their manifest abilities (as measured by performance on information-processing tasks) will approach their latent abilities which are, by definition, *uncorrelated*; (2) as speed of processing increases with development, IQ will become more dependent on the power of the specific processors. High IQ and low IQ will, therefore, increasingly select for high and low power of the specific processors, maintaining the correlation between the tasks over the population as a whole but reducing the correlation dramatically within each IQ group. For the specific model the same kind of effect occurs, but in reverse. As the specific processors develop towards their natural asymptote variation in specific processor power will reduce. Unchanging speed of processing will become, therefore, relatively more important, leading to increasing correlation between the manifest abilities of the specific processors.

What this formulation allows us to do is to look at the relationship between general and specific abilities in tandem with two alternative developmental models. This allows a richer more integrated empirical test. I am testing these predictions from the simulations currently in a longitudinal study (Project KIDS) of 240 children at the University of Western Australia.

INTEGRATING THE THREE CENTRAL CONSTRUCTS OF SPEED, CAPACITY, AND INTERFERENCE

The suggestion above does require some kind of commitment to current models. An alternative way forward might be to try and rethink the data and attempt to integrate the central constructs. Again I will offer a speculation by way of example.

What we have on the one hand are putatively different processing measures—measures of speed, capacity, and inhibition—and on the other ability measures of subjects, principally mental age (MA), our developmental measure, and IQ, our individual differences measure. One hypothesis might be:

> There is a single underlying commonality between the processing measures of speed, capacity and interference/inhibition.

What might this commonality be? It could be that a property of neurons or their connections will allow faster speeds, higher capacity, and more efficient inhibition. This would represent an all-pervasive (and implausible) *g* model. Alternatively each of these processing properties might be related to a single underlying processing parameter, which in turn is related to general ability. Although at first blush this might sound just like another rabid *g* model, it opens up other possibilities too. Although there would be a large *g* factor in both individual differences (IQ) and cognitive development (MA), it might be that each processing property is differentially related to the individual differences and developmental dimensions. This would mean that the *g* of individual differences and the *g* of development are different, a proposition tested by Helen Davis (1997). So, all well and good in theory but what might this single processing property be?

Let us take the notions of speed and interference first. In Chapter 9 Frank Dempster and Alice Corkill argue that interference is the more general case of which inhibition is but one manifestation. But maybe there is something even more fundamental than interference. One suggestion would be signal to noise ratio. What contributes to the signal and what contributes to the noise? Eysenck and Jensen have both argued that certain neural processes contribute to the fidelity of information processing as can be seen in the relationship between both speed and variability in information processing. But such a model suffers from the all-pervasive *g* problem which even Jensen (1993) has conceded is empirically untenable. And we know that some forms of information processing seem to be independent of *g* (Moore, Hobson, & Anderson, 1995; Reber, Walkenfield, & Hernstadt, 1991). So perhaps, rather than neural efficiency (and by proxy IQ) being related to signal to noise ratio, maybe it is only related to the signal. In cognitive terms, this might be manifested as the fidelity of representations or the speed at which they are assembled or accessed. This leaves open the possibility that it is the other side of the signal to noise relationship that is tapped by the construct of interference.

Mechanisms designed to reduce noise (in its many senses) in effect enhance the quality of the signal. So perhaps other neural processes (I doubt they could be the same and leave this story coherent) are responsible for reducing interference. Perhaps it is these neural processes that most obviously undergo developmental change? As summarised by Dempster and Corkill, there is a great deal of evidence to suppose this to be the case. We are left with an interesting possibility. Speed and IQ are related to properties of the signal in information processing and interference and development are related to properties of noise. Where does this leave our third construct, namely capacity?

Well, capacity might take the conceptual place of either speed or interference in the previous story but a more interesting possibility is that it has a higher order property that integrates both the individual differences and developmental dimensions. Perhaps capacity *is* signal to noise ratio. I think this might come close to Graeme Halford's cognitive conception of how the capacity of neural systems might constrain the kinds of representations that are possible (Chapter 8). Such a system would mean that information-processing constructs related to capacity, such as working memory, are higher-order constructs representing the constraint of more fundamental processes on current information processing; processes that are differentially related to individual differences and development. Take "speed" (really this means neural efficiency) out of working memory capacity and you have interference. Take interference out of working memory capacity and you have speed. Psychometrically this would mean that capacity would be mental age (MA) related and provide the primary *g* factor in developmental measures, whereas speed and interference are, primarily, IQ and chronological-age related respectively.

Considering how the three central constructs of speed, capacity, and inhibition might be related to the individual differences attributes of IQ, age, and mental age through a more fundamental processing variable might lead to other suggestions. For the moment signal to noise ratio seems to me to be a promising candidate.

INTELLIGENCE, TALENT, AND EDUCATION

Are there any implications of the research presented in this book for educational practice? Views on the nature of intelligence have influenced educational practice in the past and in a diversity of ways, from the move to more discovery-based methods of learning, supported by particular interpretations of Piaget and Vygotsky, to the justification of continuing rote learning methods for children with low IQ based on Jensen's distinction between level I and level II learning (Jensen, 1974). Again a number of the key issues discussed in this book seem particularly relevant to educational considerations—the two most important being the relationship between general intelligence and specific abilities and what causes developmental change in intelligence.

In Chapter 11 Herman Spitz shows that the understandable wish that mental retardation might be "cured" by educational intervention has led to a less than critical appraisal of research methodologies of early intervention studies. Spitz argues that contrary to this wishful thinking the evidence suggests that low intelligence is a pervasive and largely educationally resistant condition. We could generalise, wrongly, from Spitz's view to a broader conclusion that because low levels of intelligence are pervasive through the lifespan that educational intervention is of little use to the individual and their families. There are two quite distinct issues here, each of which can be informed by our scientific conclusions from this book.

First, can mental retardation be "cured" or "fixed"? The answer would seem quite clearly to be "no". Second, can the effects of mental retardation be significantly ameliorated by educational intervention? The answer would seem quite clearly to be "yes".

We know that a pervasively low IQ does *not* mean that *nothing* can be learned. However, there are constraints on what can be learned, and learning is likely to be significantly more domain specific than for the rest of the population. But, equally, what we know about intelligence and development assures us that for many children with low IQs educational intervention can significantly ameliorate the effects of their mental retardation. It is still possible to enhance their functional ability—that is, their daily life skills—and hence, the quality of life for the individual and the family. The domain specificity that characterises learning in these children may be turned to functional goals of relevance to individual children. For example, developing a depth of knowledge of horses for a child whose family breeds horses, or a knowledge of cooking for a child who is likely to remain confined to the home, or a knowledge of flowers for someone who may later find a job in a garden nursery. Their understanding of particular domains can be enhanced, albeit with greater input than is generally required and with a more limited outcome than would be possible for their siblings (but perhaps a superior level of knowledge to their same-aged peers).

When we come to the conclusion that studies show that mental retardation is resistant to educational intervention we need to be clear that this is in the sense of changing the underlying cognitive status of the child, i.e. a change in their cognitive architecture. As in other fields of psychology that have adopted the "scientist-practitioner" model, our task is to take what we know about the nature of mental retardation and use it to assist educators to moderate the impact of that condition on the life of the individual by enhancing the resources that we know the child to have. It is my view that educational interventions have had little chance of success given the slow advance in our understanding of the cognitive nature of low IQ coupled with a resistance by educational researchers (and families) to accept the theoretical advances that have been made. The resistance is explicable because at the core of these theories is the notion of a global, "unfixable", pervasive condition that is taken to imply, wrongly, that there is no point in educational intervention. It is our task to demonstrate to educators the value in having a sound theoretical basis to their intervention—one which points to differential intervention strategies with different children with the understanding that deficits in intelligence can take more than one form and that low IQ does not mean absence of ability. Reformulating educational programmes based on a theory of underlying cognitive architecture (i.e. tailoring education to the "strengths" and "weaknesses" of individual children) may bring the kinds of successful intervention strategies for the mentally handicapped that have so far eluded us. Rather than merely resting on a call to arms, let us now consider some specific options suggested by our survey of the field and broaden our scope to include the education of children in general.

What must be obvious from the contributions in this book is that any educational system must take general intelligence seriously. Spitz (1988) has argued that mental retardation is a deficit in thinking caused by a biological, most probably genetic, factor and the deficit is so severe that it is likely to render non-biological intervention strategies ineffectual. However, as we have discussed this is better viewed as an appeal to empirical realities rather than the final word on the matter. For example, the data that we have seen on savant syndrome does at least offer the possibility that impressive cognitive outcomes are still possible even given a pervasive low general intelligence. Although it would be foolish to overgeneralise from the existence of so few cases, some possibilities suggest themselves.

Clearly certain circumstances (an obsessive interest in a knowledge domain plus a great deal of exposure to relevant material) can lead to the acquisition of complex competencies. It might be argued that this is Jensen's notion of Type I (rote) learning in new cloth but I think it is more than this. For a start, the motivational component that the learner brings to the situation (and how that might be fostered) plays no part in the notion of Type I learning, neither does it in its close neighbour—implicit learning (see Anderson, 1998; Fletcher & Roberts, 1998). Second, there is the very real possibility that that many children of lower and, indeed, average IQs can possess what Nettelbeck refers to as "talents" that in their rudimentary form operate independently of general intelligence. What savant syndrome highlights is the theoretical lacuna in our understanding of how practice can transform talents into skilled performance when general intelligence is low. Research in this area will surely lead to a better taxonomy of what constitutes "talent" in this technical sense and subsequently lead to better identification. Increased theoretical under-standing should, in turn, lead to new methods of nurturing talent since it is very likely that those methods will have to differ to those used to nurture the development of "academic" talents in those children with high general intelligence. If so, it is likely to be the case also that children with "talent" and high general ability will benefit from a different regime from children with the same "talent" but poor general ability and their achievements are likely to be different.

Understanding both what general intelligence "is" and how it constrains the development of specific abilities that, unlike talents, require thought for their operation is likely to impact on educational practice—but sometimes in ways that are not currently obvious. For example if we take the view that general intelligence is based on speed of processing then it matters whether speed does or does not change with age in the normal population (an issue that, otherwise, might be thought of as arcane). For example, Brand (1996) has argued that speed is indeed the basis of g, and speed changes during development causing changes in mental age. Consequently, he proposes that children's education should be "streamed" not by their chronological ages but by their mental ages. According to Brand, optimal education would result if school classrooms contained children of a large cross-section of ages but who all were at the same developmental stage (mental age) for acquiring different types of knowledge. But let us look at some consequences of this if my alternative view of intelligence and development is correct. To briefly reiterate: Speed of processing (the fount of g) does not change through development and, since it is clear that older children are on average more cognitively capable than younger children, developmental change must be caused by some other process. I believe this to be, in part, the maturation of modular processes (as already discussed the development of inhibitory processes might depend on such a module) but it must also involve the accumulation of knowledge brought about by standard educational practices. Contrary to Brand, this suggests quite different possibilities.

First, since module maturation will be on a biological programme uncorrelated with general intelligence, streaming on the basis of mental age alone (that is, ignoring chronological age which is the likeliest closest correlate of biological growth) could lead to major intellectual mis-matches. A high IQ six- or seven-year-old does not yet have the necessary processing apparatus to cope with many learning situations that would be straightforward for a much lower IQ ten-year-old. For example, while the development of inhibitory processing may take place on average around seven to nine years of age it is at least possible that the high IQ child might remain "cognitively" handicapped in some senses compared to an average IQ seven- to nine-year-old in the sense of being unable to control the flow of their own information processing until they mature at ten (or whatever). This suggests that ignoring the chronological age of a child could be counterproductive, at least until 10 or 11 years. It also leaves open the idea that there truly is such a thing as "developmental delay" (a lag in the biological growth function) that might be independent of IQ (now best thought of in terms of an unchanging computational power). Develop-mental delay in, for example, inhibitory processes could lead to school learning difficulties that are unrelated to IQ. Another example for a younger age group might be the readiness of children to decode the phonological structure of words as one path to learning to read. I have argued (Anderson, 1992) that this "ability" may be based on modules that develop on a maturational programme that may be independent of IQ. IQ differences would only come into full bloom when children are cognitively "mature" in the developmental sense.

Having said this, certain specific "thinking" abilities (mathematics springs to mind as an obvious possibility) may have a number of features, such as a high "computational load", that lend themselves to be taught in different ways to different IQ-streams. This is a particularly relevant issue when considering education for "gifted" children where we have seen 14-year-olds completing university degrees and gifted children being placed in classes with significantly older class mates. While there is no evidence that this is inherently harmful and many child prodigies go on to do extremely well, there is room for a cautionary note that this educational path will not be appropriate for every gifted child. Optimising educational experience will require setting different goals given the needs and abilities of different children. As for educational interventions in the case of the mentally retarded, only a confident theory of intelligence *and* development, coupled with a cognitive analysis of specific educational competencies, will lead us in new and fruitful directions.

THE SHAPE OF THINGS TO COME?

So there you have it. This book is replete with data, theories and discussions about the fundamental nature of intelligence and how it develops. Each chapter tackled a different aspect of the topic but a number of strong common themes emerged, each of which is ripe for exploration. These are exciting times for the student of intelligence. There are a range of theories, the implications of which are still to be tested and contrasted, and a number of methodological tools from which to choose.

As I mentioned in the introduction to this book, the science of intelligence has been dogged by political controversy surrounding the supposed (to be kind) social consequences that follow from one theory or another. I do not think that these issues are unimportant and I do not think that we should shirk them. But to embrace them requires a different book, of which there are probably already too many. I have made my own position plain, namely that the "fact" of a major biological component to intellectual differences, which I believe to be empirically established beyond any reasonable doubt, does not predispose us to adopt any particular political stance (Anderson, 1992). Science and politics are different enterprises. I hope that some things in this book might have inspired you to consider taking up the study of the development of intelligence as a research career. As my father might have put it, it is time science had a kick of the ball.

REFERENCES

Anderson, M. (1992). *Intelligence and development: A cognitive theory.* Oxford, UK: Blackwell.

Anderson, M. (1994). Simulations of a cognitive theory of intelligence: Implications for the behaviour genetics of general intelligence and specific abilities. *Abstracts of the Annual Behaviour Genetics Conference.*

Anderson, M. (1996). A new approach to measuring intelligence in neonates: Blink reflex modification. *Infant Behaviour and Development, 19,* 67.

Anderson, M. (1998). Individual differences in intelligence. In K. Kirsner, M. Maybury, C. Speelman, A. O'Brien-Malone, C. MacLeod & M. Anderson (Eds), *Implicit and explicit mental processes.* Hillsdale, NJ: Lawrence Erlbaum Associates Inc.

Brand, C.R. (1996). *The g factor.* New York: John Wiley & Sons.

Cardon, L.R., & Fulker, D.W. (1994). A model of developmental change in hierarchical phenotypes with application to specific cognitive abilities. *Behaviour Genetics*, *24*, 1–16.

Colombo, J. (1993). *Infant cognition: Predicting childhood intelligence*. Newbury Park, CA: Sage.

Davis, H. (1997). *Cognitive development and individual differences in intelligence: Unidimensional and multidimensional models of performance on Raven's Progressive Matrices*. Unpublished PhD thesis. The University of Western Australia.

Deary, I.J., Egan, V., Gibson, G.J., Austin, E.J., Brand, C.R., & Kellaghan, T. (1996). Intelligence and the differentiation hypothesis. *Intelligence*, *23*, 105–132.

Deary, I.J., & Pagliari, C. (1991). The strength of *g* at different levels of ability: have Detterman and Daniel rediscovered Spearman's "Law of Diminishing Returns"? *Intelligence*, *15*, 247–250.

Detterman, D.K. & Daniel, M.H. (1989). Correlations of mental tests with each other and with cognitive variables are highest for low IQ groups. *Intelligence*, *13*, 349–359.

Fletcher, J., & Roberts, C. (1998). Intellectual disabilities. In, K. Kirsner, C. Speelman, M. Maybery, A. O'Brien-Malone, M. Anderson, & C. MacLeod. (Eds), *Implicit and explicit mental processes*. Hillsdale, NJ: Lawrence Erlbaum Associates Inc.

Gardner, H. (1983). *Frames of mind: The theory of multiple intelligences*. London: Heinemann.

Jensen, A.R. (1974). Interaction of level I and level II abilities with race and socioeconomic status. *Journal of Education Psychology*, *66*, 99–111.

Just, M.A., & Carpenter, P.A. (1985). Cognitive coordinate systems: accounts of mental rotation and individual differences in spatial ability. *Psychological Review*, *92*, 137–172.

Kail, R. (1988). Developmental functions for speeds of cognitive processes. *Journal of Experimental Child Psychology*, *45*, 339–364.

Kail, R. (1992). Evidence for global developmental change is intact. *Journal of Experimental Child Psychology*, *54*, 308–314.

McCall, R.B. (1994). What process mediates prediction of childhood IQ from infant habituation and recognition memory? Speculations on the roles of inhibition and rate of information processing. *Intelligence*, *18*, 107–124.

Moore, D.G., Hobson, P., & Anderson, M. (1995). Person perception: Does it involve IQ-independent perceptual processing? *Intelligence*, *20*, 65–86.

Posner, M.I., & Mitchell, R.F. (1967). Chronometric analysis of classification. *Psychological Review*, *74*, 392–409.

Reber, A.S., Walkenfield, F.F., & Hernstadt, R. (1991). Implicit and explicit learning: Individual differences and IQ. *Journal of Experiental Psychology: Learning, Memory, and Cognition*, *17*, 888–896.

Smyth, M., Anderson, M., & Hammond, G. (in press). The modified blink reflex and individual differences in speed of processing. *Intelligence*.

Spitz, H.H. (1982). Intellectual extremes, mental age, and the nature of human intelligence. *Merrill-Palmer Quarterly*, *28*, 167–192.

Spitz, H.H. (1988). Mental retardation as a thinking disorder: The rationalist alternative to empiricism. In N.W. Bray (Ed.), *International review in mental retardation* (pp. 1–32). San Diego, CA: Academic Press.

Sternberg, R.J. (1981). Novelty-seeking, novelty-finding and the developmental continuity of intelligence. *Intelligence*, *5*, 149–155.

Thurstone, L.L. (1938) *Primary mental abilities*. Chicago: University of Chicago Press.

Weiss, B., Weisz, J.R., & Bromfield, R. (1986). Performance of retarded and non-retarded persons on information processing tasks: Further tests of the similar structure hypothesis. *Psychological Bulletin, 100*, 157–175.

Zigler, E., & Balla, D. (1977). *Mental retardation: The developmental-difference controversy*. Hillsdale, NJ: Lawrence Erlbaum Associates Inc.

Author Index

333

Subject Index